Springer Texts in Business and Economics

For further volumes:
http://www.springer.com/series/10099

Klaus North • Gita Kumta

# Knowledge Management

## Value Creation Through Organizational Learning

 Springer

Klaus North
Wiesbaden Business School
Hochschule RheinMain
Wiesbaden
Germany

Gita Kumta
School of Business Management
SVKM's Narsee Monjee Institute of
    Management Studies
Mumbai
India

ISSN 2192-4333                     ISSN 2192-4341 (electronic)
ISBN 978-3-319-03697-7       ISBN 978-3-319-03698-4 (eBook)
DOI 10.1007/978-3-319-03698-4
Springer Cham Heidelberg New York Dordrecht London

Library of Congress Control Number: 2014934188

Printed on acid-free paper

Springer is part of Springer Science+Business Media (www.springer.com)

*The ability to create and maintain the knowledge infrastructure, develop knowledge workers and enhance their productivity through creation, and nurturing and exploitation of new knowledge will be the key factors in a nation becoming a knowledge superpower.*
*–APJ Abdul Kalam, (Former President of India)*

# Prologue

On the path towards a knowledge-based society, organisations – firms, public institutions, non-governmental organisations – increasingly face the challenge to mobilise knowledge resources for creating value in a sustainably manner. This book aims at providing an overview of the fields of knowledge-based management as well as offering guidance for the implementation of knowledge management.

As the fruit of more than twenty years of research and consultancy projects carried out by both authors, this is the first textbook to bring together perspectives and practices on knowledge-based value creation from all continents.

It is intended not only for academic education but also to provide guidance to managers, business consultants, trainers, coaches and those interested in learning about organisations in a knowledge economy. While the main focus of this book is on businesses, many of the approaches, methodologies and tools explained are also applicable in public administration and non-profit organisations.

The book also presents "state of the art" theory and practice. Many case studies, examples, questions, assignments as well as easy to use knowledge management tools at the end of each chapter make this work a compendium for learning and for implementing knowledge management initiatives.

The book begins with an "*Introductory summary*".

Chapter 1 deals with the changed environment of competition in knowledge-based societies and economies, and a self-assessment invites the reader to evaluate their own organisation.

Chapter 2 explains what knowledge means in organisations and clarifies the relation between information, knowledge and competitiveness.

Chapter 3 addresses the issue of finding the right organisational form to enable organisational learning, innovation and "boundaryless" knowledge flows. By using several case studies, different forms of organisations are described from the viewpoint of knowledge structure and knowledge transfer.

Chapter 4 underlines the significance of people for the knowledge of an organisation, and focuses mainly on future working methods in knowledge firms as well as new perceptions of roles of knowledge workers.

Chapter 5 concentrates on strategies for managing knowledge, and offers an explanation of the "knowledge market" concept.

Chapter 6 is devoted to knowledge management in such different contexts as managing knowledge across cultures, countries and regions as well as in small businesses.

Chapter 7 concentrates on how information and communication technologies associated with the "enterprise 2.0" paradigm can support knowledge work.

Chapter 8 addresses the issues of intellectual capital reporting and how to protect and safeguard the knowledge of an organisation.

Chapter 9 provides guidance on implementing knowledge management initiatives in practice.

This book discusses knowledge management predominantly from an organisational and business perspective, but for those readers who are interested on a knowledge worker and leadership perspective based on Peter Drucker's thinking, we recommend *North/Gueldenberg: Effective knowledge work – Answers to the Management Challenge of the 21$^{st}$ Century (Emerald Publishing)*.

Our thanks go to Deepti Parte and Virendra Degvekar for translating, formatting and editing the book and to Ian Copestake for proofreading. We also thank Silke Bartsch for designing appealing graphs and figures. Lastly we are also grateful to Springer for their support of the book.

Wiesbaden, Germany/Mumbai, India                              Klaus North
Spring 2014                                                              Gita Kumta

# About the Authors

**Klaus North** is Professor of International Management at Wiesbaden Business School, Germany. His current research covers knowledge and innovation management, particularly know how transfer within and between enterprises in an international context. He was founding president of the German Knowledge Management Association and was scientific director of the German Knowledge Management Award. He frequently consults with major firms, governments and international organisations and teaches regularly in business programmes internationally. In the last 20 years he has contributed to more than 200 knowledge management initiatives around the world.

**Gita A. Kumta** is on the Information Systems faculty at the School of Business Management, SVKM's Narsee Monjee Institute of Management Studies (Deemed-to-be-University), Mumbai, India, and specialises in enterprise systems and knowledge management and is a recognised research guide. She holds a master's degree in Statistics from the Indian Statistical Institute, Calcutta, and a Doctorate in Management Studies from the University of Mumbai. Dr. Kumta has around 30 years experience in industry predominantly in the area of business analysis and consultancy in financial systems. She actively participates and contributes papers at conferences on knowledge management, enterprise solutions and e-governance.

# Contents

# List of Figures

# List of Case Studies

# Introductory Summary

*"L' entreprise est le lieu où s'organisent les savoirs et les intelligences individuels en une intelligence collective créatrice capable d' entreprendre"*, Jacques Morin.
*(the enterprise is the place where individual knowledge and intelligence converge to form a collective and creative intelligence capable of undertaking entrepreneurial actions)*

We have tried to encapsulate the essence of this book by providing brief answers to the following ten questions regarding knowledge-based management.

- Why is "Knowledge" and knowledge management a hot topic of discussion today?
- What is the relevance of knowledge as a competitive factor?
- What does "knowledge" of an organisation actually mean?
- Is it possible to measure knowledge?
- What is knowledge management?
- What are the hurdles in the creation and use of knowledge?
- How to promote knowledge sharing?
- How can an enabling environment that promotes knowledge flows be developed?
- How can processes and structures be organised to support a "knowledge market" in a company?
- How should an organisation begin with the introduction of knowledge management?

## 1. Why is "knowledge" and "knowledge management" a hot topic of discussion today?

With globalisation, many companies realise that sustaining competitive advantage requires tapping the full creative potential and knowledge of all members of the organisation. The business environment is transforming from that which was largely dominated by physical resources to one dominated by knowledge. Companies are increasingly designing products and services which are a result of organisational learning. The companies need to become better at a faster rate because of faster changes in the markets and higher speed of innovation, resulting in fall in prices, shorter product lifecycles, personalisation of customer needs, establishment of new business areas, etc. For this purpose, it is necessary to mobilise all the knowledge resources in the company, as downsizing and re-engineering has led to loss of knowledge in many companies. Traditional potential for rationalisation and differentiation have to a large extent been exhausted. However, 'knowledge' as a resource still retains rationalisation potentials (e.g. by transferring best practices) and differentiation potentials (e.g. by combining knowledge). The developments in information technology in the last years offer the option of storing huge volumes of information at low cost, allowing people to collaborate with each other even over long distances, and so facilitate co-creation and the exchange of knowledge exchange of knowledge (see Chap. 1).

## 2. What is the relevance of knowledge as a competitive factor?

The intelligent use of knowledge about customers binds the customer to the company and enables the company to recognise the customer's present and future needs (better than the competitors). Having knowledge about competitors and other innovative companies helps a company to learn from them and position itself accordingly. Productivity and quality increase by process know-how and transfer of '*best practices*' within and across the company. It is possible to establish new processes, products, services and business areas by combining the knowledge in the company. The competition based on standard products is replaced by the offer of distinguished comprehensive services that are unique. A transparent presentation of the "*intellectual capital*" makes a company more attractive to investors. Thus, a company can achieve long-lasting competitive advantages, especially if its knowledge cannot be copied or transferred. This applies to know-how of employee teams, patents, personal and organisational networks as well as to organisation structures that promote co-operation and exchange of information. An organisation's ability to learn and discard irrelevant knowledge – i.e. to learn and unlearn – is of great importance in this age of knowledge-intensive activities (see Chap. 2).

## 3. What does "knowledge of an organisation" actually mean?

Knowledge can be classified as explicit and tacit. Explicit knowledge is formal and structured and can be codified to be shared, while tacit knowledge is experiential, consisting of lessons learned while executing tasks/projects and insights gained from continuous problem resolution. Among other things, knowledge is comprised of patents, processes, technologies, abilities, skills and experiences of employees, and information about customers, markets and suppliers. Knowledge is developed in a specific context and cannot be considered in an isolated form. It is people-specific and its availability or existence is unknown in many cases. For example, even if a painter precisely explains to us how he has made a certain painting, we are unable to reproduce the same painting. The result of this complexity of knowledge is that it cannot be completely stored and transferred detached from people. Knowledge is not "*frozen food*" that can be randomly stored, broken down and transferred. It is like preparing fresh food and learning from it every time (see Chap. 2).

## 4. Is it possible to measure knowledge?

"What cannot be measured cannot be managed" is a frequent saying in management. Therefore, some organisations structure their *"Intellectual Capital"* and have started to experiment with Intellectual Capital Reporting and to develop indicators that refer to customers, employees, processes, innovations and finance capitals. The *"Balanced Scorecard"* of Kaplan and Norton also helps in evaluating knowledge and learning associated with objectives and processes. However, at present, there is no comprehensive methodology for measuring organisational knowledge (see Chap. 8).

## 5. What is knowledge management?

Knowledge management enables individuals, teams and entire organisations to collectively and systematically create, share and apply knowledge to achieve their strategic and operational objectives. Knowledge management contributes to increasing the efficiency and effectiveness of operations on the one hand and to innovate and change the quality of competition on the other. The aim of knowledge-oriented management is to generate knowledge from information and convert this knowledge into a sustainable competitive advantage that can be measured as success in the business. In view of this, knowledge management is comprised of the following tasks and purposes:

- *Acquiring knowledge*: Ensuring that the information and knowledge necessary for business development and business processes is available.
- *Creating knowledge*: Ensuring that the knowledge is developed in the most suitable place inside or outside the company and that it leads to innovation.
- *Sharing and using knowledge*: Ensuring dissemination, learning and optimum use of knowledge.
- *Learning*: Ensuring that the organisation and each of its employees is able to learn and to reflect as well as apply what is learned.
- *Protecting knowledge*. Knowledge is an asset and its value needs to be protected by keeping it updated through contributions from people.

The challenge is to evolve the right approach for managing knowledge. It depends on the culture of the organisation and is a combination of 'people systems' and 'information systems'.

The approach of *"knowledge ecology"* emphasises that companies should achieve the right growth conditions for *"knowledge plants"* (see Chap. 5).

## 6. What are the hurdles in the creation and use of knowledge?

Hurdles in the creation and use of knowledge in many companies can be summarised using the following points:

- *Organisation structure* (e.g. line of business, establishments, and profit centre) *and values* practiced in the organisation create obstacles to knowledge flows. Knowledge is power and is therefore kept under wraps. The *"not invented here"* syndrome prevents transfer of knowledge.
- *Reward and appraisal systems* offer too little incentive to collaborate, learn and transfer knowledge.

- There are a lack of *efficient processes for creating and transferring knowledge.* Information systems are not user friendly.
- Knowledge is often confused with *information* and is therefore treated as a product such as *"frozen food"* (see Chap. 3).

## 7. How to promote knowledge sharing?

Managing a company from the knowledge point of view means aligning behaviour and cooperation directed towards goals and values of the company as a whole. This should be done in such a way that the short term success of units and the long term development of competence of the organisation as a whole can be ensured. Jack Welsh of General Electric puts this as follows:

> *What we wanted to build was a hybrid, an enterprise with the reach and resources of a big company - the body - but the thirst to learn, the compulsion to share and the bias for action - the soul - of a small company*

The following three conditions must be fulfilled in order to create and transfer knowledge effectively:

*Enabling conditions*: Corporate values, guiding principles, mission, vision and the reward systems must interconnect with the success of the business units and the contribution to the development of the whole company.

*Rules of the game*: A knowledge market should be established in the company with supply and demand. Those in need of a solution can seek knowledge and those who have insights can provide knowledge.

*Processes/structures*: Efficient processes, structures and media should be developed for creating and transferring knowledge (see Chaps. 3 and 4).

## 8. How to create a "knowledge ecology" that promotes knowledge flows and learning across the organisation?

A knowledge-promoting environment – also known as a knowledge ecology – contains a value system that is characterised by terms like trust, cooperation, and openness to continuous change.

Today, the goals and incentive systems in many of the companies are based on business units or profit centres. Individual performance is honoured more than teamwork. However, under knowledge management, companies begin to consider measurable contributions to the creation and transfer of knowledge in their appraisal systems. While rewarding knowledge workers, the success of the entire organisation is heavily weighted (e.g. using equity options) in order to encourage transfer of knowledge and teamwork across firms.

By introducing a *"Balanced Scorecard"*, the traditional financial indicators can be complemented by competence-based criteria (based on customer, employees, processes, innovations, etc.). Companies are increasingly appointing *"knowledge managers"* at senior management level. However, these efforts will be successful only if senior management is committed to knowledge management (see Chaps. 4 and 9).

## 9. How can we organise processes and structures to support a knowledge market in an organisation?

Establishing a knowledge market facilitates knowledge supply and demand, brings knowledge sellers and knowledge buyers in contact, facilitates exchange of knowledge and determines the exchange conditions.

What does this actually mean? Firstly, it is necessary to achieve transparency in terms of "who knows what in the organisation." Once the knowledge supply is presented transparently, the sellers and the buyers should be brought into contact with each other. Formal and informal networks (e.g. communities of practice) are increasingly gaining importance for this purpose. Contact fairs, approaches via the internet, debates, exchange of experiences, mentoring, etc. are other options to bring knowledge sellers and knowledge buyers in contact with each other.

The common interest of the seller and buyer is crucial for the success of the subsequent exchange of knowledge or the collective development of knowledge. Exchange and development of knowledge can take place through competence networks, cooperative projects, personnel rotation and exchange of manuals as well as process and customer information (see Chaps. 5 and 9).

## 10. How should a company introduce knowledge management?

Experience has shown that a combined change process from top to bottom (top down) and from bottom to top (bottom up) supported by appropriate information technology is promising. It is possible to adopt different ways of introducing knowledge management.

The following arrangements should be made:

Knowledge, learning and innovation are integral parts of the overall organisational strategy. *The leaders of the organisation* should be fully committed to actively managing knowledge resources: "Knowledge creation and transfer is very important for ensuring prolonged competitiveness of our company. The performance of the management and the employees is measured based on this".

*Management and reward systems* should be reformed so that learning and competence development oriented at the overall goals of the organisation are honoured. Collaboration is a defining principle across the organisation. Managers and leaders recognise and reinforce the link between knowledge, learning and performance.

Relevant knowledge is made available and enriched in processes, work flow and projects. *Competence networks and "Communities of Practice"* transfer knowledge within and outside the company (e.g. to suppliers).

The *information and communication systems* ensure that information is easy to access and retrieve. Selected information is sent to potential users in a systematic and coherent manner.

This *introduction strategy* of knowledge management leads to short-term successes that pave the path for a long-term strategy of knowledge management. The *"Twelve-point programme"* at the end of this book will assist its implementation (see Chap. 9).

# On the Way to a Knowledge Society

*In an economy where the only certainty is uncertainty, the
one sure source of lasting competitive advantage is
knowledge* – Ikujiro Nonaka

**Learning Outcomes.** After completing this chapter
- You will have gained an understanding of value creation in the knowledge economy,
- You will know challenges and approaches to managing knowledge intensive organisations;
- You will be able to assess the "fitness" of an organisation for knowledge based competition;
- You can run a knowledge café.

## 1.1 A New Perspective on Competition

'Knowledge' as a resource is gaining increasing importance. This is applicable not only at the company level but also at the economy level (Nonaka and Takeuchi 1995; Sveiby 1997; Stewart 1997). The social and organisational conditions for generating and using knowledge will effectively ascertain the innovation capability and consequent competitiveness of companies and economies in the future.

More effective learning, better use of knowledge available at different places including the knowledge of customers, citizens and suppliers, also called the "wisdom of the crowds", can significantly increase innovation, productivity and quality in firms, public administration, regions and nations.

Some typical situations are given below which the business environment is fraught with:

K. North and G. Kumta, *Knowledge Management*,
Springer Texts in Business and Economics, DOI 10.1007/978-3-319-03698-4_1,
© Springer International Publishing Switzerland 2014

- Employees are unable to find critical existing information when required. This results in employees using incomplete information or re-inventing the wheel. Information about a study conducted in a particular area, if found easily, will help reduce the time in initiating a study in another similar area and estimate the effort more realistically. Knowledge is of little value if it cannot be found when needed.
- Lessons are learned but not shared. Knowledge gained through failure is often undervalued. Events that caused a delay in the project completion or those that affected sales adversely are often forgotten. One tends to repeat past mistakes due to a lack of knowledge or the inaccessibility of the lessons learnt from failures.
- Organisations often don't know what they already know. In the knowledge-based economy survival depends on the best possible response to a multitude of challenges primarily using the knowledge gained through past experience. Due to a lack of sharing culture and facilitation, best practices of a group do not get embedded into the organisation's procedures.
- Very often individuals who have valuable information are not tracked in the organisation and this knowledge moves with them with no benefit to the organisation.

Managers interviewed by us summarised the problems and potential of knowledge management as follows:

*If we knew what our company knows, we could fulfil the customer requirements in a better way, offer innovative products earlier, react faster to the market changes and increase our productivity. In short, we could improve at a faster rate.*

## Public Sector Discovers Knowledge Management

Following the engagement of large companies and private industries in knowledge management, the public sector too has increasingly started to show significant interest in it.

Administration, health care, education, security, ministries and parliaments are predestined to turn to knowledge management: Every citizen should have access to information, consultancy services and competent contact persons. Labour administrations would like to make their knowledge of development of job markets, training and advanced training as widely accessible as possible and standardised processes enable exchange of experience and transfer of "Best Practices". The findings of the Program for International Student Assessment (Pisa Study) show how important this is in the educational sector too, as the exchange of successful pedagogic concepts across schools, didactic preparation of specific contents, supervision and tutorials on new technical developments are required everywhere.

Cooperation between various service providers, advanced training of doctors and specialists in health care, an overview of the effectiveness of medicines, and online counselling of patients are just some of the topics which highlight the significance of a systematic management of knowledge in the health care sector (see Nicolini et al. 2008).

Under the key term "New Public Management", we have a wide range of initiatives for adopting the management methods of the private sector in the public sector, in order to increase customer orientation and efficiency. Knowledge management is an important element for informing responsible citizens in a transparent way and guiding them in a competent manner.

## Improving Faster and Becoming Different

While the wish "*to improve faster*" is aimed at increasing efficiency, this only brings about short term relief in keeping a competitive lead. Take an example of a leading electronic company which sees an annual erosion of 15 % in the price of its products. Best practice transfer might lead to an increase in productivity, but is not a long lasing remedy. In order to avert such a fall in price, the competition parameters must be changed using innovation of products, processes or business models. Efforts must be taken to bring unique and inimitable products and services to the market.

Thus, knowledge-oriented management of the company not only means "*improving faster*" but also "*becoming different, gradually*".

*Different,* because it becomes impossible or very difficult to imitate the company that acquires a new configuration of resources as a result of a change in its culture. Gradually, because in most cases this means a change to a new company culture based on innovation which is a result of a highly complex process. Such a change must be initiated, organised and sustained with a lot of patience.

> In this respect **innovation** can be defined as a new configuration of knowledge resulting in new or improved processes, products or business models.

Products can be imitated in the short-term or long-term depending on their complexity. It is very difficult, however, to imitate the capability that is organised and fixed in a company to create, combine, transfer and store knowledge and to generate solutions from the knowledge for the present and future needs of customers. Thus it is a source of long-lasting competitive advantage. Knowledge competition rewards the skill of playing with an infinite number of options in order to find new and better ways of doing things (Romer 1986). For this companies need to develop "dynamic capabilities" (see Sect. 2.3).

Why can this new "*knowledge evolution*" not lead to the development of an altogether new quality of competition within and among the companies? We can take the analogous example of the development processes of life, which involves the emergence of higher forms from a constructive interaction of the different primitive forms, through a "Plus Sum Game" wherein the advantage of one form is linked with the simultaneous advantage of the other. Knowledge sharing in and across organisations is such a "Plus Sum Game" in which the sum of what is gained by all players is greater than the combined sum of what the players entered the game with (refer to the discussion of the concept of co-opetition in Sect. 3.1).

Another contributing factor to newer forms of interaction and competition is that the classical limits of companies change and even fade away at times, which, for example, applies to the concept of open innovation (Chesbrough et al. 2006).

Companies are increasingly being considered as virtual entities that revise traditional business concepts: from competitive-rivalled to cooperative appreciation of competition, from a mere task based organisation to a process-oriented organisation that is directed towards value creation, from mistrust-based alliance management to trust based alliance management. Everyone in the organisation is involved "in a non-stop process of personal and organisational self-renewal. Everyone is a knowledge worker - that is to say, an entrepreneur" (Nonaka and Takeuchi 1995). Corporate entrepreneurship can therefore be characterised by three dimensions: product innovation, risk-taking propensity and proactiveness in the pursuit of new opportunities (See Barringer and Bluedorn 1999).

## Case Study: K&P Engineering: Learning fast

K&P Engineering carries out structural analysis for complex buildings (for example bridges) at two offices with approximately 30 employees, mostly engineers. Only those engineers who handle projects efficiently and learn quickly from their mistakes as well as those who distinguish themselves as experts in a specific area are successful in this business. The brains of these employees contain highly specialised knowledge about solutions and recurring errors in construction. How can this information be stored, made available to all and used for training and continuous improvement of the younger employees?

At K&P, frequently recurring construction errors as well as good solutions are documented using a database structured according to types of buildings. If an employee has to conduct a structural analysis for a new object, he can update himself with the frequently recurring construction defects by referring to the database, detect them quickly, avoid them in his construction work if possible and learn the elements of a "good solution". This generates a commonly accessible collective knowledge of the engineering company.

Though it is easy to use the solution database, it is not always easy to convince the employees to feed their information in the system. They commit errors, since they work under high pressure, and they would not like to be linked with errors by documenting them. Further they possibly feel that the value of their expertise will reduce if others too have access to their experience. Until now, K&P has succeeded in motivating its employees to feed information by communicating with them and convincing them. With an increase in the content of the database, there is an increase in its use by the employees. Thus a culture of learning from errors begins to establish itself.

However, significant implementation problems confront the recognised potential of knowledge management in a company. Despite superior information technology, databases, exchange of experience, work groups, steering committees, etc. many companies succeed partially or fail completely in bringing transparency to the knowledge and in using synergies. Thus they end up *"reinventing the wheel"*. In many cases, employees are not aware of the developments taking place in some other area of the same organisation. When working together within a business area is a challenge in itself, it is even more difficult to cooperate across a business segment with the purpose of converting the entire available knowledge quickly and efficiently into solutions for customers' problems.

This could be viewed as a result of misunderstanding the process of knowledge creation. While one view is restricted to information processing, the more successful approach is to view knowledge creation as a process that enables the company to respond quickly to customers, create new markets and rapidly develop new products and services. Information processing only creates formal knowledge in terms of data, codified procedures and principles, and is measured using metrics such as increased efficiency, lower costs and improved return on investments (Nonaka and Takeuchi 1995).

The multi-divisional form of organisation found in a number of major enterprises often stands in the way of smooth flow of knowledge across the segments. Hence there is an argument that an efficient creation and transfer of knowledge within the framework of a hierarchical and multi-divisional organisation is difficult (Hedlund 1994). Apart from the organisation structure mentioned above, even the values that are practiced in the organisation can create restrictions, for knowledge is power and is kept under wraps. The *"not invented here"* syndrome hampers the transfer of knowledge. Often, the rewards and appraisal systems that have an individualistic orientation offer very little incentive to create and distribute knowledge (see Fig. 1.1).

However, there is an increasing awareness that *"Creation and exchange of knowledge is very important for our business and takes us forward"*.

This increasing awareness among management and employees is a good starting point for changing-over to a new quality of competition.

## What Is the Task of Knowledge Management in This New Competition?

The path to an intelligent, knowledge-oriented company initially begins with five basic questions:
1. How important is knowledge as against physical assets for the success of our business?
2. Which strategic goals do we want to support by knowledge management?
3. Which knowledge/competences do we have and which knowledge/competences do we require in the future to ensure long lasting competitiveness?
4. How do we manage the 'knowledge' resource in the company?
5. How should we organise and develop our company so that we can cope with present and future knowledge-based competition?

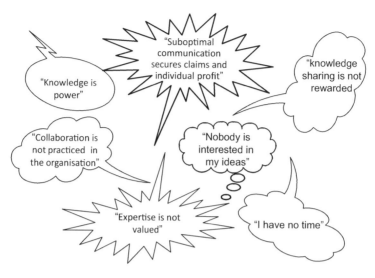

**Fig. 1.1** What hampers the creation and transfer of knowledge?

To answer these questions "over the past 15 years, knowledge management (KM) has progressed from an emergent concept to an increasingly common function in business organizations" (Zack et al. 2009, p. 392), and a search of the literature reveals a huge number of KM definitions which contain similar elements.[1]

> **Knowledge management** enables individuals, teams and entire organisations as well as networks, regions and nations to collectively and systematically create, share and apply knowledge to achieve their strategic and operational objectives. Knowledge management contributes to increase the efficiency and effectiveness of operations on the one hand and to change the quality of competition (innovation) on the other by developing a learning organisation.

The understanding of what KM is, means and does to organisations will be expanded upon throughout this book (see Fig. 1.2).

---

[1] A review of concepts of knowledge and knowledge management can be found at Anand and Singh (2011).

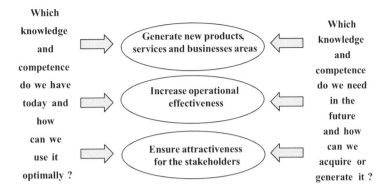

**Fig. 1.2**  Basic questions for the knowledge management of an organisation

The role of management in a learning organisation has been well formulated by Drucker:

**Management** means:
1. Making people's strengths effective and their weaknesses irrelevant
2. Enhancing the ability of people to contribute,
3. Integrating people in a common venture by thinking through, setting and exemplifying the organisational objectives, values and goals
4. Enabling the enterprise and its members to grow and develop through training, developing and teaching
5. Ensuring everyone knows what needs to be accomplished, what they can expect of you, and what is expected of them. Management allows us to coordinate hundreds or thousands of people with different skills and knowledge to achieve common goals.

## 1.2   Knowledge: Key Resource of the Post-industrial Era

### Three Driving Forces

The increasing importance of knowledge as a resource can be traced back to three interdependent driving forces:
- *Structural change*: Moving from labour and capital-intensive activities to information and knowledge-intensive activities means that the companies increasingly sell information, knowledge or intelligent products and services. Work and capital is replaced by knowledge as a scarce resource. This structural change results in changed forms of organisation and transaction within and among the companies as well as in a changing role of management and employees.
- *Globalisation*: Globalisation of the economy has changed the international division of labour. The countries known as industrial nations are now becoming knowledge nations. International learning processes are picking up pace in such

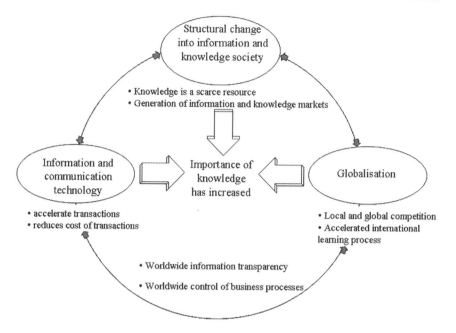

**Fig. 1.3** Three driving forces increasing the importance of 'knowledge' as a factor of competition

a manner that new competitors are emerging in the world market in a short time span due to fast learning cycles.

- *Information and Communication Technologies (ICT)*: ICT enables collaboration and interaction at low transaction costs and brings about worldwide information transparency. Thus with *"perfect information"* we can come one step closer to ideal competition. This results in fast market changes and a higher innovation rate that is reflected in price reductions, shorter product lifecycles, personalisation of customer requirements and the emergence of new business areas. A new global information market place is established and information and communication technologies represent the *wind energy* that fans structural change and globalisation.

Let us have a look at each of these developments shown in Fig. 1.3.

## Structural Change to Knowledge Society: The Kondratieff Waves

In his 1993 analysis of the post-capitalist society, Peter Drucker saw that knowledge productivity will be an increasingly decisive factor in the competitive position of a country, an industry or a company (Drucker 1993, 1997; also Hope and Hope 1997). The change to global information and knowledge society is also supported with the term of the *fifth Kondratiev wave* (Nefiodow 1990; Klodt et al. 1997). The Russian economist, Kondratiev, identified that the economic development of industrial nations was triggered by key innovations and that the development of the economy was like a roller-coaster ride that included prosperity, recession, depression and recovery from each of these phases.

The *first wave* from the end of eighteenth century up to the mid-nineteenth century briefly refers to knowledge about the use of stationary steam power that lead to an industrial revolution.

The *second wave,* which lasted from the mid-nineteenth century to the end of the nineteenth century, used the knowledge about steam power and steel for constructing railways as well as for shipping, thus changing the entire infrastructure (see Fig. 1.4).

The *third Kondratiev wave* started at the beginning of the twentieth century and lasted till the outbreak of the Second World War. It was characterised by the knowledge about chemicals, the automobile and electricity. Mass production gained acceptance and increased mass buying power. The *fourth wave* that started after 1945 and culminated at the beginning of seventies brought with it television and modes of mass transportation via road and air. This Kondratiev wave witnessed a significant growth in the world economy as the leading economies of the west set high production targets and aimed at high labour productivity.

We are now in the *fifth Kondratiev wave* wherein the information (not the labour and capital) and knowledge generated from it are the dominant resources of wealth creation. Information is the "*raw material*" that gives rise to knowledge and information builds the medium as knowledge is transferred and communicated. The contribution of physical production to the national income is decreasing against knowledge production. Tangible goods are losing weight against intangible goods. Muscle power is being replaced by the intellect (Bianchi and Labory 2004; Sreenivas 2006).

The *intangible investments* in products, development, education and training in software as well in increasing the effectiveness of management processes and information supply turn out to be the decisive indicators for the future performance of the economy. This involves expenditures that contribute in enhancing the production potential by extending the knowledge base, thus leading to profits.

> **A knowledge society** refers to any society where knowledge is the primary production resource instead of capital and labour. Such a society creates, shares and uses knowledge for the prosperity and well-being of its people.

In the United States and Europe, more than 30 % of the economically active population works in knowledge-intensive and creative professions such as engineering, science, teaching, consulting, banking, management, journalism, medical practice, law and art; in social professions; or in the information and communication sector, to name just a few (Florida 2002). In 2007, knowledge- and technology-intensive industries together contributed just under $16 trillion to global economic output – about 30 % of the world's GDP.

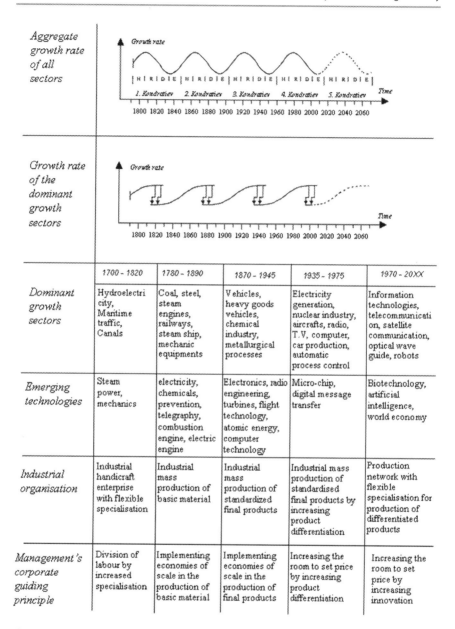

| | 1700 – 1820 | 1780 – 1890 | 1870 – 1945 | 1935 – 1975 | 1970 – 20XX |
|---|---|---|---|---|---|
| *Dominant growth sectors* | Hydroelectri city, Maritime traffic, Canals | Coal, steel, steam engines, railways, steam ship, mechanic equipments | Vehicles, heavy goods vehicles, chemical industry, metallurgical processes | Electricity generation, nuclear industry, aircrafts, radio, T.V, computer, car production, automatic process control | Information technologies, telecommunicati on, satellite communication, optical wave guide, robots |
| *Emerging technologies* | Steam power, mechanics | electricity, chemicals, prevention, telegraphy, combustion engine, electric engine | Electronics, radio engineering, turbines, flight technology, atomic energy, computer technology | Micro-chip, digital message transfer | Biotechnology, artificial intelligence, world economy |
| *Industrial organisation* | Industrial handicraft enterprise with flexible specialisation | Industrial mass production of basic material | Industrial mass production of standardized final products | Industrial mass production of standardised final products by increasing product differentiation | Production network with flexible specialisation for production of differentiated products |
| *Management's corporate guiding principle* | Division of labour by increased specialisation | Implementing economies of scale in the production of basic material | Implementing economies of scale in the production of final products | Increasing the room to set price by increasing product differentiation | Increasing the room to set price by increasing innovation |

**Fig. 1.4**  Characteristics of the economic development phase of Kondratiev waves (Source: Klodt et al. (1997), p. 63, modified by author)

In India knowledge has been recognised as the key driving force in the twenty-first century and a National Knowledge Commission (NKC) was constituted in 2005 as a high level advisory body to the Prime Minister of India. The major Terms of Reference of NKC are: Build excellence in the educational system to meet the knowledge challenges of the twenty-first century and increase India's competitive advantage in fields of knowledge as well as to promote creation of knowledge in science and technology laboratories.

### Changes in Labour Relations

The structural change to information and knowledge society also involves changes to labour relations: *The status of formal and full-time employment is increasingly complemented by free lance work, self-employment and entrepreneurial activity. Accordingly, there is neither job security provided by the government and confirmed by a collective contract nor professions that one can acquire like finished goods and practice them lifelong. For this, there is an almost endless individual freedom and lifelong flexibility in the professional life. The Employment conditions such as duties, timings, places, organisational framework etc. are normally the subject matter of independent decisions or individual negotiations between the employers and the professionals. Normally, performance and success criteria or simply the availability of certain capabilities and relation potentials are counted.* (Lutz 1997, p. 131, see also North and Gueldenberg 2011, Brinkley et al. 2009)

### Emerging Information and Knowledge Market Spaces

If information and knowledge generated from information is considered a valued resource, a market should be built for these goods wherein the supply and demand is balanced using market adjustment mechanism (Earl 1997). At present, we have seen how the internet has turned into a worldwide dominant information market as already described by the MIT researcher, *Dertouzos,* in 1991. According to him, the "information market place is an accumulation of people, computers, communications, software and services that are involved in the future information transactions within the organisations and among its people. These transactions will include processing and communicating information for the same economic motive that is presently being followed by the traditional markets for tangible goods and services." (Dertouzos 1997, p. 10)

Rayport and Sviokla (1995) talk about a "*market space*" wherein information is traded and value is created unlike "*market place*" wherein physical products are traded. Physical value chains are supplemented by virtual value chains or value networks. The development of new electronic markets exceeds a "*simple*" electrification of market processes and establishes new possibilities for interaction and the business areas resulting from it.

**Case: The rise of the knowledge market**

Today, we are beginning to see the emergence of online knowledge marketplaces where you can sell your personal knowledge. You can see its roots in the crowd sourced Question & Answer trend that spawned sites like Quora, Aardvark, Stockoverflow or Ask.com and where you can get your questions answered for free.

The Swedish start-up www.Mancx.com is proving the success of their concept of an online knowledge market to exchange personal information for money. Mancx is a fully transactional knowledge market with global paying/payout capabilities. For information buyers, Mancx is the place to go to for answers to business questions they face on a daily basis. For information sellers, Mancx offers a way to capitalise on accumulated knowledge and to build their personal brand profile as sources of valuable information. Mancx provides a secure environment and anonymity to negotiate and broker a deal of knowledge selling, taking a 20 % commission on every concluded transaction.

This is the same philosophy that www.Acabiz.com has regarding information. Acabiz is an Italian company funded by private investors and the finance arm of Lombardy's governmental body. Acabiz came up with the idea of a knowledge marketplace out of a desire to create a platform for academics to connect with businesses, governments and NGOs. It thus provides a direct link between the final consumer and supplier of specialised knowledge and cuts out middlemen or consultants.

"Accessing niche or specialized knowledge is mission-critical for any successful and targeted business activity today," said Guido Uglietti, the founding partner of Acabiz. "Everyone recognizes the importance of academia to business knowledge transfers, but has been no global platform tool to facilitate and promote knowledge transfer in any simple and scalable way."

Acabiz created a platform for academics, who they call knowledge holders, to connect with businesses, known as knowledge hunters, who are interested in their specific research expertise or knowledge. The Acabiz platform allows businesses to easily and directly tap into the knowledge network of thousands of academics worldwide who all have highly specialised knowledge in fields such as architecture, engineering, law, medicine, science, financial, economics and other areas.

Source: Adapted from: Jeniffer Hicks: The Rise of the Knowledge Market. http://www.forbes.com/sites/jenniferhicks/2011/06/27/the-rise-of-the-knowl edge-market/.

These ventures are a consequence of the fact that future-oriented investors invest in companies that are knowledge-intensive. The value of a company is therefore determined increasingly by their "*intellectual capital*" and less on the basis of book value, i.e. the physical assets of a company. Thus since the beginning of the 1980s, we can see a continuous divergent development of *book value* and *market value* of a

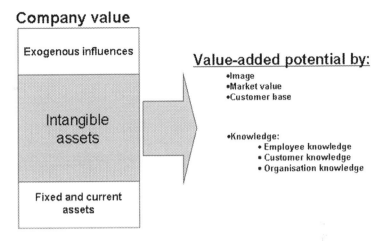

**Fig. 1.5** The value of a company is being increasingly determined based on its intangible assets

company. Companies like SAP or Microsoft are valued on the stock market at ten times their actual book value. The term *"intangible assets"* has been coined to explain the difference between both these values. The elements of these intangible assets that are traditionally called *"goodwill"* (while selling the company) include brand names, customer and supplier base, the related market knowledge, the individual competence of the employees as well as the *"collective problem-solving competence"* that is represented by employees, technologies, software, production processes, patents etc (Sveiby 1997). It is therefore not surprising that apart from the software companies, even the branded companies and manufacturers of knowledge-intensive products, such as medication, exhibit a particularly high degree of intangible assets (see Fig. 1.5).

In the fifth Kondratiev wave, investors are less interested in how physical products are generated from the physical resources. Instead, they increasingly evaluate how knowledge is generated from information and how this knowledge is converted into value for the customer. The value of organisations is increasingly determined by intangible assets.

The *"intelligent company"* is in demand and more so in the global context (Quinn 1992).

## A New International Division of Labour Based on Intangible Assets

The worldwide availability of information as well as the low-cost and efficient facilities of communication has led to an explosive rise in international trade and foreign direct investments through the participation of more and more countries.

In a generation, the proportion of the gross national product of US to world gross product has dropped from approximately 50 % to around 20 %. New competitors thrust themselves into the world market and learn fast. ACER, for example, the electronic company founded in Taiwan in 1976 with 11 employees, learnt things rapidly through joint ventures and alliances. Today, it is a leading international computer and semiconductor manufacturer.

## Knowledge Process Outsourcing (KPO)

In the new international division of labour, "selling" information and knowledge packed in products and services has gained more and more importance compared to the mere exploitation of cost differences and pure *"economies of scale"* that characterised the international division of labour in the fourth Kondratiev wave (cf. Huws 2005). In particular, trade in knowledge intensive services and international royalty and licence fee payments (as a measure for selling intellectual property) have grown significantly.[2] India is an important player in global Knowledge Process Outsourcing (KPO) including services such as research and information gathering, e.g. intellectual property research for patent applications; business and market research, legal and medical services; training, consultancy, and research and development (Mehrotra 2005; Agarwal and Nisa 2009; Contractor et al. 2010).

The advanced economies are increasingly turning into *"Knowledge nations"*. Their companies have knowledge about the worldwide markets, develop product concepts, organise production processes on an international level as well as control the international logistics of the *"supply chain"*. The physical production and to some extent even the development of product components takes place in the new industry nations or emerging markets. We call this the *impresario concept* of international division of work as described in the case study below (North 1997).

The availability of knowledge is also a criterion for decisions pertaining to where business activities are located. This involves not only the creation of local market knowledge but also the availability of corresponding qualified employees and suppliers. Firms aim to research, develop or produce in a place where one can learn the most. It is not difficult to predict that in the future, the use of comparative cost advantage will be of less importance than the use of *comparative knowledge advantage*.

Creation and transfer of knowledge play an important role even in the operative management of international companies. This involves decisions on "which knowledge is created where" and "how can knowledge be transferred efficiently". Multinational companies are turning into worldwide knowledge networks with their customers and suppliers.

---

[2] Compare the annual WTO trade statistics, www.wto.org

"How to ensure global market presence and minimize own investment?" is the
challenge for global companies. One solution is to become a "production
impresario" instead of a manufacturer with high vertical integration. A "production impresario" develops the product concept, commissions the product
modules to the system suppliers, coordinates parts production and assembly in
an international manufacturing network and undertakes the sales and distribution
of the products. The power of the production impresario lies in his knowledge of
worldwide markets, technology and innovations. In order to organise product
development, production and sales, the impresario should be in a position to
transfer relevant information along value chains, i.e. he should be capable of
controlling the international learning process and offer logistics support. The
production impresario concept has taken hold mainly in the global automobile,
textile and electronic industry.

Thus, for instance, the multi-domestic concept of a leading truck manufacturer is based on the knowledge that markets, especially in the developing
countries, cannot be captured with high-tech vehicles that are produced in high
cost countries but are to be sold on a dollar basis. Only those trucks that are
adapted to the purchasing power and conditions of use in such countries and that
possibly contain many parts from local production are suitable for these growing
markets. The basic idea is this: The truck manufacturer breaks away from the
risks of investment and in-house production with the purpose of slipping more
and more into the role of a know-how supplier, a developer and a worldwide
logistics expert. In this way the firm gets rid of the risk and becomes more agile
by passing the problems of fixed cost pools to others who are involved in
production.

Also Benetton operates as a production impresario. Till 2000 Benetton made
part of its production in its own factories and through a wide network of domestic
sub-contractors, mainly specialized in sewing. Now Benetton has drastically
moved to a new strategy, abandoning Italy and organizing production around a
dual supply chain: close locations (East Europe and North Africa) for quick
production and far away locations (Asia) for more standardized products. This
leads to a redefinition of competences for the Treviso clothing district, where
Benetton traditional sub-contractors have been in few years, drastically curtailed.
Benetton restructuring marks the transition to a new network of competences
between agents in the district. The sales network is organised through a multi-
level franchising system. Approximately 70 independent firms work as regional
dealers of the group. Over 3,000 sales outlets worldwide are operated by independent companies as franchising partners of Benetton. Benetton is responsible
worldwide for the marketing and has area representatives. Thus, with relevant
sales and market data, it is in a position to grow its low equity quickly by using
the franchising concept (Crestanello and Tatara 2009; Fornengo Pent 1992;
see also North 1997).

## 1.3    How Organisations Learn

Competing in an ever changing environment requires organistions to learn. How does this happen? The following subchapter is adapted from Brenda Barker Scott's excellent literature review on organisational learning.[3]

### What Is Learning?

The question of whether learning is a cognitive process as well as a behavioural process has practical and theoretical implications.

Theorists adhering to a **purely cognitive perspective** view learning as the development of new insights through the revision of assumptions, causal maps or interpretive schemas. An organisation has learned "if any of its units acquires knowledge that it recognizes as potentially useful to the organization".

Theorists favouring **a dual cognitive–behavioural approach** suggest that while cognitive development is necessary, action is also required for full and complete learning. Here learning is said to occur as new insights, assumptions, and causal maps lead to new behaviour or conversely, new behaviour leads to new insights. Pointing to the intimate relationship that learning has with action, Argyris (1999) suggests: "An organization may be said to learn to the extent that it identifies and corrects errors".

**Organisational knowledge (OK) theorists** have also noted the behavioural–cognitive distinction, but from the point of view of the product of learning; either the development of *know what* or *know how*.

Central to the cognition-behaviour question is the notion that learning is a function of conscious thought. Potential learning, however, is blocked when members lack the appropriate cognitive apparatus for noticing or experiencing a "learning need" and for **sensemaking**. Sensemaking has also been linked to the levels of cognitive development, whereby routine learning is associated with **single loop** learning, and **double loop** learning with deeper cognitive adjustment. Those exploring the interplay between cognition and action have delved into how action springs from, or leads to, deeper cognition through reflective processes such as action learning and after action review. Since **knowing is highly situational**, its lessons cannot be easily codified and transferred in protocols and training manuals. Rather, practitioner-developed knowing must be absorbed through interaction via improvisation, apprenticeship, conversation, and storytelling.

---

[3] The full text with all sources can be found under: http://irc.queensu.ca/gallery/1/dps-organiza tional-learning-a-literature-review.pdf

## Can Organisations Learn?

While some academics maintain that organisational learning is simply the sum of what individuals in organisations learn, others contend that organisational learning is a reflection of the collective ideas, activities, processes, systems, and structures of the organisation. Nonaka (1991), describes a **company as a living organism** with a collective sense of identity and a fundamental purpose, which in turn influences each member's commitment to learning and sharing knowledge.

Independent of the benefits to individual learning, social interaction, and common experiences also play an important role in the development and transfer of group knowledge.

Those exploring group level learning have identified how social processes enable the exchange, synthesis, and broadening of individual member knowledge into the synergistic *knowing* that resides amongst the group. Here academics have studied the many processes and conditions associated with productive learning interactions via conversation and interaction principles, and common working-in-learning experiences.

To this end practical theorists have developed social technologies like café conversations, whole systems change processes, and theory U (Scharmer 2007) to offer philosophical, procedural, and logistical tenants for the facilitation, focus, pacing and flow of productive learning experiences amongst and between groups and communities.

**The Fifth Discipline – Learning organisations are organisations** ...
...where people continually expand their capacity to create the things they truly desire,
...where new and expansive patterns of thinking are nurtured,
...where collective aspiration is set free, and where people are continually learning to see the whole together.
The elements:
1. Personal mastery
2. Mental models
3. Building shared vision
4. Team learning
5. Systems thinking
   Source: Senge (1990).

## Organisational Features That Promote Learning

Others, primarily those working from the *organisations can learn perspective*, suggest that an organisation's ability to learn is dependent on a host of organisational features. In answer to the call for adaptable and responsive organisations, ones in which learning is the norm, not the exception, scholars have identified a number of pertinent features including a firm's learning intent, strategies supporting innovation or capability development, enlightened leadership and distributed authority, norms and belief systems supporting learning, the use of whole systems planning and decision making forums, processes and tools that permit the flow or transfer of knowledge between individuals and groups, and support and legitimacy of practitioner oriented learning.

An organisation's ability to exploit new knowledge has been attributed to how well it is able to act on new insights (flexibility and speed), how extensively it is able to spread new insights to other parts of the organisation (breath), and the degree to which it embeds the learning in organisational features such as norms, protocols, products, processes and structures (depth).

Alternatively, describing **organisations as interpretive systems**, noted theorists Richard Daft and Karl Weick (1984) have attributed interpretive schemas to organisations that, in turn, influence how organisational decision-makers notice, attend to, and interpret the signals in their environments. In turn, different interpretations lead to different organisational responses, which ultimately shape strategy, norms, form and protocols for learning.

Daft and Weick's (1984) account of discovering versus enacting organisations, provides a useful lens through which to explore how different interpretive schemas influence the nature and type of organisational learning. In a *discovering organisation* managers assume that the environment is predictable and analysable. Following this, managers attempt to adapt and learn by setting predictable performance goals for continuous improvement efforts. Conversely, managers in an *enacting organisation* assume that the environment is unpredictable and malleable, and therefore innovate and learn through trial and error experimentation. Here managers understand that as they learn and apply their learnings, they in turn co–create or enact an enriched environment. The world transforms as they transform.

Independent of how a firm defines it features, it is widely appreciated that these contextual factors shape individual and group learning.

In an exploratory study Chawla and Joshi (2011) looked at the impact of knowledge management on learning organisation (LO) practices in India, and based on a small sample of firms they concluded that IT-firms and IT-enabled services score highest on most of the LO dimensions. The testing of their hypothesis revealed that most of the KM dimensions had a positive impact on LO. The type of industry, however, did not have any statistical differential impact on the dimensions of LO in most cases.

## 1.4    The Knowledge Firm: A Quick Assessment

A knowledge-based firm is characterised by its ability to learn and thus generate relevant knowledge to derive business success from this resource. The economic success of such firms is attributed to their knowledge related capabilities, which vary according to the type of business. A specific category are knowledge intensive firms or organisations,[4] such as auditing firms, consultancies, engineering firms, research labs, schools or universities which sell "packed knowledge" of highly qualified experts or organise learning processes. For a franchise company like McDonalds, the creation and transfer of knowledge means efficiently training employees with few qualifications to reach a competence level necessary for expanding the standardised and replicable processes and standardised operations of preparing a "BigMac®" worldwide. Indian IT biggies Infosys Technologies and Wipro have successfully incubated 'learning services' and are selling these to global customers struggling with technological and process changes in their companies as well as demographic shifts in the workforce. While Infosys integrated the service in its Enterprise Solutions Group in 2010, Wipro leveraged its capability in the learning space to extend it as a service to customers in terms of managing learning content, learning delivery, and hosting and managing learning platforms (Das 2010).

## Dimensions of Knowledge Intensity

Until now, we have been talking about the "knowledge-based firm" or about "knowledge-intensive firms" without explaining what knowledge intensity means. Knowledge intensity has two dimensions – *knowledge intensity of the process* and *knowledge intensity of the product/service*. We have distinguished four fields in the knowledge intensity portfolio (see Fig. 1.6):

- *Product intelligence*: Products and services vary in the degree of knowledge embedded in them. An indicator for "product intelligence" is the research and development (R&D) effort as a percentage of total cost or sales. Product intelligence is high in the case of software products, machine tools that identify their own errors, pharmaceutical products, etc.
- *Process intelligence*: Refers to the complexity of processes and the knowledge embedded in them. The amount of R&D investments in process development and improvement as well as the qualification level of people employed in production are indicators for process intelligence. High process intelligence can be found in "*Mass customisation*" (Pine 1993) wherein custom-made products are produced with over millions of variations. The resulting products, such as a bicycle or a tailor-made suit, are not particularly intelligent in themselves, but the intelligence lies in the conceptualisation and execution of the process.
- *Product and process intelligence* combines both the described phenomenon. A practical example is a firm that manufactures high-precision balances in a customer-oriented production.

---

[4] http://www.som.cranfield.ac.uk/som/dinamic-content/media/ISRC/What%20really%20is%20a%20KIF.pdf

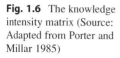

**Fig. 1.6** The knowledge intensity matrix (Source: Adapted from Porter and Millar 1985)

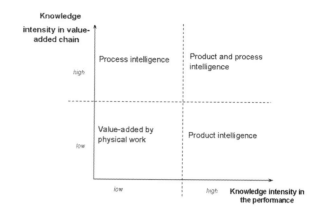

- *Value added by physical work*: Low knowledge intensity in the value added chain and in the performance is evident while selling physical work (even boxing brings money!).

> A good overall **indicator of knowledge intensity** is the added value of a product/process. This reflects the value generated by transforming an input (raw materials, components, information) into an output valued by a customer. The more specialised and unique knowledge is embedded in the transformation process the higher the value added (see Porter and Millar 1985).

## What Makes a Knowledge Firm?

What are the characteristics of a company that converts knowledge into sustainable competitive advantage? Knowledge oriented companies can be distinguished by a number of the features that are described here briefly. At the end of this chapter, the reader has the option to assess whether his company is a "*company insensitive to knowledge*" or a "*knowledge-oriented company*". This short analysis enables the raising of awareness about the subject and to take initial steps toward creating a knowledge firm. However, this does not mean that every company has to turn itself into a knowledge company, for a company that is insensitive to knowledge can also be successful (but for how long?).

We recommend the reader to look at the short analysis at the end of this chapter. The following text explains the individual sections of the subsequent analysis.

Companies will specifically develop into a knowledge firm when customer requirements are highly differentiated and demand *custom-made products*. Knowledge firms will counter a fall in the price for standard or "me-too" products and services by offering complex integrated solutions. This, for instance, applies to the supplier industry for the offer of modules and systems as opposed to production of individual parts or components. Even in a consultancy, the deployment of standard products is valued less by clients than turn-key projects or complete solution packages which demand significantly more knowledge and are therefore pay better. Markets with a high speed of innovation and short product life-cycles require speedy creation and transfer of knowledge.

A knowledge firm offers solutions for customer problems, which are less intensive in terms of labour and capital and are more and more knowledge-intensive. It is difficult to imitate and substitute them, since they draw on complex knowledge and skills. Even the ability to imitate efficiently under the *"We are unbeatable at imitation"* motto can be a successful business strategy.

### Case Study: Mumbai's Dabbawalas – "A model of managerial and organizational simplicity"

The case of Mumbai's Dabbawalas demonstrates how a simple business idea which offers solutions to customer problems can become a successful business model which is difficult to imitate when executed with discipline and dedication.

It has gained recognition world over for its service and operation and in the words of Prof. C. K. Prahlad, is *"A model of managerial and organizational simplicity"*.

'Dabbawalas', is a group of people in Mumbai, India, whose job is to carry and deliver home-made food in lunch boxes to office workers. "Dabba" means lunch box or tiffin. Daily, on the streets of Mumbai, 5,000 *dabbawalas* routinely deliver home cooked lunches in tiffin carriers to 200,000 working people all over the city.

They have been in the business for over 100 years and in 1998, Forbes Global magazine conducted an analysis and gave them a Six Sigma rating for efficiency. In the same year two Dutch filmmakers, Jascha De Wilde and Chris Relleke, made a documentary called 'Dabbawalas, Mumbai's unique lunch service'.

The system the **dabbawalas** have developed over the years revolves around strong teamwork and strict time-management. At 9 a.m. every morning, home-made meals are picked up in special boxes, which are loaded onto trolleys and pushed to a railway station. They then make their way by train to an unloading station. The boxes are rearranged so that those going to similar destinations, indicated by a system of coloured lettering, end up on the same trolley. A simple colour coding system doubles as an ID system for the destination and recipient. The meals are then delivered – 99.9999 % of the time to the right address. **The organisation relies entirely on human endeavour in the form of links in the extensive delivery chain with no technology.** The success of the system thus depends on teamwork, an attitude of **competitive collaboration** and excellent time management. Synergy and cooperation is very high, as all of them come from a single sect from remote villages around Mumbai.[5]

---

[5] Varma, Shailena; The Amazing story of Mumbai Dabbawalas http://toostep.com/insight/the-amazing-story-of-mumbai-dabbawalas

The ability to combine the knowledge of different business fields in order to innovate is gaining importance, and the same applies to the speed of generating new business fields and developing products more effectively than the competitors.

The investors in the knowledge firms are interested in a long-lasting increase in a company's value, especially those dealing in intangible goods.

Traditional companies often treat knowledge as a commodity, like information, that can be divided and stored ("*frozen food*"). But knowledge firms are aware that the creation and transfer of knowledge is an individual and collective learning process that cannot be dominated and controlled completely. Employees of such a company can discern correctly that we learn fast from other companies, we transfer knowledge effectively within the company and to/from our customers, suppliers, alliance partners and competitors.

The knowledge firm is mainly characterised by values, processes and structures, the organisational "ecology", that allows the "*plant knowledge*" to grow and prosper in a company. In this regard, we can also speak of a "*knowledge ecology*". Basic values practiced by such an organisation are trust, openness to new concepts and authenticity.

The term authenticity indicates that the employees are supported in the use of unconventional solutions, enjoy freedom in their demeanour and in organising their work and are allowed to be their own self. In knowledge firms good ideas get implemented notwithstanding who moots them.

For instance, highly-paid software specialists who often live in unconventional office environments and can afford their "*ticks*" because they are creative and encourage liberties through their creativity. Google is a good example of a firm that has understood how to nourish creativity and commitment.[6]

The corporate vision and mission emphasises the importance of knowledge for the success of business. Leadership and incentives must be organised in such a way that they reward both individual performance and the contribution to overall success of the company. This gives rise to an interest in generating good performance not only for one's own unit but also to help other units, customers and suppliers to improve.

While there are no key performance indicators (KPI) for the creation and transfer of knowledge in the traditional company, the knowledge firm measures both based on the business goals. Creation of knowledge does not make any sense if it is isolated from these goals. Such indicators are an integral part of the reporting system showing how knowledge is converted into the success of the business. Non-financial indicators that refer to customers, employees and processes gain importance over traditional financial indicators.

In a knowledge firm, a significant change as opposed to the traditional hierarchical companies is that the position of the management and experts is valued equally. In a traditional company, one requires responsibility for a certain number of employees or the responsibility for a certain budget in order to scale a position of

---

[6] Regarding inspiring office environments see http://www.youtube.com/watch?v=TaGO7XlP2EU

a department manager or chief department manager. But in a knowledge firm one achieves his position in the company by the knowledge that one has, the knowledge that one gives to the others, the ability to coach other employees, the ability to learn new things and to demonstrate expertise. The person who is in the position of an expert must continuously develop himself.

Knowledge firms develop *"knowledge markets"* wherein demand and supply are decisive for the creation and exchange of knowledge. A knowledge company achieves transparency about "who knows what" within and outside the company and knowledge transfer and development are based on common interests. Best practices and expertise are emphasised in the company thus offering a permanent stimulus for implementing good practices. Knowledge companies have overcome the "knowledge is power" syndrome; now "knowledge-sharing is power".

Various agents, processes and media support the operative tasks in our vision of a knowledge firm. In such a firm, knowledge transfer processes are defined as well as the structure of developing new business fields, products and processes. A top-ranked coach promotes knowledge creation and transfer as *"Customer Focus Coordinator"* or *"Director of Knowledge Management"*. However, these coaches do not manage knowledge the way one manages financial resources. Instead, they ensure that the *"knowledge ecology"* is right and the rules of the knowledge markets are followed. They promote the growth of employees in this new type of company.

Strategically important knowledge of an organisation is bundled in competence networks that are also responsible for the distribution and protection of this knowledge. Employees exchange knowledge in *"communities of practice"*. In a knowledge firm, a number of cooperative projects promote teamwork across the functions and business areas in a "boundaryless behaviour".

A knowledge firm practices intensive benchmarking both internally as well as externally. It finds out best practices, distributes them, enquires wholeheartedly whether such practices can be used in the individual units and if not, looks for the reasons. A number of problem-solving groups yield all the available information of their employees. The *"not invented here"* syndrome is replaced by *"implement good ideas from wherever they come"*.

Training and competence development are a high priority. Individual and collective learning processes are based on demand and joint learning happens in teams close to work situations and business units. Employees are no longer *"sent"* for training. Instead, they themselves control their own learning process actively.

While informal contacts are not appreciated in the traditional hierarchical company – *"you'd rather not talk to our colleagues in Delhi because they could snatch away our business"* – team work and informal contacts are promoted in the knowledge firm by means of knowledge fairs, knowledge brokering, attractive canteens, lounges, coffee corners and other options of informal meetings. But not all options for electronic communication are implemented in order to enable colleagues to get to know each other through personal meetings. In such a company, the office layout and the overall structure of the workplace and social spaces support interaction amongst the employees.

Information and communication technology is an important component of a knowledge firm. It connects all the employees of the organisation as well as relevant customers, suppliers and other external know-how experts. Electronic media is used intensively for discussing and transferring knowledge. The databases and other information sources are available for an updated, complete and integrated access to relevant information which is beyond the limits of functional and business units. Such databases and sources build the collective memory of the organisation. The media is user-friendly, easy to learn, adaptable to an individual's method of working and allows easy contributions (e.g. wikis, blogs).

The well-informed reader will argue that such a company described above does not exist in reality or that this utopia will also not find any practical application in the future. This argument can be countered because there are already many companies that closely match the criteria mentioned here, thus drawing us close to this vision. One such successful company is General Electric which has already gone far ahead in its "reinventions" towards a knowledge oriented company and is mentioned a number of times in this book. Phonak (Switzerland) and Oticon (Denmark), both manufacturers of hearing systems, exhibit many of the characteristics of a knowledge firm mentioned here. The list continues with Buckman Laboratories and Sequent Computers in the USA, KaO in Japan, Semco in Brazil, the MLP financial services in Germany, Infosys, Wipro, Tata Steel, Eureka Forbes, and Tata Chemicals in India, etc.

For the employees and management, a change towards a knowledge firm means a change in the working method and roles as they were described by the leading representatives of organisational learning (Argyris and Schön 1978; Senge 1990; Flood 2009). Employees of this new corporate context must be able to "to learn learning". Apart from their field-specific competence, they must have the basic ability to deal with new information and communication technologies to procure information as early as possible and convert it into knowledge. Employees are expected to have a distinct communication competency and the skill of self-management as well as an ability to be creative and solve problems themselves. The social competence or "*capability to work in a team*" involves consulting within the group, solving conflicts, dealing with stress and unexpected behaviour of the others. Management is mainly responsible for organising the above mentioned framework conditions "ecology" as well as for determining the goals and measuring the achievement of goals as per the extended criteria of a knowledge firm. The management itself is an expert – be it for a specific theme, be it for coaching others to learn or be it for communicating the values and goals.

## Short Analysis: Fitness for Knowledge Competition

Grade how you assess the position of your company in the knowledge competition between a *"knowledge-oriented company"* and *"company insensitive to knowledge"*. (You might also use the self-assessment on p. 41). Students can do the same with their university, department or teamwork with their fellow students. A good approach to sensitisation is copying and distributing the questionnaire given below among colleagues so that the results can be discussed subsequently on points such as how different the categorisation turned out to be? Where was the maximum difference in the grading? Where do we see the biggest obstacles on the way to a knowledge firm and which measures can give maximum results with less effort? How can each of us contribute to the distribution of knowledge in the company?

**Short Analysis: Fitness for knowledge based competition**

| Company insensitive to knowledge | 1 | 2 | 3 | 4 | 5 | Knowledge oriented company |
|---|---|---|---|---|---|---|
| **Our markets** | | | | | | |
| High differentiation. | | | | | | Customer requirements are highly differentiated, demand 'for custom-made' products and services |
| Demand standard products. | | | | | | Honoures customized and high value products/services. |
| Low innovation speed and long life-cycles. | | | | | | High innovation speed and short life-cycles. |
| **Our solutions for customer problems** | | | | | | |
| Work or capital intensive | | | | | | Knowledge intensive. |
| Can be imitated easily. | | | | | | Are difficult to imitate. |
| Can be substituted. | | | | | | Cannot be substituted at present. |
| The firm faces difficulties to generate new business fields. | | | | | | Generation of new business fields and products is more effective than the competitors. |
| **Our capital providers** | | | | | | |
| Are interested in short-term yield. | | | | | | Are interested in long lasting increase in the value of the company. |
| **Knowledge and learning** | | | | | | |
| We get few ideas from the employees. | | | | | | Good ideas get implemented notwithstanding where they come from |
| We learn slowly (from other companies). | | | | | | We learn fast (from other companies). |
| We do not know "who knows what?" | | | | | | We know where to locate our knowledge |
| We do not take much effort to protect our knowledge. | | | | | | We protect ourselves systematically against loss of knowledge. |
| One is afraid to emphasise best practice and expertise. | | | | | | We emphasise best practice and expertise. |
| Training does not lead to a collective learning process. | | | | | | Training practices teamwork and knowledge transfer across business units. |
| The employees are "sent" for training. | | | | | | The employees actively control their own learning processes. |
| There is no institutionalised KM. | | | | | | KM processes and roles are implemented. |

| | | | | | |
|---|---|---|---|---|---|
| Inefficient experience exchange. | | | | | Communities of practice exchange experiences. |
| We do not have systematic and open benchmarking. | | | | | By benchmarking (internal and external) we find out best practices. |
| Offices and social places are separated in our company. | | | | | Our offices and social zones encourage teamwork. |

**Basic organisational conditions**

| | | | | | |
|---|---|---|---|---|---|
| The values of our organisation foster mistrust, scepticism against innovations, conformity and formalism. | | | | | The values of our organisation promote trust, openness to innovations, authenticity and informal contacts. |
| The company goals have no relation to the knowledge goals. | | | | | KM strategy is embedded in business strategy. |
| Knowledge is power. | | | | | Knowledge sharing is power. |
| Reward systems are directed towards the performances of an individual or a single unit. | | | | | Reward systems align individual performance and contribution to the overall success of the company. |
| There are no indicators for the creation and transfer of knowledge. | | | | | We measure the creation and transfer of knowledge based on business goals. |
| Management positions are valued higher than experts' positions. | | | | | Management positions and experts' positions are valued equally. |

**Information and communication technology**

| | | | | | |
|---|---|---|---|---|---|
| Our systems are not available to all the employees. | | | | | Our systems connect all the members of the organisation. |
| Our systems are exclusively meant for matters within the company. | | | | | Relevant customers, suppliers and external knowledge-bearers also have access to our systems. |
| Stored information is incomplete and not updated. | | | | | We always have access to latest and complete information. |
| There are different isolated applications thus making it difficult to connect the systems. | | | | | We have an integrated platform that enables access to relevant information across functional units and business units. |
| There are no discussion forums, wikis, or blogs. | | | | | Discussion forums, wikis or blogs are used for discussion and transfer of knowledge. |
| The available systems are user unfriendly or are not accepted. | | | | | The systems are user friendly and are used intensively by the employees. |

## 1.5    Key Insights of Chapter 1

- Knowledge as a resource and the capacity to learn become the main ingredients for sustainable competitiveness.
- All over the world we view structural changes towards a knowledge economy and society giving rise to changed education systems, new forms of learning and valuating talent and competence.
- Intangible assets increasingly determine the value of organisations.
- Self-assessment provides insights if an organisation can be considered as "knowledge firm".

## 1.6    Questions

1. What are the characteristics of a knowledge economy?
2. What are the driving forces of knowledge based competition?
3. What is the influence of intangible assets on company value.
4. How would you define Knowledge Management? Describe at least five factors that determine the success of knowledge-based management.
5. What are the objectives and basic questions of knowledge-based management?
6. What hampers creation and transfer of knowledge in and across organisations?
7. What are the characteristics of a "knowledge firm".

## 1.7    Assignments

1. **Knowledge oriented company**
   Give examples (or prepare a poster) on firms which display the characteristics of a "knowledge oriented company" according to the criteria described in the test at the end of Chap. 1.
2. **Knowledge management definitions**
   Conduct an internet search on the definition of KM and compare them

## 1.8    KM-Tool: Knowledge Café

**What is a Knowledge Café?**
A Knowledge Café is a means of bringing a group of people together to have an open, creative conversation on a topic of mutual interest to bring to the surface their collective knowledge, to share ideas and insights and to gain a deeper understanding of the subject and the issues involved.

**Why use it?**

A Knowledge Café provides a space for people to meet, discuss and reflect. This ultimately, leads to action in the form of better decision making and innovation and thus tangible business outcomes.

**How to run it?**

A simple session may go something like this:

1. The facilitator "Coffee house owner" welcomes people to the café and explains what knowledge cafés are all about and the role of conversation in business life (max 15 min).
2. The facilitator spends 10–15 min outlining the subject or theme of the café and poses a single open-ended question. For example, if the theme is knowledge-sharing then the question for the group might be 'what are the barriers to knowledge-sharing in an organisation and how do you overcome them?'
3. The group breaks into small groups of about five each and discusses the questions for about 30–45 min and then we come back together as a whole group for the final 30–45 min where the individual groups share their thoughts.
4. **Optionally** in the small group sessions, people change tables every 15 min to broaden the number of people they get to interact with and thus the differing perspectives of the group.

Usually no attempt is made to capture the conversation as doing so tends to destroy the conversation. The value of the café is in the conversation itself and the learning that each individual takes away. In some circumstances though it makes sense to capture things from the café depending on its purpose and there are ways of doing this that interfere minimally with the dynamics of the conversation. A good idea is to have a paper table cloth and café tables on which participants can write, draw, mindmap.

For more information refer to:

http://www.gurteen.com/gurteen/gurteen.nsf/id/run-kcafe
http://en.wikipedia.org/wiki/Knowledge_Cafe
www.youtube.com/watch?v=NTZ0vf0Tmi4

# Knowledge in Organisations

**2**

*A learning organisation is an organisation skilled at creating, acquiring and transferring knowledge and at modifying its behaviour to reflect new knowledge and insights* – David A. Garvin

**Learning Outcomes.** After completing this chapter
- You will know the difference between information, knowledge and competence,
- You will be able to apply the SECI-model of explicit/tacit knowledge conversion to real organisations;
- You will be able to explain competitive advantage by the resource based view using the "VRIN"-concept and the construct of "dynamic capabilities";
- You will learn approaches to structuring organisational knowledge and assessing the value of knowledge resources;
- You will be able to run an idea competition.

## 2.1 Value Creation: Information, Knowledge and Competence

Knowledge in organisations takes many forms. It includes the competencies and capabilities of employees, a company's knowledge about customers and suppliers, know-how to deliver specific processes, intellectual property in the form of patents, licences and copyrights, systems for leveraging the company's innovative strength and so on. Knowledge is the product of individual and collective learning and is embodied in products, services and systems. Knowledge is related to experiences of people in organisations and in the society, but only a small part of knowledge is made explicit. Tacit knowledge largely determines how people behave and act.

K. North and G. Kumta, *Knowledge Management,*
Springer Texts in Business and Economics, DOI 10.1007/978-3-319-03698-4_2,
© Springer International Publishing Switzerland 2014

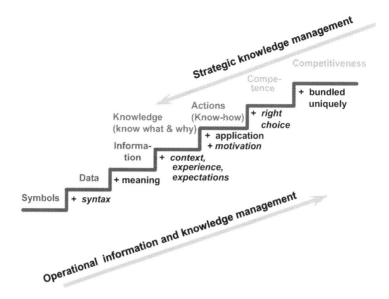

**Fig. 2.1**  The knowledge ladder

For firms knowledge is a resource, an intangible asset and forms a part of the so-called intellectual capital of an organisation. In order to enable knowledge-based value creation, management has to understand what knowledge is and how knowledge is related to competitiveness. In the following we will explain the underlying terminology of knowledge-based value creation first through a short case study and subsequently by systematising the relationship by means of the knowledge ladder (Fig. 2.1).

**Case Study: Transfer of best practice (electronic manufacturing services)**

In the morning, the factory manager, Janya Gupta clicked the inbox on the computer screen. A newsflash showed her that the results of the periodical benchmarking round the 50 electronic manufacturing units of the concern had been directly entered in the best practice database. She clicked on the news and got an overview of the graphically formatted *information*. In the benchmarking comparison, her factory was placed in the upper half. Through voicemail, she requested the best practice team of her factory to analyse the information and study the possibility to adopt the "best practices" of other factories in order to increase productivity and thus compensate for the steady price fall of electronic components. She met the best practice team in the afternoon and yet again verified the *data* of her factory that was reported to the best practice database. Everything was OK. The best practice team developed *knowledge* about the differences by establishing a relation between the benchmarking information of their own factory and that of the comparable factories. Over a video conference that was arranged at short notice with the members of the best practice teams of two "sister factories" they learned and received the *know-how.* The team received tips on how to change the configuration for assembly in their factory. The insights *motivated* them *to act.* Results were measurable just 3 days later. The best practice team of the electronic manufacturing services had demonstrated its collective problem-solving *competence.* Factory manager Janya Gupta is satisfied and stresses that in her view, the capability to learn faster than the competition is a lasting *competitive advantage.*

**Data and Information: Raw Material for Value Creation** Let us start at the bottom of the competence ladder. People communicate by means of symbols; these may be letters, numbers or signs. These symbols can be interpreted only if there are clear rules of understanding. These rules are called syntax. Symbols plus syntax become data. Combining the numbers 1, 3, 5 and the unit symbols for degree Celsius plus a point to 13.5 °C transforms symbols into data. This data can only be interpreted if it is given an exact meaning. It becomes information if we add to the data whether we talk about air temperature, the precise time and place of that temperature.

Information is organised data adding meaning to a message. This information is interpreted differently depending on context, experience and the expectations of people.

**Knowledge: Creating an Understanding as a Basis to Act**

> **Knowledge** refers to the tacit or explicit understanding of people about relationships among phenomena. It is embodied in routines for the performance of activities, in organisational structures and processes and in embedded beliefs and behaviour. Knowledge implies an ability to relate inputs to outputs, to observe regularities in information, to codify, explain and ultimately to predict (Carnegie Bosch Institute [CBI] 1995).

In the development of knowledge we distinguish between different levels. The first, **"know what"**, is a result of interiorising information. For example reading a book which only creates value for an organisation if a person is able to apply this information i.e., the "know what", is transformed into **"know-how"** by means of application. How difficult this transfer from "know what" to "know-how" can be is experienced by many people who read the operating instructions of a mobile phone for instance and want to apply the information to program specific functions. As the mental models of those who have written the operating instructions and those who apply the operating instructions are different, the user may not be able to interpret the instructions correctly. A solution could be to have potential users write the operating instructions.

Knowledge in organisations is only to a small extent explicit. Using the metaphor of the iceberg we can say that only the small part visible above the water is explicit knowledge and the big part hidden under the water is tacit knowledge. According to Polanyi (1966) tacit knowledge is personal, context-specific, often unconscious and therefore hard to formalise and communicate. Explicit or codified knowledge refers to knowledge that is transmittable in formal, systematic language. Polanyi says "that we can know more that we can tell". We shall see below how the transformation of explicit knowledge into tacit knowledge and vice versa is an important process of knowledge creation and distribution.

### Thought Experiment: Is knowledge "justified true belief"?

Philosophy professor Edmund Gettier called into question the theory of knowledge that had been dominant among philosophers for thousands of years when he defined knowledge as "justified true belief"

According to Gettier, there are certain circumstances in which one does not have knowledge, even when all of the above conditions are met. Gettier proposed two thought experiments, which have come to be known as "Gettier cases," as counter-examples to the classical account of knowledge. One of the cases involves two men, Smith and Jones, who are awaiting the results of their applications for the same job. Each man has ten coins in his pocket. Smith has excellent reasons to *believe* that Jones will get the job and, furthermore, *knows* that Jones has ten coins in his pocket (he recently counted them). From this Smith infers, "the man who will get the job has ten coins in his pocket." However, Smith is *unaware* that he also has ten coins in his own pocket. Furthermore, Smith, not Jones, is going to get the job. While Smith has *strong evidence to believe* that Jones will get the job, he is wrong. Smith has a *justified true belief* that a man with ten coins in his pocket will get the job; however, according to Gettier, Smith does not *know* that a man with ten coins in his pocket will get the job, because Smith's belief is "...true by virtue of the number of coins in *Jones's* pocket, while Smith does not know how many coins are in Smith's pocket, and bases his belief...on a count of the coins in Jones's pocket, whom he falsely believes to be the man who will get the job." (see Gettier 1963, p. 122.) These cases fail to be knowledge because the subject's belief is justified, but only happens to be true by virtue of luck. In other words, he made the correct choice (in this case predicting an outcome) for the wrong reasons. This example is similar to those often given when discussing belief and truth, wherein a person's belief of what will happen can coincidentally be correct without his or her having the actual knowledge to base it on.

Source: Gettier (1963, p. 122) cited according to http://en.wikipedia.org/wiki/Epistemology

**Competence: The Right Action at the Right Time**   The ability to apply knowledge is based on specific motives ("**know why**"). People will only act if they are motivated. Therefore, an important management task to enhance knowledge-based value creation is to ensure the right motivational set-up so that knowledge workers develop, share and apply their knowledge in line with the objective of the enterprise. Value is created when the right knowledge is applied at the right moment to solve a specific problem or to exploit a new business opportunity. The right choice of knowledge at the right moment is termed competence. With von Krogh and Roos (1996) "we view competence as an event, rather than an asset. This simply means that competencies do not exist in the way a car does; they exist only when the knowledge (and skill) meet the task."

> The term **competence (or competency)** of a person or a group describes the relationship between the tasks assigned to or assumed by the person or the group and their capability and potential to deliver a desired performance. People mobilise knowledge, skills and behaviours to "do the right thing at the right moment."

The interaction of an actor with an audience, the sales skill of a successful salesman or the adaptation of strategies by an experience consultant in order to meet the client's needs of the moment reflect competence which is often also called expertise (For a more detailed discussion see Sect. 4.3).

**Competitiveness: Bundle Competencies for Uniqueness**   If we bundle the competencies of people or organisations uniquely so that these are not matched by other organisations, then we talk about competitiveness. *Core competencies* of an organisation are considered particularly relevant for competition.

> **Core competencies** (Hamel and Prahalad 1994; Rumelt 1994) are a combination of skills and technologies that deliver value to the customer. This combination is based on explicit and hidden knowledge and is characterised by temporal stability and influence on the products. Core competencies:
> 1. Are not easy for competitors to imitate
> 2. Can be re-used widely for many products and markets
> 3. Must contribute to the end consumer's experienced benefits.

They are in synergy with other competencies and make the company unique and better than others. In this view, core competencies represent the basis for *competitiveness*. We shall elaborate on this aspect of competitive virtues of knowledge in detail in Sect. 2.3 where we also discuss the concept of "dynamic capabilities"

Coming back to the knowledge ladder we can formulate the **objective of knowledge based management** as the transformation of information into knowledge and competence in order to create measurable value in a sustainable manner.

For this, we need to build each step of the knowledge ladder. As in a real staircase you cannot say that the top stair is more important than the bottom stair, you have to build all of them. The bottom-up view reflects the operational processes of information and knowledge management whereas the top-down view reflects the strategic view of defining the competencies of an organisation and its members that will eventually lead to competitiveness.


## Fields of Action of Knowledge Management

Knowledge management of an organisation means organising all the stages of the knowledge ladder. If a certain step of the ladder is not constructed (e.g. lack of data compatibility, incomplete availability of information, lack of motivation for actions), one "*stumbles*" while climbing up and down the ladder. The implementation of business strategies or the operative business is hampered. Three fields of action of 'information and knowledge management' are deduced from the knowledge ladder:

*Strategic knowledge management* passes through the knowledge ladder from top to bottom to answer questions as to *"which competencies are required to be competitive"*, thus deducing which knowledge and know-how is necessary. Knowledge goals should be deduced from the company goals. Furthermore, strategic knowledge management should develop a company model that conceptualises the motivational and organisational structures and processes that make the company fit for knowledge-based competition.

*Operative knowledge management* particularly involves interconnecting information to knowledge, know-how and actions. The manner of organising the process of *transferring individual knowledge into collective knowledge and vice versa* is decisive for the success of knowledge-based management. Here the conversion of tacit knowledge into explicit knowledge and vice versa is of vital importance. However, this process does not take place without effective incentives. Thus operative knowledge management also entails *establishing enabling conditions that serve as stimulants for creation, distribution and use of knowledge*.

*Information and data management* is the basis for knowledge management. If we have a look at the knowledge ladder, we notice that the supply, storage and distribution of information are prerequisites for creating and transferring knowledge. From surveys, we could find that many companies begin to step towards knowledge management with information and data management measures, but eventually realise that information and communication technology cannot be used optimally without appropriate organisational and motivational conditions.

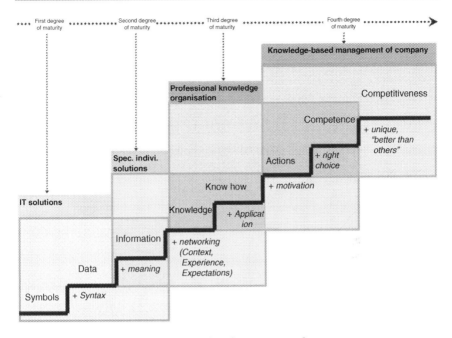

**Fig. 2.2**  Degree of maturity of knowledge-based management of a company

## Degree of Maturity of Knowledge-Based Management

Organisations vary in the degree of maturity of their knowledge-based management (see Fig. 2.2). Awareness about the importance to manage knowledge resources is a learning process and depends on the "maturity" of organisations. The change towards an "intelligent" knowledge-based organisation is a progressive endeavour involving some "trial and error".

To assess the current state of development and provide guidance for further evolvement towards a knowledge based organisation a number of maturity models have been developed. In general, a maturity model describes the development of an entity over time.

**A knowledge management maturity model** can be considered as a structured approach to knowledge management implementation. A maturity model can also provide a common understanding of the terminologies involved in knowledge management implementation to various stakeholders.[1]

---

[1] A good overview over current KM maturity models is found at Kuriakose et al. (2010). See also http://www.kmmm.org/, http://wisdomsource.com/K3MOverview.pdf

Based on empirical studies we have identified four levels of maturity in the way organisations manage their knowledge (North and Schmidt 2004):

### The first level: Information management

Companies at the *first stage of maturity* concentrate on information management. They implement an information and communication infrastructure to enable specific access to databases and documents. Accompanying organisational measures for promoting exchange of knowledge are not yet established or are established only to a certain extent. Efforts are concentrated on information and communication technology. At this level of maturity, organisations achieve an increase in process transparency and speed, avoid double work and shorten training periods for new entrants, which result in an overall increase in the quality of products and services. Examples of first level KM systems: Implementation of an intranet, development of community platforms.

### The second level: "Island" solutions

Organisations that intentionally implement knowledge management initiatives in specific areas or business units represent the *second stage of maturity*. They have realised that information and communication technology alone is not enough for knowledge-based management. Instead they have understood that a "business case" is needed to demonstrate that knowledge management yields clear benefits. Accordingly, specific solutions in specific areas are developed, e.g. service knowledge, personnel knowledge and customer knowledge. KM solutions contribute to process accelerations (fast response, for example, to customer enquiries), increase in reuse of internal knowledge (the wheel is not always reinvented) as well as improved teamwork and increase in quality. Even this approach may lead to quick wins where "KM islands" are created which might be difficult to integrate in a later comprehensive KM strategy.

Examples of second level KM systems are the establishment of Customer Relationship Management Systems integrated into sales management or a portal with "tips and tricks" for service technicians to which service technicians contribute actively.

### The third level: Professional knowledge organisation

Organisations in the *third stage of maturity* are those that have implemented a professional knowledge organisation across departments and business units and exhibit the following characteristic features:
• Information and communication infrastructure guarantees easy availability of relevant information.
• Employees are motivated and rewarded for sharing knowledge.

- Integration of knowledge management in business goals, processes and project organisation.
- Exchange of knowledge is supported through Communities of Practice (CoPs) and competence centres.
- Benefits of knowledge management are measured.

A balanced distribution of benefits resulting in improved processes, higher employee motivation and customer satisfaction is a typical feature of the professional knowledge organisation.

Examples of third level KM systems are the establishment of KM roles and responsibilities at centralised/decentralised levels of an organisation. Employees are regularly trained how to use KM-tools

At this third level KM is seen as a set of rules and tools to enhance performance. It is, however, not yet fully integrated into the minds and behaviour of people.

**The fourth level: Knowledge culture**

The *fourth level of maturity* represents an ideal condition that has been achieved only by a few organisations until now. This level of maturity is characterised by deeply shared values, teamwork, active exchange of knowledge beyond the boundaries of departments and beyond the firm, active search for innovation as well as an open and trustworthy culture that is filled with and lived by management and employees consistently. An important component of this culture is learning from the outside (e.g. markets, technologies, rivals, suppliers, customers etc.) and from the inside. The company culture is supported by a mature information and communication system and media such as CoPs, competence centres and work-outs. Collaboration, knowledge sharing and continuous search for innovation is part of such a knowledge culture. Shared values, not tools, drive knowledge creation, transfer and protection.

Such firms achieve overall levels of excellence. They would be on level 5 of the KM self-assessment as proposed by Collison and Parcell in their practical guide "Learning to fly".

---

**Case Study: Evolvement of knowledge management at Eureka Forbes Ltd.**

The case of Eureka Forbes Ltd., a USD 250 million multi-product, multi-channel corporation and a leader in domestic and industrial water purification systems, vacuum cleaning and air purification solutions in India, demonstrates how a phased approach helps in eventually gaining competitive advantage. It is a pioneer in direct selling in India and is Asia's largest direct sales organisation. Its 7,000 strong direct sales force touches about 1.5 million Indian homes, adding 1,500 customers daily. It has operations in over 135 cities and 500 towns across India. "A formal KM function has been in existence in the company for over seven years and has gone through different phases. Knowledge Management has evolved from being seen as additional work, to being recognised as providing a strategic advantage, significantly impacting both the top-line and bottom-line" says Shubha Ashraf, Knowledge Manager at Eureka. The first phase was the initial period of setting up **structural intellectual capital** as the KM function and processes to facilitate people to know about and be able to appreciate that it helps an individual to perform faster and better. The next phase was the 'value add' to **structural capital** by setting up of a portal enabling different channels and features for attracting people to it. The focus shifted from being a contact platform to being an enabling platform for the internal customers thereby improving **human intellectual capital**. The third phase focuses on improving **social intellectual capital** by leveraging knowledge gathered to improve market responsiveness, customer and employee happiness.

The success is primarily attributed to the focus being on linking Knowledge Management directly to business results, thereby providing the organisation with a distinct competitive edge. Eureka Forbes Ltd. has won the MAKE award and in January 2010 it was recognised and distinguished by three UNESCO-Water Digest Awards for Best R&D and Technological breakthrough for a new product.

KM Self-Assessment (Collision, Parcell: Learning to fly, 2004 quoted from: http://www.odi.org.uk/resources/docs/188.pdf)

|  | KM Strategy | Leadership Behaviours | Networking | Learning before, during and after | vv |
|---|---|---|---|---|---|
| Level 1 | A few people express that know-how is important to the organisation.<br><br>Isolated people with a passion for KM begin to talk and share how difficult it is. | KM viewed as a management fad. Leaders are sceptical as to the benefits.<br><br>Leaders think networking leads to lack of accountability.<br><br>"Knowledge is power" | Knowledge hoarders seem to get rewarded. | People are conscious of the need to learn from what they do but rarely get the time.<br><br>Sharing is for the benefit of the team. | Some individuals take the time to capture their lessons in any number of cupboards and databases.<br><br>They are rarely refreshed, few contribute, even fewer search. |
| Level 2 | Most people say sharing know-how is important to the organisations success.<br><br>People are using some tools to help with learning and sharing | Some managers give people the time to share and learn, but there is little visible support from the top. | Ad hoc networking to help individuals who know each other. | People learn before doing and programme review sessions.<br><br>They capture what they learn for others to access.<br><br>In practice few do access it. | Teams capture lessons learned after a project.<br><br>Teams look for knowledge before starting a project.<br><br>Access to lots of knowledge, though not summarised. |
| Level 3 | There is no framework or articulated KM strategy.<br><br>Some job descriptions include knowledge capture, sharing and distillation.<br><br>People are using a number of tools to help with learning and sharing. | KM is viewed as the responsibility of a specialist team.<br><br>Some leaders talk the talk, but don't always walk the walk! | People are networking to get results.<br><br>Networks are created | People can easily find out what the company knows. Examples of sharing and using are recognised.<br><br>Peers are helping peers across organisational boundaries. | Networks take responsibility for the knowledge, collects their subjects knowledge in one place in a common format.<br><br>Searching before doing is encouraged.<br><br>Little or no distillation. |

| Level 4 | Discussions ongoing about organisation's Intellectual assets.<br><br>A KM strategy exists but is not linked to business results.<br><br>A clear framework and set of tools for learning is widely communicated and understood. | KM is everyone's responsibility; a few jobs are dedicated to managing knowledge. "Knowledge sharing is power."<br><br>Leaders set expectations by "asking the right questions", and rewarding the right behaviours. | Networks are organised around business needs.<br><br>Networks have a clear governance document.<br><br>Supportive technology is in place and is well used. | Learning before, during and after is the way we do things around here.<br><br>"Customers" and partners participate in review sessions. | Just-in-time-knowledge is current and easily accessible.<br><br>One individual distils and refreshes it, though many contribute.<br><br>That individual acts as the owner. |
| Level 5 | Clearly identified Intellectual assets.<br><br>KM strategy is embedded in the business strategy.<br><br>Framework and tools enable learning before, during and after. | Leaders recognise the link between KM and performance<br><br>The right attitudes exist to share and use others' know-how.<br><br>Leaders reinforce the right behaviour and act as role models. | Clearly defined roles and responsibilities.<br><br>Networks and CoPs have a clear purpose, some have clear deliverables other develop capability in the organisation.<br><br>Networks meet annually. | Prompts for learning built into business processes.<br><br>People routinely find out who knows and talk with them.<br><br>Common language, templates and guidelines lead to effective sharing. | Knowledge is easy to get to, easy to retrieve. Relevant knowledge is pushed to you.<br><br>It is constantly refreshed and distilled.<br><br>Networks act as guardians of the knowledge. |

## 2.2    Dimensions of Knowledge

In order to "manage" knowledge in organisations we need to understand what type of "species" we are dealing with. We, therefore, will take a closer look at the following three dimensions of the term 'knowledge'.

- *"Nature"* of knowledge: What is knowledge? Is it considered to be an object, a result that can be shared, duplicated and transported like "frozen food" or is it an individual process that is difficult to control?
- *"Availability"* of knowledge: In which forms does knowledge become available and accessible in and across organisations? Here, we shall deal particularly with the difference between individual versus collective knowledge and tacit versus explicit knowledge.

- *"Value"* of knowledge: What is the value of knowledge? Often, knowledge is also identified as component of intangible assets or as *"Intellectual Capital"*. Knowledge is capital. The question is how can knowledge be measured?

## Nature of Knowledge

Von Krogh and Roos (1996, p. 334) contrast three epistemologies with three knowledge perspectives in a company:

- The *information processing epistemology* assumes that knowledge and information are roughly the same. In this case it is but natural to invest in the speed of information processing. From this perspective, the increase in the capacity to process information leads to an increase in the development of knowledge in the company as well. Organisations which focus on this epistemology will invest in information and communication systems such as relaunching or optimising their intranet.
- The *network epistemology* assumes that knowledge is a result of interaction of people in networks. Thus, the firm should invest to bring the employees of the organisation together. Consequently, the higher the number of opportunities for the people to meet and exchange, the greater will be the development of knowledge. Organisations which focus on this epistemology will promote communities of practice and other social networks, create meeting zones and opportunities for people to meet (e.g. brown bag lunch).
- The *self-referential epistemology* assumes that knowledge is a private *history-dependent* process within each of us. Knowledge of one person is a mere raw data for another. Each person shares organisational knowledge with another. Hence, it is necessary to find a context that stimulates continuous dialogue in the organisation. Firms which focus on this epistemology will promote small teams and task forces, create "work-out-type" problem-solving groups and provide experts with stimulating environments (see for example the design and layout of the Google Zurich office (http://www.youtube.com/watch?v=TaGO7XlP2EU)).

Von Krogh and Roos prefer the last perspective of knowledge creation. However, they emphasise that every organisation works according to all the three epistemologies at different points of time and for different functions. Therefore, knowledge can belong to both the extreme position viz. *"knowledge is object"* and *"knowledge is process"* depending on the situation. For instance, if the sales employees know the number of its A-class clients, this is information with the characteristics of an object. However, knowledge exhibits more characteristics of a process if the available information about the customer is to be used in a better way for concluding business. Gardner (1995) has described these different aspects with the terms "know-what", "know-how", "know-why", "know-where" and "know-when". Polanyi (1966) emphasised the process perspective with the following statement:

Knowledge is an activity best described as a process of knowing.

| CAPITAL | KNOWLEDGE |
|---|---|
| • Independent of person | • Dependent on person |
| • Decreases when shared | • Grows when distributed/shared |
| • Is written off in investment | • Increases in value when used |
| • Static (Object) | • Dynamic (Process) |
| • Simple to measure | • Difficult to measure |

**Fig. 2.3** Differences between capital and knowledge (Source: based on Sveiby 1997)

The extreme perspective of "*knowledge is object*" and "*knowledge is process*" are perhaps best clear if we break up the new word "*knowledge capital*" into its two components, viz. *knowledge* and *capital* and find out the difference between these two terms (refer to Fig. 2.3). Sveiby (1997) argues that the analogy between knowledge and capital does not help in the creation and transfer of knowledge because it leads to a false understanding of knowledge (see Fig. 2.3).

For creating a knowledge-based organisation – a process perspective of knowledge should be adopted. Consequently, it is necessary to develop enabling conditions that encourage the creation and transfer of knowledge.

Apart from these different perspectives – "*knowledge is object*" and "*knowledge is process*" – the nature of knowledge is determined by two features. Knowledge can be private and individual for one and public and collective for others. Furthermore, knowledge can be present in tacit and explicit forms. These aspects determine the availability of knowledge.

### Case Study: Integration of knowledge: Taking over a foreign company
The Problem:

A German enterprise takes over a French company with approximately 500 employees in order to get additional know-how quickly. On the German side, the takeover negotiations are conducted by the "Mergers and Acquisitions" department (M&A). After concluding the contract, an operative business unit takes the task of integrating the new French subsidiary in the concern without having prior experience. Though M&A knows the French company, it is only involved informally in further integration once the contract is concluded.

The French experts oppose the merger. Value of the acquisition would be reduced due to attrition. Knowledge is documented rudimentarily. The German buyer has only a few French-speaking employees who can bridge the gap towards the new subsidiary or could integrate the French employees in their teams. There is a lot of difference between the culture of the German enterprise and the medium-sized French company. The new German parent company sends a high-level management team to take over management of the French subsidiary. That's when the problems begin.

Solution Elements:

How can the integration process be arranged more effectively? The value of the acquisition is decided by the know-how of the employees. Therefore, it is useful not only to alert the Mergers and Acquisitions at an early stage but also to take actions that build faith, e.g. encouraging the employees of both the companies get to know each other, identifying the important knowledge bearers and/or teams and positively influence their attitude towards the merger. After concluding the negotiations, experienced specialists of the M&A department should start coaching the integration process. Furthermore, continuous structuring of an M&A process and the integration process is helpful. In order to ensure success, it is fundamental that knowledge and knowledge bearers are not regarded as objects that can be used freely by signing a purchase contract.

**Assignment: Identify cross border or cross regional mergers. What were the reasons for failure or success?**

## Availability of Knowledge

The "*availability*" of knowledge is affected by form, time and place. Form not only involves the "*individual* versus *collective knowledge*" aspect but also includes the "*tacit* versus *explicit knowledge*" aspect. Both these aspects are closely interlocked (Hedlund and Nonaka 1993; Nonaka and Takeuchi 1995).

The manner of organising the transfer of individual knowledge into collective knowledge and vice versa is decisive for the success of knowledge-based management. "*A company is a place wherein individual knowledge and individual intelligence converge to form a collective and creative intelligence that can be put to entrepreneurial use*" (Morin, 1997, personal communication).

There are two types of knowledge to describe this process: *explicit knowledge* and *tacit knowledge*.

***Tacit knowledge*** represents the personal knowledge of an individual. It is based on education, ideals, values and feelings of the individual person. Subjective insights and intuition embody tacit knowledge that is deeply rooted in the actions and experiences of the particular person. The term "tacit knowledge" was first introduced into philosophy by Michael Polanyi observing that "we can know more than we can tell" (Polanyi 1966, p. 4). This form of knowledge is very difficult to formulate and to pass on because it is embodied in individuals. Tacit knowledge is imparted, among other things, during our upbringing wherein we take on the behaviour patterns of parents unknowingly.

Unlike tacit knowledge, ***explicit knowledge*** is methodical and systematic and is present in an articulated form. It is stored in the media outside the brain

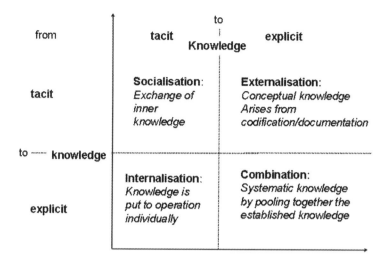

**Fig. 2.4** Four ways to create and transform knowledge (Source: Nonaka and Takeuchi 1995, p. 72)

(disembodied knowledge) of an individual and can be transferred and stored by means of information and communication technology. Examples of explicit knowledge are detailed descriptions of processes, patents, organisation trees, quality documents, etc.

Nonaka and Takeuchi have expressed that the *conversion of tacit knowledge into explicit knowledge* is the basic problem of knowledge management. The reason being that knowledge is useful for a company and can be used by individuals or groups only if it is present in an explicit form. Thus, from this point of view, it is the task of the knowledge management to arrange and direct a process of generating organisational knowledge. Nonaka and Takeuchi formulated this as follows: *"By organisational knowledge creation we mean the capability of a company as a whole to create new knowledge, distributed throughout the organisation and embodied in products, services and systems"* (*Generation of organisational knowledge means the ability of a company to generate completely new knowledge, distribute it within the organisation and incorporate it into products, services and systems*) (Nonaka and Takeuchi 1995, S. VIII; von Krogh et al. 2000).

## Basic Pattern of Knowledge Transformation: SECI-Model

Nonaka and Takeuchi (1995) assume that knowledge is created through the interaction between tacit and explicit knowledge by four different modes of conversion as shown in Fig. 2.4. We will explain all four ways of knowledge conversion as they are the basis for value creation.

**Socialisation: From Tacit to Tacit Knowledge**  The conversion from tacit knowledge of one person to tacit knowledge of another person is called socialisation. It is a process of sharing experiences and thereby creating tacit knowledge such as shared mental models and technical skills. Socialisation takes place when an apprentice observes a master, when a newly hired consultant is integrated into a project group and learns through observation, imitation and practice. Shared experience is the key of socialisation and of value creation in knowledge based organisations. The mere transfer of information will often make little sense if it is abstracted from the associated emotions and specific contexts in which shared experiences are embedded.

**Externalisation: From Tacit to Explicit**  Externalisation is the process of articulating tacit knowledge into explicit concepts. Externalisation happens when we describe a manufacturing process for the purpose of an ISO 9000 certification. In management consulting for example, externalisation takes place when a project profile is written in order to provide specific information on project development and lessons learned as a basis for future similar projects. Many firms have these type of lessons learnt on databases. Since externalisation reveals only a part of the tacit knowledge, it is good not to rely exclusively on these written statements but enable e.g. consultants who have to plan a new project to get a personal contact with those who have carried out similar projects before. Similarly, a real process will always differ from the formal project description. Externalisation is the basis for reflecting experiences, for formalised learning processes and ultimately for standardisation and process improvement.

**Combination: From Explicit to Explicit Knowledge**  Combination refers to the conversion from explicit knowledge to explicit knowledge. Individuals exchange and combine knowledge through documents, meetings, communication networks. They reconfigure existing information through sorting, adding, combining and categorising of explicit knowledge which may lead to new information. In consulting, for example, different presentations are combined and reconfigured for the purpose of a sales presentation to a new client. The combination of explicit knowledge to explicit knowledge often follows an economics of reuse and is also the basis for a cumulative innovative strategy the products and processes are improved incrementally.

**Internalisation: From Explicit to Tacit Knowledge**  Internalisation is the process of embodying explicit knowledge in tacit knowledge. It is closely related to learning by doing. A service engineer, for instance, reads an operating manual in order to program electronic equipment. A great part of our formalised learning processes happens by internalisation. According to Nonaka and Takeuchi's model, knowledge creation is a continuous and dynamic interaction between tacit and explicit knowledge which happens at the level of the individual, of the group, of the organisation, and between organisations.

It is therefore an important management task to create opportunities of interactions between these levels so that knowledge conversion can happen. According to Nonaka and Takeuchi the enabling conditions are

**Intention:** The most critical element of corporate strategy is to conceptualise a vision about what kind of knowledge should be developed and to make it operational in a management system for implementation.

**Autonomy**: At the individual level, all members of an organisation should be allowed to act autonomously as far as circumstances permit. This may increase the chance of introducing unexpected ideas and tacit opportunities.

**Fluctuation and creative chaos:** This means to adopt an open attitude towards environmental signals, to exploit those signals ambiguity, redundancy and to use fluctuation in order to break routines, habits or cognitive frameworks.

**Redundancy:** In business organisations, redundancy refers to intentional overlapping of information about business activities, management responsibilities and the company as a whole. Sharing redundant information promotes the sharing of tacit knowledge and thus speeds up the knowledge creation process.

**Requisite variety:** Based on the assumption, that an organisation's internal diversity must match the variety and complexity of the environment in order to deal with challenges posed by the environment, everyone in the organisation should be assured of quick access to necessary information and knowledge. When information differentials exist within the organisation, organisational members cannot interact on equal terms; this hinders the search for different interpretation of new information.

Nonaka and Takeuchi have assumed a "knowledge spiral" model for transforming tacit knowledge to explicit knowledge and for transferring knowledge from an individual to a group or an organisation. The starting point of the spiral is the individual employee and his/her capability to create knowledge. While communicating with the employees in a group, the individual employee gives away his own knowledge (externalisation) and transfers it to others. On the other hand, the individual internalises the experience background of the entire group (internalisation). The continuous knowledge externalisation and internalisation among employees, and teams within the organisation and beyond the organisation leads to supply of knowledge at these various levels as well as results in growth of the knowledge of the organisation. Personal communication among the employees and use of information and communication technology is a prerequisite for this entire process. The knowledge spiral runs through four phases as shown in Fig. 2.5.

- In the *socialisation* phase (exchange of tacit knowledge), the inner knowledge, e.g. mental model or technical skills are generated.
- The *externalisation* phase of knowledge (from tacit to explicit) produces the conceptual and new knowledge.
- The *combination* phase (combination of explicit knowledge) develops systematic knowledge that is manifested in prototypes, new methods or new business ideas.
- The *internalisation* phase of knowledge (from explicit to tacit) generates operative knowledge.

The following case study, "The best bread in Osaka", explains the above phases individually.

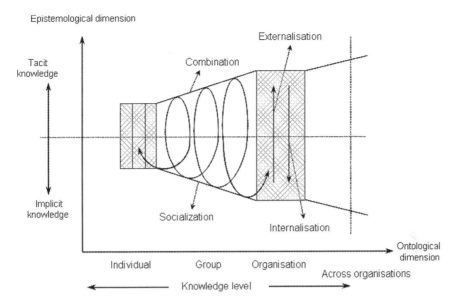

**Fig. 2.5** The spiral of creation and transfer of organisational knowledge (Source: Nonaka and Takeuchi 1995, S. 73)

**Case Study: The best bread in Osaka**

In 1985, the product developers of the Matsushita Electric Company in Osaka pondered over the construction of a bread-making machine for home use. But the prototype could not knead the dough properly and bake it thoroughly. Despite all efforts, the outer crust burnt while the bread remained raw inside. That's when software developer, Ikuko Tanaka, came up with a brilliant idea. The Osaka International Hotel basked in the glory of making the best bread in Osaka. Tanaka thought of using this to the company's advantage. She went to the master baker of the hotel to watch his kneading technique and saw how the master baker stretched the dough in a particular way. After a year of experimenting in close collaboration with the project engineers, Tanaka finally changed the construction features of the machine (by adding special ribs inside the case) in such a way that the device effectively imitated the kneading technique of the baker and baked the dough the way Tanaka had learnt in the hotel. The result was Matsushita's unique "kneading method" and a product that broke all sales records for new baking devices in the first year alone. Thus, Tanaka had converted the tacit knowledge of the baker into explicit knowledge in form of clear specification for the bread-making machine. Ikuko Tanaka first acquired the inner knowledge of the hotel's master baker (socialisation). She then converted these secrets into explicit knowledge that she could pass on to her team members and others at Matsushita (externalisation). Thereafter, the team standardised this knowledge, merged it into a guidebook and an instruction manual and let the product shape accordingly (combination). Finally, the experiences of Tanaka and the team members while constructing the new product enhanced their own tacit knowledge base (internalisation).

Source: The case study follows the description in Nonaka 1991 p. 98–99.

However, the above mentioned model describing the conversion of knowledge from private to collective and implicit to explicit does not consider **uneven distribution of knowledge** in the company that is caused by structural or motivational barriers in the organisation. On the other side, the existing knowledge is not available at the desired place at the desired time.

Knowledge management therefore should not just be restricted to the individual and organisational learning process as such but should also remove obstacles in information and communication. To put it positively, management should create conditions that promote knowledge sharing, guarantee the interaction of individual and organisational learning processes. von Hipple (1994) and Szulanski 1966) use the term "**stickiness**" to describe the fact that knowledge is freely available only up to a certain limit. Knowledge has a tendency to "*stick*". It must be set afloat by suitable organisational design measures. We will take a closer look at this topic in the sections on knowledge transfer and knowledge market (cf. Chap. 7).

The availability of knowledge is linked to the **time and place** factor. Professionals are not available round the clock worldwide, especially in companies that operate globally. A software problem that appears in a subsidiary in Europe can at times not be resolved because the specialist in India is not available or because she is on vacation. In an industry that is dependent on rapid responses, e.g. consulting firms, McKinsey has set up a rapid response network within its practice centre. The "*on-call-consultants*" in this network guarantee a qualified answer within 24 h to a field-specific question from one of the approximately 60 offices in 28 countries (Peters 1994, p. 169–171). In Eureka Forbes, the salesman in the field requires a quick response to his queries. He uses his mobile phone to connect and get his answers from the on-call consultants who have access to the knowledge repository.

Decision-making requires a full set of up-to-date information and knowledge. Today, in many companies, there is a considerable time lag in making updated information available and thus today's decisions for tomorrow's actions are based on obsolete knowledge. Company-wide availability of up-to-date knowledge and information is of vital importance particularly for companies that are surrounded by a fast-changing market environment.

Furthermore, the availability of knowledge is affected by the place where the knowledge originates or where an individual looks for knowledge. Despite electronic media, knowing people personally and the resulting trust are necessary for exchange of knowledge. It is difficult to build such trust over huge geographical distances without meeting the people regularly in person. Apart from these more motivational aspects, the creation of local and global knowledge centres and their interconnection is an important strategic task of international companies (Bartlett and Ghoshal 1989; Doz 1997). We will have a closer look at this task in Chap. 5.

## The Value Dimension of Knowledge

The 1980s witnessed the beginning of a thought process based on the observation that the market value of companies was rising in relation to their book value. The experts wondered how this gap – called "goodwill" – could be explained and concluded that the market book value gap can be attributed to the value of intangible assets, which is defined in the International Accounting Standard (IAS 38) as follows (http://www.iasplus.com/en/standards/standard37):

> An **intangible asset** is an identifiable non-monetary asset without physical substance. An asset is a resource that is controlled by the entity as a result of past events (for example, purchase or self-creation) and from which future economic benefits (inflows of cash or other assets) are expected. [IAS 38.8] Thus, the three critical attributes of an intangible asset are identifiability, control (power to obtain benefits from the asset) and future economic benefits (such as revenues or reduced future costs).

The Swedish insurance company Skandia and the Canadian Imperial Bank of Commerce were the first companies that developed a new structure of company capital. In their approach, the finance capital was complemented by "*intellectual capital*".

> **Intellectual capital** is defined as knowledge that can be converted into value (Edvinsson and Sullivan 1996, p. 358; Edvinsson and Malone 1997) or as resource utilised in future value cration without a physical embodiment (OECD 2008).

Knowledge is considered to be part of intangible assets. This integrates knowledge management in the present logic of management of financial and physical resources and helps to structure and measure the kind of 'knowledge' available in organisations (see a more detailed discussion in Chap. 6).

The "*knowledge is capital*" analogy is intriguing. However, it tends to ignore the character of knowledge as a process as we have already discussed under "*Nature of knowledge*".

The term "intangible assets" covers further resources for value creation which are not in the core 'intellectual capital'. Thus, the customer base, the image of a company or the value of the brands is only to some extent "*knowledge converted into value*". Yet these elements can be added to the value of the intangible assets.

The knowledge of and about customers that is accessible to the company as well as employee knowledge about customers, processes, technologies etc. are a part of the intellectual capital. Employees and customers do not belong to the company the way tangible assets do – the control is restricted. That is why the value of employees is not accounted for in the balance sheet (see Fig. 2.6).

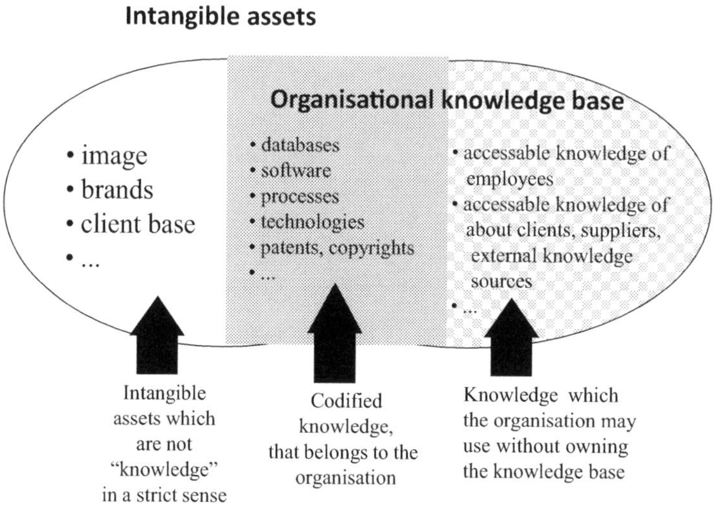

## Intangible assets

Fig. 2.6  Organisational knowledge base is part of intangible assets

How can knowledge be structured from the viewpoint of intellectual capital and which factors determine the value of knowledge?

Following the footsteps of Skandia, while structuring the company capital, the market value of a company is described by the financial capital and the intellectual capital (Skandia 1998). The intellectual capital in turn is divided into human capital, customer capital and organisational capital.

**Human capital** is comprised of the competencies of the workforce, their motivation as well as relations and values. In short we might say: **Human capital = competence × motivation**

**Customer capital** represents the value of the company's relationship with the customer. Saint-Onge defines customer capital as the depth (penetration), width (coverage) and the attachment (loyalty) of the customer base (Bontis 1996). The examples of customer capital are patients of a doctor, client base of a mail order company, branch networks of a bank and their customer relationships. Sveiby emphasised that supplier and distributor relationships must also be included in this category of capital (Sveiby 1997).

The third category of intellectual capital is **organisational or structural capital**. Skandia divided the organisational capital into innovation capital, process capital and culture. The combined value of the value-creating processes is recorded under process capital. This includes for example the value of the client order process or the value of the procurement process. The value of procurement process is based on the knowledge of employees of the purchasing department about supply markets, their ability to negotiate with the suppliers, in structuring the process cycle from a purchase requests up to finding a supplier and managing supplier relations.

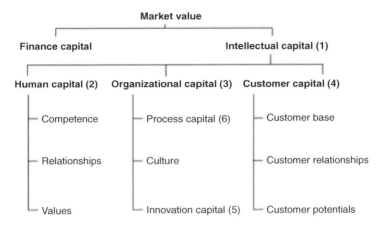

**Fig. 2.7**  Skandia's structuring of organisational capital (Source: According to Skandia 1998)

Knowledge is linked to the databases, software as well as values and goal-setting of the employees of the purchasing department.

It is often said that structural capital is the capital *"that remains when the employees go home"*. We have to note, however, that this capital comes to life and has a value only with the employees. Though information codified in the databases, software and process ensures daily operations it is valueless to a great extent if there is a massive brain drain.

*Innovation capital,* the second pillar of structural capital, is defined by Skandia as the renewal strength of a company and is evident in the protected intellectual property like patents, licences or brand names and intangible virtues that enable future cash flows. This contains, for instance, valuation of creativity. The structure of Skandia's organisational capital is illustrated in Fig. 2.7 (See also Chap. 9 for further detail).

## Criteria to Assess the Value of Knowledge

Above we have explained how to break down knowledge into components that can be assigned a value under certain conditions.

In the following we will deal with the question of how a value can be assigned to knowledge and which criteria influences this.

The value of knowledge is measured mainly on the basis of the **scarcity and the value-creating potential** of this resource. It is often difficult for both – the "seller" and the "buyer" to assess the value-creating potential of knowledge (e.g. what is the value of a patent?, What am I willing to pay for a technology consultant?)

While evaluating knowledge, the knowledge "seller" might take as a first orientation the efforts involved in acquiring the knowledge. *"I have invested so much time and money in acquiring this knowledge. Now, I want to sell it at a higher value if possible."*

The internal *sunk costs* that are incurred on, for example, the training of employees or building a team operative in software development are meaningful only to a certain extent while determining the value of knowledge resource. This is because, firstly, the expenditure incurred by the company cannot always be ascertained in terms of cost. Secondly, the expenditure could have increased because of inefficient training and advanced training measures, or the knowledge obtained can no longer be of any value because of fast changes in the market. From this viewpoint, the valuation of knowledge resources based on expenditure is inadequate. On the other hand, the knowledge "buyer" is not sure of the potential value that can be added by the transferred knowledge. This is a basic problem of the consultancy firms because the client – particularly in case of process-oriented consulting – buys learning processes without an assured result.

A better orientation might be to consider *the replacement cost of an intellectual asset*: What will it cost me to build an effective research team" and relate this to the value creation potential of the team. In Chap. 9 we discuss "Tobin's q" which relates market value of an asset to its replacement cost.

### Case Study: The value of knowledge

The tractor of a farmer stopped working. All the efforts of the farmer and his friends to repair the tractor were in vain. Finally, the farmer made up his mind to fetch a mechanic. The mechanic had a look at the tractor, activated the starter, lifted the engine bonnet and checked every detail. Finally, the mechanic took his hammer. With a single blow of the hammer at a particular place the tractor started functioning again. The engine functioned as though it had never broken down. As the mechanic handed over an invoice to the farmer, the farmer was completely shocked and angry and said, "What? You want fifty Toman for one strike of a hammer!" The mechanic said, "My dear friend, I charge only one Toman for the hammer strike. But I have to charge forty-nine Toman for knowing where to strike."

The following key questions introduce knowledge "sellers", knowledge "buyers" and investors to the valuation of knowledge:

- Knowledge users: For which purpose do I use the knowledge and what is the 'value adding potential' related to this knowledge?
- Knowledge "sellers": What was my cost for acquiring this knowledge and how can I make this knowledge valuable in the market? Investor: How will the knowledge of this company contribute to its success in the market? What is the relation between market value and replacement cost?

The knowledge sellers, knowledge buyers and investors will assess the knowledge implicitly by means of a range of criteria which we will discuss in the following:

**Specificity:** We assume that the more specific the knowledge, the higher its value. Users value ready made and tailored solutions of their problems. Knowledge contributing to this will be higher valued than general principles. This leads, for example, to a strategic discussion in consultancy companies about the value of standard methodologies versus individualised advice.

**The validity** of knowledge can be seen from a content perspective and a time perspective. The content perspective refers to the way in which knowledge is created and validated.

- Scientifically accepted knowledge that has universal validity under precisely defined conditions
- Judgements and evaluations that can be traced objectively
- Individual or collective experiences and acting potential derived from such experiences.

There is an argument that the cost of acquiring knowledge – and in certain respect, the value – is lowest for the accepted knowledge and highest for the potential knowledge. Researchers in pharmaceutics might buy accepted knowledge in the form of a scientific database at a relatively low price, but the cost of molecular modelling or acquiring advice from experienced experts will be much higher. Therefore, the value of a research team or a strategic alliance with a laboratory should be estimated as significantly higher than the accumulation of accepted knowledge.

The **temporal validity** of knowledge refers to its "expiry date". A general technological knowledge base has a longer validity than market knowledge that can drop to zero value just within days or weeks.

Yet another criterion of valuating knowledge is its uniqueness or its **scarcity** value. However, there should be a corresponding demand when knowledge is to be evaluated this way. An expert might be the only person with knowledge about a specific subject without there being any demand for his knowledge. Equally important is the speed at which this knowledge can be imitated or substituted.

All these perspectives are considered while valuating knowledge.

## 2.3   Knowledge as Competitive Factor

### Knowledge-Based Theory of the Firm

Morin recognises the company as a place where individual knowledge and individual intelligence converge to form a collective and creative intelligence that can be put to entrepreneurial use. From this viewpoint, companies exist because they are in the position to convert individual knowledge into collective knowledge and employ it for an entrepreneurial purpose. Accordingly, the business is successful:

- If individuals make their relevant knowledge and experience available for the operation of the firm and
- If there is an effective knowledge transformation process from individual to collective level and
- If activities are aligned in an entrepreneurial spirit to achieve the objectives of the firm.

However, this description of a company from the knowledge point of view does not explain the existence of the company. Individuals could get together in order to share their knowledge, to create collective knowledge and thus to transact business (Spender 1996; Grant 1996; Tsoukas 1996; Kogut and Zander 1992). According to Grant (Grant 1996, p. 112), the existence of a company is a result of the restricted capacity of a human brain to acquire, store and to process knowledge. This gives rise to individual specialisation in several fields of knowledge. However, offering complex solutions to problems requires coordinated efforts of various specialists. Markets alone are incapable of taking up the role of this coordination because they cannot mobilise tacit knowledge and cannot answer the risk of theft of intellectual property (in case of explicit knowledge) by a potential knowledge buyer. Thus, companies exist because they are capable of creating conditions that favour the production of goods and services and enable individuals to integrate their specialised knowledge. Hence, an important task of the knowledge-based management of a company is to establish conditions so that employees with specific knowledge are in a position to create collective knowledge and to implement it to ensure business success.

## Knowledge as Strategic Competitive Factor

But how to ensure business success in a competitive environment? In this respect, knowledge is increasingly being considered as a *strategic competitive factor*. This has formed complementary viewpoints – the market based view (Porter 1985) and the resource-based view (Penrose 1959; Hamel and Heene 1994) further developed by the theory of "dynamic capabilities" (Teece 2009, see also Teece 2007; Teece et al. 1997, 2000).

The *environment related view* assumes that competitive advantage arises out of uneven distribution of information and knowledge between two companies. Since individual companies are ahead of competitors in terms of information and knowledge, they recognise market opportunities earlier than the competition. Since they have the corresponding competencies, they convert these opportunities into business. From this perspective, entrepreneurship involves detecting relevant differences in information and knowledge as well as conversion of this difference into business. But this results in a dynamic competition wherein the actions of the successful company are imitated and thus competitive advantages are continuously lost and it becomes necessary to identify new developments in information and knowledge as well as implement them in entrepreneurial activities. Hence, this type of competition requires a company to be faster than its competitors while it is difficult to build lasting competitive advantage.

In the resource-based view (Penrose 1959; Nelson and Winter 1982), companies achieve competitive advantages by being and acting differently than its competitors. As opposed to the environment-oriented approach, this approach enables continuous differentiation between companies. These differentiations are difficult to imitate.[2] Considering the potential of the resources to achieve continuous competitive advantage, Barney (1992) reviewed them in four criteria which are often abbreviated as "VRIN":

- Valuable (for the customer)
- Rare as compared to the rivals
- Imperfectly imitable due to unique historical conditions, causal ambiguity and social complexity
- Non-substitutable

The last two criteria are seen as particularly relevant for achieving continuous competitive advantages. *Obstacles in imitation* arise firstly because knowledge is codified but legally protected, e.g. brands or patents. Secondly, because knowledge exists in tacit form and through facts that even explicit knowledge is related to persons and groups of persons. The obstacles in imitation are linked directly or indirectly to the knowledge or the development of knowledge. Furthermore, it is argued that intangible assets are the real source of competitive strength and key factors in the adaptability of the company because of the following three reasons: Intangible assets are difficult to accumulate, they can be used a number of times simultaneously and they are both inputs and outputs of business activities (Itami and Roehl 1987, p.13/14).

Does this hold also for fast moving business environments open to global competition, and characterised by dispersion in the geographical and organisational sources of innovation and manufacturing? Teece (2009, p. 4) argues that *sustainable* advantage requires more than the ownership of difficult-to-replicate (knowledge) assets. According to Teece this also requires unique and difficult-to-replicate so-called "dynamic capabilities". These capabilities can be harnessed to continuously create, extend, upgrade, protect, and keep relevant the enterprise's unique asset base.

**Dynamic capabilities** are the ability to reconfigure, redirect, transform, and appropriately shape and integrate existing core competences with external resources and strategic and complementary assets to meet the challenges of a time-pressured, rapidly changing Schumpeterian world of competition and imitation (Teece et al. 2000, p. 339).

For analytical purposes, dynamic capabilities can be disaggregated into the capacity (1) to sense and shape opportunities and threats, (2) to seize opportunities, and (3) to maintain competitiveness through enhancing, combining, protecting, and when necessary, reconfiguring the business enterprise's intangible and tangible assets. Dynamic capabilities include difficult-to-replicate enterprise capabilities required to adapt to changing customer and technological opportunities. They also embrace the enterprise's capacity to shape the ecosystem it occupies, develop new products and processes, and design and implement viable business models. (Teece 2009, p. 4)

---

[2] Barney (1992), see also http://www.valuebasedmanagement.net/methods_barney_resource_based_view_firm.html

How are these competitive advantages developed out of production factors that can be bought on the market? Let us consider the following example:

A laboratory recruits graduates (*production factor*) on the labour market and integrate them into a team of experienced R&D staff in order to develop an innovative, specialised group of developers. The team becomes a *resource* which is difficult to imitate due to shared values and tacit understanding. The lab has established *routines* and processes of technology and project management over the years through which the individual *skills and competences* of R&D teams are organised to deliver unique and difficult to imitate development services. Content and type of development work are continuously reflected in a strategic dialogue with leading research institutes and customers. Based on this new areas of knowledge are integrated and thus an enrichment and of existing core competences is ensured. *Dynamic capabilities* are developed to sustain uniqueness.

It is clear from this chapter that compared to the physical resources, knowledge is a more difficult to imitate and rarer company resource that offers a very high potential for generation of value. Knowledge is increasingly being considered as "a justification of existence"; as a determining factor for existence and size of a company.

The analysis of what organisations are should be grounded in the understanding of what they know how to do. (Kogut and Zander 1992, p. 383)

## 2.4    Key Insights of Chapter 2

- Knowledge in an organisation can be classified in different ways and can be evaluated. The handling of information is affected by the perspective "What is knowledge and how important is it for our organisation."
- The knowledge ladder describe value creation linking information, knowledge, competence and competitiveness
- There are at least three knowledge epistemologies. Depending on the situation, knowledge can be viewed as an object or a process. The process perspective of knowledge is explained in this book.
- The SEICI model describes the transformation of knowledge from individual to collective and from tacit to explicit.
- Knowledge is viewed as a component of intangible assets or "intellectual capital". The value of knowledge is based on its scarcity and potential to add value.
- Knowledge is considered as a factor of production, a strategic competitive factor and basis of the existence of a company. Knowledge can be imitated and substituted – these two aspects of knowledge are the decisive criteria for sustainable competitive advantage.

## 2.5   Questions

1. Explain the difference between information and knowledge and knowledge and competence.
2. What is the difference of tacit and explicit knowledge? Is explicit knowledge only "information"
3. How would you interpret Knowledge Maturity in an organisation?
4. Assess the value of a five person research and development team. Which criteria would you use?
5. What are criteria to evaluate core competencies?

## 2.6   Assignments

1. **Transferring successful sales practices**

   In your company several of the experienced sales representatives are close to retirement. A number of new sales reps. have been recruited.

   *You are asked to propose how to structure an effective knowledge transfer between old and new sales reps. You remember the SEICI model of Nonaka and Takeuchi and think that this might be a good basis for developing a proposal.*

2. **Core competence analysis**

   Apple is often cited as a successful and innovative company. Analyse the core competencies of Apple.

## 2.7   KM-Tool: Idea Competition

**What is an idea competition:**

Leveraging employees' creative imagination in conjunction with the thrill of competition is a powerful way to source compelling, well-articulated ideas.

An idea competition is a well focused way to access innovative ideas and solutions from employees, users, potential clients. **The quality of ideas increases exponentially when participants' are given a clear and focused challenge question.**

Idea competitions build on the nature of competition as a means to encourage participation in an open innovation process, to inspire their creativity, and to increase the quality and focus of submissions. When the contest ends, submissions are evaluated by an expert panel. Those whose submissions score highest usually receive a bonus or an award.

**Why use idea competitions?**

- In many organisations suggestion schemes do or work well. People do not submit their ideas because of bureaucratic procedures. Idea competitions open a change for a focused, timely and simple collection of ideas.

- Tapping ideas from "the crowd" of users or other people outside the organisation has a huge value creation potential
- Idea competitions create a spirit of interaction and challenge current practices and wisdom

### How to organise idea competitions?
### Prepare a clear and transparent process:

Idea competitions involve multiple participants including sponsors, administrators, contestants and judges. The responsibilities of administrators include:

1. **Design:** Prior to launching a competition it is important to set the rules, design the structure, select prizes and incentives and determine the timeline.
2. **Planning:** It is essential to carefully plan, anticipate the number of submissions and define the various roles and responsibilities during the various stages of the process.
3. **Prioritisation:** If hundreds of ideas are submitted, it is important to efficiently sift through the submissions to quickly identify the best ideas.
4. **Providing a delightful experience:** Each participant must feel energised to participate and feel the competition process is fun and easy to engage in.
5. **Transparency:** Respond to participants in a timely fashion and make information accessible to reduce administrative bottlenecks and make them feel important.
6. **Fair evaluation:** Uniform judging is critical to fair competition. Judges should be provided with a scorecard and evaluation criteria to fairly rate each concept plan/idea.
7. **Managing scale:** Due to the viral nature of online competitions, administrators must be prepared to handle hundreds or perhaps thousands of entries. Using a robust and proven web-based system will prevent the administration from being burdened.

### Ensure participation and prepare for high quality results.

How can an employee-driven idea competition process be designed to deliver better ideas? A few important guidelines are as follows:

1. **Executive-level sponsorship:** Have a senior executive sponsor the competition, play a role in defining the strategic focus, and communicate the importance of the effort in supporting corporate strategy.
2. **Participant section:** Recruit creative, passionate participants with complementary skill sets and perspectives (marketing, consumer insights, R&D, channel sales, production, etc.) and assemble them into teams. Involving key stakeholders in the innovation process fosters conversations that lead to higher quality ideas. It also creates the ownership that accelerates the decision-making process and builds the buy-in necessary for implementation.
3. **Participant preparation:** Treat idea competitions (and *any* innovation effort) as a process – not as an event. Expecting participants to innovate without any meaningful preparation, context or inspiration typically leads to irrelevant "ideas in a vacuum".
4. **Consumer Insight:** Ensure that participants have insight into consumer needs – both articulated and unarticulated. Go beyond historical consumer data and

usage patterns, and seek to understand the voice, heart and mind of consumers. At a bare minimum increase participants' awareness of known issues that consumers have with current products, services and solutions, but for better results build in a "consumer experience" module (such as a field trip) that has participants observe consumers using the current product or service.

5. **Industry Foresight:** Create an orientation towards future-oriented thinking. Help participants identify *emerging* trends along several dimensions, for example: "bleeding edge" technologies, anticipated shifts in the competitive landscape, unusual business models, hypotheses about societal trends, anticipated regulatory shifts, emerging sales channels, new manufacturing practices, etc. Be aware that focusing on historical data and *established* trends is easy to do but typically limits the output to closer-in, incremental ideas such as line extensions. Most companies are familiar with historical trend data but are uncomfortable thinking about "emerging trends" – and yet it is critical.

6. **Strategic, imaginative thinking:** Push participants to break out of traditional thinking modes and challenge their own assumptions. Have them look for lessons and analogs from other industries. At a minimum, introduce interactive stimuli (videos, advertisements, "user scenarios", customer testimonials, etc.). Old habits and thinking patterns are hard to break – stretching participants' thinking to entirely new levels calls for a radically different approach.
Sources/links:

http://www.innovation-point.com/Idea%20Competitions%20and%20Break through%20Innovation.pdf

Jeff Howe (2006) The Rise of Crowdsourcing. http://www.wired.com/wired/archive/14.06/crowds.html

http://www.knowledgeboard.com/item/1286/23/5/3

Erlach, Thier, Neubauer 2005; *Swiss Agency for Development and cooperation: Story Guide- Building bridges using narrative techniques* www.youtube.com/watch?v=UFC-URW6wkU&feature=player_embedded.

Brown JS, Denning S, Groh K, Prusak L Storytelling in organisations. www.amazon.com/dp/0750678208

# Organisational Forms to Leverage Knowledge

**3**

*Innovation would take place if we let people with different backgrounds work together and inspire each other* – Lars Kolind, CEO, Oticon

**Learning Outcomes.** After completing this chapter
- You will know what are organisational challenges and approaches to find a balance between stability/renewal and competition/collaboration;
- You will be able to apply game theory to knowledge sharing behaviour;
- You will know the strengths and weaknesses of different organisational forms regarding knowledge flows
- You will be able to evaluate and determine an appropriate organisational form for a specific business setting
- You will be able to run an After Action Review;

## 3.1    Balancing Antagonisms

How can we create a boundaryless organisation where knowledge flows in and out, from top to bottom and bottom-up, where knowledge flows across units and "knowledge silos" do not exist? How can we create an organisation which learns quickly, innovates and performs its day to day routines in an effective manner?

In this chapter we will deal with the challenges to find the right organisational forms to make a reality this vision.

The art of organising is related to balancing antagonisms: To be successful in knowledge competition organisations must learn to balance *stability and renewal* as well as *cooperation and competition*. An excess of stability can obstruct renewal. At the same time, excess renewal could mean that a regulated business process is no longer possible. This is seen in companies that have to struggle with "*the curse of high growth rates*". The same applies to the act of balancing cooperation and

K. North and G. Kumta, *Knowledge Management,*
Springer Texts in Business and Economics, DOI 10.1007/978-3-319-03698-4_3,
© Springer International Publishing Switzerland 2014

competition within and among companies. Excess competition – e.g. while selecting a supplier company – might bring high returns in a short term. However, this may result in extreme price wars, quality problems and cutting-off from knowledge sources. An excess of internal competition in companies limits knowledge exchange. Too much cooperation makes competitive knowledge accessible to competitors or obstructs cost-effective solutions because the similarities and teamwork are searched at every price (Hansen 2009). Stability and renewal as well as cooperation and competition are the keys to knowledge-based management of a company as we will see subsequently.

## Stability Versus Renewal

In a highly global competitive environment companies need to address a few critical questions – How do companies balance the two conflicting factors of stability and renewal? How do companies enhance order and control while responding to challenges and how do they renew themselves and learn new things? How can companies establish relatively stable general conditions that provide flexibility in organising and combining employees and t resources? (Ciborra 1996, p. 113). On the one hand, organisations must constantly strive to be "different" by re-combining their resources. Knowledge represents a portfolio of options and a platform for future developments. The concept of "*platform organisation*" (Ciborra 1996; Kogut and Zander 1992) discussed below facilitates this perspective. On the other hand, companies must be in a position to enhance their operational efficiency, i.e. to use their competence and skill as optimally as possible in short-term competitive situations. How can companies balance these factors as shown in Fig. 3.1?

In an ***evolutionary perspective***,[1] a company accumulates knowledge over the course of its existence. This knowledge is a source of specific competence of the firm. In its development over time certain thinking pattern are adopted by the employees of the companies, certain behaviour is expected and practiced and particular decision processes are built into the operating procedures and inculcated in the minds of the employees. In this sense, these "*core competencies*" can become "*core rigidities*": "Firms are stuck with what they have and have to live with what they lack" (Leonard-Barton 1992a, b; Burgelmann 1994).

In successful cases, this accumulated knowledge enables the company to process its operative business effectively, strengthens the unique advantages of the company further and contributes to continuous and progressive development of knowledge. *Quality Management* is based on this type of stability focussing on processes and routines.

Renewal – the other side of the balance – implies an ability of the organisation to develop and change its resources and capabilities through learning and innovation.

---

[1] On evolutionary theory see Nelson and Winter (1982).

**Fig. 3.1** Balancing stability and renewal

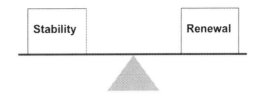

This includes continuous improvement processes as well as disruptive change challenging current wisdom and accepted patterns of action. As we will see in the Oticon case below, it is not easy to institutionalise a renewal process in organisations.

How can firms balance stability – exploiting current capabilities- and renewal – exploring fundamentally new competencies – in order to achieve long-term success? While earlier studies often regarded the trade-offs between these two activities as insurmountable, more recent research describes ***ambidextrous organisations*** (Tushman and O'Reilly 1996; Raisch et al. 2009) that are capable of simultaneously exploiting existing competencies and exploring new opportunities.

> Organisational ambidexterity refers to an organisation's ability to be efficient in their management of today's business and also adaptable for coping with tomorrow's changing demands (Raisch and Birkinshaw 2008).

To compete, companies must continually pursue many types of innovation aimed at existing and new customers (O'Reilly and Tushman 2004):

- Incremental innovations = small improvements in existing products and operations
- "Architectural" innovations = technology or process advances to fundamentally change a component or element of the business
- Discontinuous innovation = radical advances that profoundly alter the basis for competition in an industry

It is not easy to combine these various types of innovation. Kodak for example has long time excelled at analog photography but hasn't been able to make the leap to digital cameras.

Table 3.1 shows that exploitative and explorative business develop different mind sets (tacit knowledge) thus making it so difficult to excel at both.

For discontinuous and sometimes also for architectural innovation it is therefore recommended to set up as an independent unit with its own culture, processes, and structure, but the unit is still integrated within the existing management hierarchy.

What does it take to become ambidextrous?

Based on a number of case studies O'Reilly and Tushman conclude that ambidextrous organisations need ambidextrous senior teams and managers – executives who have the ability to understand and be sensitive to the needs of very different kinds of businesses. Combining the attributes of rigorous cost cutters and

**Table 3.1** The scope of the ambidextrous organisation

| Alignment of: | Exploitative business | Exploratory business |
| --- | --- | --- |
| Strategic intent | Cost, profit | Innovation, growth |
| Critical tasks | Operations, efficiency, incremental innovation | Adaptability, new products, breakthrough innovation |
| Competencies | Operational | Entrepreneurial |
| Structure | Formal, mechanistic | Adaptive, loose |
| Controls, rewards | Margins, productivity | Milestones, growth |
| Culture | Efficiency, low risk, quality, customers | Risk taking, speed, flexibility, experimentation |
| Leadership role | Authoritative, top down | Visionary, involved |

Adapted from O'Reilly and Tushman (2004), p. 80

free-thinking entrepreneurs while maintaining the objectivity required to make difficult trade-offs, such managers are a rare but essential breed. Organisational units should operate in a separated manner, but the senior team needs to be integrated.

Furthermore, a company's senior team must be committed to operating ambidextrously even if its members aren't ambidextrous themselves. Resistance at the top levels of an organisation can't be tolerated, which means that a shift to an ambidextrous organisation can be a wrenching experience.

The authors also have found that a clear and compelling vision, relentlessly communicated by a company's senior team, is crucial in building ambidextrous designs. These aspirations provide an overarching goal that permits exploitation and exploration to coexist. For example Ciba's "Healthy Eyes for Life" were compelling visions that underscored the strategic necessity of ambidexterity and the benefits for all employees, both those in the traditional units and those in the breakthrough initiatives. To maintain momentum and overcome inertia it is important to highlight the concrete accomplishments of the new approach.

### Case Study: Oticon – The spaghetti organisation

Oticon, the Danish hearing aid technology company, was a world leader in behind the ear hearing aids but its market share began to decline, as people moved to 'in the ear' models. Just as the company's market share had dropped from 15 % to 7 % and it was starting to lose money, Lars Kolind took over as CEO to turn its performance around.

A former management consultant and associate Professor at Copenhagen University, Kolind embarked on a classic turnaround strategy: he pared the company down, shed staff and improved efficiency. And he re-focused the business on its key markets. One year later, the strategy seemed to be working and Oticon returned to profit. But Kolind knew that the changes were not enough. "It was clear that we could not survive over the next five years without taking a radical step" he remembers. "Where was our competitive edge? Nowhere".

It was at that point that we reached a sort of breakpoint. I realised the competitive situation was extremely difficult because we were up against all the big boys you can imagine – Siemens, Philips, Sony, 3M, and AT&T. My analysis was that we could never beat them in financial resources; we could never beat them at marketing or at the brand level because they all had fantastic brands. We could never beat them at technology, so we had to find something that we could do in a unique fashion. That led me to believe that if we could design a uniquely innovative, fast moving, efficient organisation, then this is something they could never replicate.

Kolind's response to this problem was a radical new organisational model with no formal hierarchical reporting relationships, a resource allocation system built around self-organised project teams, and an entirely open-plan physical layout. He called it the spaghetti organisation, to symbolise the organic and non-formal structure he was trying to create.

In his concept of the perfect corporate organisation, Kolind placed the interaction, collaboration, and connectivity of people, customers, suppliers, and ideas at the company's heart. Kolind called it "a spaghetti organisation of rich strands in a chaotic network". The key characteristics of a spaghetti organisation are choice (staff initiate projects and assemble teams; individuals invited to join a project can decline); multiple roles (the project approach creates multi-disciplined individuals); and transparency (knowledge is shared throughout the organisation). The organisation is knowledge based and is driven internally by free market forces.

My thinking went like this. If Oticon was to compete with a serious competitor like Siemens, we had to do something radically different. You can't just do it 10 percent different. You have to do it radically different and use your imagination, gut feeling, whatever it is, and hope it will work. So I was aware that I couldn't simply read the same books as the MBAs at Siemens. I had to find something that was unique and better.

So how does the spaghetti organisation work? Any individual who comes up with a good idea is free to assemble a team and act as project leader. Each project, however, then has to compete with all the other projects trying to get off the ground at any time. In true Darwinian fashion, an employee must attract sufficient resources and support for his or her project or it will perish.

Key to freeing up the way people think and work is Oticon's mobile office system. Employees carry their office with them wherever they go at Oticon's headquarters. Desks are not allocated; instead workers use the nearest available workstation, rolling their personal "Rullemaries" (mobile carts) around the hardwood floor to wherever they need to be in the building.

The new way of working seems to have worked. During the following recession, Oticon's industry experienced some of the toughest trading conditions in its history. During those dark days, however, Oticon proved the exception to the rule. It published figures showing an increase of 100 % on revenue and a ten-fold increase in profits in relation to figures of 5 years earlier.

But Kolind sensed that something wasn't right. It had been a hard year, with the company almost exclusively focused on developing and releasing a new line of digital hearing aids. The new products epitomised the breakthrough culture.

The problem was that the temporary teams created to push them through had assumed an air of permanence.

The unorganised company was becoming dangerously organised. Kolind's solution was to "explode Oticon in a new direction". Projects were re-arranged geographically within the building. He described the result as "total chaos" – precisely what he was looking for.

When Lars Kolind stepped down from Oticon after 10 years as CEO he left it in a strong competitive position.

**Source:** *'Rethinking management's first principles – Oticon'*
New frontiers Tomorrow's management innovation today
http://www.managementlab.org/files/u2/pdf/case%20studies/OticonCase
Study_.pdf.

## Competition Versus Cooperation

When should management, business units or research teams go for competition and when would collaboration be more effective? What does collaboration or competition mean for knowledge flows?

To answer these questions consider these two different organisational arrangements:

(a) A firm creates profit centres in order to introduce competitive forces into the organisation. Profit centres might compete for clients and performance of profit centres is ranked so that managers compete for the best rank. They will focus on their individual bottom lines and avoid sharing best practices as each manager would like to stay at the top of the performance ranking and keep the profit centre's "secrets".

(b) A big international firm promotes cross-unit collaboration. Leaders are encouraged to form cross-unit networks focused on areas of shared interest. Over time, this idea flowers into an unforeseen number of networks and sub-networks sharing best practices. But increasingly, the firm finds that people are flying around the world and are simply sharing ideas without always having a strong focus on the bottom line. With this example Hansen (2009, p.12) illustrate the "collaboration trap" that when leaders promote collaboration in their companies, they get more than they bargain for; people often overdo it.

The challenge to balance competition and cooperation is typical for a knowledge-based firm. Different branches of the same consulting firm or an insurance company like to compete with each other for the same customers. However, this competition should not result in loss of a customer because they cannot come to an agreement among themselves on who "*shoots the bear*". Competition must not lead to a conflicting situation wherein revenue targets of one branch inhibit allocation of right resources available in another branch.

**Fig. 3.2** Balancing
competition and cooperation

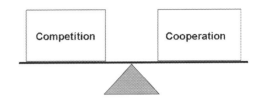

Hansen advocates a "disciplined collaboration" and defines it as "*the leadership practice of properly assessing when to collaborate (and when not to) and instilling in people both the willingness and the ability to collaborate when required*"(Hansen 2009, p. 15).

To accomplish disciplined collaboration Hansen proposes three steps:

***Step 1*: *Evaluate opportunities for collaboration.*** Ask the question: What will we gain from collaboration and what is the cost of collaboration? Make sure that collaboration is not an end in itself.

***Step 2*: *Spot barriers to collaboration.*** What are the barriers blocking people form collaborating well? Particularly look out at the "not–invented-here" barrier, the "hoarding" barrier, the "search" barrier (people are not able to find what they are looking for) and the "transfer" barrier (people are not able to understand and transfer knowledge and practices to different contexts).

***Step 3*: *Tailor solutions to tear down the barriers.*** How to motivate for collaboration and develop the required competences? To overcome the barriers Hansen proposes three levers. The "unification lever" refers to compelling common goals and articulating a strong value of cross-company teamwork. The "people lever" refers to get the right people to collaborate on the right projects. The "network lever" focuses on interpersonal networks and less on formal hierarchies.

### Case Study: Competence networks

The cooperation in networks, communities of practice, marketing teams, core service teams, research groups and specialised teams is gaining more and more importance for a systematic creation and transfer of knowledge. The functions of these networks include the identification, transfer and development of knowledge relevant to the business. For this purpose, teams involved in the competence network conduct benchmarking activities and meet periodically to discuss certain topics. They are the competent 'drop-in centres' for queries. They coach and conduct projects and are responsible for creating and maintaining the contents of databases as well as Intranet.

**IBM** has competence networks that are initiated by the management. There are competence networks for specific business processes, technologies and industry segments. A full-time or a part-time coordinator is appointed. The coordinator meets regularly and otherwise communicates using Lotus notes. Competence networks operate as filter for information that is subsequently also adopted in the network-specific databases. 'Hit lists' serve as a performance measure indicating the most sought after information in the database. There are periodical "health checks" wherein the activities of the network are evaluated by the company management. Furthermore, user polls are conducted periodically. These polls evaluate the value of knowledge gained from networks.

At **McKinsey**, creation and transfer of knowledge is supported practice centres (Peters 1994, p. 170). These practice centres are structured not only as per market segments but also as per service divisions. In these practice centres, one can find company specialists that market their knowledge aggressively. The purpose is establishing a dynamic market of ideas. Every centre tries to increase their knowledge share or "mindshare" (analogous to "market share") in terms of consultants in the company. The practice centres themselves measure the number of internal customers who use their material, presentations, information, methods, etc. Requests for quotation are called as "sales leads". Bestseller lists of project descriptions are published. The method of functioning of a practice centre can be explained well with the example of the Organization Performance Practice Center. The practice centre comprises of approximately 70 consultants worldwide and a support group of four members. This support group operates a "rapid response network" that guarantees a quick response from the consultants. Every member of the practice centre is available as on-call consultant for a certain number of weeks per year and assures an answer within 24 h to the questions coming from any of about 60 offices across approximately 30 countries. The support group evaluates the level of customer satisfaction and a yearly business report about activities and progress of the Performance Practice Centre is published.

## Two-Person Knowledge-Sharing Dilemma[2]

The issue of collaboration versus competition (see Fig. 3.2) has been explored by game theory. When would people be willing to share knowledge and when not?

Knowledge sharing between individuals can possibly result in a benefit for both, but game-theoretically it might not be the equilibrium strategy. We analyse a situation with only two people and two possible actions. The action space (A) per player consists of the two possibilities: knowledge sharing (s) and knowledge hoarding (h).

There are four possible outcomes with the respective payoffs (see Fig. 3.3):

hs: Utility of hoarding while the partner shares his knowledge
ss: Utility of mutual knowledge sharing
hh: Utility of mutual knowledge hoarding
sh: Utility of sharing while the partner is hoarding

---

[2] Text based on http://www.diss.fu-berlin.de/diss/servlets/MCRFileNodeServlet/FUDISS_derivate_000000002325/03_chap3.pdf;jsessionid=DCC25A49443797BEC2C730833FD9884D?hosts=, p. 60–61.

**Fig. 3.3** Payoff matrix of a two-person knowledge-sharing dilemma

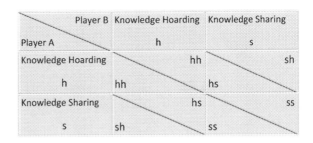

The best situation for a player is to hoard the knowledge while the other player shares the knowledge (hs). The second best outcome is that both share their knowledge (ss). This difference between hs and ss comes from the cost of knowledge sharing and the benefit of being the only one who has this particular knowledge. The third best option is the mutual knowledge hoarding (hh). Therefore, both would be better off if they share mutually instead of mutual hoarding. The worst option is that the player spends the time and effort to share knowledge while the other player hoards his (sh). This leads to the following ranking of the payoffs: hs > ss > hh > sh.

We also assume a situation where the best collective strategy would be mutual knowledge sharing rather than a collusion of sharing and hoarding.

The ranking of the payoffs corresponds to the prisoner's dilemma game. In this situation, it is always individually best not to share the knowledge, independent of the choice of the other person, i.e. knowledge hoarding is a strictly dominant strategy. Consequently mutual hoarding is the equilibrium. Caused by the payoff structure, the players are trapped in a social dilemma. In a social dilemma, optimal individual behaviour has the effect that everybody is worse off than they would be otherwise. Individual rationality leads to collective irrationality. In a social dilemma there is at least one outcome in which every person would be better off than in the equilibrium.

This analysis helps to understand why knowledge sharing is not a dominant strategy in many organisations and hence the need to create convincing motives for cooperation.

From a market related game theory perspective, Nalebuff and Brandenburger have coined the term "*co-opetition*" (Nalebuff and Brandenburger 1996). Co-opetition is a business strategy based on a combination of cooperation and competition, derived from an understanding that business competitors can benefit when they work together. Companies participate in "*competitive collaboration*" in order to get access to knowledge and acquire knowledge collectively. They compete with each other in exploiting this knowledge.

The relation between automobile manufacturers and their suppliers is a good example of competition and cooperation from the knowledge perspective. While selecting the suppliers, the buyers exploit the competitive situation very well. However, they stick to the supplier for longer periods and develop competencies together with the suppliers (North 1997). Competition takes place increasingly at the level of clearly distinct end products and not at the component level or module level.

*Benchmarking* between competitors is another example of this strategy of competition and cooperation. In large companies, some business divisions cooperate through strategic alliances while some business divisions are strong competitors. If such an organisational design is well conceptualised, the competitive collaboration turns into a Plus Sum Game that strengthens the competitiveness of both the partners for a long time.

Cooperation need not always be planned and agreed formally at the management level. It can also take place informally. Thus, with an example of competing steel companies in the USA, Stadler and von Hipple (Stadler 1995; von Hipple 1987) could prove that employees handled information based on mutuality according to the "*GIGI principle*: *give information, get information*" Fig. 3.4 summarizes criteria of people whether to share or not to share knowledge.

Balancing cooperation and competition requires choosing the right organisational setting. Before deciding on organisational structures it is advisable to make clear what are the guiding principles of a business:

"*Success of a unit has a priority over success of a company*": This perspective emphasises competition as a driving force for success. It is assumed that entrepreneurs (or "intranpreneurs" in a company, e.g. a profit centre) act with a motive of optimising unit performance and are therefore interested in optimum use of the resources of their unit. A global control cannot assure this optimum utilisation. Company units that are operated in this manner must be exposed to internal and external competition. Manufacturing plants compete with each other. If the profit objective is not achieved, the business unit is closed down. Profit incentives are dominant. Knowledge is transferred selectively considering the cost-benefit ratio. Often, in such a mindset, the entire company turns into a meaningless financial holding with individual "knowledge silos" that do not cooperate considering that "knowledge is power and must be concealed". Customer benefits and capacity use are suboptimal because units never or rarely work together. The customer does not get a comprehensive service or advice from one source.

"*Searching for synergies is the basis of success*": The synergy or cooperation theory assumes that the possible total performance of the company is higher than the sum of the individual performances of units. Search for synergies and cooperation avoids double work and enables a complete customer service cutting across all the functions of the company. Competitive advantages can be materialised depending on the size of the company and the variety of activities. On the negative side, search for synergy if not leveraged, can be an end in itself. Work groups, professional discussion groups etc. do not convert the transferred knowledge into business success adequately and can lead to long-term strategic disorientation.

"*Segmenting with synergy brings lasting success*": Examples of successful companies show that neither too much segmentation nor too much search for synergy lead to the success of the company. Instead, it is necessary to find a

| Criteria for knowledge sharing or hoarding | What do I gain if I share my knowledge? | What do I loose if I share my knowledge? |
|---|---|---|
| Reputation as "expert" | | |
| Uniqueness of my knowledge | | |
| Job security | | |
| Trust in the organisation | | |
| Value of my knowledge | | |
| Incentives/ rewards/ punishment for (not) sharing | | |
| Time and opportunities to acquire new knowledge | | |
| Others: | | |

**Fig. 3.4** Criteria to decide whether to share or not to share knowledge

*synthesis* between both guiding principles as "*segmenting with synergy*" (Goold and Campbell 1998). Businesses are tied together by strong shared values, aligned towards common goals and moral concepts of the entire company. They combine short-term success of the units with the long-term competence development of the entire company. This concept considers short-term as well as long-term competitiveness of the company. The flexibility of a small company is combined with the resources – especially the knowledge – of a big company. Such a company can offer complete and complex solutions that are difficult to imitate and can be redeemed for suitable prices. The restructuring of General Electric aimed at such segmentation with synergy. In his introduction to the annual report 1995 Jack Welsh, the then Chief Executive Officer, General Electric, has expressed this as follows:

What we wanted to built was a hybrid, an enterprise with the reach and resources of a big company – the body – but the thirst to learn, the compulsion to share and the bias for action – the soul – of a small company.

**Minicase: Mindtree I**

Full dependence on directed structures is not enough for the new era the Indian software company MindTree www.mindtree.com has prepared to meet. MindTree views a new era organisation as a set of interdependent, collaborating, interacting knowledge workers who are autonomous and who configure and reconfigure their people-networks dynamically to achieve a purpose determined by them in the fast-moving environment they work in.

As knowledge workers accomplish their work, they step across their task boundaries, collaborate, seek knowledge and so on, to accomplish the task not as originally perceived, but as the solution emerges. *"This creates a highly scalable and agile model of the organisation, and in the long run creates an organisation capable of self-transformation"* says Datta.

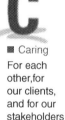    

■ Caring
For each
other,for
our clients,
and for our
stakeholders

■ Learning
Personal
development
and innovation

■ Achieving
Aspiration,
accountability,
and action
orientation

■ Sharing
Team work
and
knowledge
creation

■ Social
Responsibility
Corporate
citizenship
and integrity

MindTree's vision reads as follows: *"What brings MindTree Minds (what we call our employees) together in building an organisation that has a unique culture is our value system. Every MindTree Mind is driven by CLASS, the acronym for our core values of Caring, Learning, Achieving, Sharing, and Social Responsibility. Everything we are, everything we do, and everything we believe in revolves around our CLASS values and the distinct culture that we have built. The two main attributes that characterize our culture are high achievement orientation and high caring."*

**Case Study: Allianz Group Business Services (AGBS) encourages knowledge synergies**

Allianz Insurance Group is made up of huge number of subsidiaries worldwide. These companies are operated as per the decentralised philosophy (business is local). However, the continuous utilisation of synergies within the global network of companies is a critical success factor of this business model. The prerequisite for this is a pragmatic knowledge identification and transfer process that is practiced and encouraged by the management and the employees in all the companies of the group.

AGBS is a unit in the Group Centre which facilitates the global process of knowledge transfer and provides suitable tools and methods. The following figure gives an overview of the approach of AGBS's knowledge management.

First, priority topics are selected based on expected benefits. Secondly, best practices and expertise are identified and in a third step discussed and transferred by workshops, community interaction and an IT platform. It follows a localised implementation process as well as an evaluation. Results are made public via a "synergy balance sheet". The following arrangements are considered of particular importance for the success of the programme:

*Expert teams*: These are groups of five to eight members comprising international experts from different specialised fields. These groups are germ cells of new knowledge and work predominantly on strategic questions. Every expert team has a basic "mission" as well as an annual goal that is decided together by the expert team manager and AGBS. The expert teams share their knowledge and the outcome of their work with the practitioners around the world through online communities as well as in regular workshops. Furthermore, they document the developed knowledge in the "Expert Team Reports" that are provided in the communities and in compass with others.

*Incentive systems*: Knowledge management is also integrated in an established incentive system. Participation in the activities of knowledge management (e.g. expert team) is a criterion for achieving a certain level of management. This is documented in a policy in "Group HR Handbook". Furthermore, specific incentives were created for knowledge sellers and knowledge buyers, e.g. awards such as Knowledge Manager of the Year, Expert Team of the Year, etc. Targets are set for knowledge management actors such as expert team managers. These target agreements can be considered according to their bonus relevance.

| Theme selection/ demand | Identification/ development of knowledge | Distribution of knowledge | Application of knowledge | Evaluation of knowledge | |
|---|---|---|---|---|---|
| • OE demand<br>• Business volumes<br>• effects on *value driver*<br>• setting targets strategically driven by groups | Identification, development and supply of best practice along the value creation chain | Distributing identified/ developed good practices over suitable media and channels | Implementation of good practices in organizational units | Measuring (qualitative and quantitative) and balancing success | Synergies |
| • AGBS Steering Committee<br>• Matching Service | • Expert Teams<br>• Yellow Pages<br>• Compass | • Workshops<br>• Communities<br>• Compass | • Consultancy projects<br>• Group Consultants<br>• OPEX | Synergy Balance | |

Basic conditions: knowledge manager network, IT infrastructure, incentive systems and marketing

*IT infrastructure*: AGBS supports the knowledge transfer process using (web-based) IT infrastructure such as yellow pages; Compass database of "good practice"; Online communities, Communication platforms for communities of practice; Info miner, Intelligent search engine; Virtual project offices, Online team space for collaborations in projects. All the IT components are based on a uniform IT platform (Group Intranet) and linked with each other in such a way that usage barriers such as multiple logins or redundant data entries are avoided.

*Synergy portal*: There is a synergy portal for internal marketing. This portal provides access to the knowledge documents and experts as well as gives an overview of the knowledge management activities organised by AGBS (workshops, expert teams, projects etc.). Synergy Review, a quarterly magazine, presents the results and connects the community with the management.

*Synergy balance*: Cost and benefits of the described tools and methods are incorporated in the "Synergy Balance" that is created by AGBS on a quarterly basis. Benefits of projects are measured on the basis of calculated "Fair Values" and the benefits of knowledge management tools are measured on the basis of calculation of opportunity cost. Trends and developments are identified earlier thus enabling the company to react to the changes earlier and effectively. This reduces the "time to market" of new products. Increasing efficiency and effectiveness by using internal best practice as well as avoiding mistakes has positive impacts on the Economic Value Added (EVA).

**Source:** based on material provided by Allianz AGBS

## 3.2   Platforms for Knowledge Creation

Apart from reformulating the entire organisation of the company in order to convert the dialectics between renewal and stability, cooperation and competition into short-term and long-term business goals, there are approaches designed to maintain the existing organisational forms and also to institutionalise supplementary or parallel ad hoc organisational forms such as process and project organisation. Knowledge is linked to departments, projects and business processes. In most cases, it is not processed, shared and transferred beyond the limits of organisational entities systematically.

While the traditional organisation guarantees stability and short-term business results, the ad hoc forms create contexts for the renewal that can then be docked to the existing organisation. From a somewhat different viewpoint, the existing organisation turns into a platform that offers a certain framework, an infrastructure and a basic layout from which the new developments can "*take off*" and also land again accordingly.

Let us have a closer look at two of these approaches –the *hypertext organisation* as described by Nonaka and Takeuchi and the *platform organisation* as described by Ciborra.

## The Hypertext Organisation

The model of the hypertext organisation (Nonaka and Takeuchi 1995, p. 169ff) assumes that a company can have a non-hierarchical and self-organised structure that cooperates with the hierarchical formal structure. While the latter ensures stability, the hypertext organisation equips the company with the strategic capability to acquire, recreate and use new knowledge continuously in a cyclic process. Like a hypertext, this organisation comprises of a number of interconnected levels or contexts, especially the levels of business systems, project teams and knowledge bases (see Fig. 3.5).

- The operative business is conducted at the central *level of business system*. This can happen not only through a traditional bureaucratic structure but also through entrepreneurial processes meant for building an entrepreneurial corporation.
- At the *project team level*, a number of project teams are engaged in the development of new knowledge, e.g. development of a new product. The team members are recruited from various units of the business system and are allotted to the project team until the end of the project.
- At the *knowledge base level*, the knowledge created in the upper level is re-categorised and placed in a new context so that is available commonly in the company thereafter. The knowledge basis level does not exist as an independently organised unit. Instead, it gains its existence from the knowledge workers of a company and the corresponding systems for saving information or safeguarding knowledge.

The remarkable feature of the hypertext organisation is that three different levels or contexts co-exist in the same organisation. The process of knowledge creation is a dynamic cycle that is set in motion effortlessly by these three levels. The project team members who were selected from different functions and departments of the business system level perform knowledge-creating activities. Once the project team functions are completed, the members take to the knowledge level. They pass their knowledge on through internal seminars or workshops, make project reports or enter information in the company's information system. After re-categorising and re-contextualising, the project team members go to the business system level wherein they again dedicate themselves to the operative business until they are reallocated to another project team. According to Nonaka and Takeuchi, the feasibility of switching in and out of different knowledge contexts quickly and with flexibility and thus building a dynamic cycle of knowledge creation determines the organisational capability to create knowledge.

**Case Study: Hypertext: Creating organisational linkages**
**Case1: The Eureka Forbes Senate**

   When Eureka Forbes (EFL), a multi-product, multi-channel corporation and a leader in domestic and industrial water purification systems, vacuum cleaning and air purification solutions in India, was searching for a way to connect with all its employees, it found a model right in its backyard – in the Indian Parliament

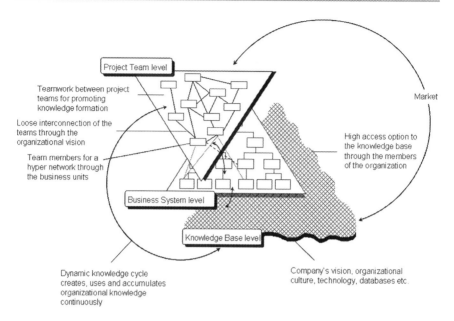

**Fig. 3.5** The hypertext organisation (Source: Nonaka and Takeuchi 1995, p.169)

(Ghosh 2010). EFL decided to create a senate, a sort of a parallel governing body, which would have representatives from all Eureka Forbes' centres across the country. "The idea was to make sure each and every one of our employees has a voice," says Marzin R Shroff, CEO, direct sales. "We wanted to tell them that they will be heard. The senate, as we see it, is an important empowerment initiative."

At the heart of the set-up is the EuroSenate, a 14-member body of elected representatives – one each from Eureka Forbes' 14 strategic business units, or geographic zones. The representatives, called senators, are assisted by a three-member council, also elected from the SBU or the 'constituency'. The 42 councillors and the 14 senators report in to six governors, regional heads of the company. There is also a president, speaker and a Senate Administration Committee. "The senate has taken care of so many of our problems, both big and small," says H R Ganesh, senator for the Karnataka region. "Many things were difficult to bring to the notice of the head office before. We didn't have an opportunity to meet the Directors either, and tell them about our problems. Now, as part of the senate, we get to interact with them at least once every three months."

The senators and their councillors have a clear mandate. They are to be the emissaries of the head office in the zones, and a conduit between workers and the HQ. "They must have their ear to the ground, and their eyes on their teams," says Shubha Ashraf, deputy general manager of the Knowledge Management team, which came up with the idea of the senate.

Source: Interview with Eurekoa Forbes.

### Case 2: Sharp – hypertext in research and development

Since its inception in the 1912, Sharp has had a reputation of a "*new product*" company. The constant pursuit of creativity and originality is represented in its slogan "do not imitate". We find all the three levels of the hypertext organisation in Sharp's research and development.

- *Business system level*: The day-to-day business of the R&D is organised in the traditional hierarchical form. The central R&D is responsible for basic developments that take three or more years, the company's laboratories cover specific themes with a time frame of approximately one and a half to 3 years and the R&D in the business segments works based on product and process for a time frame of less than a year and a half. The R&D facility communicates hierarchically from the centre to the business segments. Conferences, meetings and workgroups coordinate the exchange of explicit knowledge of all the facilities.
- *Project team level*: New products are developed by "*Task Forces*" that operate quite independently and parallel to the R&D structure at the business system level. While new products are normally developed in the projects of the business segments, the strategically important development projects are allocated to the "*Urgent Project System*". Employees of these projects leave their position in the business segments and work exclusively for the strategic project for a period of 1–2 years without any budget limitations enjoying the privileges of directors.
- *Knowledge basis level*: Sharp's knowledge base can be described by explicit knowledge in the field of optoelectronics and tacit knowledge that is symbolised by the "*do not imitate*" slogan. The knowledge generated at the business system level and project team level is re-categorised and placed in a new context with a view to develop optoelectronics systematically. The constant exchange within the business systems as well as with the project teams and process of storage and transfer of explicit knowledge revive the knowledge base. The tacit knowledge "*do not imitate*" is strengthened by frequent exchange and inner R&D culture.

Source: According to Nonaka and Takeuchi (1995), p. 181–190.

## The Platform Organisation

Inspired by his Italian experience and a case study at Olivetti, Ciborra (1996) had suggested a meta-organisation in order to react adequately to surprises in unstable circumstances. Management assumes that managers direct their decisions towards clear goals and strategies based on a rational problem solving process. Ciborra contrasts this fiction of a systematic management process, with his view of management that is characterised by the French term *"Bricolage"* (repairing, tinkering or improvising like a jazz ensemble).

Similar to jazz ensemble, the employees in the company have learnt to play and improvise together in order to solve the arising problems quickly, respond to unexpected customer demands or implement and test new product ideas without long justification and approval processes. Ciborra cites Mary C. Bateson (1994):

> Men and women confronting change are never fully prepared for the demand of the moment but they are strengthened to meet uncertainty if they can claim a history of improvisation and a habit of reflection.

Ciborra argues that in a fast changing environment, none of the organisational forms are in a position to optimise the use of resources. A "formless" chameleonic organisation that generates new forms through frequent recombination would be most suitable here. From the structural view, the platform is a result of the union of existing organisational mechanisms and forms selected and assembled together by the management according to subjective and situational plans and interpretations (Weick 1993).

The platform organisation is identified by its flexibility, mobility and continuous transformation that results from overlapping, intersecting and juxtaposing different organisation arrangements such as network, matrix or even hierarchy. A platform organisation appears fragmented and interwoven at the same time. However, it could be the only form that survives the high-tech industry wherein a monolithic and fixed company identity would not have been in the position to cope up with the fast technological changes. Unlike every traditional form of organisation, platform organisation features a collection of all the qualities of a clear, seemingly opposite as well as surprising coincidence. This platform contains an exciting mixture of prefabricated arrangements and interpretations as well as solutions and visions that are either found or provided incompletely or have not yet materialised. It is a model that completely changes our opinion about structural and permanent or subjective, informal and short-lived. It is the function of a platform organisation, to cope not only with the often sudden and radical changes to the products, markets and technologies but also with changes – to the identity of the business fields or industry segments – that are sensed by the organisation incidentally over time.

According to Ciborra, the ability to leave old identities and develop a new identity that is adapted to the respective technological phase represents a key to this fast sequence of unexpected and unplanned transformation processes.

The platform organisation is inspired by computer or car platforms on which a huge number of models are produced. Individual components of the organisational platforms can represent the organisational units, departments, functions and division. Every defined unit has a mission and eases the control at least at local level. The integration of different components is flexible and not represented in an organogram. Units and organisations outside the limits of companies are also integrated. Common research and development projects and global alliances are built and disintegrated according to the requirements.

Thanks to the existence of platform standards, technologies are developed independent of products. Thus, technologies can be combined at *"last minute"* and bundled into specific products for which a market demand is identified or into products that react to the activities of competitors. The research and development must work closely with the marketing function in such an organisation in order to exploit the market opportunities quickly.

How does a platform organisation differ from a network? The platform organisation acts at two levels. Firstly, it works at a structural level wherein routines and transactions function like those in a network. Secondly, it acts at the higher level wherein the frequent structural changes are organised. The dynamic recombination of routines and transactions is important at this level and not the features of a specific organisational arrangement such as that of a network. *How to form a relatively stable environment wherein the employees and resources can be used with flexibility?* – This important question for high tech companies was answered by Olivetti in its own way: the formal structure changes frequently and abruptly while the informal networks remain relatively stable.

**Minicase: WIPRO as a platform organisation**

WIPRO was initially set up in 1945 with main product of producing sunflower Vanaspati oil and various soaps. At that time the company was called Western India Vegetable Products Limited with representative offices in Maharashtra and Madhya Pradesh states of India. During the 1970s and 1980s it shifted its focus and begin to look into business opportunities in IT and the computing industry which was at nascent stages in India at that time. WIPRO was the first company which marketed the first indigenous homemade PC from India in 1975.

In 1966 Azim Premji, still the majority shareholder in WIPRO, took over as the chairman of the company at the age of 21 and with the passage of time transformed it into one of the finest and largest IT outsourcing services provider of the world. It is now considered the world's largest independent R&D service provider and offers different technology driven services all over the globe with 46 development centres.

In the following section we shall have a look at selected organisational forms from the perspective of knowledge creation and knowledge transfer.

## 3.3   From "Infinitely Flat" to "Star Burst"

Commonly companies structure their organisation according to product groups, process investments, geographical necessities or functions in order to increase effectiveness and efficiency. These organisational forms follow the criteria of stability – especially that of control. Request for renewal, the demands of many employees for more freedom and creativity as well as the information and communication technology, have given rise to a complete range of new organisational forms. Four such ideal types can be described as follows (Quinn et al. 1996).

From the knowledge viewpoint, these forms of organisations – viz. "infinitely flat", "inverted", "star burst" and "spider" – are different from each other in the following aspects:

- *Localisation of knowledge*: Where can one actually find the deep knowledge that presents the core competencies of a company?
- *Localisation of "customisation"*: Where is knowledge converted into customer solutions?
- *Direction of the knowledge flow*: In which direction does the value-creating knowledge flow?
- *Method of leverage*: How does an organisation transform the knowledge from individual to collective knowledge?

All the aforementioned forms of organisation tend to delegate responsibility to the part where the company comes in contact with the customers. All the forms create a flat organisation and remove hierarchies. They all seek fast, adequate and individual customer communication. All these forms require that you overlook the traditional mindset about command lines, "one employee one boss" structure, centre being the leading power and management of tangible assets being a key to success. But each of these organisational forms varies significantly in terms of their purpose and management. Let us have a closer look at these different forms of organisation from the knowledge viewpoints You can see the comparison of these organisational forms at the end of this chapter. Every type of organisation is described theoretically as well and is followed by a case study.

## The Infinitely Flat Organisation: Effective Replication of Routines

The centre of this organisation stays in contact with infinite nodes, e.g. individual field staff, branch offices of franchise partners etc. The leading competence or the knowledge on how to create and operate a fast food chain or how to sell Tupperware and Avon cosmetics lies at the centre. The knowledge about the customers lies with the employees of the branches that work parallel with less direct communication. Thus, the centre is the source of information, coordinator, place of transfer of best practices and problem solver. It is the core of the growth process. In the market, new nodes, i.e. branch offices or franchise partners are constantly added to the centre. Furthermore, the centre continuously generates new products and services packages that are then provided to the nodes by means of intensive training and e-learning.

Such flat organisational structures are particularly effective when it is possible to break up the activities of the nodes in individual sections and to optimise these activities. This is the case with the recipes and the operating guidelines of a fast food chain or the basic components of financial transactions of financial brokers and banks. In the best case scenario, the training curve is accelerated through the information system across the company in such a way that employees with relatively few qualifications are capable of giving higher performance relatively quickly.

This reminds us of a *"Tayloristic"* division of work wherein the higher efficiency is linked to fast growth and a continuous innovation process. However, there is no traditional career path anymore in such infinitely flat organisations. Wage-incentive systems must contain a balance of qualitative and quantitative performance parameters. This type of infinitely flat organisation presents an option to create a *"highly intelligent"* organisation with employees having relatively less education and knowledge. It also gives an option to respond quickly to the market changes by being equipped with *"efficient market antennae"*.

### Case Study: Financial Service provider: Replicating financial services

The operative business of a financial service provider is carried out by approximately 18,000 brokers in over 500 business units scattered over a wide region. The company offers custom-made solutions to its customers. The local brokers act as independent entrepreneurs. Generally, they are not those clever investment experts who have undergone long years of training. Yet, by means of information transfer using a widely developed information system, they are able to provide investment advice as well as detailed and precise information about huge volumes of complicated financial instruments. These brokers are supported by the centre wherein a few financial experts work with outstanding analytical skills. They cooperate closely with the other external specialists as well as the "inventors" of the investment model. They analyse the previously concluded business transactions and bring in their expert knowledge in the company's software model and databases. The on-site brokers have access to the detailed analysis of financial markets, economic trends etc. Thus, the centre breaks down the process of investment advice in individual replicable steps and provides them to the on-site broker. The electronic network of the company guarantees that the broker is always updated with the latest information. They are informed extensively by the centre about concluding business transactions, commercial guidelines, profit, conditions of commercial paper, investment options, fiscal considerations and new offers of commercial paper. The software of the company is available online and also serves as a medium of imparting fast training. Thus, it is ensured that all the brokers work as per valid rules, all the calculation and typing errors are eliminated to a large extent and the customers are supplied with the latest marketing information. In short, the entire knowledge is available to each and every broker. Ad hoc teams are built in case of huge and complicated projects with a purpose to pool the widely scattered talent temporarily in order to solve a particular customer problem. Thus, in one year, the brokers work together with different colleagues on various projects. Therefore, in order to develop the business, the infinitely flat organisation is supplemented by network structures wherein the reward is linked to the cooperation between development projects and customer projects. Those who do not work in a team or do not aim at customer satisfaction are penalised (see Quinn et al. 1996, S. 99ff.).

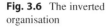

**Fig. 3.6** The inverted organisation

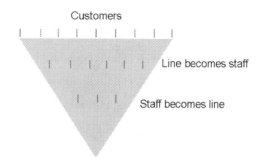

## The Inverted Organisation: Support to Individual Expertise

The traditional hierarchical pyramid, shown in Fig. 3.6, is turned upside down in this organisational form. The core competencies of the company as well as the customer knowledge are found at the nodes and not at the centre. Examples of such organisations are hospitals, consultancy firms or engineering firms (here, the nodes are the doctors, the partners of the consultancy firm, the engineering experts, etc.).

Generally, in an inverted organisation, the exchange of knowledge between the individual nodes tends to happen informally while exchange of knowledge between a node and the centre is a formal process. This is distributive allocation of knowledge, i.e. the organisation offers logistic or administrative support of experts but it does not give instructions or control the business operations. The function of a line manager is restricted to overcoming the bottlenecks, developing the company culture, providing advice on request, starting exchange of experiences and cooperation as well as providing a range of services offered to the experts. Hierarchy can exist to a certain extent in order to ensure consistency in carrying out a task as per corresponding rules, e.g. statutory orders. In a way, the line management adopts the functions of the staff.

Inverted organisations function well if the employee handling the customer has more information and knowledge about the customer's problem and possible solutions than the centre and if experts are willing to learn jointly. Safeguarding effective knowledge transfer and competence development of the entire organisation (collective thinking) is a special challenge for such inverted organisations so that on the one hand knowledge is retained when a specialist or a team leaves the company and on the other hand it is possible to create new business fields.

Furthermore, the loss of formal authority can be traumatic for earlier management of the classical type. Specialists gladly ignore the rules and the norms of the company. As a result, a strong common value system and incentive system that honours not only the individual performance but also the contribution to the development of the entire company is necessary for the functioning of an inverted organisation. If this does not happen, the individual competence that is generally high cannot be converted into high competence of the entire company.

Colleges are a good example of this scenario. Generally, the individual high-school teachers or institutes have high field-specific competence that is used only in rare cases through effective cooperation to increase the competence and the renewal ability of the entire entity.

### Case Study: NovaCare – The rehabilitation service provider

With the reform in the public health sectors worldwide, there is a search for new organisational structures. The service provider, NovaCare is an interesting benchmark for the organisation of paramedical occupations. NovaCare comprises over 5,000 occupational therapists, speech therapists and physiotherapists who operate in a type of franchising system. These specialists offer their knowledge at more than 2,000 locations all over the country. The centre undertakes the administrative and commercial functions of the therapists by signing contracts with rehabilitation services, retirement homes, etc., by undertaking the accounting as well as supporting the scheduling and reporting over the course of the therapy. Furthermore, vocational training is organised and the performance of the therapists is marketed in order to achieve stability and increase in the income.

NovaCare has saved a major part of the knowledge of its therapist in its software system. The information about patients, scheduling and invoicing is added through administrative procedures such as guidelines. The therapist must follow these procedures. From NovaNet, the company management can get information on trends or problems that would need consideration in the near future. NovaNet collects information about costs and service features from all the therapists, particularly effective treatments as well as information about changing medical care model in different areas. This information is very important for recruiting, training, motivating and further training of the therapists. NovaCare records the work of its therapists in 10-min blocks so that it is easier to record and analyse all the knowledge. This detailed information is saved in the database that can be used by anyone who is interested, e.g. care facilities, hospitals, rehabilitation clinics, health insurance companies, etc. NovaCare uses detailed reports of colleagues and patients in order to evaluate the performance of its therapists and to pay them according the quality and scope of their service.

The therapists are independent, especially when it comes to treating a patient. The company's regional administrative offices responsible for accounting, marketing and logistics are primarily meant to support the therapists. Thus, the organisational structure is distributive. Logistics, analyses and administrative support are the function of the structure. These functions are carried out by qualified therapists (see Quinn et al. 1996, p. 191ff.).

## The Starburst Organisation: The New Business Creator

Organisations that are depicted in the form of a *star burst* have specialised and value creating knowledge in the branches as well as at the centre. These companies continuously generate new business fields or companies that in turn build new companies. The branch operates largely independently in the market and raises its capital in the market.

In the analogy to financial holding, the star burst organisation is a *"knowledge holding"* wherein new companies are formed continuously based on the specialised competence. Examples of such companies are film studios, insurance companies or even software companies that open different markets and market niche with their firms with the help of a certain basic software. Large companies which embarked on implementation of ERP systems set up IT departments to support the company. When these developed expertise in implementation of IT solutions, the companies leveraged this expertise and created another company whose main business was IT solutions. There are a number of examples of these in India – L&T Infotech from Larsen & Toubro, an engineering company, 3i Infotech was promoted by ICICI Bank, India's largest private sector bank, and NSE.IT Limited, a 100 % subsidiary of the National Stock Exchange of India Limited (NSEIL) which is a Vertical Specialist Enterprise, specialising in providing complete IT solutions to stock exchanges, clearing corporations, brokerage firms, insurance firms and other organisations in the financial sector.

The constant renewal and recombination of knowledge through cooperation is more important for these companies as compared to components of stabilisation.

Starburst organisations (Fig. 3.7) are particularly successful when they have expensive or complex know-how on the one hand and on the other hand operate in a business environment that changes quickly and for which entrepreneurship becomes essential.

In this way, it is possible to amortise expensive and specialised knowledge immediately in different markets. Thus, the company can penetrate the differentiated markets quickly with minimum equity and high competence. The centre designs the organisational culture, cultivates innovation and risk, sets priorities, selects key persons (an entrepreneur in a company or important know-how bearers) and procures resources more efficiently than the branch. However, the actual entrepreneurial activities take place in the branches that have extensive freedom in organising their business fields as long as such branches are commercially successful. A classical problem in this form of organisation is that, often the central management loses faith in the branches very quickly if the desired market results do not appear rapidly enough. Efforts are made to consolidate such branches thus disturbing its energy. Yet another problem arises when the branch develops a very high capital requirement that is not covered by the centre and capitalisation through the market is undesirable.

**Fig. 3.7** The starburst organisation

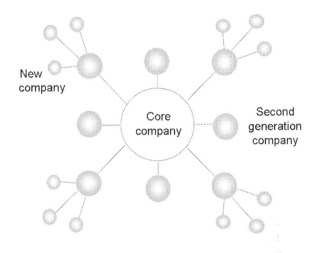

New
company

Core
company

Second
generation
company

---

### Case Study: 3M – The product generator

The Minnesota Mining and Manufacturing Company (3M) is less known for a long-term strategically planned product development process than for its "bottom up" approach towards mobilising capabilities, inventive talent and organisational activities. 3M's obsession to generate new products was given a form by the "Eleventh Commandment" – "thou shall not kill ideas for new products". As opposed to the traditional decision process, if someone thinks that the idea is not good, the burden of proof is on the person who thinks that the idea is not good and not on the person who has proposed the idea. 3M researchers and developers enjoy a free time of up to 15 % of their work time to pursue their own dreams and ideas ("15-percent-rule"). The performance of every business unit is graded on whether at least 25 % of their turnover is achieved with products that are younger than 5 years. In reality, the share of such products in the company's turnover has gone beyond 30 %.

3M has announced that an individual inventor or entrepreneur can develop their ideas and establish new business units continuously under the slogan "grow and divide". This growth is supported by a categorisation of core technologies, range of technical forums, cross-functional teams and a fault tolerance. If a business idea fails, an inventor or entrepreneur shall have the guarantee of being transferred back to their old position. The company encourages creation of legends of successful inventors or entrepreneurs and motivates the others to imitate the same. Thus, stories of how Art Fry sang in the church choir and his makeshift bookmarks fell off his prayer book will be narrated again and again. He came up with the idea of developing the "Post-it" note, materialising this idea technically, overcoming opposition ("we do not need anything like that") and making a successful business (see Nonaka and Takeuchi 1995).

## The Spider Organisation: Creating Value by Networks

The spider's web is a metaphor for an ideal type of network. Company networks are an organisational form of economic activities. Such organisational form binds the coordination potentials of market and hierarchy (organisation) with each other in an intelligent manner and is distinguished by cooperative – rather than competitive – and relatively stable relationships between more than two legally independent companies or company units that are financially more or less dependent (Sydow and van Well 1996, p. 197). The nodes can be products, services or competence centres for specific technologies. They can bear regional responsibility, have a long-term existence or can be installed temporarily as projects. Knowledge is mobilised in the presence of projects or order situations – "*the spider starts running to hunt down the prey*". Knowledge flows within numerous nodes. Typically, the individual nodes work together only temporarily in order to develop specific customer solutions. See Fig. 3.8.

Knowledge development is exponential. Very few nodes give rise to several combination options. Such project-related or order-related networks exist already since hundreds of years, e.g. universities or networks of trading groups. The advantage of the networks is that they can successfully facilitate high specialisation and handling of different geographical regions and simultaneously focus on a specific problem of a specific customer. Hence, the network model is also used in the management of international companies, e.g. in the form of model of a transnational corporation (Bartlett and Ghoshal 1989).

Although the network is good for a fast response and for ad hoc problem solutions, it poses difficulties in developing long-term business strategies. Competition between individual nodes can obstruct the distribution of knowledge. Networks function properly only if there is an open culture and a willingness to cooperate. The grading systems must rate the networks based on their individual success and their contribution to the total success of the organisation or other network nodes. Common interests of the members of a network, a common value system or intersecting value system and profit – all of which is achieved by teamwork – is essential for functioning of every network. According to Quinn (1996, p. 22) the following must be considered for an *effective network management*:

- Networks must overlap each other in order to increase exchange of information and the process of learning.
- Hierarchical structures should remain undefined deliberately.
- Network purposes (project purposes) should be set and strengthened continuously.
- Too much elaboration should be avoided in case of rules meant for appropriation of funds or distribution of profit to individual nodes.
- Continuous mechanisms must be developed in order to provide the nodes with latest information about the external business environment.

**Fig. 3.8** The spider organisation

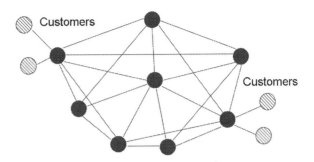

- Customers as well as the colleagues should evaluate the performance of the nodes.
- The members of the nodes should be rewarded with individual and group incentives for their teamwork.

### Case Study: The Indian Youth Climate Network (IYCN)

The Indian Youth Climate Network (IYCN) is a network uniting Indian youth and youth oriented organisations who are concerned about climate change and environmental issues. Since it was founded in 2008 it has grown rapidly and has today offices in six locations, with sub groups in 18 different states reaching out to thousands of youth in colleges, schools, corporations and institutions.

IYCN works on three levels – as a network of people, as a network of partners and support- groups, and as a provider of services and projects. By working in this way the organisation is able to do a wide range of activities to achieve its aims of generating awareness about and establish consensus on what role India should play in the global debate on climate change. IYCN also addresses national issues related to the environment and climate change. The three strategies IYCN uses to achieve this are awareness campaigns, policy advocacy and results oriented projects. Through these three platforms IYCN organises a range of different activities such as Youth summits and solutions fairs, Environmental Audits for corporations, ongoing campaigns, policy tracking, advisory work and giving young people a voice in the international climate change debate by sending youth delegations to international conventions.

Source: www.iycn.in.

Generally, we find that more of these ideal types of organisational forms co-exist in real organisations. For instance, the reservation system of one airline and the respective operative systems are linked but are designed in a completely different manner in their organisation. The reservation service is a spider's web, the flight operations are infinitely flat, the financial administration is conservative and hierarchical, the maintenance and ground service is decentralised and hierarchical and the training and advanced training are organised functionally. Thus, different organisational structures and contexts can co-exist in one company as long as it makes sense for the functions that are to be completed.

## 3.4    Overcoming Deficiencies of the Multidivisional Organisation

In the last 50 years, enterprises, particularly the big ones, across the world have focused largely on independent and mostly product-related divisions or segments. These enterprises were and are still successful in markets and company environments that are relatively stable. Multidivisional companies are best equipped to react to *linear and incremental changes* in the company environment. However, an organisation with a constantly improved organisational processes and rules of conduct – wherein everything is governed – has become an Achilles' heel of the company in a changing competitive environment. Such an environment requires acting under turbulent changes that are often unpredictable and are of discontinuous type (Ghoshal and Bartlett 1995). A multidivisional company is poorly equipped for strategic renewal and largely incapable of developing new business fields within the company. Growth in such a company is mostly restricted to existing business fields by means of economies of scale, economies of scope or by huge financial power. New activities tend to be launched by acquisition of smaller create companies.

The independent nature of individual business units create obstacles in the path towards success in a knowledge competition wherein products and services bundle different competencies of a company and create value for customers in an integrated manner. The premise of independence is preventing the companies from integrating their diverse research, development, production and marketing resources into a coherent system for value delivery. The multidivisional company is built on the assumption of horizontal independence and vertical dependence and in its pure form does not have any effective mechanism for managing the interdependencies. Horizontal interdependence is not a part of the mindset of this form of organisation.

Ghoshal and Bartlett (1995, p. 143–144) argue that the strength of the multidivisional companies in a linear and increasingly changing competitive environment is a result of efficient ways of processing information and knowledge development derived from such processing. In such companies, information processing is structured according to business unit level, divisional level and corporate level. Business units deliver data. This data is analysed and organised into business-relevant information at the business unit level and division level. The entire company (corporate staff groups) combines information from different sources for the purpose of generating value. The company management absorbs and institutionalises this knowledge in order to derive "*wisdom*" that becomes a part of the accepted perspective and standards of a company. Mechanisms and routines of budgeting, planning and control represent the dominating strength of divisionalised company through efficient work allocation and specialisation in procurement, analysis and interpretation of data in the stages of information, knowledge and "*wisdom*". The hierarchical multidivisional company is well-equipped if the information cost is high and the company environment is stable (Klodt et al. 1997, p. 70ff), as shown in Fig. 3.9. Organisational knowledge is generated and used increasingly for improving the operating process of existing activities.

However, these companies lack the antithesis of this sequential and incremental knowledge-building process that is necessary for strategic renewal. Multidivisional companies do not have a process that is capable of challenging institutionalised wisdom, overturning existing knowledge bases and re-configuring the sources of data. Companies become immobilised in the absence of these challenges. Too many "sacred cows" hinder the action-oriented and anticipation process beyond the boundaries of divisions.

This criticism of Ghoshal and Bartlett is shared by another management researcher, particularly from the viewpoint of multinational companies. In contrast to M-form (m = multidivisional), Hedlund (1994) proposed a new form of organisation called N-form (n = new) that is better at dealing with wide variation and fast changes in knowledge inside the companies. Instead of bringing information to a given decision point, the decisions should be shifted to where the knowledge is available. Let us have a look at the concept of firm that is more capable of renewal as compared to the traditional multidivisional organisation.

## The Entrepreneurial Corporation

Ghoshal and Bartlett (1995) have developed an organisational form called as "*Entrepreneurial Corporation*".

The entrepreneurial corporation contains three processes – entrepreneurial process, renewal process and integration process that links the earlier two processes. These processes are given a definite form by the *front line entrepreneurs, corporate leaders and the senior level coaches* (see Fig. 3.10).

While the processes described below and the tasks of the actors are commonly found in all companies, the type of implementation is completely different in each case.
- The entrepreneurial process represents search for business opportunities and externally-focused ability of the organisation to create new business fields
- The integration process allows the entrepreneurial corporation to link and leverage its dispersed resources to build a successful company
- The renewal process maintains the capacity of entrepreneurial corporation to challenge its own beliefs and practices and to continuously revitalise itself so as to develop an enduring institution.

Each of these processes requires certain organisational infrastructures and mechanisms (Bartlett and Ghoshal 1993) that we shall see in detail subsequently.

**Fig. 3.9** Evaluation of forms of organisation as per stability of the company environment and information costs (Source: Klodt et al. 1997, p. 73)

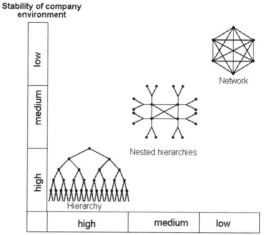

**Minicase: Mindtree II**

*MindTree, a mid-sized Indian IT services company* is known for its knowledge management practices, its collaborative communities, and its strong culture and values. At MindTree, innovation, knowledge sharing, and collaboration is a way of life. It extends through all three of their DNA elements, beginning with imagination (idea), extending into action (implementation), and culminating in joy (new product or service). The company strongly believes that the human ability to create new knowledge and lead with ideas is central to personal as well as business success.

MindTree's knowledge management function enables the organisation to harness the knowledge and ideas of its people, resulting in innovation, better service delivery and organisational learning. MindTree's approach to knowledge management is holistic and focused on building a knowledge ecosystem which MindTree defines as four spaces within which its people interact to create value: physical space, virtual space, social space, and mind space. The key thrust areas of knowledge management in MindTree are innovation, collaboration and reuse. This has all been realised by deploying multiple platforms that impact people's behaviour, creativity, and productivity.[3]

---

[3] http://www.mindtree.com/about-us/knowledge-ecosystem/our-knowledge-ecosystem

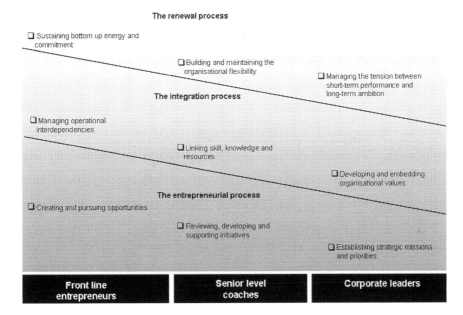

**Fig. 3.10** The processes and roles in an entrepreneurial corporation (Source: Ghoshal and Bartlett 1995, p. 153)

## The Entrepreneurial Process

> The entrepreneurial corporation is a company built around a core entrepreneurial process that drives everybody and everything, the company does. (Ghoshal and Bartlett 1995, p. 145)

An entrepreneurial process requires a close interplay among three management roles. The frontline entrepreneurs are the spearheads of the company. It is their responsibility to create and pursue new growth opportunities. The coaches in the middle and senior management positions play a pivotal role in reviewing. They develop and support the initiatives of the entrepreneurs. The corporate leaders at the top of the organisation establish the company's overall strategic mission that sets the boundary for entrepreneurial initiatives and also sets the highly demanding performance standards that these initiatives must meet. We can find four attributes in companies that have institutionalised a successful entrepreneurial process:

- Firstly, the organisations are built around relatively small units. Matsushita launched a new company for every new product according to the "one product – one division" concept. ABB is known as a network of 1,300 separate companies with an average of 200 employees per company. One can observe the same practice in many companies. To build such small units, these companies have abandoned the notion of functionally complete strategic business units that had all the key resources so as to be in full control of their performance. Instead, they have structured incomplete 'performance units' that are interdependent and must use each other's resources to achieve their own goals. From the viewpoint of creation and transfer of knowledge, this is an important observation because the basis of knowledge integration is laid after considering the business objectives. We shall come back to this aspect when dealing with the integration process.

- Secondly, in every stage from the initial idea to product development, prototyping, market testing and commercialisation, it is necessary to compile and propose a specific budget. The necessary resources are allocated in multiple stages (*multistage resource allocation process*) instead of committing to clearly articulated long-term plan right from the beginning. Thus, at 3M, any employee can propose to a business idea and a single coherent sentence can often suffice as a starting plan.

- Thirdly, the highly structured and rigorously implemented financial control system ensures that the failures are detected immediately, risks are minimised and successful businesses are encouraged accordingly.

- Fourthly, successful entrepreneurial corporations have a clearly articulated and widely shared understanding of which activities are meant for the company and which results should be expected in which time horizon. The actual boundaries that are to be borne in mind by the entrepreneur can be formulated considering either the technology or specific customer groups. These boundaries serve as a guideline for the entrepreneurs to focus their own creative energy.

## The Integration Process

The entrepreneurial process alone is not sufficient for an entrepreneurial corporation that threatens to fall apart or is not in the position to offer complete customer solution if the integration processes is underdeveloped. In the absence of such an integration process, decentralised entrepreneurship may lead to some temporary performance improvement as the existing slack is harnessed, but long-term development of new capabilities or businesses is neglected. The integration process in companies has three components:

- *Value-based integration* that should be achieved by the company management along with the coaches. It is necessary to develop a company culture wherein qualities such as teamwork, openness to problems and solutions of others and being supportive and helpful are accepted as values of the business (see the case study of Kao). This works in an entrepreneurial corporation only when charismatic management sets an example by following these values and demands the same from the employees and when the incentive systems are directed towards the success of a unit and overall success of the company.

- *Knowledge-based integration* of a company involves effective transfer of knowledge – be it customer knowledge, be it best practices or be it medium-term and long-term creation of competencies.

- *Operative integration* aims at managing interdependence and potentials of the operative business. One such function involves offering solutions to key customers. Yet another function involves letting a number of entrepreneurs carry out business – e.g. huge projects – together. Operative integration can also mean organising the purchasing process in such a manner that it is possible to increase the purchasing power and reduce price due to high purchase volumes.

In the integration process, coaches play an important role in knowledge transfer. They co-ordinate teamwork and show who knows what in the company, gather initiatives of entrepreneurs in order to be in a position to offer complete solutions. Enterprise level programmes such as cross-functional projects or total quality management, can contribute in sustaining a target-oriented coaching process which gives comparable and measurable results. Furthermore, the integration process in a company can be given a specific form through company-wide benchmarking and evolving a common learning process resulting from such benchmarking.

## The Renewal Process

While the integration process links and leverages the existing competencies of the organisation, the renewal process questions the strategies and their underlying assumptions continuously and inspires in achieving new competencies in order to be prepared for the competition in the future. In any large organisation, there is a need for a structured learning environment which facilitates continuous learning so as to enable the people to reach out to end users. This requires content to be prepared as new systems come on board and processes keep changing. A renewal process comprises of two symbiotic components:

- *Rationalisation and restructuring of* existing business units to achieve continuous improvement in operational performance.
- The second part of renewal process is *revitalisation*. This involves the creation of new competencies and new businesses, challenging and changing the existing rules of the game and leap frogging of competition through "quantum leaps".

The renewal process is built on the premise of *"business not as usual"*. The renewal process lays emphasis on the significant symbiosis between the present and the future. There is no long-term success without short-term performance just as short-term results mean little unless they contribute to building long-term vision of the company.

In the renewal process, it is the task of the company management to maintain a balance between short-term success and long-term vision and the competence required for this purpose. Finally, the capability of a company to continuously renew itself depends on the ability of its front line managers to motivate their employees for continuous rationalisation and revitalisation. The improvement suggestions and new ideas are brought in by the sales person, the operator in the plant or the research and development engineers. They are not willing to accept the possibility that the company may not be in the position to implement these ideas or present clearly in the short-term why this or any suggestion cannot be implemented in its existing form.

Coaches are the motivators of the renewal process just as the trainer of a team who urges, motivates and communicates vision to the team members. Simultaneous and equal development of all the three processes is crucial for the success of entrepreneurial corporation. An entrepreneurial process without integration will give as few results as an integration process that is not led by clear business objectives of entrepreneurial process. We have explained this model of entrepreneurial corporation in such a manner that it provides a basis for our concrete suggestions on implementation of knowledge management in later chapters.

### Case Study: KAO – Creative in Japan

KAO is known as one of the most creative companies in Japan. The traditional soap manufacturer has expanded successfully in the field of hygiene and cosmetic products. The core of its innovative ability is an entrepreneurial process with small, functional and incomplete units, aggressive goals, rigorous financial discipline and a structured product development process supported by a flexible and multi-staged resource allocation system. Furthermore, the strategic missions are clearly defined in order to use basic technologies to develop products with increased customer network.

This entrepreneurial process is incorporated in a value system that is built on the values of Buddhism and in an open information exchange that is supported by personal meetings and teamwork as well as by a highly developed information system. Dr. Yoshio Maruta, Former Chairman, KAO describes the concept behind this entrepreneurial process as "biological self-control". The value system of KAO aims at harmony and social integration following the "everyone is equal" spirit. These values of equality and free information exchange are continuously observed by Dr. Maruta and other members of top management and are anchored deeply in organisational routines.

A large part of the work of the top management functions in "Decision Spaces" where everyone participates in the discussion and the decision-making process. Furthermore, the company has an extensive system of function-related and cross-business meetings for exchanging ideas and encouraging shared development of new initiatives and projects. The "open space meetings" that allow the participation of people from any part of the organisations takes place every week in different business units. The "total creative revolution project" is an institutionalised coaching process that constantly pulls together teams and task forces from different parts of the company to perform specific tasks in order to find creative solutions for a problem or identify new business potentials. This total creative revolution aims at achieving innovation through shared learning process. The senior managers are formally expected to be priests – those who facilitate the process of shared learning.

KAO is an example of a successful entrepreneurial corporation that developed itself very fast from a traditional soap manufacturer to a leader provider in the wide field of hygiene and cosmetic products.

Sources: Ghoshal and Bartlett (1995), p. 148ff; Graham and Pizzo (1996), p. 342.

## 3.5     Knowledge Alliances

Companies take different forms of long term cooperation in order to form a cartel, to distribute risks, pool complementary resources together and overcome market barriers together.

A **strategic knowledge alliance** is an agreement of two companies or independent business units of a company for common use and development of knowledge resources.

That is how competitors work together in the development of, for example, electronic components.

Knowledge alliance can contain cross-shareholding (joint ventures). It can be almost permanent or designed as a project over a course of time. Experts (research and development employees) can be brought together in a new independent organisational unit or they can collaborate from their respective units towards the goals of the alliance. In many cases, such knowledge alliances are also referred to as networks of companies that cooperate through multiple nodes.

Knowledge creation and transfer in alliances is influenced by three criteria: the organisational level, positioning of the alliance in the value-creation chain and its (organisational) form. Contrary to the narrow definition of alliance as a basic agreement of a number of companies, we think that an alliance is also possible within a company. In a company, wherein the business units operate independently, alliances of business units are as significant as the alliances across companies.

However, there are indeed a lot of differences in creation and transfer of knowledge. *Intra-organisational alliances* operate in an environment that is characterised by a common corporate guiding principle, a company culture and an incentive system that is consistent in positive case and combines the result of the units as well as the entire company. In case of *inter-organisational alliances*, it is necessary to "*tolerate*" different organisational identities, guiding principles and incentive systems. If employees of a company have a certain tacit knowledge on how development work takes place, how new business fields are generated or which behaviour is desirable, this tacit knowledge of an employee of one company can be at odds with the tacit knowledge of an employee of another company.

Therefore, the process of converting tacit knowledge into explicit knowledge across the company is important for the functioning of knowledge alliances. On the other hand, it is possible for business units operating in similar markets but belonging to different companies to have built similar identities and feel closer to the business units of the alliance partners than those of their own company. This is applicable particularly when companies are structured as finance holdings with individual business units that do not have common interests pertaining to technology, products or market. Yet another influential factor in the creation and transfer of knowledge is the positioning of the alliance based on the value creation chain. Alliances can be horizontal and vertical.

In *Vertical alliances* partners complement each other in the value creation chain. This applies for example to supply chains. The same applies to logistics alliances in which the manufacturing or the trading companies work on a long-term basis with the forwarding agents that undertake the distribution and some parts of order processing (Bowersox 1990). In such a relation, each partner keeps the knowledge necessary for his part of the value creating chain secret. The commonly created knowledge refers to the standardisation as well as documentation of processes considering overall quality management, continuous improvement and exchange of best practices resulting in increased efficiency of the entire value chain.

Withdrawal of a partner from an alliance can break the entire value chain. The alliance loses the knowledge of the withdrawing alliance partner because it is generally not recorded jointly in the alliance related knowledge documentation system. Thus, withdrawal of a logistics partner can result in loss of important customer information. Vehicle manufacturing companies are increasingly wondering whether a reduction in the value creation of up to 20 % of the vehicle value would lead to a loss of critical knowledge in the company.

*Horizontal alliances* are characterised by cooperation of the partners belonging to the same level of the value creation chain. Prominent representatives of a horizontal alliance are the development partnerships between companies that are not linked otherwise and could even be competitors. In the automotive industry, such development partnerships can be seen between Renault and Volvo or Daimler Benz and Mitsubishi in order to bolster engine development. High cost of developing new memory chips can be financed only through the alliance of multiple companies. The success or failure of such an alliance can be determined by the capability to integrate highly qualified experts of both the companies in a functional team as well as creation of an open cooperation within the framework of the alliance between the companies that are possibly strong competitors in other fields. Furthermore, it must be ensured that the cooperation within the alliance does not lead to a knowledge-flow to the third party.

## Forms of Alliances

The form of alliance is important to the alliance partner while creating and transferring the knowledge. Based on the classification of networks (Richter and Wakuta 1993), we can classify the form of alliances as open, permeable and closed.

- *Open alliances* aim for a short-term opportunistic cooperation with the changing partner constellation in order to acquire projects of higher volume. In such an alliance, the knowledge transfer and creation takes place depending on the opportunity and in accordance with a specific purpose. Only a little collective learning takes place. The alliance partners open up only to an extent that appears to be necessary for the momentary situation. However, by means of such ad hoc alliances, different partners bring in new knowledge that contributes to the transparency in knowledge about markets, competitors and potential partners.

- Contrary to the open alliance, the *close alliances* are characterised by stable partner constellations. Partners are under the obligation to cooperate only within the alliance and have a share in each other's company capital. A typical example of a closed alliance is the Japanese Keiretsu with clear division of roles, long-term arrangement, a Keiretsu culture and identity and common tacit knowledge. However, the know-how lying beyond the experience horizon and the competencies of the partner are not used because of this stability.
- The *permeable alliance* represents the combination of open and closed alliance forms. Permeable alliance contains a relatively stable partner constellation wherein the partners can belong to multiple alliances and thus transfer knowledge across the boundaries of an alliance. Examples of permeable alliance are the distributing companies that develop product components jointly with the competing buyers [purchasing companies]. These components are then used in the end products that compete in the market. Ideally, permeable networks combine the stability of an alliance that is necessary for mid-term creation and transfer of knowledge with the option to transfer new know-how into the alliance. Thus, permeable alliances are the best structures if we consider the viewpoint of creation and transfer of knowledge. However, there is a risk of knowledge being transferred outside the alliance undesirably because knowledge is safeguarded only to a certain extent in permeable alliances.

## 3.6   Groups as Knowledge-Promoting Forms of Organisations

Group structures have a special meaning in the process of creation and transfer of knowledge, especially while converting the individual knowledge into collective knowledge. In many cases, groups build the smallest organisational unit that then operate in the above mentioned structural model at the department level of a business unit or the entire company. We can consider groups as formal or informal alliances of the employees. The significance of groups in solving problems and in decentralised creation of knowledge has become popular under *Total Quality Management*. The group performance is also considered as crucial for the "*Lean Production*" (Womack et al. 1990). Ultimately, the success of a group-based organisational structure is determined not only by the ability of the individual groups and their members to solve the problem but also by the knowledge transfer across groups. While the work groups undertake the operative business – e.g. the final assembly of a vehicle or guiding specific customer groups – in the long run, they increasingly have the task of reflecting upon their activities and improving their own activities continuously. Thus, quality circles are small groups created for longer periods. The members of these groups have a common experience background. They get together voluntarily at regular intervals in order to analyse the problems of separate work segments under the guidance of a trained moderator, they process and present solution proposals with the help of specially learnt techniques of problem-solving and creativity, convert the suggestions independently as much as possible and take up the verification process.

*The Emotional Intelligence of Groups*

Groups have an IQ which is a result of the talent and capabilities of all the participants. The efficiency in the functioning of a group depends on the "level" of this IQ. The average "IQ" has turned out to be the most important element of group intelligence in the emotional sense and not in terms of academic performance. Social harmony is decisive for a high group IQ. The difference in the performance of two equally talented and competent groups could be explained by the harmony or the lack thereof within these groups. Even if one talented member of a group contributes to the total performance of the group, other competent members of the group cannot reap the benefits if there are major conflicts within the group. One particularly talented member contributes to the total performance of a harmonic group.

The members cannot give their best in a group wherein emotional and social tensions are high because of fear, anger, rivalries or resentment. As opposed to this, if there is harmony in a group, it can reap the biggest possible benefits from the capabilities of its most creative and most talented members. Thus, knowledge does not have a mere cognitive component. The collective ability to solve a problem influences the emotional intelligence radically.

Source: According to Goleman (1997), p. 205, 206.

A group-related activity can be restricted temporally as in the case of *learning centres* wherein the workers meet in the premises close to the respective production plant at regular intervals with a purpose to share their experiences, enhance their basic knowledge and to improve and combine the communication and teamwork under the guidance of moderators.

However, like the *quality circle*, it is equally important that the results of individual groups are disclosed and provided to the other groups as well so that each group does not have to "*reinvent the wheel*".

Ad hoc problem solution groups are also arranged quite often under the workout approach of General Electric. The main activity here is to include various perspectives and interests in a problem solving process. External factors such as customers, suppliers or the administration are equally integrated in the internal problem solving processes like various business segments and company levels.

Yet another more strategically oriented type of groups is the *technology group* that deals with new upcoming technologies and looks around for their possible application in the company. Such groups are in a way binoculars or antennae of the company for learning and testing the new upcoming technologies to find out how these technologies can be introduced and implemented in the company.

Apart from these formal groups, there are a number of informal groups in the company that arise from the common leisure activities, training and advanced training, past teamwork etc. These informal groups often outlive a formal group culture and are profitable for the transfer of knowledge. An example of such group are "Communities of Practice" (see section 4.5).

**Table 3.2** Forms of organisations from the viewpoint of knowledge-oriented management of a company

| Organizational form | Stability | Renewal | Competition | Cooperation | Knowledge creation and transfer |
|---|---|---|---|---|---|
| Infinitely flat | Knowledge passed over in replicable routines | Growth by replication | "Grazing" interlocking customer groups | While replicating business units, not otherwise | Efficient codification and replication of existing knowledge |
| Inverted | Through logistic support | Rather incidental, depends on individual initiative | Dependent on positioning of knowledge bearers | Rather low | Overall value and incentive system is needed to convert individual knowledge into collective competence |
| Star burst | Low | Continuous generation of new business units | Competition for ideas, competition for searching suitable entrepreneurs | Rather low | Branches acquire (pull) knowledge. Systematic creation and transfer of knowledge between the branches is problematic |
| Network | Routines supplemented by ad hoc teamwork | Can be planned and controlled up to a limit | Takes a backseat in presence of cooperation | Between many nodes (formal, informal) | Large number of contacts promote knowledge transfer; targeted knowledge creation is problematic under optimum resource utilization |
| Multidivisional | High | Incremental, else by acquisition of know-how | High | Low | Operation use of knowledge divisions, less knowledge creation across boundaries of divisions |
| Entrepreneurial | Through comprehensive processes | From the company | High using 'entrepreneurial process' | High using 'integration process' | Good combination of all the criteria |
| Hypertext | At business system level | By cooperation of project teams and business systems | Competition for expert | In projects | Through knowledge basis level |
| Platform | Low | Continuous and chaotic to an extent | Only short-term/medium-term success is ensured | Occasional, coincidental to some extent | Rather intuitive, mostly through alliances |
| Alliance | (Rather low) depending on the duration and purposes of alliance | Especially in R&D alliances | Simultaneous competition to some extent and cooperation in defined areas | Low | Overall knowledge creation and conversion is problematic in the specific contexts of alliance partners |

## Evaluation of Organisational Forms

In the following table 3.2 the above discussed organisational forms are evaluated according to their capacity for renewal versus stability and competition versus collaboration. The dominant form of knowledge creation and transfer is described.

## 3.7    Key Insights of Chapter 3

- Organisations need to balance stability and renewal as well as collaboration and competition. Creation and transfer of knowledge is best supported by organisational forms that accentuate cooperation and renewal.
- The concept of "disciplined collaboration" is an effective way to harvest synergies oriented towards clear business related goals.
- In Table 3.2 we have juxtaposed the above-mentioned organisational forms under the criteria of "stability versus renewal", "competition versus cooperation" and "knowledge creation and transfer".
- An entrepreneurial corporation is one that can fulfil the requirements of stability as well as renewal, competition and cooperation very well.
- Fast growth in new business units is achieved effectively from the star burst organisation.
- The "infinitely flat organisation" is suitable for growth by replication (increase in the number of franchise partners or business locations).
- The concept of platform organisation is suitable for the turbulent and chaotic conditions found particularly in "high-tech" industries.
- Networks are being used increasingly in order to bring independent organisations as well as units of a company in contact with each other.
- The inverted form of organisation is particularly suitable when highly qualified experts render services widely and independent of each other and one wants a logical support or bundling of their services in form of a complete service.

## 3.8    Questions

1. What does "co-opetition" mean? And how is it related to knowledge sharing?
2. Provide examples of situations where "disciplined collaboration" makes sense.
3. What distinguishes an "entrepreneurial corporation" from a classical "multidivisional firm"?
4. Which organisational form would you recommend for a consulting firm? Discuss advantages and disadvantages of such an organisation.
5. What is a hypertext organisation? What would it mean in practice to implement this organisational concept?

## 3.9    Assignments

1. **Organising for innovation**
   You are hired as a trainee for the organisational development unit of a big firm which operates in a highly innovative industry.
   *You are asked to propose organisational forms which could increase innovativeness. Discuss various organisational forms (Pros and cons) and prepare a short presentation for a board meeting.*

2. **Franchising in small business "Mary's cup cakes"**
   You have opened a shop, a friend has designed it nicely for you and you are successfully baking and selling a variety of cup cakes.
   *As you have little capital but are convinced that your business idea would be ideal for franchising, you want to transfer your business concept and know-how to franchising partners. What are the steps for transferring your knowledge? Which type of organisation would you have in mind?*

## 3.10    KM-Tool: After Action Review (AAR)

**What is an After Action Review?**
An After Action Review (AAR) is a simple process used by a team to capture the lessons learned from past successes and failures, with the goal of improving future performance. It is an opportunity for a team to reflect on a project, activity, event or task so that they can do better the next time. It can also be employed in the course of a project to learn while doing. AARs should be carried out with an open spirit and no intention to blame.

**Why use it:**
- The AAR is the basis for learning from project success and failures. It is the starting point for improvements in future projects.
- Team members can identify strengths and weaknesses and determine how to improve performance in the future by focusing on the desired outcome and describing specific observations.
- The project team can document the lessons learned and make it available to the rest of the organisation to improve decision-making.

**How to apply it?**
1. Hold the AAR immediately whilst all of the participants are still available, and their memories are fresh. Learning can then be applied right away, even on the next day.
2. Create the right climate. The ideal climate for an AAR to be successful is one of openness and commitment to learning. Everyone should participate in an atmosphere free from the concept of seniority or rank. AARs are learning events rather than critiques. They certainly should not be treated as personal performance evaluations.

3. Appoint a facilitator. The facilitator of an AAR is not there to 'have' answers, but to help the team to 'learn' answers. People must be drawn out, both for their own learning and the group's learning.
4. Ask 'what was supposed to happen?' The facilitator should start by dividing the event into discrete activities, each of which had (or should have had) an identifiable objective and plan of action. The discussion begins with the first activity: 'What was supposed to happen?'
5. Ask 'what actually happened?' This means the team must understand and agree facts about what happened. Remember, though, that the aim is to identify a problem not a culprit.
6. Now compare the plan with reality. The real learning begins as the team of teams compares the plan to what actually happened in reality and determines 'Why were there differences?' and 'What did we learn?' Identify and discuss successes and shortfalls. Put in place action plans to sustain the successes and to improve upon the shortfalls.
7. Record the key points. Recording the key elements of an AAR clarifies what happened and compares it to what was supposed to happen. It facilitates sharing of learning experiences within the team and provides the basis for a broader learning programme in the organisation.

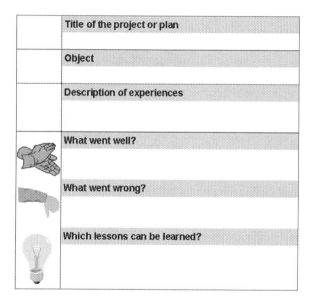

Source/link:  www.kstoolkit.org/After+Action+Review,  www.skyrme.com/tools/ index.htm.

# Knowledge Is Human

**4**

*The most valuable assets of a 20th-century company were its
production equipment. The most valuable asset of a 21st-
century institution, whether business or non-business, will be
its knowledge workers and their productivity* – Peter Drucker
(1999, p. 135)

**Learning Outcomes.** After completing this chapter
- You will know about the characteristics of knowledge workers and their evolving contractual relationships;
- You will be able to name and explain the six major factors determining knowledge worker productivity according to Drucker;
- You will know the roles and tasks of the five groups of actors of the knowledge firm;
- You will know how to motivate knowledge workers
- You will be able to evaluate and develop competencies of employees
- You will know what makes a CoP successful or fail;
- You will be able to develop a competence matrix for a specific unit.

## 4.1 A New Social Contract

As we have seen in Chap. 2 knowledge materialises in the minds of people.

Therefore, knowledge intensive companies are hunting for "brains" rather than traditional "manpower". Florida (2002) postulates the rise of a new social stratum, the Creative Class, whose values comprise of creativity, individuality and being unique and performance oriented. 'Value creation through knowledge' is becoming the dominant source of our prosperity, but we can maintain and multiply this prosperity only if it is based on effective and creative knowledge work.

K. North and G. Kumta, *Knowledge Management*,
Springer Texts in Business and Economics, DOI 10.1007/978-3-319-03698-4_4,
© Springer International Publishing Switzerland 2014

**Knowledge work** is an activity based on cognitive skills that has an intangible result and whose value added relies on information processing and creativity, and consequently on the creation and communication of knowledge. **Knowledge workers** are people who primarily engage in knowledge work.

Along the same lines, Davenport describes a knowledge worker as someone whose principal activity consists of acquiring, generating, packaging or applying knowledge; in other words 'knowledge workers think for a living' (Davenport 2005).

What does this mean in terms of work? Until recently, most employees performed a pre-structured and clearly defined task for which they were paid. They were assured that they would be employed in the company as long as this task existed in the company and as long as they met a certain standard while carrying out their tasks. To a certain extent, they were assured a work place for a certain period of time.

"Knowledge workers are going to be the primary force determining which economies are successful and which aren't," says Thomas Davenport, professor of information technology and management at Babson College, in Wellesley, Mass.

They are the key source of growth in most organisations. New products and services, new approaches to marketing, new business models—all these come from knowledge workers. So if you want your economy to grow, your knowledge workers had better be doing a good job. (Alter 2005)

Peter Drucker suggests that **knowledge worker productivity** is the most important challenge for management in the twenty-first century. He describes six major factors determining knowledge worker productivity (Drucker 1999, p. 142, see also North and Gueldenberg 2011):

1. "Knowledge worker productivity demands that we ask the question: "What is the task?"
2. It demands that we impose the responsibility for their productivity on the individual knowledge workers themselves. Knowledge workers have to manage themselves. They have to have autonomy.
3. Continuing innovation has to be part of the work, the task and the responsibility of knowledge workers.
4. Knowledge work requires not just continuous learning but also continuous teaching on the part of the knowledge worker.
5. Productivity of the knowledge worker is not – at least not primarily – a matter of the quantity of output. Quality is at least as important.
6. Finally, knowledge worker productivity requires that the knowledge worker is both seen and treated as an 'asset' rather than a 'cost'. It requires

(continued)

that knowledge workers want to work for the organization in preference to all other opportunities."

He also adds that to be successful, the knowledge work must be focused as part of a system, on the needs of the customer and business strategy.

The new viewpoint of the company means a change in the social contract. Employees provide their intelligence, learning aptitude and knowledge to the company. In return, the company is bound to use, develop and safeguard these individual capabilities and skills with the purpose to convert them into "*organisational knowledge assets*" (collective intelligence) and create value out of it. Flexibility in allocation of resources is the need of the hour.

### Case Study: The "workforce 21" initiative of AT&T (Escher and Bajenaru 1997)

A corporation flexible in its allocation of resources and competencies stands a better chance of being successful. Workforce 21 is meant to be a tool for securing flexibility in resource allocation throughout AT&T and also supporting an efficient diffusion and proliferation of organizational and individual competences.

AT&T's Workforce 21 initiative is aimed at being better equipped for achieving the strategic objectives of the company in an ever strongly liberalised and competitive communication market by undertaking personnel development and targeted knowledge creation. The efficient and effective conversion of individual and organisational knowledge into innovative services is considered as a primary differentiation option in the market. This also means developing new forms of social contracts between the employer and the employees. In the Workforce 21 team, AT&T ponders particularly about how the company can assure the access to knowledge resources on the one hand and get enough flexibility for an operation in the fast changing markets. The core of these thoughts establishes the form of future teamwork with different employee groups and a new definition of affiliation to the company. The Workforce 21 in the AT&T model comprises "core employees" who will decrease in number in the future and who will be assigned to the operative business units. These employees are supported by the internal "knowledge centres" that develop and process highly specialised knowledge and implement it in customer solutions together with the operative employees. External employees, customers and suppliers also come along to provide additional knowledge of the organisation on a contractual basis. As a result, the borders between internal and external blur. The organisation turns into a contract network that comes into being under the criteria of knowledge creation and conversion of knowledge into customer solutions. Core employees and core work are ascertained by necessary or provided knowledge and the cohesion of core work. Thus, processes such as customer order processes require close collaboration of employees and therefore have high cohesion. The consideration for structuring the Workforce 21 are visualised in Fig. 4.1.

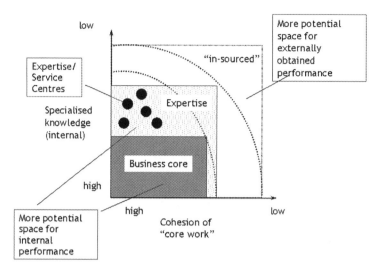

**Fig. 4.1** Possible structuring of work (Source: Escher and Bajenaru 1997)

Compensation patterns have also changed over the years. An individual is paid as per his/her contribution to the company's value creation. The company pays not only in monetary form but also offers the individual a chance to develop his capabilities and skills further and apply them in challenging tasks. The classical barriers between employees, customers and suppliers fade out. Thus, customers can contribute in the development of new products and can be remunerated for their efforts – similar to the existing practice of remunerating the suppliers for their contribution. Employees develop and control their own competence portfolio that must then stand the test of time in an operation portfolio that gets reconfigured time and again.

## Drivers and Obstacles of Effective Knowledge Work

In order to find answers to Drucker's challenge formulated above organisations should consider the following questions:
1. What performance are knowledge workers capable of achieving if they work under ideal conditions, and what fraction of these results do they deliver in a real organisation or as independent knowledge workers in a real work environment?
2. Under what conditions will knowledge workers be ready to tap their talents and utilise their potential for the benefit of organisations they work for?
3. How should an organisation therefore manage employees who align themselves to the organisation's goals, are self-driven and co-operative, detect opportunities and solve problems proactively?

*Effective knowledge work* is not merely a term that indicates efficiency and focus on the "right" issues; it also comprises conditions and resources which help harnessing and developing the performance potential of knowledge workers. Effective knowledge in our extended view comprises such factors as quality, creativity, ability to innovate, efficiency, effectiveness, and – from the individual's point of view – self-realisation, satisfaction and fun at work, development of one's own competencies, and maintenance of good health.

The dilemma of knowledge-intensive jobs is due to the organisation's dependency on the commitment and knowledge of its employees. Having said that, these are perhaps unaware of their own potential and the potential "best result" which could be achieved under ideal conditions is not known. *"The passion to go well beyond the extra mile is what drives people to create insanely great products and services."* says Christopher Meyer (1997).

Kim and Mauborgne (2003) reason that it all depends on designing a "fair process". This process should be based on consistent, transparent, and comprehensible decision-making processes by involving the employees. In order to do so, all of those involved in the decision making processes should be equal as regards access to information. If the decision-making process and the teamwork are perceived as fair by the employees, they will be willing to accept responsibility for the decisions and work actively towards their implementation even if they do not wholly agree with what the decision entails.

### Fairness increases efficiency – Two lab experiments

Numerous experiments have shown that employees respond to fair management with higher performance. Two lab examples conducted by Prof. Falk of the Laboratory for Experimental Economic Research at the University of Bonn (Germany) make this clear.

**Experiment one** shows that fairness leads to an increased efficiency. In this lab experiment, the employer pays a salary to the employee and the employee is requested to give an output as he deems appropriate. An absolutely self-interested employee would give the lowest possible output, irrespective of how high the salary is.

The management therefore has no reason to pay any salary, if all the employees start behaving like the "homo economicus". However, the experiment shows that many employees reward fair salaries. The more the salary, the more willing the employees are to take up more work. Companies which paid higher salaries earned more in the experiment than those which were willing to pay the bare minimum. Thus, it would be worthwhile for companies to handle their employees with a sense of fairness. This fairness also includes social recognition of performance (compare the economic model of efficiency wages[1]).

---

[1] http://en.wikipedia.org/wiki/Efficiency_wages

**Experiment two** proves that mistrust can be de-motivating. Employers in the experiment had the option to either limit the scope of action of their employees or let them make a largely autonomous decision regarding a productive task. In practice, examples of such limitations are rigid work instructions, strict attendance rules or checking of workflows. Keeping in mind the self-interest hypothesis, it would always be better to closely monitor employees and limit their scope of action so as to curb opportunistic behaviour at the earliest. In reality though, the experiment showed that the output level was higher if the employees were not restricted in thought and action; in fact, too many controls proved detrimental to employee commitment. When questioned after the experiment, the employees indicated that they interpreted the restrictions as mistrust and reacted with restrained output.

Falk's conclusion of the experiments: Instead of working solely with incentive and compliance mechanisms in human resource management, it would be useful to create freedom, give more responsibilities, and thus show trust in the employees. In doing so, the management obviously runs a risk, but also reaps profits from it.

Source: Falk (2008)

Buckingham and Coffman (1999, p. 21) studied the factors which are essential to recruit top-class knowledge workers, to retain them, and engage them in productive work. The following six factors have a highly positive correlation with productivity, profitability, employee retention, and customer satisfaction:
1. Knowing exactly what is expected of you at work
2. Availability of resources to execute the job correctly
3. Opportunity to do what one can do best
4. Regular recognition and appreciation for the work done
5. Recognition of an employee as a human being
6. Having a mentor at work who supports your development

While these factors are also relevant in industrial work they are, however, critical for enabling effective knowledge work, which in its core is often an activity involving little structure, a lot of novelty, and dependence on individual expertise. Moreover, well-being and team spirit in the workplace also affect the productivity of knowledge work (Hube 2005). Another factor negatively affecting productivity is the situation wherein knowledge workers increasingly have to start freelancing, or are employed on short-term contracts, and perceive a high risk of losing their job (Dostal et al. 2001). In such situations knowledge workers would spend much energy to safeguard oneself, to position oneself vis-à-vis colleagues, and to put one's own future above everything else.

Therefore, one of the main tasks of top management is to **provide an environment where work is rewarding and fun**. The strategy of managing knowledge workers keeps the focus on people. With the provision of conditions that promote employee's initiative, creativity and knowledge transfer, companies expect to make intensive use of this freedom to create value. Effectiveness of knowledge workers is based on results and credibility, perceived reputation, and network of relationships rather than formal authority, job description, or position in the hierarchy (Saxenian 1996).

Freedom to create value goes along in many cases with high work loads. A software developer reports, *"Earlier, after closing a project, we had time for post-processing. Today, a project is immediately followed by a new one. Earlier, we had time for learning phases but today a couple of hours in the day-to-day business are supposed to be adequate."*

Individuals to be employed for this type of work are mostly independent and extremely flexible in terms of time. Therefore, 75 % of the employees in the development centres are young singles. On the other hand, giving freedom without specifying clear targets leads to certain arbitrariness like in the motto, *"Do what you want to but be profitable."*

According to Meyer (1997) knowledge workers

- Primarily identify themselves with their profession rather than workplace; more sensitive to the kudos and esteem they receive from their peers than those they receive from management
- Are highly mobile and quick to change jobs
- Are driven primarily by the pride of accomplishment
- Have strong beliefs and personalities; they respond much better to being pulled than being pushed
- Have an informal network with peers, inside and outside their own company, which helps them benchmark their personal efforts and their company's competitiveness

Quinn et al. (1996) recommend how to make use of the potential of *"professionals"*: Employ only the best ones and let them ponder over new problems under high pressure to succeed. After initial training, these *"potentials"* are confronted immediately with the complexity of real problems. New employees are assigned to small teams that contain three to seven people – as found in Microsoft. The new employees participate immediately in the development of new complicated software systems under the guidance of their mentors. The legendary 80-h weeks and long nights praised by investment bankers and software engineers serve the purpose of advance training that is to be taken seriously. They enable the best employees to move up along the learning curve that turns out to be steeper than that of the other employees. Training on the job, guidance by mentors as well as pressure of competition among colleagues helps the experts to reach the highest possible level of knowledge in their field. Quinn et al. are of the opinion that the specialised knowledge of these experts increases faster when they have to comply with tough demands.

The specification of targets that demand apparently impossible things (*stretched goals*) (Thompson et al. 1997) (such as the achievement of "*Six Sigma*" standard at Motorola, doubling of number of components per chip at Intel or increasing only the capacity by 50 % as in the case of Hewlett Packard devices) leaves the knowledge workers with two options – they can either sustain the pressure and go along with it or search other tasks within or outside the company. "*Top companies push their experts constantly from barricading themselves comfortably behind clever books, simulation models or even monitored laboratories. These companies mess around mercilessly with the most difficult tasks that exist such as the real customer outside, the existing system as well as highly complicated external circumstances and cultural differences. This is not seen in middle mediocre companies*" (Quinn et al. 1996, S. 98).

These companies not only have a tough internal competition, regular performance evaluation and feedbacks but also nurture a culture of sharing knowledge. This is because if one does not cooperate, one will also not succeed in the competition and have no chance of progressing in the company.

Even at the worker level in the production department, the pressure resulting from the expectation of better performance – as compared to the organisation based on division of labour – increases with the increased freedom of decision. When the employees decide their own work process, it is also expected that they examine their own work carefully and continuously and make improvements. It is also expected that they pass on their knowledge about process and product improvements as part of their normal activities and not as an extra remunerative service.

### Risk of Burn-Out

However, not all employees will be ready to face this pressure. For instance, some may decide to cooperate as an external developer in specific projects or to be available as a company consultant in consulting firms only for X number of days. Others undertake repairs and maintenance tasks assigned externally or participate in the production network as sub-contractors. They earn less but may be able to organise their time freely. They may voluntarily or forcibly become "life entrepreneurs."

Psychological overload occurs especially when workers are confronted with discrepancies between work requirements, rules and available re-sources that inhibit them from reaching their goals and that are linked to immediate negative consequences for them.

Reflect a bit on whether you feel overwhelmed with the following five types of disparities:

1. **Contradictory work goals**: Additional requests and tasks have to be accomplished and simultaneously the originally delegated tasks have to be completed within the given time without requiring additional resources.

2. **Disparity between tasks and execution framework**: Colleagues meant to provide help are not available or occupied elsewhere. The promised resources and tools are not provided.
3. **Disparity between tasks and learning framework** (i.e. learning restrictions): The necessary knowledge or concrete experience cannot be acquired due to lack of sufficient freedom of action. For instance, solutions have to be developed without proper knowledge of customer requirements.
4. **Disparity between individual and professional goals and expectations:** Due to unfulfilled technical and organisational prerequisites, knowledge workers are not able to do fulfil their professional standards. They are obliged to work under conditions that they normally cannot support.
5. **Conflict between professional and personal life**: There is a lot of stress caused by having to balance familial roles and responsibilities along with professional obligations such as long working hours, working over the weekends, etc.

**Making time-off predictable & required**

People in professional services believe a 24/7 work ethic is essential for getting ahead, and so they work 60-plus hours a week and are slaves to their Blackberrys. Perlow and Porter based on their research in several offices of the Boston Consulting Group, however, suggest that consultants and other professionals can meet the highest standards of service and still have planned, uninterrupted time off – whether in good economic times or bad. In the action research a requirement that everyone on the team take one full day off a week was imposed. Since that meant everyone was now working 80 %, another consultant was added to the team to ensure that the client would still have the equivalent of four full-time people on the project. Once it was demonstrated that taking full days off (working 80 %) was possible, the researchers approached a further challenge whether people working full time could have predictable time off and still achieve similar benefits for themselves and the organisation. In a second experiment, they required each consultant to take one scheduled night off a week, during which he or she could not work after 6 PM – not even check or respond to e-mails or other messages. After initial resistance 5 months later participants reported more open communication, increased learning and development, and a better product delivered to the client. Perlow and Porter (2009) conclude that imposing a strict mechanism for taking time off works if it is accompanied by encouraging lots of talk about what's working and what isn't, promoting experimentation with different ways of working, and ensuring top level support

Source: Adapted from Perlow and Porter (2009), pp. 102–109

For more information on the (self-) management of knowledge workers see North and Gueldenberg (2011).

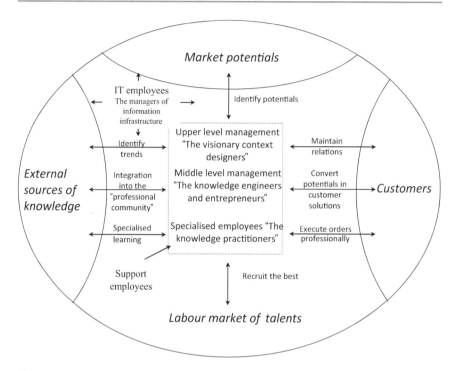

**Fig. 4.2**  Actors in a knowledge-oriented company

After this description of the ways of working in the knowledge society or knowledge firm, we will look at the different employee groups in a knowledge-based company.

## 4.2    Co-thinkers of the Knowledge Firm

We distinguish five specific groups of employees who are the main actors in the knowledge firm – see Fig. 4.2:

- *Knowledge practitioners:* Expert employees, the "knowledge practitioners" carry out mainly operational tasks professionally while they gain specialised knowledge continuously.
- *Knowledge engineers and entrepreneurs:* The second group of personnel comprises of middle level management, who convert market potential or customer problems into solutions. Middle managers are in fact knowledge engineers who gather the knowledge of their knowledge workers and convert it for internal use and package it as per customer requirements.
- *Visionaries and context designers:* Upper level management comprises of "visionaries and context designers", who identify the market potential, create a

knowledge-ecology, act as leaders as well as keep a check on the focus of entrepreneurial activities.

- *Information brokers and infrastructure managers:* The fourth employee group that is to be attributed to the expert employees based on their qualification are the information and communication employees. They develop and manage the information and communication infrastructure of a company in terms of both technologies as well as content.
- *Support employees:* The fifth group of employees is the "support employees" comprising secretaries, back office, call centres, reception etc. which support the remaining employees. They are capable of influencing the image of the organisation decisively in the minds of the customers.

The functions and roles of these groups of persons are largely determined by the organisational concept or management approaches. Nonaka and Takeuchi analysed the top-down and bottom-up approaches from the viewpoint of knowledge creation (Nonaka and Takeuchi 1995, p. 125ff) and came to a conclusion that a third way, "*middle-up-down approach*", is more suitable for promoting knowledge creation in the company.

- *Top-down approach:* In the "*top-down approach*", upper management receives simplified and selected information through the hierarchical pyramid. From this information, upper management develops plans, orders and instructions that are binding on the middle management and are implemented by the "*knowledge practitioners*".
- *Bottom-up approach:* In contrast to the top-down approach, the "*bottom-up approach*" aims at the autonomy of entrepreneurially operating individuals without interaction. Tacit knowledge is gained at the lower levels but is not shared and converted into explicit knowledge. Development of knowledge does not have a clear target course.
- *Middle-up-down approach:* Unlike the aforementioned approaches, the "middle up-down approach" plays a key role in the process of organisational knowledge creation. In the middle up-down approach, upper management develops a vision or a "dream" while the middle management develops concrete concepts that can be understood and implemented by the employees at the front, i.e. the specialised employees. Middle management tries to resolve the discrepancy between the goals that the upper level management hopes to achieve and the reality at that point of time. To some extent, middle management is a *translator* that finds the right words, metaphors and slogans that can be understood by the specialised employees as well as the customers and inspire them to perform a task or develop a product concept.

Table 4.1 juxtaposes the three management approaches referring to knowledge creation. Successful knowledge engineers and entrepreneurs display the ability of the middle level management of packing and bundling the specialised knowledge of the employees in such a way that the customers find a solution to their problems in it and are willing to buy these solutions. We shall now take a closer

**Table 4.1**  Comparison of management approaches with respect to knowledge creation

|  |  | Top-down | Bottom-up | Middle-up-down |
|---|---|---|---|---|
| WHO | Main knowledge creator | Top management | Entrepreneurially operating individuals | Team with middle level management as knowledge engineers |
|  | Role of upper level management | "Commander" | Sponsor/mentor | Promoter |
|  | Role of middle level management | Processor of information | Autonomous entrepreneur | Team leader |
| WHAT | Accumulated knowledge | Explicit | Tacit | Explicit and tacit |
|  | Conversion of knowledge | Partial, focused on combination/ internalisation | Partial, focused on socialisation/ externalisation | Spiral internalisation/ externalisation/ combination/socialisation |
| WHERE | Storage of knowledge | In databases/ manuals | In individuals | In organisational knowledge base |
| HOW | Type of organisation | Hierarchical | Project groups and informal networks | Hierarchical and "task force" (and principles of the hypertext organisation) |
|  | Communication | Orders/ instructions | Principle of self-organisation | Dialog and usage of metaphors/analogies |
|  | Tolerance to ambiguity | Chaos/ fluctuations are not allowed | Chaos/fluctuations are required | Establishing and strengthening chaos/ fluctuations |
|  | Weakness | High dependence in upper level management | Time-consuming, coordination costs of individuals | Exhaustion of employee, redundancy costs |

Source: Adapted from Nonaka and Takeuchi (1995), p. 130

look at the roles and functions of individual employee groups from the viewpoint of an entrepreneurially oriented middle-up-down approach.

## Middle Management: Rebirth of a Presumably Extinct Species

With the restructuring of the hierarchical organisation, reduction in management levels and self-organisation of semi-autonomous groups, middle management was often considered an obstacle to change. Management gurus explained that the companies of the future can manage almost without middle management (Kanter 1989; Quinn 1992). In reality, middle management has in many ways lost its traditional function as implementers of strategies or respected experts in the sense of traditional masters, while employee groups gained stature through the concepts of semi-autonomous teamwork and "*empowerment.*"

However, knowledge-oriented management of a company assigns a key role to middle management. Despite the heterogeneity in their roles (e.g. manager of a consulting firm, an operations manager of an electronic goods company or a manager of a developmental project), middle managers are characterised by common biographical elements that predestine them for these new functions of bundling knowledge and packaging it as per customer requirements. By the time the members of the middle management reach this level – after having worked in the company for a few years – they understand the rules of the organisation and take positions because they are competent and enjoy the confidence not only of their superiors but also of their subordinates. They are not at a level in the organisation to lose contact with the customers and the ideas of employees. They are motivated and have the skill to initiate and implement changes and innovations.

This experience background helps them to carry out their tasks. "Instead of giving orders, they now put away obstacles, accelerate the granting of funds, conduct investigations and act as advisors" (Quinn et al. 1996, p. 102). This task description applies very well to the operative engineer, who has been turned from a disciplinary superior into a coach of work groups in the production department. The manager in a consulting firm acts as an entrepreneur to identify the potential of the consultation demand for a client and conduct acquisitions.

Lars Kolind, CEO of the innovative Danish hearing device manufacturer Oticon (see case study in Sect. 3.1), added yet another management task for middle management: the ability to make the employees "*happy*" and give them a feeling of security while they work in a very unstructured, chaotic, difficult and constantly changing environment (La Barre 1996, p. 50). Middle management, the knowledge engineers (Nonaka and Takeuchi 1995, p. 154), are intermediaries between what actually exists and what will exist. They *merge* the tacit knowledge of the specialists and that of the upper-level management, and convert it into explicit knowledge for integrating it into new technologies, products or systems. Furthermore, they also ensure that knowledge of an individual is transferred throughout the organisation; as shown in our case study on development of Matsushita "*Home Bakery*" (see Chap. 2).

Figure 4.3 illustrates important functions of middle management. You can enter you personal role profile according to the actual and ideal profile. Every criterion can be evaluated based on its priority (how important it is. . .) and its time allotment (which part of my working time do I spend for. . .).

Following the logic of the middle-up-down approach, we will now describe the roles and functions of upper management in a knowledge-oriented company before turning to specialists and employees of information and communication technology.

## Upper Management: Visionary Context Designers

Bearing in mind the concept of the Entrepreneurial Corporation as discussed in Chap. 3, upper level management performs the main tasks as shown below:

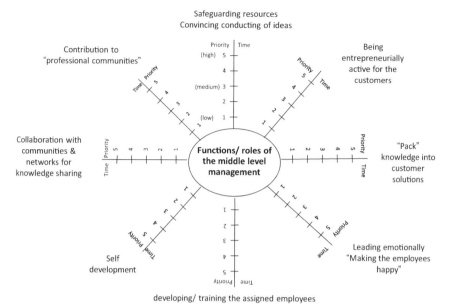

**Fig. 4.3**  Functions and roles of middle management

- Managing the tension between short-term success and long-term ambition
- Developing and incorporating values
- Setting strategic goals (guiding principle) and priorities.

The change from hierarchical to entrepreneurial action requires the management to change its role perception:

> Management should leave most of the decisions to the market, establish an organisational infrastructure that governs the behaviour and encourages teamwork within the company. (Halal 1994, p. 69)

While management in today's real companies spend a lot of time solving the problems of the operative business and grappling with the repercussions of misled incentive systems, the concept of knowledge-oriented management of a company considers upper management as visionary context designers. They identify market potential beforehand, create a buzz around the product and organise framework conditions, especially through incentive systems that promote creation and transfer of knowledge. They describe and evaluate the behaviour expected from the managers and the employees and exemplify it themselves by behaving accordingly. They develop leaders.

As individuals they represent the values of the organisation and are the highest moral entity in the company. Their actions are conducted by "*wisdom*" comprising the rules of conduct which govern the behaviour of the employees of the entire organisation (Galvin 1996).

**Minicase: The "gardener" at MindTree Consulting**

Subroto Bagchi is best known for co-founding **MindTree Consulting** in 1999 where he started as the Chief Operating Officer. MindTree is a global Information Technology services company with head-quarters in Bangalore, India. Bagchi has now taken on the role of a 'Gardener' who develops leaders/entrepreneurs. This role is based on the concept that a gardener understands the requirements of each plant and nurtures it accordingly; the plants don't go to the gardener but the gardener identifies and nurtures the plants. Bagchi spends one-on-one time with the Top-100 leaders at MindTree on their "personal-professional" issues to expand leadership capacity and build readiness for taking MindTree into the billion-dollar league. In addition, Bagchi works at the grass-roots by making himself available to its 45 Communities of Practice that foster organisational learning, innovation and volunteerism within the organisation.[2]

Upper management harmonises different interests, coaches middle management, discovers and develops talent and simultaneously keeps a check on whether the results of the entrepreneurial activity of the middle level matches the target specifications. Upper management urges all the others in the company to learn and to develop themselves continuously. However, it should also reserve a certain amount of time for its own development.

Nonaka and Takeuchi describe upper management as "*Knowledge Officers*" (Nonaka and Takeuchi 1995, p. 156). They say that these knowledge officers direct the activities of knowledge creation in a company firstly by articulating how the company should be, secondly by establishing a knowledge-oriented vision in form of a guiding principle, and thirdly by setting standards for the value of knowledge that is created. Chapter 7 contains the description of how of these individual actions materialise.

In Fig. 4.4 we have compiled a range of functions and roles for upper-level management. You can enter your personal role profile as per priority and time allotment of the function and compare it with the actual situation at a given point in time.

## Professionals: The Knowledge Practitioners

"Knowledge practitioners" often called professionals, specialists or subject matter experts are the primary knowledge resource of a company. They convert their specialised knowledge into customer solutions with the instructions and coordination of the middle level management under the context defined by upper

---

[2] www.mindtree.com.

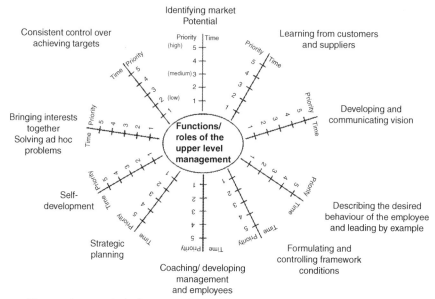

Please enter your desired target profile and compare it with the actual profile

**Fig. 4.4** Functions and roles of upper management

management. In many cases, they convert the efforts of the company to products/ services for customers which form the image of the company. They are capable of influencing customer satisfaction significantly. The value of specialists is equal to their knowledge. It is therefore in their best interest to gain new knowledge continuously and to confront new tasks so that they do not lose their value in the constantly changing environment.

> *What experts like and do not like* (Sveiby 1997, p. 57)
> - Experts are characterised by profound knowledge of the field in which they specialise. They contribute actively to this field.
> - Experts like complicated problems, progress in their occupational area, freedom to search new solutions, well-equipped work place/laboratories and public recognition of their services.
> - Experts loathe routine work, bureaucracy and rules that restrict their freedom.
> - Experts often lack distinct management skills.
> - Experts admire specialists who are better than them.
> - Experts condemn power oriented persons.

Sveiby (1997, p. 72) has explained this phenomenon as the life-cycle of professionals (see Fig. 4.5). Stated generally, the competence of an employee

**Fig. 4.5** Life-cycle model of
the market value of
specialised competence
(Source: Diagrammatic
presentation based on Sveiby
1997, p. 72)

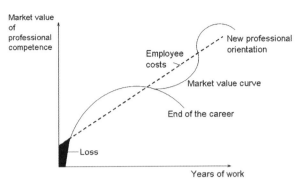

increases with age or the years of work he puts in. In positive cases, the company finds this increase to be higher than the employee cost. At the beginning of the career, the employee cost is higher due to training or restricted commitment. In succession, the market value increases at a faster rate than the employee cost; the employee "*rents himself*", "*brings in more than his cost*". At some point of time, a level is reached wherein the increase in the salary level does not bring in corresponding increase in the value of the employee's competence. At the latest before reaching this level, the company and the employee should think about profitable options of using the experience of the employee by undertaking new functions or a new qualification. Otherwise, the company will be inclined to part with this employee in the short-term or long-term. In reality, the competence and cost of an employee increase intermittently. Knowledge-oriented companies will increasingly evaluate the commercial value of the specialised competence of their employees. This is easily possible in consulting firms using the realised daily rate.

Apart from updating competences continuously, professionals have other options to make themselves indispensable in the company, e.g. by customer relations created by them. If a customer always wishes to work with Ms. X or Mr. Y, the transfer of this employee may affect the company's relation with such a customer adversely. From this viewpoint, in order to safeguard their position, it is important for professionals to work intensively with fewer customers than anonymously with large number of customers.

Another option of positioning the professional in the company is through cooperation in formal and informal networks and communities. Here, the employees provide their knowledge, distinguish themselves as experts of a topic, contribute to the company's internal information system or are available as contact persons for certain topics. Even though many experts are sceptical of self-marketing, it should be considered as an important component within the framework of career development in a knowledge-oriented organisation.

On the one hand, professionals will be interested in safeguarding their commercial value and their position in the company, while on the other hand the knowledge-oriented company will try its best to motivate them and develop their capabilities to gain as much value as possible with this "*human investment*". Studies show that the returns on human capital investment are significantly higher than the returns from investments in intangible assets (Klodt et al. 1997, p. 123). However, investment decisions in *"human capital"* have their perils. An investor cannot estimate the value creation potential of a potential employee for accumulating human capital in the same way as for tangible investments. Hence, the risk of unprofitable investment is accordingly higher. From the investor's view, investments in employees do not offer the options of collateralisation unlike real capital investment. In other words, the specific features of the *"human capital"* lead to increased risk as compared to the risk involved in the investment of tangible assets. How can the companies alleviate this risk in practice? Let us have a look at three elements: Recruiting, motivating and career development of professionals

## Recruiting Professionals

Targeted knowledge creation and transfer appears to be possible in a company when a relatively stable pool of employees works together for a long time in changing combinations (Hedlund 1994). This means that the company primarily selects the employees with the aim of a long-term cooperation with changing functions instead of selecting them on the basis of knowledge required for the latest project. The past years have witnessed the establishment of elaborate selection processes for recruiting people (e.g. multi-staged Assessment Centre). These selection processes test people not just for their latest knowledge, but also their ability to blend well with the company culture, and their flexibility and willingness to work in different teams.

Once employed, there is a modular qualification process wherein the new employees are confronted quickly with real customer problems as they are work together with experienced colleagues. Training involves cooperation beyond the limits of functions. This helps in building informal networks that can then be used if required.

---

*Individual knowledge management*

Information overload and varied knowledge gives a feeling of helplessness and the pressure to react fast. Therefore, individuals need to develop strategies for dealing with information and knowledge personally. Here are some tips (Reinmann-Rothmeier and Mandl 2000; Reinmann and Eppler 2008):

- *View and throw*: Ask yourself which information you need and how often do you need it. Separate the wheat from the chaff courageously.
- *Reduce systematically*: Reduce the amount of information coming to you regularly. Are the distribution lists, mailing lists, magazines, etc. really relevant to you?
- *Filter instead of collecting*: Do not collect information without selecting. Instead, keep a record of where you can find information if required.

(continued)

- *Set limits*: Say no to yourself when you are confronted with information overloads.
- *Courage for a break*: Call it a break when the effort of searching and collecting information exceeds the achievable benefits by gaining information.
- *Practice composure*: Develop an approach as per the motto "*No one knows everything but everyone knows something*". A solid personal knowledge base promises success more than a possibly complete information pool.
- *Use technologies that work for you*: You should not use every new technology just because it is new. Use the options of new media to adjust the time for feedback of requirements of your work situation.

## Career Development

Career development of professionals in flat hierarchies is a challenge faced by knowledge-based companies. On the one hand, these companies have very few levels of hierarchy and on the other hand not all the specialised employees are interested or suitable to undertake management functions. There is a growth option towards middle level management for those employees, who wish to take up management positions and are capable of holding it. Generally, growth is possible after hard – but not necessarily uncooperative – internal competition, regular performance evaluations and feedbacks. Talent is always screened to its finest. That is why in a consultancy firm, only about 10 % of the carefully searched advisors have the chance of becoming a partner and that might take 9–12 years (Quinn et al. 1996, p. 97).

Fast growth is possible only when the company grows proportionately. Hence, growth inside the knowledge firm is connected very closely to the rate of the growth of the company.

Highly qualified researchers who do not aim at management functions or whose specialised competence is too valuable for the company to place them in management positions, can opt for a separate **expert career** and can be drawn close to the status of the upper-level management in terms of their compensation or competencies. In hierarchical companies, a chief department manager requires a specific number of employees or a certain budget to be able to rise to this position. This "*head count*" is not applicable to a knowledge-oriented company. Along these lines, the World Health Organisation, for example – an otherwise hierarchically organised body – has opened up career options to their qualified experts, other firms create positions of "chief scientist" or "chief technical advisor" ranking at upper management levels.

*Personnel development* *with perspective: lateral thinkers instead of upward climbers*[3]
What does career actually mean?
- If one asks you,
- If one takes your advice,
- If one gives you information,
- If one has trust and confidence in you,
- If one gives you lot of space,
- If one gives you responsibility, then
- You have made a career at the firm.
in short, when you are in demand among customers and colleagues.

Despite all these retention efforts, companies continue to lose qualified employees. However, there are ways of losing the employee without losing their knowledge completely. Knowledge-based companies should ensure that professionals pass on their knowledge to team colleagues and save their information continuously in the information system of the company, pass on their knowledge in company's internal competence networks and familiarise new employees with the work and coach them.

In Fig. 4.6, you find functions and roles of professionals. Based on these elements and according to the priorities and time allotment, we have created a target profile that can be compared with an actual personal profile.

## Information Brokers and Infrastructure Managers

The development of the knowledge firm gives rise to a new group of employees (a specific group of professionals) who operate the information and communication system of the company both in terms of content and technology. This group ensures that the different available sources of information are made available to the employees in the company or external customers by filtering such sources and making them user-specific and function-specific. While the technical operation of the information and communication system can be assigned partly or entirely to an external service provider, content management should be carried in-house.

Knowledge of experts must be codified and stored. Journalists edit project reports to make them understandable to a third party. The knowledge of competence networks should be stored in a structured form and made available round the clock throughout the world. Expert systems should also be updated.

---

[3] CSC Ploenzke information brochure

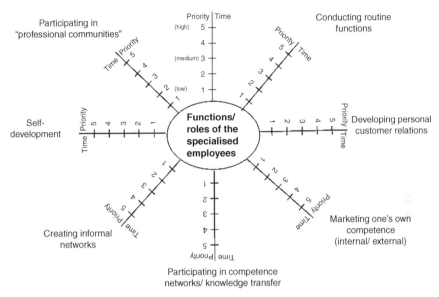

*Please enter your desired target profile and compare it with the actual profile*

**Fig. 4.6** Functions and roles of professionals

Social software such as wikis and blogs require co-ordination and often editing support. Information 'brokers' motivate colleagues to contribute content like writing wikis for important topic areas.

Furthermore, research is getting more and more complex and needs to be carried out in very short intervals. The client, the prospective customer or the senior employee expect to be informed quickly and comprehensively about a subject area. Basic research can be conducted by the end user himself on the internet or through the company's internal high-capacity search engines. In contrast to this, complex research or selective search requires specific information or information experts who carry out a search professionally.

## Support Employees

It is often said that offices, communication centres and secretarial pools will become unnecessary following the improvements in information and communication technology. This might be true in drafting simple texts or the increase in email communication. On the other side, there is a rise in demand for quality of presentations, updating content on the internet, organising the appointment book, conducting simple research and answering standard customer queries.

Hence, back office support gains importance with an increase in the variety of functions. A good command over text processing, graphical presentation and use of software tools as well as complex communication systems is a part of general qualification requirement of these employees; professionals, increasingly working under tight time constraints and with constantly changing tasks, become increasingly dependent on back office support to complete routine tasks.

**Gamification: get employees to share knowledge and expertise by making fun**

Gamification is about taking the essence of games – fun, play, transparency, design, and challenge – and applying it to real-world objectives rather than pure entertainment.

Over the past several years, companies like Samsung and Nike have added gamification to their consumer websites to get customers to engage with them and take certain actions – anything from buying a particular product to answering questions in an online forum. Now, firms are starting to apply these tactics internally to motivate their work forces.

The major gamification factors can be classified into the following aspects:

A Scoring System where points are awarded for completion of tasks and accumulate over time. A progress bar which shows how close a user is to completing a task once the bar is full, the user is awarded a certificate or a badge as a token for achievement. This is reflected in the contributor's profile and signifies his expertise in a particular area. He/she can also appear on a public score board that displays the 'Top 10 High Achievers' points tally which in itself is an award. The contributor can also be assigned a level which may signify a users' proficiency in the area such as beginner, intermediate, advanced.

Gamification has a potential for increasing user generated content and engagement which enhances use of knowledge management systems by employees within organisations. Some examples are Deloitte and Accenture. Deloitte has successfully implemented gamification with applications such as Yammer and Badgeville. At Accenture – a management consulting, technology and outsourcing company – gamification techniques are being deployed to, quite literally, 'change the game' when it comes to encouraging and empowering its people to collaborate and share with one another across its global network of more than 250,000 employees. According to Gartner, gamification is "positioned to become a highly significant trend over the next five years," with more than 70 % of Global 2000 organisations set to have at least one 'gamified' application by 2014.

Sources: Palmer et al. (2012), Rosenbaum (2012), APQC (2013)

## 4.3   Competencies for the 'Intelligent Firm'

In a knowledge-oriented company management of competencies goes beyond the traditional concept of training. It includes self-learning, taking responsibility for one's own competence portfolio, using and marketing the competencies (see Sect. 4.5 Knowledge Communities). This will be clear when we see typical problems that can be solved using competence management.

- *Project staffing based on competence*: We often assign projects to employees that we know, without knowing whether there are even more suitable colleagues. The "*competence profiles*" that describe the competencies of an employee offer the option to identify suitable employees for the project.
- *Identifying competency gap*: Imagine you have come from a strategy workshop and would like to realign your business units. You ask yourself questions – "*Do my employees have the competencies necessary for the future alignment? How can we impart selective training to the employees or which profiles should we hire?*" Increasing the present competencies, deriving the necessary competencies as well as the "actual-target" comparison enables us to take appropriate measures.
- *Passing on knowledge across employee generations*: Highly specialised employees work in the development, production, sales and IT department. The firm often does not know what individual experts know. The value of the knowledge that is lost becomes clear only after these employees have left the unit or firm. A customer complained that she is no longer advised as before, there are unexpected problems in the production process or crucial technology know-how is not available. Competence descriptions help identify the "*hidden experts*" to pass on knowledge to the employee generations.
- *Career by developing competence*: In flat hierarchies, it is often not possible for the employees to make a career by climbing up the greasy pole or promotion. Yet, we can offer a long-term development perspective and retain qualified employees in the company by means of competence extension and consolidation. The agreed development is incorporated in target agreements as well as appraisal and incentive systems.
- *Finding competent contact person*: Very often the company is on the look out for a particular skill/profile and is confronted with questions like-who is good at database programming? Who can help me quickly with the supply and knows the customer? Who is an expert on US accounting in our company? We can locate expertise quickly using "*skill databases*" and take measures. Software solution of "*skill based routing*" can be used for this purpose to reach out to a wider circle.
- *Evaluating training needs and effectiveness*: A training provider serves many small companies with the function of determining training requirement of the employees and structuring a specific program. The training department within the company has a similar function. Employees often register for seminars without finding out how such seminar would contribute in developing their competence or of the working group. How can training needs be assessed and training effectiveness evaluated systematically? How can the employees manage their own "*competence portfolio*", especially if they change the companies more often and wish to increase their "*employability*" in the market?

The answer is provided by mapping a company's competence requirements of jobs with competence of existing employees. After assessing this, improvements in performance and changes required in behaviour can be evaluated.

## Short Analysis: Competence Muffle or Competent Organisation

In the short analysis that follows, you can evaluate the competence management of your company by means of eight criteria. Assess to see how you estimate the position of your company between "competence muffle" and "competent organisation".

A good approach to raise awareness would be to copy and distribute the form given below among your colleagues in order to discuss the results subsequently and answer the following questions:

- How different was the categorisation?
- Where was the maximum difference in grading?
- Where do we see the biggest obstacles towards a competent organisation and which measures should we take?
- What can each of us contribute to ensure that the required competencies are developed and the existing competencies are used optimally?

Grade each point according to the school grades: from 1 = very good to 5 = unsatisfactory.

### Short Analysis: Competent organisation or competence muffle

| "Competence muffle" | 5 4 3 2 1 "Competent organisation" |
|---|---|
| 1. Core competencies are not defined. | Core competencies are defined and updated regularly. |
| 2. Employees do not have a competence profile. | Employees have a competence profile for core processes, core functions. Profiles are updated regularly. |
| 3. Competence development is not interconnected with human resource development. | Human resource development is based on a systematic competence evaluation |
| 4. In case of time pressure, learning and advance training must take a back seat to operative functions. | Learning has a high priority (time and budget for every employee provided). |
| 5. Informal learning at work is not recognised. | Informal learning is supported with suitable measures (Coaching, mentoring, etc.). |
| 6. There are no development plans for individuals. | Individual development plans are implemented consistently. |
| 7. Training and application are not interlocked. | Training is always connected to the application. |
| 8. Employees do not get incentives for developing competence. | Competence development is supported consistently by incentive systems. |

## Developing Competence

The objective of learning of knowledge workers is to develop professional skills and proficiencies. Knowledge, experience, intuition come together in concrete situations that require action. Competence (or competency) is therefore the capability to act adequately in a given situation. This includes the capability of self-organisation. Competency comes into effect in the interplay of individuals, groups and organisations.

Competence materialises at the time of knowledge application and can be measured with the result achieved from the action. These actions are more or less pre-defined by instruction or an action framework. Appropriate action therefore requires a disposition to self-organisation. Competency is therefore also defined as one's disposition to self-organisation.

> The term **competence** of a person or a group describes the relationship between the tasks assigned to or assumed by the person or the group and their capability and potential to deliver the desired performance. People mobilise knowledge, skills and behaviour to "do the right thing at the right moment".

The competence of a person is understood as an individual quality that cannot be replicated. Competency development depends on the activity exercised, the experience gathered, and the corresponding environment. We should note that competency is:

(a) *Context-specific*: It is related to the activity performed and materialises at the time of problem solving and application.
(b) *Person-specific*: It is embedded in the *"experience record"* and personality of a person and determines his/her conduct with respect to the task/situation (e.g. social engagement).

There exist many competency models for professions or roles which need to be adapted to the specific context.

The typical components of a competency-based approach are as follows (Draganidis and Mentzas 2006):

1. Identify the desired results: Which output or result is desired for a "successful" completion of a role or a job?
2. Describe the competencies that truly have an impact on results based on a competency model.
3. Evaluate employee competency using a competency model and grade the level of proficiency. Usually one would combine self-evaluation and peer–to-peer or rating by a superior.
4. Implement employee development strategies and resources to close the gap between real and desired competency level.

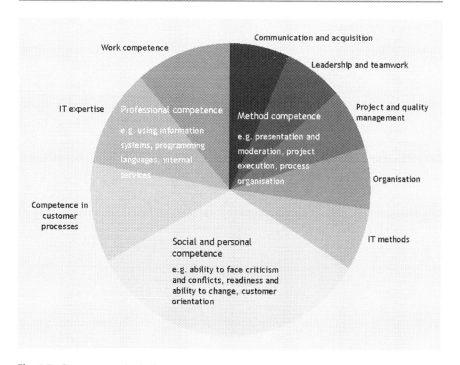

**Fig. 4.7**  Competence wheel of an insurance company

The more unstructured a job is and the more freedom knowledge workers have to reach their goals the more difficult is it to answer the question "which competencies are required in a specific job or role?" as people with different sets of competencies might achieve similar results.

Competencies can be visualised as a competence profile. Figure 4.7 shows an example of an insurance company to describe the competencies considered as necessary to fulfil a role (e.g. project manager, customer advisor etc.).

For each of the competencies a description and proficiency level need to be formulated. For the purpose of structuring commonly competencies are categorised in "hard" and "soft" where technical and functional competencies are considered as hard competencies whereas creativity, interpersonal, and behavioural skills are soft competencies. Other frameworks classify competencies into functional, managerial, methodological as well as social and personality related competence (cf. Janjua et al. 2012), in reality these competencies interact and are difficult to separate.

After describing individual competencies, the level of each of the competencies should be evaluated. Different expertise models are recommended in the literature wherein the three tier evaluation of professional and method competence has established itself in reality.

**Beginners** have theoretical knowledge with less experience of application of such knowledge and are able to use the pre-structured solutions of problem in theory on real problems (e.g. project management course was conducted successfully and the first experience of executing project was collected).

*The proficient* have multiple experience in application and can react appropriately even to new unforeseen situations (e.g. multiple projects of different complexities were carried out at one's own authority).

*Experts* are capable of anticipating problems to a large extent by means of self-organisation and intuition. They are also capable of solving such problems. They stand out through profound knowledge of topics (e.g. managing complex and novel projects, contributing to further development in methods of project management). Further nuances are possible depending on the desired degree of differentiation. Social competence can be gauged with the levels such as *"less distinct"*, *"distinct"* and *"more distinct"*.

---

**Case Study: Career in the CSC world: Become more precious**

In the service model of an organisational unit, the service know-how that is offered is presented in segments of a circle. This "competence wheel" describes the know-how of an employee and his/her know-how careers in the medium term (earn more during stability phase). The segments of the service model stand for the service spectrum that is relevant for the respective organisational unit with key elements from industry and technology. Thus, the main features of the fields of activity that are to be observed by the employees are documented. Simultaneously, it is shown which topics should be covered. One such sheet is a component of all the documents required for an employee review and is used to discuss medium-term career planning. Information on the segment wherein an employee works at present and the segments wherein he is supposed to go through in the next 3–10 years is also documented. This concept of personal development will promote not only multiple qualifications but also creativity, initiative, ability to learn and the courage to try new things (Fig. 4.8).

---

## Various Methods of Competency Development

Knowledge workers use various methods of competency development.

Mainly, the execution of new challenging tasks is a motivation and an opportunity for learning. The challenge for highly differentiated knowledge work is to be able to better integrate learning and work. The opportunities offered by *e-learning and blended learning* approaches support this.

The time consuming activity of following knowledge domains through newsletter subscriptions, observing technical portals, or reading through technical journals can be better organised. Colleagues can mutually assign topics and exchange knowledge periodically; for instance as a recurring item in the agenda of regular meetings. Initiatives such as *"colleagues learn from colleagues"* support this sort of mutual learning. This can also foster learning across professional groups.

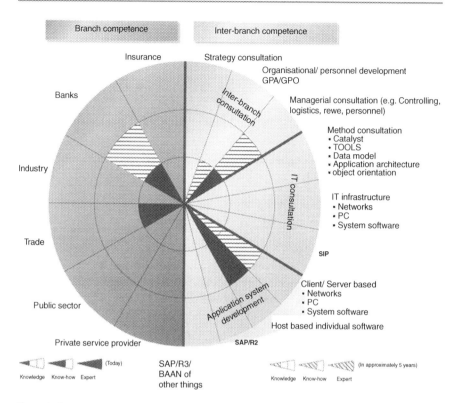

**Fig. 4.8** Branch competence and inter-branch competence

Source: Guidelines for junior advisors in the brochure of CSC Ploenzke AG

In a survey of staff, British Telecom (BT) found out that 78 % of its engineers preferred to learn from their peers, but to date, very little money or attention had been focused on affecting and improving the learning and development that naturally takes place in the workplace. Following the survey, BT replaced much of its traditional formal training programmes for its engineers with a social media, contribution-based platform that they called Dare2Share. The company deployed a YouTube-like platform that allowed engineers to pull learning content, in the form of content contributed by other engineers, when they need to do so. The overall outcome has been an increase in sharing and network building, faster problem resolution, lower costs and the replacement of off-the-job training with performance support.

If you want to know more about BT's Dare2Share visit http://www.youtube.com/watch?v¼gtVYkEdGtfo.

*Coaching and supervision* help knowledge workers reflect upon their learning process and reflect self and peer assessment. In the predominantly individualistic cultures of many professional circles, there are barriers to open up to colleagues and superiors. Coaching and supervision can provide personal support and also allow for taking individual learning to group learning sessions.

A fantastic form of combined learning is possible in *projects* where new interdisciplinary questions are tackled. Team members gain experiences which are of great value for the members themselves and for future teams with similar questions. In a process of self-reflection, every team has to summarise all the critical experiences gathered and what future teams with similar problems must pay particular attention to. Often different perspectives emerge only in such reflection sessions, which can thus prove to be a valuable source for the participants to evaluate their own work.

Under the point "lessons learned" we urge organisations to more frequently revisit the experiences and learning experiences from their successes as well as from their failures. Lessons learned represent the essence of all experiences that were made during a project or in a particular position. In order to make adequate use of lessons learned, there should above all be a suitable framework for recording them.

What are your objectives for competence development and how do you want to achieve it?

## 4.4 Motivating Knowledge Workers

Motivation is an often discussed and controversial issue in theory and practice. Current thinking based on advances in neurological research argues that motivation means creating enabling conditions that reinforce personal motives and thus make people contribute and in a positive case give their best to achieve the goals of the organisation as long as they are in line with personal goals.[4]

In this respect we have to understand the difference between intrinsic and extrinsic motivation.

**Extrinsic motivation** functions via an indirect satisfaction of needs, mainly through factors like money or power. In this case, achievement of organisational goals is linked with monetary or career boosting incentive systems for the employee.

Against this, **intrinsic motivation** underlines the aspects of direct fulfilment of needs. Intrinsic motivation may be rooted in the joy of doing the work itself or in a perceived commitment. Commitment may result from a self-commitment – e.g. due

---

[4] An overview of work motivation research can be found at Latham and Pinder (2005), an overview over motivation theories can be found under http://www.goldsmithibs.com/resources/free/motivation/notes/summary%20-%20motivation.pdf.

to personally defined goals – or from commitment to other people, groups, or the society as a whole.

As a rule, the ideal incentive system for intrinsic motivation is the work itself, along with freedom and conditions which help establish a personal identification with this work and with the existing values. These three challenges are central in this context:

- Intrinsic and extrinsic motivation cannot be generated and changed to the same degree in every person.
- Intrinsic and extrinsic motivation cannot be considered independent of each other.
- Intrinsic motivation needs not be in line with the goals of the organisation and is very difficult to change.

Pink (2009) has identified three key factors that drive motivation in humans. These are the quest for autonomy, the innate desire for mastery and the need for purpose. These drivers are strong in knowledge workers. Therefore management styles that support autonomy, mastery, and purpose are required to enable a significant shift in the performance and productivity of knowledge workers. Carleton (2011) suggest for the retention of knowledge workers giving them attention, providing challenging work, offering developmental opportunities, providing appropriate resources, placing them in a supportive environment, and recognizing their contributions.

Table 4.2 describes important extrinsic and intrinsic work motives and incentives that support them.

While traditional forms of performance related payment is largely based on the extrinsic motivation, the intrinsic motivation gains importance when it comes to sharing and developing knowledge. An intrinsic motivation compatible with the objectives of the company is necessary for promoting the transfer of knowledge. With regard to knowledge development, one can say that the creative activities rest largely on intrinsic motivation.

Learning processes in particular are boosted by intrinsic motivation ("I learn because I like the topic" as opposed to the extrinsic motivation "I learn because I get something in return").

While designing a knowledge-oriented incentive system it is to be borne in mind that every employee is a knowledge source for the company and it is essential to motivate him/her through individually configurable incentive systems for knowledge objectives and objectives of the company.

How can well-trained professionals be motivated? Initially through a task or varying tasks that *challenge their specialised knowledge* and give them a chance to grow. The practice of assigning young employees with easy routine jobs at the beginning is disastrous from the knowledge viewpoint. Accomplishing challenging tasks leads to learning and a demonstration of competence which is motivating. Recognition from customers as well as from experts with higher qualification is generally considered as a very important motivational factor (Sveiby 1997; Maister 1993).

**Table 4.2**  Work motive and incentive

| Work motive | Incentive |
|---|---|
| *Extrinsic work motives* | *Material and status related incentives* |
| Money | Salary, bonus |
| Security | Pension, loans |
| Prestige | Status symbols |
| *Intrinsic work motives* | *Options to interact and personal development* |
| Contacts | Belonging to the professional community |
| Performance | Feedback about one's own performance (e.g. by appreciation and constructive critique) |
| Self-realisation | Independence (e.g. flexible working times empowerment) |
| | Learning options through challenging activities |
| | Good working conditions |
| | Job rotation, job enlargement and job enrichment |

A further source of motivation is *enabling advanced learning*. From an employee perspective, an opportunity to participate in a highly rated seminar (thanks to his/her outstanding performance) or to train under the guidance of top experts in his/her field of specialisation is of much more value than an increase in the salary.

Another motivational factor is *efficient work equipment and a stimulating office environment*. This relates to an open information culture as well as workplace lay-out and equipment such as a high-performance computer or a laboratory that eases the work of a specialist on the one hand and accords a certain status among colleagues on the other, because traditional status symbols loose importance in a knowledge-oriented company.

### Case: The company breakfast

In order to establish an open exchange of information as a component of the company culture, a manufacturer of optical and electronic equipments has introduced a regular practice of a common breakfast of all 150 employees approximately four times a year. There is a name card for each employee. These name tags are mixed like playing cards and distributed on the tables of the canteen randomly. Thus, employees from different departments and hierarchies sit together. Thereafter, over the course of the entire breakfast, the company management gives information about different topics like current business situation, new interesting projects, personnel changes or internal and external problems and gives an insight into the future. In turn, the employees are requested to ask questions, bring forth problems and give suggestions to the management.

*Monetary rewards,* naturally, continue to be yet another motivational factor. Incentive systems (e.g. share options) that are based on the success of the entire company can stimulate a positive behaviour and be supplementary to incentive systems designed exclusively for individuals (For more details see Sect. 4.4).

There are a number of options for *promoting teamwork* directed towards the interest of the entire company. One such option is paying the employees as a group instead of paying them individually. This compensates the success of the group and not the individual performance. Furthermore, there is an option of connecting a significant part of the salary to the success of the entire company. This is particularly important for the upper level management. For instance, in General Electric over 22,000 employees at all levels have share options in the company and thus a clear financial incentive to have the overall success of the company in view. Thus, the support of the colleagues in the same or in other business units contributes simultaneously to the improvement in the entire situation of the company. The rewards from the shares are often significantly higher than the bonus that is linked to the performance of the individual business unit. A number of companies have abolished the individual-oriented bonus systems and award fringe benefits depending on the results of teams, units and the entire company. Even improvement suggestions can be arranged keeping the group in mind. Thus, the employees are motivated to work on and implement the improvement suggestions together.

In case of *"Management by Objectives"*, the targets are agreed upon between the seniors and the coordinators, the responsibility of every individual is defined in form of results expected from them and the result is measured based on the "target-actual" comparison. Extending the target catalogue by individual knowledge objects is called as *"Management by Knowledge Objectives"*. Here, the operative and strategic knowledge objectives are the source of agreements on objectives. These objectives can be directed not only towards the enhancing personal competence but also towards passing the knowledge further (e.g. briefing a new employee about work). Qualification objectives are measured and adapted periodically. Employees are encouraged to participate in the development of objectives.

A firm has integrated incentives – in form of bonuses – into agreements on objectives. For this purpose, knowledge required for certain tasks was defined in *"skill blocks"*. A successful completion of a *"skill-block"* leads to an increase in the salary. For this, the employee has to take a test that is assessed by seniors and colleagues who already have a command over these skill blocks. This incentive system resulted in an increased flexibility and improvement in the work processes.

Another version of objective agreements is the integration of knowledge objectives in the work process which is then linked to payment. In case of a consulting firm, the performance of the advisor is evaluated based on five categories, one of them being "contribution to the knowledge of the company and its benefits." In another company, a part of the salary of an individual employee is ascertained based on his activities to share his knowledge (e.g. lessons learned). Even the **employee appraisal** or the periodical employee discussion has a place for creation and transfer of knowledge. A management consultancy has developed these questions related to the topic of dealing with knowledge resources.

Employees are asked the following:
- What have you done in the last year to increase your own competence?
- How have you contributed to the further development of the knowledge base of the company (e.g. by cooperating with networks, inserting presentations in the information system, by presenting project reports, project profiles etc.)?

In addition to the above questions, the management is asked the following:
- How have you encouraged your employees to build up their competence?
- Have you managed to increase the revenue per employee?
- Have you contributed to innovations, to improve processes or to build new business areas?

The integration of *knowledge related criteria into employee appraisal* ensures that the employees are retained in the long run to generate and share knowledge in order to develop themselves in the company. However, this also means that "career" has gained a new definition that is based on the recognition of professional and social competence. Appreciating the know-how in a certain field is an important incentive for strengthening the intrinsic motive. At the same time, the belongingness to a social group is connected to this appreciation. The common engagement in trade unions, trade organisations and honorary office shows the effectiveness of motivation by appreciation. The option of presenting oneself as an employee with one's own homepage in the intranet, a competition of the documents downloaded from individual homepages are the options of rewarding the involvement in sharing the knowledge.

For example, a company has installed a *"Virtual Knowledge Centre"*. The documents of which that are used most often are published in a "hitlist". The advisors who have placed the highest ranked case studies have the option to participate in the annual event of *"Knowledge Centre Conference"*.

For a knowledge worker, time is becoming more scarce day-by-day. Sharing and developing knowledge can therefore be rewarded by giving time and space to the employees. The option to take a vacation for half a month, to attend an MBA program or *"10 percent of total work time at the employees' free disposal"* can be stronger incentives than payment and promotions. Employees are motivated by the option of working in a project team with the leading experts, solving complicated problems, making technical advances in their field, freedom of searching new solutions, well-equipped work places/laboratories and appreciation of their performance.

The 'fun' incentives that supplement the formal incentives are useful for creating awareness and motivation for knowledge management. Following this, a consultancy firm launched the *"sharing knowledge earns you miles"* initiative that was used by a number of companies ever since it was coined (see also Box "gamification on p. 128).

**Case: "Sharing knowledge earns you miles" – Initiative of a Management Consultancy**

Consultants are often under enormous time pressure and therefore, are often not completely willing to spend time on documenting and passing on their knowledge. Apart from the comprehensive incentive systems of the company, playful incentives can contribute in creating awareness about transfer of knowledge. Hence, analogous to the miles collection of airline companies, the "Sharing knowledge earns you miles" initiative was launched in one of the branches of the management consultancy. The message conveyed by this initiative can be articulated as follows:

We want to motivate you to share knowledge, offer help to your colleagues and contribute successful concepts and lessons learned from project work. In order to achieve this, we want to find the "knowledge leaders" in our organisation, i.e. the employees who transfer knowledge actively to others.

The rules: Every quarter, you receive 50 points which, if you wish to, you may distribute among the colleagues who have supported you. Every employee thinks about the following questions: Who has helped me actively in solving a problem, shared his experiences with me and particularly encouraged the creation and transfer of knowledge in our company? At the end of the quarter, you send the distribution of your points to the miles office through email. Colleagues considered for the points collect these points in their miles account and can pick up a gift from a range of gifts depending on the number of miles (e.g. top-class seminars of their choice, including seminar fees and travelling expenses). The redemption of "miles" should contribute to further creation of knowledge leaders.

If a company succeeds in developing in enabling conditions required for leveraging the motives of its employees, the "motivation spring" is twisted in the right direction. High motivation leads to higher productivity and quality of work that in turn leads to success in terms of customers. This success results in the success of the company which in turn is reflected in generous compensation in form of further training options and career development.

## 4.5   Communities of Practice: A Learning Approach

Value creation in a knowledge-based organisation and beyond the limits of that organisation is determined considerably by the ability to mobilise the shared knowledge across markets, customers, products and processes with a specific purpose and generate a value out of it for customers.

However, traditional and formalised structures of hierarchy and business units are equipped inadequately to perform such functions. Hence, self-organised communities that take initiative, learn together, share experiences or develop new products and services thus overcoming the boundaries of hierarchy and organisational units gain importance. Innovation circles, experts, groups become increasingly popular.

### Case: Knowledge communities at MindTree

MindTree is a mid-sized Indian IT services company known for its knowledge management practices, its collaborative communities, and its strong culture and values. From the beginning, MindTree has considered communities as all those self-organised groups which take on a mission. They don't appear on the organisational chart and they don't report to anyone. Yet, they are driven by their self-defined objectives. These could be focused short-term goals (for example, building a software component) or broader, long-term goals (such as building capability in a domain).

At MindTree, communities with long-term goals are called 'knowledge communities'. The company has more than 30 of them and they are highly visible, while others with short-term goals use the available infrastructure, but are not tracked in the same manner as knowledge communities. "Overall, communities create the fractal structure – and the feeling of belonging – that keeps smallness alive," says Datta.[5]

The various forms of learning and exchanging knowledge are discussed under the terms *"Communities of Practice"* (Wenger 1998a, b) or learning communities, or knowledge communities

**Communities of practice** are groups of people who share a concern, a set of problems, or a passion about a topic, and who deepen their knowledge and expertise in this area by interacting on an ongoing basis. (Wenger et al. 2002, p. 4)

Communities of practice have a range of functions for procuring, accumulating and distributing knowledge in the organisation and beyond the boundaries of the organisation (Wenger 1998a, b; Wenger et al. 2002):

- They are nodes for the exchange and interpretation of information. Since the employees involved in communities of practice have a common understanding, they know which information is relevant and can be passed on and how it can be presented in a useful manner. From this point of view, the communities of practice are also ideal for spreading information beyond the boundaries of the organisation.

---

[5] Ash, Jerry, 'Ideas Emerging', Case Report on Mindtree

- They can keep knowledge alive unlike databases or manuals. The tacit elements of knowledge are maintained and passed on and adapted to the local terms of use. Thus, these communities are also ideal for inducting new employees, educating them and sharing experiences with them.
- They help develop competencies further and bring about the latest developments in the organisation. They are often faster and less clumsy than the business units. The feeling of getting into the act at the start of latest developments gives an identity to the members of communities of practice.
- They are a 'home' for identities. In times when the project, short-term teams and allocations to the business units change faster than ever, the communities of practice build a long-term professional identity for their employees. In flat hierarchies, the communities of practice build a space for experimenting and learning in which the employees can often exchange ideas.

According to Wenger, the approach of situational learning or social learning becomes important in contrast to a traditional view of learning and advanced training in the company:

> Our institutions, to the extent that they address issues of learning explicitly, are largely based on the assumption that learning is an individual process, that it has a beginning and an end, that it is best separated from the rest of our activities, and that it is the result of teaching. Thus, we learn in seminar rooms and organised computer-aided training programmes with individual sessions. We test the success of teaching by means of individual tests. Wenger argues that as a result a huge part of our institutionalised training and advance training is considered as boring and irrelevant to practical application (Wenger 1998a, b, p. 3).

In contrast to this, the basic assumptions of the social and situational learning define learning as a group process that is not restricted by time and takes place unknowingly to some extent. Learning takes place in the context of activities. Instead of directing training primarily towards abstract process descriptions, learning involves handling situations together (e.g. meetings with customer) and discussing how one can improve these situations or even sharing experiences. Situational learning or social learning is based further on a variety of forms of teaching and learning as close as possible to the environment experienced by the one who learns and the one who teaches. The following checklist provides ten factors of success of CoP. In the following we will discuss in more detail how to ensure that communities create value for its members and the organisation.

### Checklist: CoP –10 factors of success: How do your communities perform?
*Management Challenge*
1. Focus on topics important to the business and community members.
2. Find a well-respected community member to coordinate the community.
3. Make sure people have time and encouragement to participate.
4. Build on the core values of the organisation.
   *Community Challenge*
5. Get key thought leaders involved.
6. Build personal relationships among community members.
7. Develop an active passionate core group.

8. Create forums for thinking together as well as systems for sharing information. *Technical Challenge*
9. Make it easy to contribute and access the community's knowledge and practices. *Personal Challenge*
10. Create real dialogue about cutting edge issues.

Source: Richard McDermott http://www.co-i-l.com/coil/knowledge-garden/cop/knowing.shtml.

## Ideal Type of Communities of Practice

We need a vision or guiding principle to launch communities of practice. *North* et al. (2000) have identified the features of an ideal type of community of practice from their personal experience with a number of knowledge communities.

Ideally, a community of practice is a community of people:
- Who wish to cut through a topic
- Who consider themselves to be teachers or students
- Who open themselves completely to a topic
- Who let others express their beliefs and experiences
- Who talk openly about mistakes and failures
- Who have enough time and space for sharing this information
- Who protect each other
- Who do not cling to the existing concepts and are open to think about new things
- Who listen to each other and try to understand each other
- Who do not wish to enter commercial competition with their knowledge

It seems to be plausible that such communities of practice can be effective only if they are embedded in a nurturing organisational culture. Therefore, the following four framework conditions are the essential components of a typical community of practice:
- The *inner values of the organisation,* inculcated in the members of the communities of practice, should be as follows: trust, openness to new things, individual responsibility, authenticity (of one's identity) and so-called "*boundary-less behaviour*", i.e. a behaviour that encourages teamwork beyond the boundaries of organisational units. Communities of practice will not flourish in a command and control culture.
- *A balance between short-term, medium-term and long-term results*: If we think about the events in the ecology, we can also formulate a balance between sowing and yielding. Predominantly short-term company objectives and short-term objectives of the communities of practice mean that we want the yield too soon without having sowed enough. The controller breathes down the neck of

the researcher with a deadline. This appears to be a problem in many real research groups and competence networks.

- *Incentives for common activities*: Regulated communities of practices rarely prosper. The comparatively stable factors in such communities are a shared interest for the selected domain or shared values that can be followed or transported using the content of the communities of practice. Opportunism and differences in interests are bad starting points for working together in a domain. Incentive should never be searched in monetary form. However, many companies have introduced incentive mechanisms that are highly successful and motivating. (cf. Sects. 4.4 and 7.3).

- *Balance between implementing and experimenting*: Finally, companies should put the knowledge of the communities of practice to a practical application and incorporate it in the value creation process. But what could be a solution that can be realised? A visible product or a document? What about the participants' learning experience which is used in several other activities? Leonard Barton (1992b) has shown the importance of experimenting to generate knowledge. This can mean that the communities of practice get resources for pilot applications and implementations. Thus, while restructuring the exchange of information in a company it was ensured that the members of the research groups comprised experts as well as members from the management who were competent to take decisions for implementing the targeted results.

### Case Study: Two examples of communities of practice

Case I: Sharing tipps and tricks

In a work analysis, a manufacturer of a photocopying machine found that the customer service employees spent a considerable amount of time chatting with each other in the warehouse or kitchen and not with the customers. A traditional rationalisation measure would have been elimination of this time so that the employees could focus only on the customers. However, the anthropologist who conducted the analysis found that the chats provided a forum to exchange important knowledge about improving maintenance or tips on techniques of repairing. Hence, the company encouraged this exchange by establishing framework conditions for communication among the technicians even when they were in transit. Thus, a second frequency was installed in the radio of the technicians which turned into a knowledge channel. The French subsidiary established an information system in which one could enter important experiences of the service technicians so that they could also be provided to other groups of people (Brown and Gray 1999). This example shows that even self-organised informal groups can be supported by the organisation.

Case II: TechClubs

A car manufacturer operates since 20 years with Tech Clubs that reflect the problems of car platform structure. They are informal groups organised along disciplines like electronics or chassis. They take responsibility for the further development of relevant knowledge, innovation and new skills. They have provided a basis for and ensured success of the "Engineering Books of Knowledge" for reducing development cycle time (a group of 60 for 30 months) and development cost. These tech clubs have developed through different phases. In the first few years, the supervisors came together to discuss the problems pertaining to certain parts, suppliers or new technologies. In the second phase, they tried to carry the learning processes further by inviting all the engineers of a certain domain such as representatives of purchase, scientific laboratories, etc. In the subsequent phase, the tech clubs took over more responsibility, checked the plans for products and processes and recorded important knowledge in a Lotus notes database. Today, these forms of generation and exchange of knowledge should be spread worldwide and encouraged. However, the company is still searching for options to support these communities of practices all over the world (Blair 1997; Karlenzig 1999).

## Dimensions of Communities of Practice

Raj Datta of MindTree believes that KM and community movements are inter-dependent. The fact is, KM will fail if you don't allow people to channel their passions and the best way to do that is to let them self-organise to create the right kind of conditions and enabling environments. The other fundamental shift – psychologically speaking – is to believe that people are intrinsically motivated to share and don't necessarily need to be motivated by external factors

The contexts for active communities of practice can be developed consciously. The MIEO-Model shown in Fig. 4.9 comprises four dimensions (North et al. 2004): Members, interactive community, effect (result), organisational support.

According to the model, the individuals – through interaction in the communities of practice – contribute to a transformation of knowledge of the entire organisation and thus, change the value creation process of the company. Some of the dimensions are directly controllable, e.g. the membership criteria or the selection of people for communities of practice. Others can be influenced only indirectly by establishing valid framework conditions, e.g. the motivation of the members of communities of practice. We will now discuss the most important dimensions.

### The "Member" Dimension: Challenging and Manageable Topics

The motivation for teamwork in communities of practice can be influenced indi-rectly by organising contexts that are conducive. The commitment to the challeng-ing quantitative or qualitative objectives of the company such as "*increasing the productivity of all the factories by ten percent every year*" or "*increasing customer satisfaction*" can work as short-term motivation for exchanging experience. How-ever, reasonable objectives that the groups of employees set for themselves and inspiring groups and meaningful meetings motivate the employees for high and long-term commitment. How is membership regulated in the communities of practice? Generally, the community of practice itself decides who can be a member. A number of difficulties may result if the self-organised selection process is impaired from outside in order to retain or retrieve "*control*". Members appointed by the management can easily become foreign bodies that can damage the trust that has developed, bring in an unwanted sense of hierarchy and damage the matured

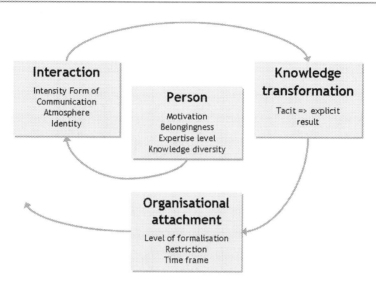

**Fig. 4.9** Dimensions of communities of practice: the MIEO model

work culture. As CoP are learning instruments it is advisable to include members with different *levels of expertise* and k*nowledge diversity* be it functional experience (e.g. marketing, sales or product development) or cultural experiences (e.g. languages, courses, hierarchy levels).

Based on their study of 45 successful CoPs of multinational companies Probst and Borzillo recommend sticking to strategic objectives. They found evidence that setting clear and measurable objectives provides COP members with a concrete direction to follow. Such quantifiable objectives limit COP members to specific metrics (% of cost reduction, % of revenue increase, % of time reduction, increase in customer satisfaction, etc.) that must be respected when they participate in the process of developing and sharing best practices with other members. They also argue that classifying objectives into subtopics gives COP members absolute clarity regarding the goals that a COP must achieve (Probst and Borzillo 2008, p. 338).

## The "Interactive Community" Dimension

The work of the people in communities of practice is characterised by their interaction that can be described in terms of intensity, communication form, atmosphere and identity.

The *intensity* is identified particularly by the frequency and duration of the meeting or contacts of the members of communities of practice. The form of these contacts – e.g. regular personal meeting, video conferences, and chat rooms on the internet or different seminars – determines the type of contact alternatives and options and limitations in the exchange of knowledge.

The selection of the *form of communication* is decisive for the quality of interaction. The authors have polled the members of communities of practice on the form of communication. The unanimous opinion was that the personal acquaintance of members of communities of practice simplifies the subsequent exchange through electronic media. The adequate form of communication is further dependent on the type of the knowledge exchanged. The higher the exchange of tacit knowledge, the higher is the reliance on the face to face personal communication. The higher the exchange of explicit knowledge, the higher is the suitability to use the electronic media.

The interaction of people in a community of practice is further characterised by the *atmosphere* in which they work together. For instance, a code of conduct that takes up the aforementioned rules of an ideal type of communities of practice and defines the behavioural rules of the members can be helpful here. Addressing each other with names and avoiding titles encourages an interaction at the same level. Atmosphere also includes selecting attractive venues for meetings.

Apart from the corporate identity of a company, one can also support in building an *identity* of the community of practice. Communities of practice can be given a space on the internet to showcase themselves or they can develop their own logo. The community can develop its own language over a course of time and perhaps even its own methods, rules and tools that mark the independent identity as an outline from the rest of the organisation.

### The "Effect" (Result) Dimension

Interaction between people not only involves exchange of knowledge but also creates new knowledge. Communities of practice contribute in transporting knowledge to the company on the one hand and are germ cells for new thoughts on the other hand. Many thoughts that are developed and shared in communities of practice are not conveyed directly to the third party. A person who has not shared certain processes has a tough time understanding their cognition. In many cases, the trust in the integrity of the members of community of practice is given importance as against exact verifiability.

Parts of knowledge can be visualised, fixed and evaluated as result of knowledge transformation.

> The questions at the individual level are:
> - What have I learnt?
> - What can I implement in my daily practice?
>   The questions at the level of communities of practice are:
> - Which knowledge was created?
> - Which parts of our work have the highest demand?
> - How have we developed our common resources (methods, language, etc.) further?
> - How have we contributed to the value creation process of the entire company?

This analysis helps to connect to the entire organisation or to a network with other communities of practice.

### The "Organisational Support" Dimension

The organisational support is decisive in implementing the knowledge for creation of value. This dimension considers the criteria of level of formalisation, restriction and time frame.

While some authors see CoPs as widely self-organised entities which are not accountable to anybody (Wenger 1998a) others argue that CoP must be tightly managed. Along these lines Probst and Borzillo (2008) recommend having a sponsor and a COP leader who are "best practice control agents" and that the COP leader must have a driver and promoter role.

The *extent of formalisation* of communities of practice ranges from complete "indefiniteness" to recognised strategic meaning. Wenger (1998b) came up with five categories of relation to formal organisation (extent of formalisation):

- *Unknown:* unknown to the entire organisation and to some extent even to the member of communities of practice
- *"Illegal"*: visible only informally for a group of people in the environment
- *Legitimised*: approved officially as useful unit
- *Strategic*: widely known as centrally important for the success of the organisation
- *Transformative*: capable of redefining their surrounding and the direction of the organisation

The organisational support from the communities of practice is further characterised by its boundaries or demarcations. Here, one should differentiate between communities of practice within the business units and those that exceed the business units or organisational boundaries. Yet another factor is the geographical distribution of its members. Thus, in terms of boundaries, we can differentiate between local, regional, national, international and global communities of practice.

Another aspect of communities of practice is their demarcation from each other. In reality, the communities of practice often overlap because no clear organisational limits are defined. For instance, this applies to a community of practice that is oriented towards customer satisfaction and other communities of practice that are oriented towards quality where customer satisfaction obviously constitutes the aspect of quality. A conscious overlapping by twin membership helps prevent later conflicts in coordination. Probst and Borzillo recommend forming governance committees with sponsors and COP leaders which discuss and assesses the overall activity of the various COPs in their specific functional area of the organisation.

The following checklist allows the reader to plan communities for success:

### Study: Why Communities of Practice Succeed and Why They Fail

(Probst and Borzillo 2008)

An investigation of 57 COPs from major European and US companies led to the discovery of ten "commandments" that lead to the successful development and sharing of best practices. It also identified five main reasons for failure.

The ten commandments of successful COP governance

1. Stick to strategic objectives
2. Divide objectives into sub-topics
3. Form governance committees with sponsors and COP -Leaders
4. Have a sponsor and a COP leader who are "best practice control agents
5. Regularly feed the COP with external expertise
6. Promote access to other intra- and interorganizational Networks
7. The COP leader must have a driver and promoter role

8. Overcome hierarchy-related pressures
9. Provide the sponsor with measurable performance
10. Illustrate results for COP members

The main reasons for failure of cops

1. Lack of a core group
2. Low level of one-to-one interaction between
3. Members
4. Practice intangibility

## 4.6    Key Insights of Chapter 4

- There is an increasing international competition for talent.
- We witness the development of a "multiple-class knowledge working society" with different contractual bonds with the company. The roles of upper-level management, middle-level management and specialised employees have been redefined. Same applies to the functions of ICT employees and support employees.
- The knowledge of the company is to a great extent located in the brains of its employees. The evaluation of employee competencies and their targeted development are of great importance.
- Knowledge-based management of a company means creating motives and inspiring environments for employees to convert their creativity knowledge to profit the company and their own development.
- Incentive systems are essential for aligning behaviour for sharing and developing knowledge.
- Knowledge workers increasingly work and interact in (social) networks and share their experiences via communities. Companies should know how to support communities.

## 4.7    Questions

1. What are the differences between intrinsic and extrinsic motivation? And which are the implications for incentive systems?
2. Please name at least five success factors of communities of practice.
3. The need to share knowledge more broadly has increased as decision making has been pushed down to more people within organisations. While sharing knowledge is important, simply opening the floodgates is risky. Discuss.
4. Which factors influence/determine knowledge worker productivity?
5. List some important competences of a sales representative.

## 4.8   Assignments

### 1. Making knowledge sharing happen

For 3 months you have been working in a consulting company. The firm has invited you to join a working group to improve knowledge sharing. The company has an intranet platform, a number of discussion forums and expert groups, but consultants keep important knowledge for themselves and share only information which is not central to their activities. Particular senior consultants are reluctant to share. They have been working for many years in their area of expertise, each of them has a different work style, some think that they are better experts than their colleagues, some of them believe that the firm depends on them and behave like this.

*The working group is asked to analyse the reasons for this behaviour and to propose possible solutions.*

### 2. "We have to have ideas"

The reason that we have to involve everyone in the process,' says Dr. Geoffrey Nicholson, Vice President, Corporate Technical Planning and International Technology Operations, 3M 'is because we can't schedule creativity. We don't know who is going to have a good idea. But we do know that to have good ideas, we have to have ideas – the good, bad and the ugly. We must empower the individual to pursue his or her dream to help the good ideas survive.'

*You are asked to propose possible measures. Be inspired by examples of creative firms.*

## 4.9   KM-Tool: The Skill or Competence Matrix

### What is a skill or competence matrix?

A skill or competence matrix is a widely proven and suitable method for structuring, evaluating and visualising the distribution of skill or competencies in a unit or a firm (an example is shown. in Fig. 4.10). It is also easy to apply SMEs.

### Why use a skill/competence matrix?
- The matrix shows were skills/competences are lacking or a unevenly distributed
- The matrix helps you to assess training needs
- By the matrix recruitment of new staff (which competences and skills do we need?) and succession planning is supported
- A wider skill/competence distribution (multiskilling) increases the flexibility of the organisation.

### How to create a skill/competence matrix?
1. List tasks and skills/competences needes to carry-out these tasks.
2. The employees and skills/competencies are placed together in a matrix (see Fig. 4.10). Thus, you get an overview of the performance profile of your company.

**Fig. 4.10** The competence matrix: who can do what and how well?

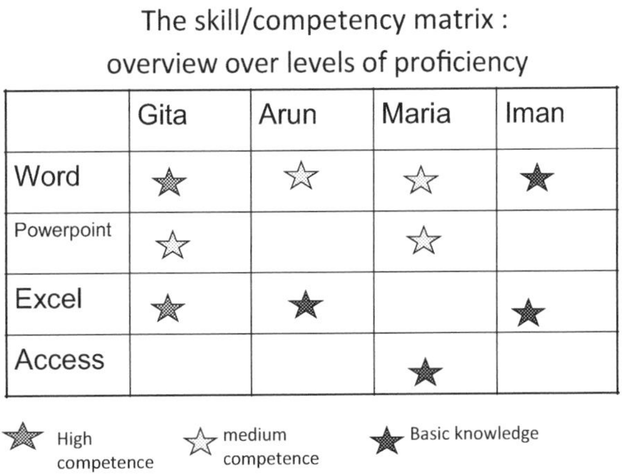

The skill/competency matrix :
overview over levels of proficiency

|          | Gita | Arun | Maria | Iman |
|----------|------|------|-------|------|
| Word     | ★ | ☆ | ☆ | ★ |
| Powerpoint | ☆ | | ☆ | |
| Excel    | ★ | ★ | | ★ |
| Access   | | | ★ | |

★ High competence      ☆ medium competence      ★ Basic knowledge

You can see whether particular competencies are covered satisfactorily and plan the creation of new competencies systematically. In a table, the skills that are typically found in daily work in the company are placed next to the employees. You might structure skills/competences according to process steps, technologies, language and social competences .

3. Every employee does his/her own evaluation and in parallel the supervisor assesses the competencies of collaborators. In an appraisal meeting evaluations of both sides are discussed and unified.

4. You can read the competence profile of an individual employee vertically. If you see horizontally, you get an idea of how well the respective competence is covered in the company. Set minimum standards. Depending on the size of the company, one or more employee should have top grades in each competence.

5. Knowledge gaps are formed if none or only one employee has top grades for a competence category. If this person is missing, the efficiency of the company reduces because no employee can fill in with matching skills. You should fill in such knowledge gaps. Create a goal for yourself: For example, in my company, each competence category should have three employees with "+++" and two employees with "++".

6. You can extend the table by entering new competencies. The central question is, *"which skills/competences must be available in the company in one, five or ten years?"* Subdivide the objectives in smaller actions or necessary individual skills. You can set a deadline in the table for these tasks. It would be useful to note down not only the name of the employees but also further information such as cost centre, scope of work, activities or qualifications (for instance, ability to operate certain machines, first-aid knowledge etc.).

7. You can also use the table to set incentives for the employees. For instance, an employee who has top grades in four competencies would get a bonus.

# Strategies for Managing Knowledge

**5**

*A resource-based approach tends to place more emphasis on the organisation's capabilities or core competences. A knowledge-based strategy formulation should thus start with the primary intangible resource: the competence of people –*
K.E. Sveiby (2001)

**Learning Outcomes.** After completing this chapter
- You will be aware of guiding principles for a successful KM strategy;
- You will be able to develop a KM strategy guided by five questions;
- You will know how to develop a "Best Practice" process;
- You can name the differences of KM strategies for process and project oriented organisations;
- You will be able to run a knowledge market.

## 5.1 The Need for a Knowledge-Oriented Strategy

Typically most organisations develop their strategy around a well-recognised business model. Therefore it would seem logical to map Knowledge Management (KM) issues to a recognised business model. The idea is to articulate the issues around business terms and not KM by itself. KM should be seen as a set of concepts that could be tailored to meet business needs (Dilip Bhatt 2000).

> While talking about knowledge management in companies, we should also see how organisational knowledge potential is converted every single day into successful practices that increase market share, strengthen competitive advantages and satisfy/inspire stakeholders. (Deiser 1996, p. 49)

K. North and G. Kumta, *Knowledge Management*,
Springer Texts in Business and Economics, DOI 10.1007/978-3-319-03698-4_5,
© Springer International Publishing Switzerland 2014

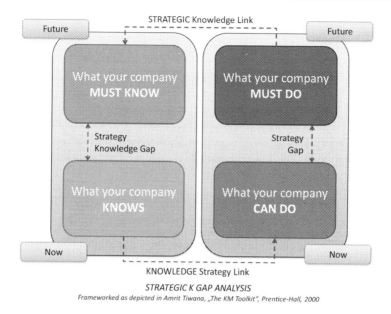

**Fig. 5.1**  Strategic K gap analysis

**The question therefore is:**

- How can organisations leverage past experiences to be able to cope with today's dynamic business environment?
- How can firms develop the competences needed to compete successfully in the future?
- How can business strategy be driven by knowledge that can enhance the quality of products and services and accelerate the time to market thus giving the organisation a competitive edge. What we need is a sort of mental clearing house where knowledge and ideas are received, sorted, summarised, digested, clarified and compared.

A strategic knowledge gap analysis as shown in Fig. 5.1 might be helpful to answer these questions and identify knowledge and competence gaps to be closed.

## Guiding Principles for a Successful Knowledge Management Strategy

In developing a knowledge-oriented strategy firms should take into account the following guiding principles which we have identified based on an analysis of knowledge management initiatives:

*Total Knowledge Management:* This involves integration of knowledge management in all the business processes. On the lines of Total Quality

Management (TQM) which assumes that *"there is quality in everything we do"*, one could also talk about Total Knowledge Management (TKM) in terms of creating, protecting and using knowledge in all business processes. Knowledge management will have a lasting and professional effect only after one realises that "knowledge organisation" is an independent organisational dimension with corresponding resources and processes. However, just as a quality manager or an environment protection officer is not solely responsible for quality and environment in a company, a knowledge manager can take the responsibility of creation and transfer of knowledge only to a certain extent. The principles of knowledge management should be followed by everyone – be it inspirers, coaches or sponsors of knowledge.

*Value-based knowledge management:* Knowledge management should be linked clearly to the objectives of a company. Generation of knowledge, transfer of knowledge and *"feeding"* the information system are not objectives by themselves. The purpose is not managing knowledge, instead managing the company under optimum utilisation of knowledge resource – *adding value by knowledge*. Value-based knowledge management can be considered similar to value-based management. From the viewpoint of knowledge management projects, this means concentrating on few definite objectives.

*Personal interaction and codification:* It is necessary to select the suitable mix of personal interaction to share and learn and codification. Knowledge management initiatives often debate whether knowledge should be documented in databases or exchanged personally. Experience shows that both options complement each other. It is advisable to document knowledge that can be standardised, needs less explanation, is reusable and has a long period of validity. Individual, specific and complex solutions that are also based on personal relations or experiences should be transferred personally. According to Hansen, Nohria and Tierney (1999) you need to start by identifying what kind of organisation you have and what your information needs are, and then primarily focus either on a "personalisation" strategy (putting up infrastructure such as Communities of Practice to help people find each other and tap rich contextual information from other people) or a "codification" strategy, where information is identified, codified, and stored for later retrieval in some kind of effective information store.

*Knowledge has a market value:* If knowledge is a valuable resource, it is bound to build a market for itself. There are knowledge sellers and knowledge buyers who operate through market balancing mechanisms under certain conditions. In a traditional hierarchical company or a bureaucratic organisation, it is often decided as to who knows what and who is responsible for a certain task. However, in a market-oriented control, the competences and service offers are built in the interplay of supply and demand. This is ensured through inevitable use of knowledge/information in the workflow.

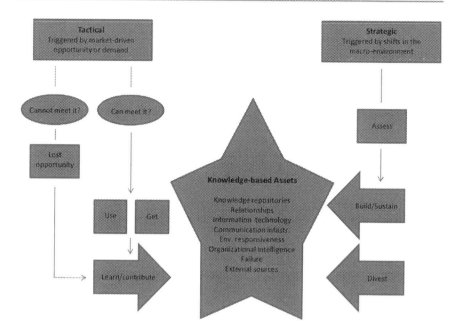

**Fig. 5.2** The KM process framework by Buckowitz and Williams (1999) (Source: http://www.knowledge-management-tools.net/three-km-models.html)

## Knowledge Management as Response to Tactical and Strategic Changes

According to Bukowitz and Williams (1999), KM initiatives are the result of the response to tactical and strategic changes and needs. Their model provides an overview of the strategy behind KM and depicts the process that defines the management strategy in order to build, sustain, divest and enhance assets. The model is based on the tactical processes of get, use, learn and contribute. It is a model that emphasises the "why" and "when" aspects. The strength of this model rests on its strategic focus based on the tactical processes, which essentially puts knowledge management action into context. The model is depicted in Fig. 5.2.

Knowledge is useful for a company and can be used by individuals or groups only if it is present in an explicit form. Thus, from this point of view, it is the task of the knowledge management team to arrange and direct a process of generating organisational knowledge. As discussed in Chap. 2, Nonaka and Takeuchi have defined organisational knowledge creation as the capability of a company as a whole to create new knowledge, distribute it throughout the organisation and embed it in products, services and systems. Their Spiral Model SECI demonstrates how tacit knowledge gets converted to explicit and then back again to tacit. Strategies should therefore revolve around the tactical processes which focus on capturing and converting individual knowledge for achieving organisational goals.

## 5.2 Developing a Knowledge Management Strategy: Five Questions

The strategic objective of knowledge management is to convert knowledge into competitive advantages that can be measured as business success. Considering the content of the objectives, we can express them as normative, strategic and operative knowledge objectives that vary in significance in different phases of business development.

*Normative knowledge objectives (know-why)* refer to the desired values and behaviour that are relevant for a long-term and lasting competitiveness.

*Strategic knowledge objectives (know-what)* shape the manner in which we can convert our existing knowledge into success of the business and help identify knowledge required for producing new strategic options in order to get the desired growth.

*Operative knowledge objectives (know-how)* refer to "*daily business*", i.e. control over processes and project. Mobilising operative knowledge to create value and satisfy customers.

Implementing knowledge management firstly means making oneself aware of the importance of knowledge as a competitive resource. In order to develop a knowledge management strategy the following five questions can provide guidance:

**Question 1:** Are our stakeholders (especially management, employees and investors) sensitive to the importance of knowledge as resource for our business success?

**Question 2:** Which strategies do we want to support by mobilising knowledge?

**Question 3:** Which knowledge do we have today and which knowledge do we need in the future to sustain competitiveness?

**Question 4:** How do we handle our knowledge resources, which factors promote creation and use of knowledge and what are the barriers to it?

**Question 5:** How should we organise and develop our knowledge to cope with present and future knowledge competition?

Let us look at each question.

### Question 1: Are our stakeholders sensitive to the importance of knowledge as resource for the business success?

We will start by coming back to the analysis presented in Chap. 1 considering markets, solutions for customer problems and investors. It is recommended to reflect on the role of specific knowledge and competences to strengthen unique selling propositions of products and services and how to inhibit imitation and create sustainable competitive advantage based on our knowledge.

Another way of identifying 'knowledge sensitivity' of an organisation is to ask the employees and management to identify specific instances relating to timely access to relevant information and knowledge. It would be interesting to find some answers to the following questions:

- Have we lost orders because we could not mobilise the right information about customer requirements and because of the solutions we offered?

- Have we put ourselves in an embarrassing situation in front of customers because we have no information about what we had offered 2 years back?
- Was the profit margin low because we did not use our experience?
- Have we hired a consultant in the company because we do not know that similar competence is present in our company?
- Are best practices in terms of knowledge documentation, transfer and learning from each other documented?
- Are investors evaluing intellectual capital before taking investment decisions or lending capital?

Based on the responses to these questions, if we come to a conclusion that managing knowledge resources systematically contributes largely to business success, we should move to the next step:

## Question 2: Which strategies do we want to support by mobilising knowledge?

Successful organisations concentrate their efforts on a particular area and excel at it, rather than trying to offer everything to everyone and failing to excel at anything. According to Traecy und Wiersema (1993), there are three higher-level strategic company objectives: Product Leadership, Customer Intimacy and Operational Excellence

This suggests that there are three primary elements to any competitive business: the business itself, its product(s) and its customers – see Fig. 5.3. Each of these components represents the focus of attention for one of the value disciplines. The focus is on the product(s) when pursuing "Product Leadership"; the focus is on the customers and their requirements when pursuing "Customer Intimacy"; and the focus is on the organisation itself and its delivery processes, when pursuing "Operational Excellence". Depending on the organisation's focus KM strategies are developed.

| Focus area | Objective of KM strategy |
|---|---|
| Products | Constantly developing new ideas and launching them in the market quickly |
| Relationship with their customers | Increase customer satisfaction and retention by better understanding the customer's needs and preferences |
| Internal processes | Sharing best practices between different units, reducing costs and improving efficiency |

**Product leadership** strives at capturing and creating market shares with new and innovative products. Ideally, product leadership means being the first company to bring a new product in the market and create market potential for it. Product leadership is achieved by continuous technological innovations, their conversion into product innovations and consequent formation of new business fields.

From the knowledge viewpoint, product leadership requires high renewal power from within, a process of knowledge creation in which new knowledge is created continuously using existing knowledge (according to principles described by Nonaka

**Fig. 5.3** Strategic objectives according to Traecy and Wiersema

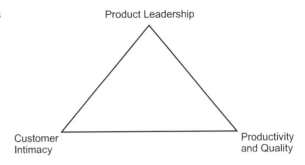

Product Leadership

Customer Intimacy

Productivity and Quality

and Takeuchi). Early identification or anticipation of market trends as well as basic technological developments is necessary for achieving product leadership.

The second strategic objective is called "**Customer Intimacy**" which is not the same as closeness to the customer or the term "*customer as partner*" (Wiersema 1996). Customer Intimacy means knowing more about the requirements and preferences of customers than the competitors, guiding customer individually and building trust in order to learn and grow together. The Individual Inc. Clipping-Service (see case study) is a good example of this customer intimacy. Knowledge is built keeping the customer in mind which benefits the customer because of more focused supply of information and therefore the customer feels better served and is bonded to the company. From knowledge viewpoint, the learning process here is structured by and with the customers. Customer order processes are redesigned from the knowledge perspectives. Customer intimacy also means customer-related information management and offering complete solutions under the "*one face to the customer*" motto.

Productivity and quality (**Operational Excellence**) is the third strategic objective of a company. This includes learning quickly using intelligent processes, not repeating mistakes, avoiding double work and transferring best practices efficiently. Fast learning processes in and across the company are vital to survive, especially in markets with high price deterioration and short product lifecycles. If an electronics manufacturing company is expected to register a price fall of 10–20 % every year, it should be compensated widely by more efficient processes.

All the three objectives can be achieved only if necessary financial and knowledge resources are available. Therefore, fulfilment of strategic goals is supported by sensitising the stakeholders to the importance of knowledge for achieving company's objectives. A transparent presentation of Intellectual Capital can be the first step in this direction.

## Question 3: What knowledge do we have today and what knowledge will we need in the future to sustain competitiveness?

While we can describe and evaluate our present knowledge, there are limits on determining which knowledge we need in future in a turbulent market environment.

# Strategic knowledge analysis

1. Which capabilities/competencies    ➢  What should we do to develop these
   do our **customers** expect in the next    capabilities?
   3 years?

2. What are we doing better than our    ➢  How can we fortify these strengths?
   **competitors**?

3. What are our competitors doing
   better than we?                       ➢  What can we learn?

**Fig. 5.4**  Strategic knowledge analysis

However, there are certain approaches which help in foreseeing the future. Using the concept of *"Technology Road Maps"* which describe the development of future technologies and build specific, definable competences, we can create knowledge Road Maps to identify future needs.

As core competences (we have discussed the concept in Chap. 2) are of particular importance for sustaining competitive advantage think about the knowledge and competences (i.e. the ability to apply your knowledge to take the right actions in the right moment) you have and you will need to support your core competences. Think in terms of which knowledge we need to mobilise and to develop to support the criteria of relevance, difficulty of imitation and breadth of application:

1. Relevance: Firstly, the competence must give your customer something that strongly influences him or her to choose your product or service. If it does not, then it has no effect on your competitive position and is not a core competence.
2. Difficulty of Imitation: Secondly, the core competence should be difficult to imitate. This allows you to provide products that are better than those of your competition. And because you're continually working to improve these skills, means that you can sustain its competitive position.
3. Breadth of Application: Thirdly, it should be something that opens up a good number of potential markets. If it only opens up a few small, niche markets, then success in these markets will not be enough to sustain significant growth.

A simple approach to define knowledge and competence needs in the future is to focus on customers, own strengths and competitors and develop answers to the following questions of a **strategic knowledge analysis** (see Fig. 5.4). A workshop with employees across hierarchies and departments helps to unify perceptions and create a joint vision where the organisation stands and needs to go.

While taking the step from strategic to operative knowledge management, we should ask ourselves the following question.

## Question 4: How do we handle our knowledge resources, which factors promote creation and use of knowledge and what are the barriers to it?

As in the earlier sections, we here invite you to assess your actual situation in this short analysis of "knowledge and learning" (see Fig. 5.5).

If one does not want to be oriented to a pre-structured questionnaire, one has other options like the *fishbone diagram* (also called Ishikawa diagram), well-known in quality management, mind-mapping or a strength-weakness analysis in order to compile problem areas of knowledge management and their correlation. This compilation takes place in a structured manner in a research group. The method suggested here helps the company develop objectives for knowledge-oriented management in a structured manner. They can then be included in the overall concept. For this purpose, it is necessary to answer question 5.

*Empirical surveys of knowledge management*

In numerous empirical surveys, organizations were asked which benefits they expect from KM and which factors promote or prevent creation and transfer of knowledge. The result of the selected surveys is summed up in the following table. It becomes clear that the company culture, incentive systems and management support are more important than the technical systems.

| Expectation from knowledge management | Prevents creation and transfer of knowledge | Promotes creation and transfer of knowledge |
|---|---|---|
| Increasing product quality | Lack of time | Company culture |
| Increasing innovative ability | Lack of awareness | Support by/responsibility of the upper level management |
| Improving customer proximity | Inadequate incentive systems | Push and pull of information and knowledge |
| Using resources efficiently | Incomplete and user-unfriendly IT | Contributions to knowledge management are important for career development |
| Safeguarding the capacity to compete | Inner values create barriers | IT as integrator and catalyst for exchange of knowledge |
| Asserting/creating market position | Fear of change | Organised exchange options |
| Increasing performance | Lack of management support | Increasing freedom of action, autonomy of the smallest unit |
|  |  | Transparency in knowledge requirements |

| Company insensitive to knowledge | 1 | 2 | 3 | 4 | 5 | Knowledge-intensive company |
|---|---|---|---|---|---|---|
| **Knowledge and learning** | | | | | | |
| Information is synonymous to knowledge | | | | | | Knowledge is developed from Information |
| We learn slowly from other companies | | | | | | We learn quickly from other companies |
| We transfer knowledge ineffectively in our company | | | | | | We have effective knowledge transfer within the organisation |
| There is no transparency in knowledge | | | | | | Transparency in knowledge is established through yellow pages, knowledge maps etc. |
| We do very little to protect our knowledge | | | | | | We protect ourselves from loss of knowledge |
| We are shy of emphasising best practices | | | | | | We emphasise best practices and expertise |
| Training and development is directed towards individual learning processes | | | | | | Training and development practices teamwork and knowledge transfer beyond business units |
| Employees are "sent" for training | | | | | | Employees control their own learning process actively |
| There is no institutionalised KM | | | | | | KM, processes and roles are implemented |
| Inefficient groups of transfer of knowledge | | | | | | Competence networks gather and transfer know-how |
| We don't have any cooperative projects | | | | | | Cooperative projects in the company encourage teamwork |
| We don't have any systematic and open benchmarking | | | | | | We emphasise best practices through benchmarking (internal and external) |
| In our company, offices and social rooms are demarcated | | | | | | Our offices and social rooms encourage teamwork |

**Fig. 5.5**   Assessment of knowledge management situation

## Question 5: How should we organise to cope with current and future knowledge competition?

In order to answer this question it is necessary to decide on the approach which we want to take towards a knowledge organisation.

Development of knowledge, generation of new business fields, internal develop-ment as well as learning from external knowledge resources requires the *cultivation of knowledge ecologies*, i.e. contexts favourable for developing knowledge and motivating employees to create, share and use knowledge across business units and the entire company. The knowledge ecology emphasises the process character of knowledge and the elements of self-organisation in order to function in a fast changing environment. Organisations are recognised as dynamically learning systems that revolve in a continuous process by examining their own surroundings and themselves (the autopoietic systems).

In this sense Nonaka and Konno (Nonaka and Konno 1998) applied the Japanese *concept of "Ba"* to organisational theory. Ba (equivalent to "place" in English) is a shared space for emerging relationships. It can be a physical, virtual, or mental space. Knowledge, in contrast to information, cannot be separated from the context – it is embedded in Ba. To support the process of knowledge creation, a foundation in Ba is required.

Efforts to understand the complex dynamics of self-creating organisation through rigid regulations and control fail in the light of complexity and speed of the change. A company that has open culture, provides space and offers incentives for entrepreneurial initiative as well as teamwork forms the basis of knowledge ecology. Development and utilisation of knowledge cannot always be planned. Instead, this process is ad hoc, intuitive and left to coincidence to some extent.

In practice, we find a wide variety of approaches to knowledge-based management depending on the characteristics of firms, sectors and countries.[1] We will first quote some examples of KM initiatives of different firms and subsequently take a deeper look into knowledge management approaches.

For *Chevron*, knowledge management is largely identical to effective transfer of knowledge within and into the company. Knowledge transfer is connected to the Total Quality Management of a company. *"ShareNet"* and best-practice processes are some of the ways used by *Siemens* to design its knowledge transfer. It also encourages *"knowledge networking"* in sales and creates communities of practice. A team at the company level coordinates numerous initiatives of the departments (Davenport and Probst 2000). At MindTree, communities of practice plays an important role while at Eureka Forbes, the Senate helps to capture organisational learning. Learning from the projects is considered of great importance particularly in consulting firms.

Some companies incorporate knowledge management in the functional areas, especially research and development. The benchmarking survey of the American Productivity and Quality Centre (APQC 1996) showed that US companies have varying perceptions and approaches towards knowledge management. Majority of the 11 *best practice companies* that were compared consider knowledge management synonymous to knowledge transfer.

Other companies see knowledge management from the aspect of management of the intellectual capital. The Swiss hearing aid manufacturer, *Phonak*, encourages open communication beyond the hierarchical and professional boundaries thus turning a canteen into a market place of ideas. An environment is created to encourage exchange of information and teamwork. *General Electric* sets ambitious objectives and value systems supported by an incentive system that promotes teamwork beyond the boundaries of business units and encourages openness to learn from outside. An insurance company relies on international synergy

---

[1] There is no comprehensive and up-to date overview, for summarising statements refer to http://www.kbos.net/uploadfiles/Knowledge%20Management%20implementation%20trends.pdf or see the annual results of the "MAKE"-award.

management in order to make expert knowledge available to its groups. Even the small and medium enterprises are increasingly recognising the importance of knowledge management.

All the aforementioned companies attribute their success to the fact that they used knowledge to gain competitive advantage. In other words, the investors get good returns through nurturing and exploitation of "intellectual capital". Analyses of the case studies published about knowledge-based management reveal a lot of emphasis on better use of the available knowledge ("*Economies of re-use*") by disseminating "Best Practices", making knowledge available in processes or learning from past project experience. The ability to act in turbulent and fast changing environments requires merging innovation and knowledge management. New knowledge is generated at the boundary of the existing knowledge.

In the following we will look deeper at four typical KM strategies or approaches which are not exclusive but can be combined.

## 5.3   Focused Strategies: Innovation, Process and Project Perspectives

### Innovation-Oriented KM Strategy

Innovation means systematically combining knowledge afresh to generate value for the customer. Successful innovation management is thus based on a conscious handling of knowledge as a resource. On the other hand, innovation problems are knowledge problems. Let us look at the most important reasons for the failure of innovation projects: The inability to align technological innovations to the needs of the market and of the customers is rooted in a lack of knowledge transparency across markets and customers and an inefficient knowledge transfer across functional boundaries. Strategy, Marketing and R&D fail to share their knowledge. Innovations do not materialise or they fail, because the entire Know-How available in the organisation is not applied in the product. Innovations also fail because organisations do not learn systematically from successful projects or from the failed ones. Experts are not encouraged and fostered in a focused manner, and knowledge is lost.

Organisations and employees are rarely short of knowledge and ideas. The implementation of these ideas and knowledge in new or improved products, processes and business areas is the main problem.

An innovation oriented KM strategy should put particular emphasis in the *cultivation of knowledge ecologies*, i.e. contexts favourable for developing knowledge and motivating employees to create, share and use knowledge across business units and the entire company. In the following we will some important elements of an innovation oriented KM strategy:

*Setting knowledge goals:* Based on the organisational goals and innovation strategy, it should be determined which knowledge (e.g. core technologies) represents a relevant resource from the strategic point of view, and which capabilities need to be worked upon. These goals could be normative, strategic and/or operative in nature.

*Identifying knowledge:* To start with, transparency has to be established as to which knowledge and competence is available internally and externally with regard to experts, capabilities and experiences. Knowledge maps, knowledge brokers and scouts, etc. make their way into the organisations only gradually.

*Acquiring knowledge:* Concerted external procurement of knowledge by taking over innovative companies, forming alliances or recruiting experts etc. helps build future competencies faster than may be possible through own resources and efforts. "Shopping" in international knowledge markets is an important part of innovation processes. Crowd sourcing and innovation jams tap resources of employees and their families, clients and the interested public at large.

---

**Minicase: www.innocentive.com – A platform to tap external knowledge[2]**

InnoCentive was launched by the pharmaceutical company Eli Lilly to connect with people who could help develop drugs and speed them to market by inviting other organisations to join. It has since become a major platform to draw upon outside expertise. The process works in the following way:

1. Open a project room. When you find a challenge summary of interest, log in and the challenge agreement in order to open a project room. A project room is a secure space where you can view the confidential detailed description, see technical requirements, ask the Seeker questions, and submit solutions.
2. Let your creative juices flow! If you get stuck, consider finding a teammate, reviewing the solver resources, or messaging the seeker from within your project room.
3. Submit a solution. You can modify or replace your solutions up until the deadline.

The companies – or seekers – pay solvers anywhere from $5,000 to $1,000,000 per solution. (They also pay InnoCentive a fee to participate.) Some of the most prolific solvers have even quit their day jobs to focus on finding the answers to problems full-time.

---

*Developing knowledge:* New forms of development processes in networks and teams, better idea generation and evaluation and more efficient processes are central to this element of knowledge. The analysis of knowledge development – e.g. using the Nonaka and Takeuchi model of knowledge spiral – forms the basis for understanding innovation processes.

*Sharing knowledge:* In order to make isolated knowledge in the organisation of use for the whole organisation, "Knowledge sharing" is an imperative prerequisite.

---

[2] For more information on crowdsourcing see Howe (2006); Chesbrough et al. (2006).

The key question is: Who needs to know or do what and to what extent, and how can I facilitate knowledge sharing?

*Utilising knowledge:* The willingness to share knowledge must be accompanied by the willingness of employees to put this knowledge to use. Through appropriate motivation, Organisations should ensure that knowledge created with great efforts and identified as strategically important is also applied in the day to day activities, and that such knowledge does not fall prey to the general reluctance of the organisation.

*Retaining knowledge:* To avoid loosing valuable expertise easily, know-how risks must be managed; i.e. the processes of selecting the know-how that is worthy of protection, storing it appropriately and of its regular update must be designed consciously. Also, measures and instruments for protecting the know-how must be implemented on time.

*Evaluating knowledge:* In accordance with the formulated knowledge goals, methods for measuring normative, strategic and operative knowledge goals are necessary. The quality of the formulated goals is revealed latest at the time of evaluation. Abstract goal formulations such as "We want to become a learning organisation", can have negative consequences in this case. Knowledge-oriented cultural analyses, intensifying of methods of training control as well as the comprehensive concept of Balanced Scorecard are the steps in the right direction. Only by measuring the central variables of the knowledge management process, the management loop can be closed.

These core processes of knowledge management will be successful, if they are embedded in environments conducive for fostering knowledge. They are based on one vision "Adding value through knowledge – The basis of our success". This vision should be implemented by practicing values such as trust, openness for innovations, fault tolerance, authenticity, just to name a few. The desired behaviour of executives and of employees on the basis of these values should be described, and the actual behaviour should be measured. Reward systems should honour cooperation and collective knowledge development based on the overall performance of the organisation. A culture of innovation and knowledge rests on people and their motivation to build knowledge. A project manager of an innovation project summarises his experiences thus: "Perhaps, right from the beginning, one should have addressed the human aspect of the issue instead of prioritising information and communications technology".

### "Sense" increases innovation performance

A rather unusual knowledge management was established in the pharmaceutical development unit of a major drug firm. The unit had 50 employees (chemists, pharmacists, biologists, chemical engineers, laboratory assistants) responsible for developing generic dosage form into product form ready for the market. Thus, the concerned employees take a centre stage apparently linked to the targeted results. To improve performance and reduce stress the "Sense" initiative was launched by middle management.

$$\text{Sense}^2 = \text{sense (by being human)} \times \text{sense (by visible results)}$$

Sense by being human is based on the following three elements: building trust, creating space and giving time. A monthly orientation meeting was arranged in order to build trust. The members of management speak openly and frankly about how they are handling things they like and things that disturb them. This increased the estimation of trust enormously. Extremely high common goals were set, thus demanding strong trust. Successes were celebrated spontaneously and conspicuously.

In order to create space, a recreation room was converted into a creative kitchen (physical space) wherein the employees could meet each other and share knowledge. Four completely integrated development teams were created with experts from all the departments (physical space). Each of these teams was assigned a clearly defined number of projects to be handled. Furthermore, three IT communication platforms were arranged (virtual space) that enable fast exchange of information (laboratory results, project advancement etc.).

In order to give time, the overhead presentations were skipped to a large extent in the monthly meetings so that one could explain the team results in form of stories (story telling) and hold discussions accordingly. Posters highlighting the mottos "*You explain, I will listen, I will ask questions*" and "*operative rush does not replace mental calm*" were displayed in all laboratories and offices.

Knowledge can come into being, grow, be shared and used by building trust, creating space and giving time. The following **results** were achieved based on the criteria of speed, innovation and networking: development time was brought down by 25–50 % (speed). The number of patent applications increased three-fold (innovation). The cooperation projects with universities and other external specialised institutions were enhanced significantly (networking).

Source: Adapted from Krischker and Raneburger. Presentation for the competition "the 10 most effective KM tools".

## Process-Oriented KM Strategy

The late 1980s and early 1990s saw a widespread focus on business process reengineering, peaking at the time that Hammer & Champy published in (1993) "Reengineering the Corporation", along with an increased recognition of the importance of business processes as a primary means of adding value. A number of authors such as Davenport & Prusak (1998) in "Working Knowledge" discussed the issues relevant to applying process models to knowledge work while differentiating between processes that apply knowledge and processes intended to create knowledge. Business processes are both knowledge demanding and knowledge generating (see Fig. 5.6). Process-oriented knowledge management initiatives are designed to provide employees with task-related knowledge in the organisation's operative business processes.

A process-oriented KM strategy should therefore begin with an information and knowledge analysis of business processes as shown in Fig. 5.6. Based on this, expertise and knowledge sources should be made transparent for every stage of the process. Knowledge supply should be integrated in the work process so that using knowledge becomes inevitable. There are a number of software solutions available for this purpose.

Apart from transferring knowledge within the business processes, knowledge should also be exchanged beyond processes. The significance of the integration process with three components – value-based integration, operative integration and knowledge-based integration – was emphasised for the organisational concept of Entrepreneurial Corporation.

"*Knowledge integration processes*" in a company can be designed analogous to its business processes. Take for example three typical processes of a manufacturing company – product engineering process, order process and purchasing process. These similar processes largely take place independent of each other in different business areas or units of a company. The knowledge integration process superimposes the business processes by interweaving the otherwise loose threads of business processes. Knowledge integration processes can aim at optimising the purchasing processes throughout the divisions of a company. The product engineering processes, order processes and buying processes can also be harmonised better within and across business units. For this competence centres, teams or Communities of Practice should be established (p.e purchasing competence centre, global purchasing team, Purchasing CoP).

## Best Practice KM Strategy

A typical knowledge integration process is the "Best Practice process" with the goal to improve business processes by learning from others. A Best Practice process can be structured within and across organisations

A Best Practice process can be structured within and across organisations

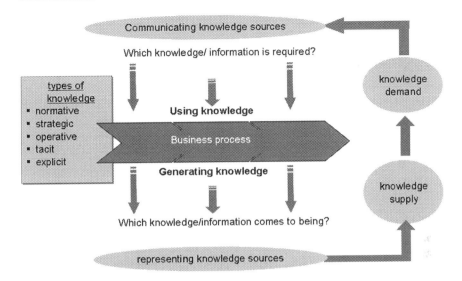

**Fig. 5.6** Information and knowledge analyses of business processes

Best Practices in organisations generally comprise of methods, procedures and ways of working which lead to higher productivity, quality, added value and higher customer benefits. Best Practices change continuously with our learning processes. The potential earnings of transfer from Best Practices are usually very high (see Fig. 5.7).

**Best practices** are those practices that have been shown to produce superior results; selected by a systematic process; and judged as exemplary, good, or successfully demonstrated. "Best Practices" are a moving target as they change with experience and innovation

## From "Good Practices" to Standards[3]

In the following five steps, we describe how, based on (intuitively) realised good practices, an understanding process for standardisation gradually results in a specialised community or in a professional field.

*Step 1: Identification and exchange of Good Practices:* Collection of "Success Stories", of narrations of what, as perceived by the practitioners, "worked". Here intuition plays a big role.

*Step 2: Understanding of indicators for Good Practices:* The "Community" of practitioners works out criteria which indicate a "Good Practice". For instance, such criteria could be effectiveness, productivity and social effects. This step is a

---

[3] This section was authored by Dr. Thomas Rieger, ComoConsult.

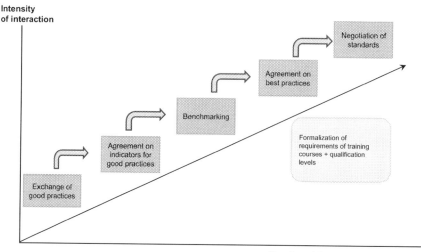

**Fig. 5.7** How best practices emerge (Source: Thomas Rieger)

"start" of systematisation. Resistance may result from the apprehension that individually reported Good Practices may not suffice the indicators or criteria.

*Step 3: Benchmarking:* Ideally, benchmarking is formalised, although often it takes the form of sum of specific interactions such as conferences, congresses, discussions in scientific publications for instance (refer remarks on benchmarking given below). Possible sources of resistance are rooted in problems of trust and the tendency to avoid the high effort involved in the benchmarking procedure, or the fear of not being "good" or "the first".

*Step 4: Understanding of "Best Practices":* Based on the benchmarking, evaluation criteria are refined and Best Practices are described in detail. From this level onwards, a significant pressure for standardisation begins; these "tricks of the trade" can also be used as standard for executing work in a professional manner. Resistance may arise from the fear for the pressure to change, if (among others due to Benchmarking) it is assumed that one's practices are not accepted as Best Practices.

*Step 5: Standardisation:* In this step, the defined "Best Practices" are described in detail. They are stipulated in a work instruction, a standard, and a regulation or in some other form as a recommendation or mandatory procedure. This level is the most "politicised": Deviations may have immediate economic and legal consequences (non-saleability of goods and services, liability claims etc.). The significance of trade and commercial instrumentalisation increases. Source of resistance: Is the same as in case of transition to Best Practices; although now driven by significantly stronger conflicts of interests, since deviations from standards have consequences.

A French industrial enterprise optimises its production with the "best in class" programme, i.e. with a competition of production centres of its subsidiaries in France, Thailand, Philippines, Brazil, Mexico and USA. Every month, the manufacturing plants compare their data pertaining to productivity, quality and effectiveness. What do the better plants do? Everyone is allowed to copy. In a quarterly newsletter, the best subsidiaries express their views yet again in detail. The managers meet all 6 months for intensive exchange of information and knowledge.

Source: Seifert (1996), p. 134.


## Benchmarking: Learning to Improve Processes

Benchmarking, the structured comparison of processes and activities is an indispensable part of knowledge transfer, learning and "negotiation" what is Best Practice. First of all, benchmarking makes us aware of what we are doing. Benchmarking often turns implicit knowledge into explicit. Processes are questioned and success criteria are made transparent. We can accelerate our learning processes and create pressure to change through comparison with other business units or companies (Camp 1989).

There are several suggestions of benchmarking steps, which all include the following elements[4]

1. **Demarcate area of analysis:** Because benchmarking can be applied to any business process or function, an exploratory research might be useful to know better on which aspects to concentrate in order to have a high return in relation to the effort.
2. **Identify other organisations that have similar processes or activities:** For instance, if one were interested in improving hand-offs in addiction treatment one would identify other fields that also have hand-off challenges. These could include air traffic control, cell phone switching between towers, transfer of patients from surgery to recovery rooms.
3. **Identify organisations that are leaders in these areas:** Look for the very best units within an organisation, in any industry or in any country. Consult customers, suppliers, financial analysts, trade associations, and magazines to determine which companies are worthy of study.
4. **Develop metrics for practices and survey:** Develop detailed surveys of measures and practices used to identify business process alternatives and leading companies. Surveys are typically masked to protect confidential data by neutral associations and consultants.

---

[4] Adapted from Camp (1989) and http://en.wikipedia.org/wiki/Benchmarking.

5. **Exchange detailed information and learn jointly, identify leading edge practices:** Companies typically agree to mutually exchange information beneficial to all parties in a benchmarking group and share the results within the group. This might include company visits, experts rounds and practitioner workshops

6. **Implement new and improved business practices:** Take the leading edge practices and develop implementation plans which include identification of specific opportunities, funding the project and selling the ideas to the organisation for the purpose of gaining demonstrated value from the process.

Benchmarking results should be accessible to the interested employees. In this process, similar business units, plants and projects think together about ways of making improvements. However, benchmarking is restricted by the fact that it is based on the actual situation. It is not directed at *"what would have been possible"* or to *"next practice"*.

Benchmarking should be conducted on a regularly basis. Thus, the criterion is improved, development becomes visible and learning process is accelerated. From a *"best-practices database"*, it should be possible to pull out information on which methods and processes were used, what were the experiences with new methods etc. Hence, creation and maintenance of best-practices databases is an important component of knowledge management.

> ### Case: Learning to improve processes – two examples
>
> **Electronics manufacturer:** Through knowledge transfer, an electronics manufacturer was in a position to create the capacity equivalent to an entirely new chip factory from the existing fabrication plant, thereby avoiding approximately $ 500 million investment. The impetus for improvement came from benchmarking of 12 wafer fabrications of the company that were distributed in several business areas. The firm supported knowledge transfer that motivated exchange process, updated a best practices database continuously and created Best Practices Facilitator Network. These facilitators are employees who collect best practices under the framework of their functions of quality management and transfer them in a systematic form.
>
> An **Oil and Gas company** has introduced a best practice process under its total quality management and communicates this process in its "Best Practice Resource Map." This "knowledge map" that is available electronically as well as in paper form contains a list of experts classified as per the topics of quality management (criteria of American Baldrich Quality Award). The company's vision states "create an organization that learns faster and better than competitors through benchmarking, sharing and implementing best practices, learning from experience and continual individual learning and personal growth." There are two reasons for the success of this approach. Transfer of knowledge is integrated in the total quality management and is therefore not an

additional independent approach in the company. The course of knowledge transfer is visualised in comprehensive form, knowledge sellers are identified so that knowledge buyers can orient themselves quickly from the "who knows what" perspective.

## Project-Oriented KM Strategy

In project-based organisations like consulting or construction firms knowledge management has to support the project cycle. A knowledge organisation encourages and supports learning from projects and ensures an efficient and effective progress right from initiation of the project up to the final processing of project results (cf. Yeong and Lim 2010). Figure 5.8 describes how knowledge can be used or processed at every step of a project cycle.

**In the project initiation phase**, it is possible to resort to organisational knowledge about customers, processes or methods by means of process documentations, customer relationship management (CRM) systems or databases on project experiences. **While preparing an offer**, templates, profiles, support of reference projects and lessons learnt from similar projects provide guidance. Experts and project personnel can be identified by means of competence pools, yellow pages or networks. While **executing the project**, it is possible to resort to organisational knowledge sources such as methods handbook, manuals, help desks, competence centres, CoPs and project databases in order to ensure that existing knowledge is used and learning speed increases. The knowledge organisation keeps instruments like supervision and in-flight review ready in order to **identify and solve the problems** in the ongoing process.

At the end of a project cycle, it is necessary to transfer the knowledge that is generated in the organisation by means like systematic project documentation or lessons learnt reports or a debriefing or in the form of consolidation and transfer of experiences through the network.

In every project, the members of the team get experiences that could be of great significance to the future teams with similar problems. Often, these experiences are not raised systematically at the end of a project and are therefore available as a whole for the organisation.

'Lessons learnt' represent the essence of experiences collected in a project or in a position. In order to gain suitable benefits from lessons learnt, it is first necessary to have a suitable context for its safety. Lack of time, different priorities and lack of readiness of the participants often hinders systematic regeneration of organisational activities. However, subsequent benefit is not possible unless experiences are safeguarded. (see KM-Tool "after action review" at the end of Chap. 3)

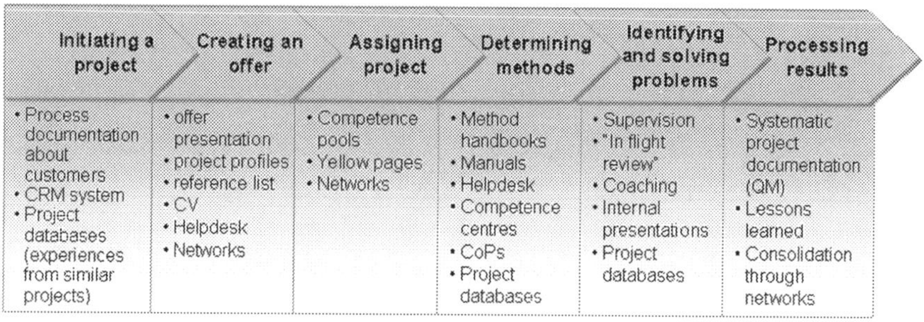

| Initiating a project | Creating an offer | Assigning project | Determining methods | Identifying and solving problems | Processing results |
|---|---|---|---|---|---|
| • Process documentation about customers<br>• CRM system<br>• Project databases (experiences from similar projects) | • offer presentation<br>• project profiles<br>• reference list<br>• CV<br>• Helpdesk<br>• Networks | • Competence pools<br>• Yellow pages<br>• Networks | • Method handbooks<br>• Manuals<br>• Helpdesk<br>• Competence centres<br>• CoPs<br>• Project databases | • Supervision<br>• "In flight review"<br>• Coaching<br>• Internal presentations<br>• Project databases | • Systematic project documentation (QM)<br>• Lessons learned<br>• Consolidation through networks |

**Fig. 5.8** Knowledge organisation in project cycles

**Debriefing**

Debriefing is a method for simple, systematic collection and documentation of know-how obtained from an experience. By means of interviews and workshops, a trained "*third person*" collects knowledge of an individual employee (in an interview) or a team (in a workshop). The documentation of this knowledge is likewise undertaken by the "*third person*" who is also called "debriefer". He puts the collected know-how in an agreed form that enables future users to see the content quickly without any expert support.

Debriefers should be adequately trained to be able to conduct a workshop or an interview systematically even on difficult, conflict-laden subjects. Even for documentation, one requires an equally huge know-how. In order to be accepted as competent dialog partners, the debriefers should have at least their own basic know-how in subjects handled by them. They should take a neutral position and should not be involved directly in the topic to be handled or in the project being considered.

The subject to be handled in an interview or a workshop should be selected in such a way that the interview does not last more than 2–3 h. Even a workshop for collecting the knowledge of a team should remain restricted to half or one day. Longer debriefings neither cater to the scope of the information to be recorded nor to its documentation. If the subjects are comprehensive, it is better to conduct more debriefings restricted to each topic.

## 5.4     Organisations as Knowledge Markets

In organisations continuously new knowledge is created, people gain experiences, thus creating a wide ranging offer of knowledge. On the other hand people are continuously seeking information and knowledge in order to solve specific problems. Knowledge moves through organisations, it is exchanged, bought, found, generated and applied to work. We can therefore describe organisations

| Social network | Internal social market economy | Free market |
|---|---|---|
| ◆ Family/clan | ◆ Internal exchange | ◆ Competition |
| ◆ Public relations | ◆ Take-over negotiations | ◆ Full competition |
| ◆ Free services | ◆ Internal stock price | ◆ Market price |
| ◆ Satisfaction | ◆ Value creation | ◆ Profit |
| ◆ Group bonding | ◆ Customer orientation | ◆ Market rule |
| ◆ Homo Socialis | ◆ Co-entrepreneur | ◆ Homo economicus |

**Fig. 5.9** Governance concept of knowledge markets as "internal social market economy" (Source: Wunderer 1996, p. 7)

using the metaphor of knowledge markets. The market metaphor helps to understand the driving forces and barriers of managing knowledge and to develop effective enabling conditions and market mechanisms for the generation and exchange of knowledge. Markets have multiple functions and like markets for physical goods or financial markets there are knowledge markets.

> **Why go to a market?**
> ... I have something to sell,
> ... I need to buy a specific good,
> ... I have no specific need, but want to be seduced by attractive of,
> ... I want to get the news,
> ... markets inspire me.

Following this metaphor in an organisation, we have knowledge sellers and knowledge buyers and intermediaries such as knowledge brokers and market places and (virtual) spaces which allow knowledge sellers and buyers to interact. In order to create knowledge markets and make them work we have to define enabling conditions as well as principles and rules and develop the supporting knowledge media and infrastructure. In the following we will deal with each of these aspects.

A market-oriented concept of knowledge management establishes an internal social market economy, in other words, internal knowledge-based market economy[5] (Fig. 5.9).

## The Knowledge Market Concept

The knowledge market concept was developed by North (1998) based on many action research projects. This concept should encourage entrepreneurial action and cooperation by directing it towards objectives and values of the entire company so

---

[5] General Electric, Annual Reports 1994, 1995, 1996.

as to ensure short-term success of business units and long-term competence creation of entire company.

In order to achieve this, it is necessary to fulfil three conditions for effective creation and transfer of knowledge in a company (see Fig. 5.10):

*Enabling framework conditions:* Create attractive market conditions . Corporate mission statements, management principles and incentive systems should connect the success of business units and contribution to development of the entire company. Individual competence creation as well as their contributions to the organisational knowledge base should be rewarded.

*Players and rules of game:* Rules for knowledge markets should be defined. The manner of articulating supply and demand of knowledge, bringing sellers and buyers in contact and exchanging knowledge should be decided using these rules of the game. They should also be used to set rules for exchanging knowledge.

*Instruments, processes and structures for interaction on the knowledge market:* For the creation and transfer of knowledge, it is necessary to develop efficient instruments and media that implement rules in their knowledge game. What does this actually mean? Firstly, it is necessary to achieve transparency with regards to **who knows what** in the company. For this purpose, companies have developed various instruments and approaches such as *"yellow pages" or "knowledge maps"* often linked to telephone directories, instant messaging to internal facebook-like applications (p.e. Yammer)

Once knowledge supply is made transparent, it is time to bring sellers and buyers in contact with each other. There are many ways of establishing an exchange: Formal and informal, personal interaction or via electronic platforms. The informal and formal networks, often called as Knowledge can be exchanged and developed for example by networks, collaborative projects consisting of cross-functional employee groups, exchange of manuals, process descriptions and customer information.

---

**Checklist for knowledge sellers and buyers**

"Sellers" should ask themselves:

- To whom am I "selling" my knowledge, what are their needs, level of understanding, and their motivation to seek my knowledge?
- Is my knowledge well structured and presented in an attractive form, ready for use?
- What can I learn from the interaction with knowledge buyers?
- How can I create a demand for my knowledge and increase my "mindshare"

Buyers should ask themselves:

- Am I able to articulate well my demand?
- Where can my demand for knowledge be best satisfied? Inside or outside the firm?
- How can increase my attractiveness as knowledge buyer so that sellers are eager to transfer their knowledge

| Framework conditions | Players and rules of game | Instruments and processes |
|---|---|---|
| 1.1 Incorporate values and importance of knowledge in company's mission statement | 2.1 Develop knowledge market: set goals that are challenging and encourage cooperation and measure their achievement | 3.1 Integrate knowledge management in workflows (project or process perspective) |
| 1.2 Describe and develop desired behaviour of employees and management, measure actual behaviour accordingly | 2.2 Establish actors (players) of knowledge markets | 3.2 Implement media and organisation structures |
| 1.3  Describe roles and competences of employees | 2.2 Define market equilibrium mechanisms (rules of game) and let them be effective<br>• Interest cluster principle<br>• Lighthouse principle<br>• Push and pull principle | 3.3 Information and Communication |
| 1.4 Reward the cooperation and overall success of entire company in the appraisal and incentive system | | |

**Fig. 5.10**  The knowledge market concept

We shall now describe these elements with the help of corporate examples. The knowledge market concept is also a reference model using which companies can measure the development stage of its knowledge management. We will start with the question how corporations can create a demand for interaction.

## Creating a Knowledge Market: Setting Demanding Goals

Apart from organising the behaviour-oriented and motivational framework conditions, it is necessary to organise contextual framework conditions, i.e. formulate goals, which create a demand for knowledge flows. For example, demanding environmental standards formulated by public administration trigger innovations in this area. Alternatively, new solutions are developed because of ambitious corporate objectives ("we want to be the leaders in a new technological field"). For example, 3 M's business objective is to achieve 25 % of turnover from the products that have been around for less than 5 years. Another firm has started a company-wide increase in productivity and quality with its Six-Sigma program. The objectives of Six-Sigma are applicable to the entire company but they are formulated in such a way that every business unit can use them as per their

| Company insensitive to knowledge | 1 | 2 | 3 | 4 | 5 | Knowledge-oriented company |
|---|---|---|---|---|---|---|
| **Rules of game in a knowledge market** | | | | | | |
| Knowledge exchange is governed by administration | | | | | | Knowledge exchange is encouraged in company by knowledge market |
| There is no transparency in knowledge | | | | | | There is no transparency on who knows what within and outside the company |
| There are no clear criteria for creation and transfer of knowledge | | | | | | Creation and transfer of knowledge is based on common interests |
| People are shy of emphasising best practices | | | | | | Best practices are emphasised |
| Knowledge/ information is "forced" on employees based on its supply | | | | | | Knowledge buyers can retrieve selective knowledge/ information |

**Fig. 5.11** Extract from the short analysis of knowledge-oriented company

requirement. This encourages exchange of knowledge, a common improvement culture and transfer of best practices. The resulting behaviour was called as *boundary-less behaviour* by General Electric. How demanding can the goals be? General Electric formulated *"stretched goals"* that were impossible to achieve. They could be achieved only by the utmost effort, mobilising all resources, avoiding double work, cooperation and by learning quickly from others.

Thompson et al. (1997) emphasise that setting ambitious goals makes sense only when supported by a corresponding organisation culture, as we have seen before. Setting ambitious goal does not make sense if management and organisational structure deter employees from fulfilling them. Figure 5.11 invites you assess the rules.

## Establishing Actors in Knowledge Markets

A knowledge market is formed by the interplay of knowledge buyers and knowledge sellers that should be brought in contact with each other. For this purpose, there are knowledge brokers that act as internal service providers. They create contacts systematically or randomly, transfer best practices, provide information, etc. (see Fig. 5.12).

In knowledge management, successful companies have shown that structuring the processes of creating and transferring knowledge alone does not help accomplish goals. Knowledge sellers and knowledge buyers should be motivated to work together. They should live and observe the rules of knowledge market.

Knowledge markets function well in an *"Entrepreneurial Corporation"*[6] (see Sect. 3.4).

---

[6] See also v. Krogh et al. (1997).

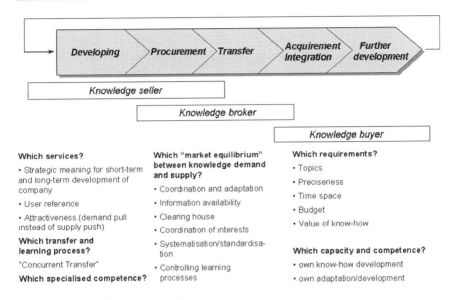

**Fig. 5.12** Actors of knowledge market

*Upper level management* formulate and control goals and provide enabling contexts for knowledge markets conditions.

*The front line entrepreneurs* are responsible for operative business. They motivate coaches for cooperation, harmonise interests, identify best practices and support future competence development of the company.

*Coaches* play a central role in the concept of knowledge market. They promote relationships that keep the knowledge spiral going. Coaching functions are not restricted to one person. They can be observed by organisational entities such as competence networks, lead factories or lead functions as well as by training and development.

## Knowledge Managers and Coaches

A range of leading companies have entrusted top-ranking management with the task of leaders and coaches of knowledge markets. The more diverse the titles, the more diverse are the functions and settlement of this management. A part of the company sets up motivation for knowledge management in the personnel department. Knowledge management and organisational learning are widely considered as synonymous. Dow Chemical has appointed a Global Director to look after Intellectual Asset and Capital Management especially for better use and marketing of patents. At ABB, knowledge management is strongly linked with the "*Customer Focus*". At General Electric, the vice-president of Leadership and Development is responsible for tapping new best practices and for promoting them (Fig. 5.13).

Special training units, strategic participation in projects as well as networking in a community of practice equips the designated knowledge brokers with

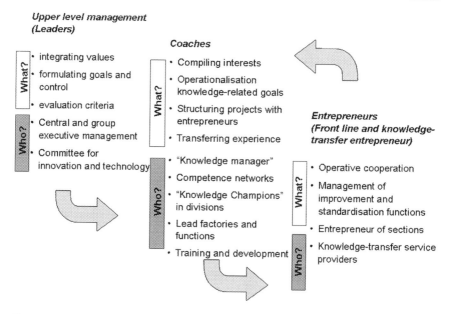

**Fig. 5.13** Coaches = catalysts of knowledge management

competencies required to fulfil their functions. According to Earl and Scott (Earl and Scott 1999), the Chief Knowledge Officers (CKOs) should fulfil the following four roles: Start new and even venturous initiatives *as an entrepreneur*, harmonise new ideas with necessities of business *as a consultant*, be familiar with the latest facilities in information and communication technology *as an IT technologist* and establish knowledge-promoting framework conditions and processes *as an "environmentalist."*

**Case Study: Job description of a Knowledge Manager**

The main function of a knowledge manager would be to help champion organisation-wide knowledge sharing, so that the organisation's know-how, information and experience is shared inside and (as appropriate) outside the organisation with clients, partners and stakeholders. Key responsibilities include:

– **Promote knowledge sharing** through the organisation's operational business processes and systems by, among others, strengthening links between knowledge sharing and the information systems, and improving integration among information systems in the organisation, to facilitate seamless exchange of information across systems;

– **Promote collaborative tools** such as activity rooms to facilitate sharing of ideas and work among internal teams and external partners;

– **Provide support** for the establishment and nurturing of communities of practice, including workshops, one-on-one guidance and troubleshooting;

- **Share experiences across communities** of practice, business units, and networks on innovative approaches in knowledge sharing, including preparation of case studies;
- **Help monitor and evaluate** the knowledge sharing program, including external benchmarking and evaluation programs/opportunities;
- **Help disseminate information** about the organisation's knowledge sharing program to internal and external audiences, including organising knowledge sharing events (such as knowledge fairs, site visits, interviews), maintaining communications on knowledge sharing across the organisation, participation in orientation and training sessions, and preparation of brochures/presentations.

**Skills of a knowledge manager:**

**Communications:** Ability to get consensus and collaboration across many business units; ability to explain complex concepts in layman's language; ability to generate enthusiasm; ability to communicate with all levels of management and staff. Establishing straightforward, productive relationships; treating all individuals with fairness and respect, demonstrating sensitivity for cultural and gender differences; showing great drive and commitment to the organisation's mission; inspires others: Maintaining high standards of personal integrity; coaching experience would be helpful.

**Client Orientation:** Understands clients' needs and concerns; responds promptly and effectively to client needs; Customises services and products as appropriate

**Drive for Results:** Makes things happen; Is proactive; balances "analysis" with "doing"; sets high standards for self; Commits to organisational goals

**Teamwork:** Collaborates with others in own unit and across boundaries; acknowledges others' contributions; works effectively with individuals of different culture and gender; willing to seek help as needed. Influencing and resolving differences across organisational boundaries: Gaining support and commitment from others even without formal authority; resolving differences by determining needs and forging solutions that benefit all parties; promoting collaboration and facilitating teamwork across organisational boundaries.

**Learning and knowledge sharing:** open to new ideas; shares own knowledge; applies knowledge in daily work; builds partnerships for learning and knowledge sharing

**Analytical Thinking and Decisive Judgment** – analysing issues and problems systematically, gathering broad and balanced input, drawing sound conclusions and translating conclusions into timely decisions and actions.

Source: adapted from: http://www.stevedenning.com/Knowledge-Management/KM-job-description.aspx.

Companies that practise knowledge management, however, often lack structured information about the effectiveness of such coaches. As mentioned earlier, coaches can be successful only if they operate under knowledge-promoting conditions. They do not have a fig-leaf function. They are not the only ones responsible for knowledge management. They are most successful when they become redundant.

We will come back to the role of knowledge mangers as coaches and brokers in Chap. 9, when we discuss the implementation of knowledge management initiatives.

## Defining the Rules of the Knowledge Market

With the rules of knowledge market we define how the actors, knowledge seller, knowledge buyers and knowledge brokers cooperate under the given conditions.

Our knowledge game has four rules that have been formulated as principles:

- The common *interest principle* helps us find common interests.
- The *lighthouse principle* supports in achieving knowledge transparency and highlighting best practices and leading competence.
- The *push and pull principle* makes knowledge available according to use.
- The *give and take principle* ensures reciprocity of knowledge exchange.

Let us have a look at the three principles one by one.

### The Common Interest Principle

This principle states that collective creation and transfer of knowledge will be successful only if the participants have common interests. If the benefit is one-sided, the displayed cooperation will function as coming together of employees who have just a few common interests. Often employees, who do not have common interests otherwise, are brought together according to technological criteria. They meet for the sake of meeting without achieving anything concrete. However, if one uses the common interest principle, one succeeds in bringing together persons, units, and business areas etc. that have similar development or improvement interests. Target groups of similar characteristics can be grouped under multiple criteria. The common interest principle is used while structuring networks, introducing discussion forums on intranet of the company or conceptualising training and development courses. We suggest configuring "clusters" of common interest. The word cluster is taken from statistical analysis wherein objects are grouped as per multiple criteria. Clusters are groups of persons or objects that feature similar characteristics considering various criteria.

For instance, in order to encourage exchange of best practices in manufacturing, the experience exchange should not be selected simply from technological perspective. By grouping for example electronics manufacturing plants as per criteria of production volumes, complexity of integrated circuit, lifecycle of product, range of services and development of components, it was possible to bring together plants and production lines that have common interests pertaining to business divisions.

The interest-cluster principle helps to answer the main question "do the people working there together have common interests?"

## The Lighthouse Principle

Lighthouses stand high and emit light far and wide. They clearly indicate the source of knowledge and highlight leading competence or best practices of individual experts, units, competence centres, practice groups, lead factories or networks. They lead in specific processes or have role model or forerunner functions. For instance, we can identify lighthouses by benchmarking inside or outside the company. We can locate lighthouses in a sales organisation by measuring customer satisfaction. In short, lighthouses are competent and contribute to business success. Emphasising leading competence through friendly competition, letting factories compete against each other, assigning challenge cup to the best process, highest quality or best expertise in a field has become quite common. However, in companies, there is a frequent argument that the emphasis on competence and excellence devaluates the other business units. Then, very soon, a defensive position is created which tries to explain benchmarking criteria as irrelevant or argues that, *"everything is entirely different in our unit"*.

In contrast to this, a knowledge firm creates a culture of exchange. Lighthouses are tapped as knowledge sources. On behalf of the emphasised units, in the traditional companies it is argued that answering all the questions is an additional load. The mindset *'we are paid to do our work and not to help others.'* has to be overcome. Even here, there are many options to encourage this readiness to a certain extent in knowledge firms. Hence, teamwork and sharing knowledge is rewarded in appraisal and incentive system. Furthermore, the lighthouse function, for example of a plant, can be accompanied with employees being financed as *"knowledge brokers"* who then undertake the function of transferring knowledge.

A lighthouse function can also be converted into cash in the market as shown by many consulting units created out of internal department offering their Know-How to external clients. Leading competence can be emphasised, e.g. in company's yellow pages which lists information on *"who knows what"*. Employees can present themselves in the Intranet of the company and offer their competence, showcase their knowledge maps that state which knowledge is available at which position.

> **Case: Transferring knowledge through a "Listeners Program" at TCL, India**
>
> Established in 1939, Tata Chemicals Limited (TCL) is the world's second largest producer of soda ash, with manufacturing facilities in India, the UK, Kenya and the US – but the company's products cover a huge range of chemicals, from fertilisers to branded, iodised salt.
>
> At TCL, it was recognised that every employee has much more to contribute than simply their specialised knowledge in a particular domain. For example: An experienced soda ash kiln operator will notice the colour of the kiln stack when he enters the plant, and based on his observations, he's able to make predictions about the success of a particular job and the general health of the kiln. This shows that there are useful "knowledge nuggets" across the workforce,

regardless of hierarchy. Such important observations, heuristics and learning must be captured and refined, systematically and continuously – but in addition, they should also be shared and disseminated across the organisation.

In order to do that, a KM initiative called "TITLI" was launched at TCL in 2005. The project name TITLI (the Hindi word for butterfly) was chosen because the diversity of colours of the butterfly and its role in cross-pollination was seen to embody TCL's KM ambitions. The TITLI program is intended to facilitate the cross-pollination of ideas, experiences and learning and to embrace the varied hues of each individual's perceptions in the form of "anubhav", or stories, as its core inputs. TCL's KM team launched a "Listeners Program" as part of TITLI.

The aim of the listeners program is to create involvement, engagement and participation throughout TCL and make all aspects of capturing, sharing and seeking knowledge effective. As employees have come to realise that the tacit knowledge captured really makes a difference in terms of solving day-to-day problems and enhancing productivity, their engagement and participation has increased. Likewise, both contributors and listeners are recognised by TCL for their insights and inputs (Kruthiventi et al. 2009).

Source: *Knowledge Management Review, June Edition, 2009.* http://www. melcrum.com/kmreview/kmreview_0609.shtml.

## The Push and Pull Principle

Traditionally, following the push principle, information and knowledge was often circulated in the company in form of reports. However, knowledge firms are increasingly switching over to the pull principle by letting users retrieve information or knowledge required by them.

Push principle is supply-oriented. The know-how provider is dominant with his knowledge, often causes high transaction costs, has low accuracy (if feedback loops are not incorporated) and often encounters implementation resistances from users. The push principle was typically used by central departments that designed production processes and transferred them in standardised manner to the plants for implementation. This often resulted in resistance because the centrally designed production processes did not meet different requirements of the plants. The result was poor performance against very high expenditure.

According to the pull principle, units decide on their own with whom they develop new production processes/products/services and from where they pull relevant knowledge. The central control should maintain itself as a service provider and prove its competence. This process brings about an increase in accuracy. Generally, better performance can be achieved with lesser expenditure if the right information is given to the right users at the right time. However, this requires the knowledge user to have special competence to select suitable collaborators and pull the right actionable information.

In its benchmarking survey on knowledge management, the American Productivity and Quality Center discovered that it is necessary to combine the pull and push principle:

> Push approaches are characterized by a desire to capture knowledge in central repositories than "push" it out onto the organisation. "Pull" approaches, in contrast, expect people to seek the knowledge they need. Neither seems to work well by itself. (APQC 1996, p. 8)

An information push by management creates a pressure of change by publishing best practices and benchmarking results. The same applies to information on market tendencies, losing market shares, winning huge projects through competition and also positive news about market development of one's own company. This information should motivate the employees to think about changes and improvements. This "*information push*" is supplemented by "*knowledge pull*", i.e. the users decide themselves which knowledge is transferred and who they want to work with etc.

## The Give and Take Principle

Knowledge will only flow in an organisation if people adopt a give and take philosophy. Davenport and Prusak (1998) call this reciprocity: "A knowledge seller will stand the time and effort needed to share knowledge effectively if he/she expects the buyers to be willing sellers when he/she is in the market for their knowledge." Reciprocity may be achieved less directly than by getting knowledge back from others as payment for providing it to them. Knowledge sharing that improves profitability will return a benefit to the sharer now and in the future. Whether or not a knowledge seller expects to be paid with equally valuable knowledge from the buyer, he/she may believe that being known for sharing knowledge will make others in the company more willing to share with him/her. To promote the give and take principle, a number of companies have established "miles for knowledge" programs. In such programs professionals get a number of credit points which they can distribute to those colleagues which have helped them particularly in the solution of problems, have provided valuable knowledge for a project and so on. (see case "Sharing knowledge earns you miles on p. 140)

The four principles of interest-cluster, lighthouse, pull and push and give and take are reflected in the processes and structures of knowledge management. Monitoring the adherence to these rules, implementation of these rules, and supporting employees and business units in implementing them are tasks of the knowledge managers.

## Enabling Framework Conditions

Corporate mission statements, management principles and incentive systems should reflect company's values. They must ensure that success of a segment (business unit) and contribution to the development of the entire company gets enough attention. Incentive systems should not just reward creation and transfer of

| Company insensitive to knowledge | 1 | 2 | 3 | 4 | 5 | Knowledge-intensive company |
|---|---|---|---|---|---|---|
| **Organisational framework conditions** | | | | | | |
| The lived values of our organisation encourage mistrust, scepticism against innovations, conformity and formalism | | | | | | The lived values of our organisation encourage trust, openness to innovations, authenticity and informal contacts |
| Company objectives are not connected to knowledge objectives | | | | | | KM strategy is embedded in business strategy |
| Management principles and incentive systems are directed towards performance of an individual or individual units. ☞ *Description of jobs and roles is not associated with competence development and knowledge transfer* ☞ *Knowledge transfer and competence development are not mentioned explicitly in employee appraisals* | | | | | | Management principles and incentive systems connect individual performance and contribution to overall success of the company ☞ *Description of jobs and roles is associated with competence development and knowledge transfer* ☞ *Knowledge transfer and competence development are mentioned explicitly in employee appraisals* |
| There are no key figures for creation and transfer of knowledge | | | | | | Key figures are used to measure creation and transfer of knowledge with reference to business objectives |
| Reporting contains only financial indicators | | | | | | Financial indicators (employees, processes etc.) have no importance in reports. |
| Management positions are enjoy higher status than expert positions | | | | | | Management positions have the same status as expert positions |

**Fig. 5.14** Extract from the short analysis of knowledge-oriented company

knowledge but also conversion of this knowledge into success of the business (see Fig. 5.14).

This would help in evaluating the framework conditions in the company. Later on, using a range of examples, we shall show how the described criteria of a knowledge company can be put to practice. We shall describe the formulation and control of the framework conditions with a universal example of the company General Electric[7] and add further selective examples.

As we have already seen in the earlier chapters, the main feature of a knowledge firm is that it creates strong shared values. Values are more important than structures. Structures can be defined but values enable teamwork of employees in different projects, represent tacit knowledge and ease the association with each other. From the knowledge perspectives, we had mentioned trust, openness to

---

[7] General Electric, Annual Reports 1994, 1995, 1996.

innovations and authenticity as particularly important. Take for example Koziol, a gift article manufacturer with 180 employees, the most innovative company in its industry. At Koziol, the corporate mission statement incorporates teamwork and autonomy according to the motto "*instruct yourself, organise yourself, motivate yourself and control yourself*". One also experiences a regular exchange in product development teams across departments. For the management it is important that all the employees participate actively in the "*company project*".

However, having these values somewhere on the paper is not important. They should be lived. They should be lived at all the levels – including management. Formulating such values is less problematic than living them in day-to-day life.

In order to implement the values of a company in daily life, it is advisable to describe explicitly the behaviour expected from employees and management and compare their present behaviour with expected behaviour in e.g. periodic employee appraisals.

---

**Case: Restructuring General Electric towards a boundary-less organisation[8]**

During restructuring, General Electric experienced how difficult it was to change behaviour of management and employees. "*During the workout sessions, it was clear that creating presentation techniques at management level including employees, enthusiasm and free space did not match with the reality of business units. The problem was that some of our members of management were unwilling or incapable of leaving the "autocracy of large-scale enterprise" and take in values that we wished to build. Therefore, we defined our management style or types and how they either blocked or encouraged our values. We then acted accordingly.*"

General Electric defines four types of management behaviour:

- *Type 1* not only guarantees its performance but also believes and develops the enterprise values of General Electric. The way to this group is "*onward and upward*". Men and women who embody these values will take our company to the next millennium.
- *Type 2* neither guarantees its performance nor does it share our values and will not stay very long in General Electric.
- *Type 3* believes in values of the company but is not capable of fulfilling the received commitments. They are encouraged to change, resulting in type 3 typically getting an additional chance.
- *Type 4* is the most difficult. One is always tempted not to take action because the fourth management type has short-term success. This group takes actions without considering the values. Some of them learnt to change themselves while most of them did not. The decision of removing the fourth management type from the company was a "*turning point*" and proved that the company was serious about its values.

---

[8] General Electric, Annual Reports 1994, 1995, 1996.

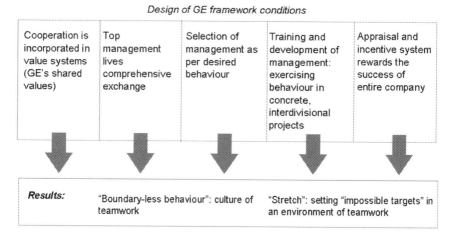

*Design of GE framework conditions*

| Cooperation is incorporated in value systems (GE's shared values) | Top management lives comprehensive exchange | Selection of management as per desired behaviour | Training and development of management: exercising behaviour in concrete, interdivisional projects | Appraisal and incentive system rewards the success of entire company |

| **Results:** | "Boundary-less behaviour": culture of teamwork | | "Stretch": setting "impossible targets" in an environment of teamwork | |

**Fig. 5.15** The framework conditions at General Electric encourage creation and transfer of knowledge

At General Electric, employees and management are constantly evaluated to find out whether they uphold the values of the company. Evaluation takes place as per the expected behaviour.

Values are reinforced or destructed by incentive systems.

The incentive systems directed towards the performance of an individual or individual units are considered as significant barriers to the creation and transfer of knowledge. However, as we have seen in Chap. 4, there are a number of options for encouraging teamwork oriented towards overall interest of a company. However, incentive systems cannot be ignored as they play an important role in getting started.

All the described framework conditions should together form an optimal *"organisational mix"* that encourages creation and transfer of knowledge. Individual elements of these conditions alone cannot guarantee success. Interaction of all these conditions is yet again clear from the example of General Electric. The value system, behaviour of the top level management, promotion and selection of managers according to their behaviour, practising teamwork by training and development and evaluating in the incentive system that rewards the overall success of the company lead to a culture of openness (boundary-less behaviour) which allows setting of *"stretched goals"* in an environment of trust (see Fig. 5.15).

## 5.5     Spaces for Interaction: The Physical Layout

With virtual interaction one might think that office architecture and design of social zones is of less importance. Employees increasingly use the option of working from home or work at the customers' premises and rarely meet their colleagues. On the other hand, researches show[9] that innovative thoughts arise through personal communication and often through unplanned meetings in the case of informal information exchange.

If you view the You Tube video about Google's office in Zurich[10] you will be puzzled about such an innovative office design to foster innovation. The Swiss hearing aid manufacturer, Phonak, allows for this fact by turning the staff canteen into a common meeting place. In many huge Japanese enterprises, the management board does not have independent offices. Instead, they have a vast open board room which facilitates inevitable interaction among them. Some companies go to such lengths that the members of the management board have only one working and meeting room wherein they are meant to work and take decisions together. In new plants, such as those in the automobile industry, it has already become standard for operations engineers and production engineers sit close to each other, often in offices that are separated from the production division simply with a glass window. This encourages the ability to solve problems quickly and the feeling togetherness through the architecture. The same applies in designing the office premises.

Knowledge-oriented companies should therefore design offices, break rooms and circulation areas in such a way that they support function-based cooperation, employees meet each other randomly and can communicate with each other. The Munich based architecture firm, Henn, has developed a concept for the offices called as knowledge stock exchange.[11]

While the physical material flow is visible inside a building and inadequacies are noticed, the flow of intellectual material is not visible in an organisation. Incomplete thoughts and solutions are often concealed because they do not pile up in boxes. Though they also block the ways to solutions, they do not stand out directly. Based on this thought, Henn developed or adapted a process to capture the communication in the building. The result was visualised in a '*netgraph*'. Office concepts that encouraged communication were developed based on this. Figure 5.16 shows three different types of offices – traditional office cubicles, group space and combi-office with communication zone – under the criteria of concentration and communication.

A suitable interior decoration encourages teamwork and symbolises, through the type of design, trust and openness to innovation. Some companies have created employee lounges, based on the concept of airport waiting rooms, for employees who come to the office randomly. The employees can work, meet or relax in these employee lounges. One requires variable work places like a room in a hotel.

---

[9] Allen (no year).

[10] http://www.youtube.com/watch?v=TaGO7XlP2EU

[11] The text widely follows Henn (1995).

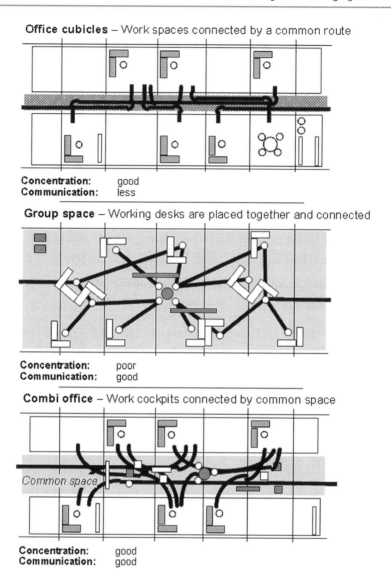

**Office cubicles** – Work spaces connected by a common route

Concentration:        good
Communication:     less

**Group space** – Working desks are placed together and connected

Concentration:        poor
Communication:     good

**Combi office** – Work cockpits connected by common space

Common space

Concentration:        good
Communication:     good

**Fig. 5.16**  Types of offices (Source: Henn Architects)

If knowledge is not visible directly, it is possible to present process intelligence and product intelligence symbolically through a suitable architectural design.

## 5.6    Key Insights of Chapter 5

- The business environment is rampant with situations that require information about products, about activities done in the past and their result, about effective ways of executing a process and interpretations of various outcomes. The question therefore is: how can organisations leverage experiences to be able to cope with today's and tomorrow's dynamic business environment?

- The approaches of company practice can be described with a basic concept of a knowledge ecology, which creates enabling conditions for creativity, innovation and knowledge flows.
- Normative, strategic and operational knowledge objectives are starting points for interventions in organisational knowledge base in order to convert knowledge into competitive advantages.
- Organisations can be regarded as knowledge markets. The following are the three elements of the knowledge market concept .
  a. Framework conditions,
  b. Players and rules of game
  c. Processes/Structures,
- According to Traecy and Wiersema, there are three higher-level strategic company objectives. The fulfilment of these objectives is supported by respective creation and transfer of knowledge. The three areas are:
  a. Product Leadership
  b. Customer Intimacy
  c. Operational Excellence
- The model defined by Bukowitz and Williams (1999) rests on the premise that KM initiatives are the result of the response to tactical and strategic changes and needs. The strength of this model is the strategic focus based on the tactical processes, which essentially puts knowledge management action into context.
- The main feature of a knowledge firm is that it creates common moral concepts of employees. Values are more important than structures. Structures can be defined but values enable teamwork of employees in different projects, represent tacit knowledge and ease the association with each other.
- The successful implementation of knowledge management often rests on two aspects: firstly, on the ability and readiness of employees to share knowledge with other employees and secondly, on the focus on technology as an enabler.

## 5.7 Questions

1. How can an organisation align its knowledge management strategy to the business strategy? How can effective knowledge management provide the competitive edge?
2. How do you identify the strategic positions of the company in terms of the knowledge assets so as to determine the areas where the knowledge management efforts need to be enhanced?
3. How can knowledge management enhance operational effectiveness?

4. How can a knowledge management strategy contribute to improved innovativeness? What would be concrete measures to be implemented?
5. In an organisation following the knowledge market metaphor, how can you create demand for knowledge (and the consequent sharing of it)?

## 5.8    Assignments

1. **Improve customer response**

    Atul Corporation is a large corporate, manufacturing and supplying engineering goods to the industry. It has four divisional offices. A customer survey showed that clients of two divisions were not happy with its ability to deliver orders on time, in proper condition and at the proper location.

    *How can a knowledge management solution help the company address this problem? Identify the knowledge assets and the implementation challenges?*

2. **Star bakery**

    You're a new manager of a chain of 10 bakeries located in a region of 50 miles. Sales performance, customer satisfaction and profitability of the bakeries vary substantially.

    *Apply the four principles of a knowledge market (common-interest, lighthouse, push-pull, give and take) to improve performance. Which concrete measures would you take?*

## 5.9    KM-Tool: Knowledge Market

### What is a knowledge market?

A knowledge market relates offer and demand of information and knowledge and enables contacts and transfer between buyers and sellers. Knowledge markets operate over the internet or an intranet or on a physical knowledge marketplace (buyers and sellers are in a room). A knowledge market can be organised within units, across units and also open up a firm to the outside (e.g. knowledge market with customers or suppliers). It provides a different way of experience exchange than the traditional slide presentation and discussions.

**Why use a knowledge market**
- The knowledge market helps resolve problems using the "wisdom of the crowd"
- Good practices are made public
- Colleagues find that they are working on similar problems and have similar interests. A knowledge market can be a start of a community, a form to organise experience exchange-group form
- Market participants learn to present their knowledge and to ask precisely.
  In the following we will present ways of organising a knowledge market:

**The prearranged market stand version**
This version is similar to an "open space" meeting.
1. In participatory process (usually some weeks or days before the market session) decide on priority topics of interest or define a problem to be solved/questions to be discussed
2. Set up a number of market stands/tables in a large foyer. Each stand presents a topic, a solution, a good practice related to the market topic. Each table/theme is "hosted" by two resource persons who moderate the discussions.
3. Participants go from stand to stand according to their interests and interact.
4. The contents of the market and discussions might be summed up by a short video, which might be made available
5. Market discussions might be continued in an intranet discussion form or in community meetings.

**The spontaneous market**
1. The "market master" (facilitator) prepares presentation two boards or wall paper on two sides of a room. Write on one the title *"I offer,"* the other *"I'm looking for."*
2. Participants write their offers and requests on paper cards or "post-it", and add their name/nickname. The number of cards may be limited, for example, three offer and three demand cards per participant.
3. Participant put their cards on demand or offer side.
4. If no categories were predetermined, the market master may arrange the cards thematically.
5. Participants have time to become familiar with supply and demand (about 15 min).
6. Market Master asks buyers to contact vendors: Those participants who have found an answer (offer) to their query take their question cards from the "search" wall and attach it to the appropriate offer (15–20 min).
7. Buyers and suppliers get into contact personally and discuss/resolve the issue. If necessary, the market master calls out the names of seller and buyer. The

issues might be deepened in small groups or appointments for follow-up can be made (20–30 min).

8. If there are still unanswered questions on the "I'm looking for" board: The market masters may read them out individually or bundled together thematically and asks who can contribute to the solution, if necessary, who could answer the question outside the present group. If the question is not answered, or it includes a more complex problem, the market master decides with the participants, whether the question is so important that it should be pursued. The market master takes the unanswered questions and contacts relevant experts to provide the answers. For example, answers to questions will be posted under the heading "knowledge market" on the intranet.

9. If there are offers which did not find a "buyer" the market-master asks briefly the "seller" provider to explain and clarify their respective offer and ask participants if they are interested in the offer.

10. The market concludes with a summary of the transactions and asks participants to evaluate the quality of the exchange.

# Context Specific Knowledge Management Strategies

6

*"Sannin yoreba monju no chie" (a gathering of three people will result in wisdom equivalent to that of Monju Bodhisattva) – Japanese Proverb* (APO 2010)

**Learning Outcomes.** After completing this chapter
- You will know the challenges of knowledge transfer across cultures,
- You will be able to develop KM activities based on the projection, orchestration and integration approaches;
- You will know how international service organisations design their KM activities;
- You will be aware of KM solutions for small businesses
- You will have an idea how to organise KM at regional and country level
- You will be able to apply storytelling in your own context.

## 6.1 Knowledge Management in International Contexts

Knowledge management in an international context poses specific challenges in addition to those mentioned until now.

*Integration of geographically scattered knowledge* that is of no value without context or that is integrated in different cultural contexts: Transferring it detached from these contexts is not possible. Cross-cultural management (cf. Hampden-Turner and Trompenaars 2000) taught us that tacit knowledge developed in long socialisation processes of countries and regions goes along with different beliefs and behaviour. This leads in particular to variations in relations between people, motivational orientation and attitudes toward time. Thus, when the American parent company Disney transferred its amusement park concept to Euro Disney close to Paris, it discovered that the concept did not match with European customs of recreational activities. Another example is the transfer of total quality management

K. North and G. Kumta, *Knowledge Management*,
Springer Texts in Business and Economics, DOI 10.1007/978-3-319-03698-4_6,
© Springer International Publishing Switzerland 2014

approaches beyond the boundaries of countries which is successful only if an equally encouraging company culture is either present in context or is established (North 1997).

*Complexity in acquiring, developing, transferring, using and safeguarding knowledge in the international context*: With their network of "international sensors", companies should manage to find out early where new knowledge is created, safeguard knowledge sources from the competitors, make knowledge within the company useable worldwide and enhance it further. In doing so, companies should combine *local differentiation* and *global standardisation*. Thus, worldwide standardised products are developed in information and communication technology, produced using local cost advantages and sold over locally differentiated distribution channels. This involves setting up the function of research and development in a place where best talent is available, undertaking production where the labour is inexpensive and qualified, transferring best practices quickly across the world and finding efficient local partner for distribution.

Products in the automobile industry are adapted to the local market requirements based on common platforms and components, thus reducing the complexity of required knowledge. Platforms and components are increasingly being developed centrally and specific market requirements are introduced locally. However, this may give rise to experiences that could be of global interests, e.g. experiences of renewable raw material in Brazil were transferred to an automobile manufacturer in South Africa.

### Minicase Study: Knowledge work across the world

An automobile manufacturer works on building up a global development network. The largest vehicle manufacturer of Europe is thinking seriously about developing parts such as transmission, engines or chassis not just predominantly in the German locations but also in other continents via computers in order to develop the entire product. Accordingly, a developer in Germany starts working on a plan for a new brake in the morning. By evening, he transfers the design for further processing to his colleague in America, where the working day has just begun. By evening, the colleague in USA sends his work, his developed plans, to the operations in Asia. From there, the design plan comes back to Germany. The design time can be reduced to its one-third if this networking idea is implemented successfully. It will then be possible to work on the plans round the clock.

How can the principle "*being local worldwide*" be implemented from a viewpoint of learning and sharing knowledge across cultures? For this purpose, Doz et al. (1997) described three approaches viz. projection, integration and orchestration.

## From Projection to Orchestration

How to exploit the benefits of home base knowledge leadership in a way that is sufficiently sensitive to the deeper differences between their home environment and the new international environments in which they are attempting to operate?

The basic question of **projection** is how knowledge advantage that is available in the home country and that is to be incorporated in products, service packages and related logistics in foreign markets, be transferred considering its characteristics. From the projection viewpoint, it is the function of management to find a balance between blind transfer of experience from the home country and over-conformity to the local conditions. This balance can rarely be determined beforehand. That's how McDonalds established its US concept worldwide in a standardised form, yet varied the local taste through specific local products. Coca Cola tastes the same throughout the world. However, the selection of distribution channels and logistics varies significantly. Product knowledge is projected internationally by the centre while local partners undertake distribution based on their market knowledge. Projection requires an efficient knowledge transfer from the centre to the branches throughout the world. It also requires an efficient feedback system so that it is possible to distribute commonly relevant local experiences through the centre. International management and identifying the distinction between the culture of local company and that of the homeland, simplifies the process of internationalisation.

The advantage of the projection approach is that knowledge and standards can be "pushed-out" quickly to subsidiaries. Disadvantages are related to a mind-set *"we are headquarters and know what needs to be done"* and consequently an inefficient learning between centre and branches (see Fig. 6.1).

**Integration** goes a step ahead of projection. It not only involves learning from one's own company worldwide but also from outside. Similar to the inverted organisation, knowledge resides in the branches across the world, centres of excellence or alliance partners. The centre integrates a part of this knowledge without representing the leading competence. Detachment of knowledge from specific contexts can be problematic in this case.

A range of worldwide operational consultancies and auditing firms work according to the principle of integration. Decentralised networks develop core services that can be implemented locally. Quality guidelines and routines for executing orders apply to all the branches overall. The centre itself has less knowledge than the external nodes in case of integration. This gives rise to the question whether partial management without the centre is possible under knowledge viewpoint. This results in orchestration. The box below shows how these different concepts are applied to organising international research and development (see Fig. 6.2).

**Orchestration** brings together and fuses multiple capabilities and insights from different environments. In an extreme case, orchestration means collaboration of units of a company, alliance partners, customers and suppliers in a global network

**Fig. 6.1** Projection: push-
out knowledge to subsidiaries

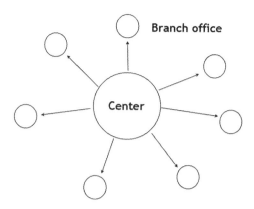

without a centre or headquarters. Units of a company work together in different
coalitions in order to convert new knowledge into market solutions (see Fig. 6.3).

Specialised units build knowledge alliances in order to offer complete solutions
to the customers. Research and development centres pursue the know-how. Intensively decentralised international companies, such as ABB, work according to this
principle. In an orchestrated company subsidiaries are empowered by taking global
responsibilities for competence areas, business units, product groups or services.

Doz et al. describe three pre-requisites for effective implementation of orchestration, which they also term a *"meta-national strategy"*[1]:

- *Effective Sensors:* Presence of effective sensors in important markets and
  regions with critical knowledge. These sensors can come into effect through
  linkages to leading research institutes that develop knowledge in new areas by
  relocating critical functions- for example research functions from homeland can
  be linked to the leading regions by establishing branch offices, development
  centres and manufacturing plants in critical locations. The entities could be
  central functions at the headquarters, customer or product management
  structures, global platforms, comprehensive projects, logistics systems and
  global centre of excellence.
- *Attractors*: Establishing attractors, i.e. leading competence that focuses, gathers
  and provides distributed market knowledge, product knowledge and technological knowledge.
- *Exchange of knowledge:* Ensuring effective and efficient knowledge transfer
  between the nodes of a network. In order to encourage common creation and
  transfer of knowledge between the nodes of the *"orchestrated network"* it is first
  necessary to control the behaviour of the employee. Common ideals, common
  interests, common language and terminology are very important for creating and
  transferring knowledge in network structures. Companies with a distinctive
  company culture, such as Hewlett Packard or Motorola, move knowledge largely

[1] See also Bartlett and Ghoshal (1989) and the concept of the Transnational Corporation developed
by them.

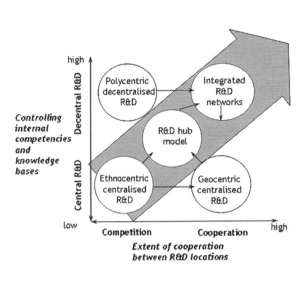

**Trends**

1. The RD& processes are strongly oriented towards international markets and technical knowledge centres, e.g. Mercedes, BMW, Volvo, Toyota, Volkswagen

2. Establishing firmly controlled and technologically sound listening posts, foremost being Japanese companies with basic research laboratories in Europe, e.g. Hitachi's research centres in Dublin (information science) and Cambridge (microelectronics)

3. Enhancing competencies and empowering the foreign R&D sites; assigning a strategically active role e.g. Sony

4. Increased integration of decentral R&D sites, e.g. Philips or General Motors (building competence centres for component groups - used in worldwide vehicle manufacturing - in Rüsselsheim)

5. Tightening the coordination and recentralising R&D activities to a few competence centres for increasing efficiency, e.g. ABB, IBM, Hoechst

**Fig. 6.2**  Different organisational models of international research and development
Research and development is increasingly internationalised and carried-out distributed over several locations worldwide. From an analysis of 25 huge companies with headquarters in Europe, Japan and US five trends can be identified:
**Trend 1**: Many companies with a centralised R&D are strongly oriented to their international surroundings.
**Trend 2**: Build technological listening posts in the technological centres of excellence of trade.
**Trend 3**: Companies with centrally regulated foreign R&D locations enhance their competency.
**Trend 4**: Companies grown through acquisitions and having widely autonomous subsidiaries recognise the integration potentials and link their R&D activities more intensively. There is a trend towards an integrated R&D network.
**Trend 5**: However, one can also notice a trend within the integrated networks. There is an increased focus on fewer centres of excellence and centralisation of decision processes in fewer competence centres.
A lot of importance is being given again to focus on cost reduction. Consolidation aims at better use of economies of scale by increasing the coordination between R&D activities worldwide and reducing double developments if there is simultaneous intensification of international transfers within the company.
Source: Based on Grassmann (1997)

independent of the country culture (North 1997). International managers, who are committed to their company, are guarantors of such worldwide company culture (Doz et al. 1997).
• *Local employees*: Thorough selection of local employees and their intensive introduction to the values and work methods of the organisation are important measures to achieve same ideals and shared tacit knowledge.

**Fig. 6.3** Orchestration fuses
multiple capabilities

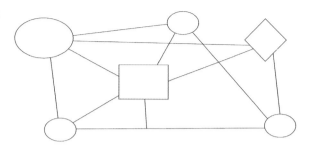

- *International incentive systems*: Yet another requirement for the orchestrated company is internationally oriented incentive systems. These could exist in shares options for the entire organisation as found in General Electric or be oriented towards the worldwide results of company units. That is how Texas Instruments promotes knowledge exchange between their factories by determining a global responsibility for wafer fabrication (APQC 1996).
- *Intensity of communication:* The orchestration is further supported by the intensity of communication, especially the scope of information. It is not enough to provide information only through Intranet. This should be supplemented by personal meetings, video conferences, emails, discussion forums, etc.

Even in the international context, it is apparent that company culture, incentive systems as well as information and communication become central components for creation and transfer of knowledge.

It becomes more and more difficult to achieve global competitive advantages by dominating one domestic market. In the knowledge competition, the competitive advantages are achieved increasingly by "*global orchestration*".

**Case: GIZ: from worldwide project experience to service products**

The services delivered by the GIZ, the German International co-operation agency, draw on a wealth of regional and technical expertise and tried and tested management know-how. As a federal enterprise, GIZ supports the German Government in achieving its objectives in the field of international cooperation for sustainable development. GIZ operates in more than 130 countries worldwide with more than 17,000 staff members across the globe – some 70 % of whom are employed locally as national personnel.

GIZ starts hundreds of projects every year throughout the world for improving the living and working conditions of people across the globe. GIZ is increasingly starting projects even for non-government entities.

How can the experiences of one project be used again for a new project? How can the organisation learn systematically from the projects?

For this purpose, GIZ introduced a "product-based knowledge management" concept. The core of the initiative is the classification of the GIZ services in about 100 product groups, such as "clean air in cities", each with a product manager who operates like a knowledge broker. This gives rise to systematisation because different repeatable service packages are available which should be adapted only in rare cases. The respective product team works worldwide and mostly meets virtually. The product knowledge that originates from such interaction is made accessible to all the GIZ employees through a product database and virtual product teams. A knowledge manager coordinates further development of the "knowledge organisation" which results in the following benefits:

- Availability of information at a faster rate
- A more efficient use of human resources
- Safeguarding of strategically important knowledge and reduced in loss of knowledge due to employee turnover.
- Better communication within the GIZ
- The objectives of development policies can be achieved more efficiently by faster access to knowledge available worldwide.

Bundling the available knowledge helps in optimum utilisation of synergies from the worldwide projects. Thus, development projects become more effectively as per the benefit of the giver and receiver. With the introduction of product-based knowledge management, GIZ has increased market and customer orientation and has thus improved its lasting competitiveness even further. For this, GIZ won the special price of public companies – "Knowledge manager of the year 2005".

Source: www.wissensmanager-des-jahres.de.

## Knowledge-Oriented Project Planning[2]

Opening new markets, developing global products, planning new factories or technical cooperation in development require knowledge-oriented project management that harmonises different ideals, experiences and interests. Traditional concepts of projection of knowledge are always less suitable for setting up operations that are efficient, fast-learning and connected worldwide.

New approaches should be found in order to consider the socio-cultural environment of a country, integrate international best practices in new manufacturing plants and transfer know-how efficiently in a network of globally operating manufacturing plants. We shall now discuss different approaches of dealing with planning of an overseas factory.

In the "state of the art" approach towards planning, the project management team undertakes a key role as a generalist with high autonomy of decision making while handling a plan. The management coordinates team specialists of different

---

[2] Description according to North and Aukamm (1996).

divisions of the company. Recruiting key personnel from other leading local companies as early as possible can be very helpful while setting up operations in a foreign country. It is equally important to review the allocation of roles while working in a team with a local partner.

"T*winning*" of management of both the partners in all the important divisions of a company as well as in planning teams helps to integrate different views. Even when it takes long at the beginning to make such double allocations or mixed teams, it accelerates the overall planning and implementation.

**Twinning and shadowing**

Experts, colleagues or managers working in different contexts, countries, subsidiaries, branches can learn from each other by carrying out work together as "twins". For example, staff of the Cairo underground worked together as twins with their Paris homologues in Paris and in Cairo. Thus common understanding (tacit knowledge) about contexts was created and advanced practices were transferred in close interaction.

In twinning the twins together take responsibility for their actions, while in "shadowing" one partner follows the other like a shadow and learns, reflects and discusses without taking responsibility.

Traditionally, while planning a factory the subsequent operator replaces the planner and finds himself in such an environment that it is either difficult or impossible for him to participate if he has not been a part of the planning process. The planners of the overseas factory should be aware of the local environment and the involvement of local operators increases motivation and ensures a plan that is feasible as the project team knows that later on it is responsible for the execution of the plan.

*Push* versus *Pull approach:* It is important to abandon the know-how provider's "push system" (normally that of the parent company) under which turn-key factories are centrally planned. Such a system does not allow a person who is ultimately responsible for the operations enough freedom in planning his work environment. On the contrary, in a pull principle, the subsequent operators are also the ones who have to decide which technology is best suitable under which circumstances. An important advantage of the pull of know-how by the on-site project team is that the transferred know-how is accepted locally and knowledge that is really necessary is requested. The use of this principle creates advantages not only while transferring knowledge to subsequent operators but also while bringing the local employees together with their management. It is necessary to structure an intensive exchange between the planning teams and competencies linked world-wide during and after the planning phase in order to transfer knowledge throughout the project.

*Selection and training of employees* is one of the most important planning functions. The employees recruited during the planning process should take up the role of pioneers who are in a position to pass on their knowledge to their colleagues after undergoing a separate training for this purpose. Therefore, it is necessary to send them to the country of the know-how provider before starting subsequent operations in order to see and understand the new company philosophy. Thus, as planners they can learn new production system and works, for example by creating documentation necessary for production in the language of their country/ company. The documents can thus be processed by those who are supposed to use their own perceptions later in the operation. It is also customary that employees in the production are able to practise a true-to-life imitation of all the production processes of a vehicle in the simulators in training centres before they start with the production. Thus, the necessary controls can be practised without any time pressure.

One can also support the production process by producing the first products in cooperation with experts of the know-how provider. This ensures establishment of the *"We" feeling* right from the beginning and those participating can identify with the product in a better way. The arrogance of the know-how providers in doing everything better than the local employees should be avoided. Perhaps it is easier to repair the defects occurring in a vehicle rather than changing an unhealthy company culture.

In a nutshell, planning a manufacturing plant should involve a process that integrates important elements of socio-cultural environment of the country where the plant is located with the company philosophy and production philosophy of the know-how provider.

## Bridging the "Know-Do" Gap in International Service Organisations: Three Cases

### Knowledge for Global Health: World Health Organisation

The increasing resources for international health aid and growing demand to improve health systems offer an opportunity to foster health equity in countries that need it the most. Many solutions are available to tackle the health problems of the poor but these are not implemented, leading to what is called the "know-do" gap: the gap between what is known and what is done in practice. The mission of World Health Organisation (WHO) Knowledge Management (KM) is to help by fostering an environment that encourages the creation, sharing, and effective application of knowledge to improve health.[3]

The KM strategy of WHO (shown in Fig. 6.4) focuses on national policymakers, WHO programmes, and health professionals. The objectives of the strategy cover three main areas:

- Strengthening health systems in different countries through better knowledge management,
- Establishing KM in public health, and

---

[3] World Health Organisation, Knowledge Management Strategy, WHO/EIP/KMS/2005.1.

## Knowledge Management Strategy at WHO

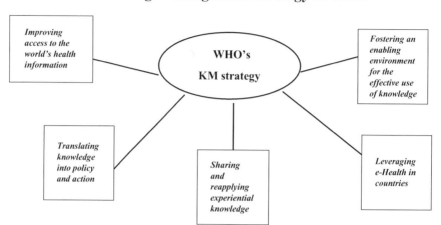

**Fig. 6.4** Knowledge management strategy at WHO

- Enabling WHO to become a better learning organisation.

   In order to achieve these objectives WHO has defined the following KM core functions:

### Improving access to the world's health information

1. Support for WHO publishing. Publish, market and disseminate in priority languages, relevant and high-quality information products reaching a widespread, targeted readership in both print and electronic formats. Establish publishing policies and guidelines to ensure efficiency and quality of WHO publications.
2. WHO flagship publications. Publish WHO global and regional flagship products to communicate key issues and effective practices in the field of public health. Major products include the World Health Report, Bulletin of the WHO, regional medical journals, and regional director reports.
3. WHO network of libraries. Provide access for key audiences to scientific and health information in print and electronic media via the WHO library and initiatives such as, such as the Global Health Library and HINARI.
4. WHO Web communications. Provide multi-lingual access for millions of users worldwide to WHO health information via WHO websites at global, regional and country level. Provide guidance to health authorities and other institutions on effective use of the internet and web technologies.

**Translating knowledge into policy and action**

5. Good practice and guidance on knowledge translation and scale-up. Following on the recommendations of the Mexico Summit for Health Research in 2004, identify and disseminate good practice in translating health knowledge into policy and action.
6. Build capability in KM methods in public health practice. Assist public health communities to develop the capacity to translate knowledge into policy and action in their local context.
7. Promote evidence for policy and decision making tailored for key audiences, through programmes such as EURO's Health Evidence Network. Sharing and applying experiential knowledge
8. Improve ability to share knowledge in public health through KM processes. Employ KM techniques, including communities of practice, to assist countries and technical programmes to manage and use knowledge.
9. WHO and Global Health Histories. Document and analyse significant public health developments, milestones, trends and perspectives. Develop expertise in extracting and applying the lessons learned in public health.
10. WHO Collaborating Centres. Improve the use of the knowledge held by WHO Collaborating Centres through peer networks.

**Leveraging e-Health in countries**

11. e-Health frameworks, guidelines and tools. Make available evidence-based e-Health frameworks, guidelines and tools to support policy and practice in health systems and technical programmes.
12. e-Health services in countries. Provide technical assistance for governance, monitoring and improvement of e-Health services in countries.
13. Country capacity building via ICT. Utilise ICT tools to build capacity in the health sector in countries.
14. Public-private partnerships in ICT. Develop and utilise public-private partnerships in ICT to address priority issues in health systems and technical programmes.

**Fostering an enabling environment**

15. Foster a knowledge management culture. Promote a culture at WHO and the public health sector that encourages the routine capturing, sharing and application of knowledge to better deliver expected results.
16. Develop and deliver KM training programmes to build WHO and country capacity with emphasis on innovation, knowledge sharing and translation, and managing the reapplication and scaling-up of successful interventions.
17. Support countries, technical programmes and partners with KM approaches. Work directly with countries, technical programmes, and partner organisations to identify knowledge needs and opportunities, to develop and implement KM plans.

## Asian Development Bank (ADB): A Pragmatic KM Approach

At the 42nd Annual Meeting of the Board of Governors, ADB President Haruhiko Kuroda stressed the importance of knowledge for an organisation: "To be fully effective, we must also consciously and actively blend knowledge with financing. We will focus on developing, capturing, and sharing knowledge in all our work, ensuring that ADB serves an intermediary role for both financing and knowledge".[4]

ADB's plan of action for knowledge management connotes a pragmatic, step-by-step approach. With the objective of enhancing Knowledge Management under Strategy 2020, in July 2009 President Kuroda approved actions/outputs to advance the knowledge management agenda for Asian Development Bank. The strategy focused on four pillars:

- Sharpening the knowledge focus in all ADB operations,
- Promoting and empowering communities of practice for knowledge generation and sharing,
- Strengthening external knowledge partnerships to develop and disseminate knowledge, and
- Enhancing staff development programs to improve technical skills and manage knowledge.

The **Knowledge Management Results Framework** is an important instrument at ADB to assess and improve performance and help identify problems and their solutions. It was prepared after extensive internal consultations and is the basis for reporting. The highlights of the framework are:

Enhanced appreciation for ADB's *flagship knowledge products*, such as the Asian Development Outlook, Key Indicators for Asia and the Pacific, and Asia Economic Monitor among many others.

Launch of *communities of practice* and the establishment of regional knowledge hubs, both adding to ADB's growing array of knowledge partnerships.

Improved coordination mechanisms that govern *cooperation between the knowledge and operations departments*, and encouraged development of approaches such as the Technical Assistance Strategic Forum.

Nomination of *focal persons for knowledge management* in the operations departments, and establishment of knowledge management units in several departments.

New *information technology solutions* for improved knowledge sharing in ADB, such as C-Cube and e-Star.

Corporate-level *recognition of knowledge management and learning* by inclusion of chapters on sector and thematic highlights, generating and sharing knowledge, and independent evaluation in ADB's annual reports.

*Transformation of the ADB library* into a knowledge hub to encourage knowledge networking.

---

[4] Enhancing Knowledge Management under Strategy 2020- Plan of Action 2009–2011 http://www.adb.org/documents/books/km-action-plan/enhancing-knowledge-management-under-strategy-2020.pdf

The framework created the following structure to ensure smooth implementation:

**Technical Assistance Strategic Forum** at the **regional level**, to coordinate the medium-term research and sector work among the knowledge and operations departments.

**Country Partnership Strategies (CPS)** will explicitly reflect knowledge management as part of CPS formulation and implementation at the **country level**.

**Teams** at project level were created to identify how the project can be designed to support rigorous impact evaluation, forge knowledge partnerships, harness sector and thematic know-how, and encourage learning and knowledge sharing.

## World Bank "Knowledge Services"[5]

In the document "State of World bank Knowledge Services" the President of the World Bank describes the rationale of the bank for engaging in KM activities *"The value the World Bank Group brings to our clients, and to the world, is grounded in developing and sharing knowledge. Our financial resources are significant—but they are finite. By contrast, knowledge is potentially unlimited: the more it is shared, the more new ideas develop, and the more improvement is possible. When strands of knowledge are connected, the possibilities for increased prosperity and improvements in human welfare multiply.*

*The more people know, the more they can expect, and the more they can do. As we consider the ways the Bank Group will support development in the 21st century, we understand that change and reform are dynamic processes involving the active participation of all segments of societies. My vision is for a World Bank Group that plays a catalytic role in linking up data, information, and ideas with those in search of development solutions—in ensuring that knowledge for development is readily available to citizens, civil society, opinion makers, researchers, and government policy makers at all levels. My aim is to sponsor a Bank Group that reaches out to better encompass the experiences of successful developing countries—not with ordered templates, blueprints, or prescriptions—but with inquiry, innovation, cooperation, and openness."*

### The Bank's Knowledge Services

As the bank adapts its knowledge services to current demands, all three of the bank's knowledge roles are changing. As a ***knowledge producer***, the bank is doing less economic and sector work and more technical assistance. Its research activities are becoming more open and collaborative, and independent researchers worldwide are being empowered by access to the bank's open data and robust tools. As a ***knowledge customiser***, the bank is fostering more collaboration between and among bank teams, government teams, civil society, and academia to apply global knowledge to pressing development challenges. As a ***knowledge connector***, the bank links practitioners and development professionals across the globe. Increasingly, the focus is on empowering non-state actors to press for greater

---

[5] The following text is based on World Bank (2011).

accountability through their engagement in public debate and policy formulation (in the past the focus was primarily on state actors). Knowledge activities exist not only as standalone services; they are also integrated with the bank's operations and underpin its lending activities.

Following the 2010 Knowledge Strategy and the bank-wide effort in preparing this first Knowledge Report, the extent of the bank's knowledge activities is becoming clearer. But the bank has only one lens through which to view its knowledge work – the management information system and the defined knowledge "products" it captures. That system has its roots in enterprise software developed to manage discrete or industrialised processes, built on the notion that individual products have defined starting and finishing points. This report deals mostly with the defined knowledge products and how they are produced. But that presents an incomplete picture of the bank's knowledge activities. And even as we speak about "knowledge products" and "product lines," it is important to situate the discussion in a broader universe of World Bank–sponsored knowledge activities. These are as follows:

**Core knowledge activities** funded by the bank's budget or by trust funds and subjected to one or another type of bank process for quality assurance;

**Noncore knowledge activities** prepared for other bank management purposes (for example, country and sector strategies);

**Noncore knowledge activities** for which the bank works within the organisational goals of a partnership, but for which the partnership itself retains responsibility for quality;

**Knowledge activities** embedded in lending operations as part of project preparation and implementation

## 6.2 Knowledge Management in SMEs

Knowledge management is often associated with firms operating in multi-locations with thousands of employees working on the same or similar projects who need to share information in order to be responsive and competitive in the market. Most of the literature also focuses on big businesses. But in fact it is the small businesses that have much more at stake because every employee has knowledge that is important to the continuity of business due to the size of the organisation. Therefore, even if one employee separates, a significant part of business expertise and experience is lost. Knowledge is the key resource – and perhaps the only resource – capable of creating sustainable competitive advantage (Teece 1998).

The small and medium enterprises (SMEs) focus on running the business on a day-to-day basis and find no time to manage knowledge. Formal 'knowledge management' is therefore not a common terminology that one hears in SMEs who perceive it as an 'overhead'. This could be due to several reasons, some of which are listed below:

• SMEs are too busy with running the business on a day-to-day basis and perhaps find little time to analyse it and retain the learning.

- SMEs already have a large enough informal network to enable people to get the job done which also makes them more flexible. It is generally felt that knowledge management is required only when there are a large number of employees.
- Risk of separation of key employees is not perceived as a big threat due to the informal network and the embedding of knowledge in the products and services (Kumta 2008).

Awazu and Desouza have identified five peculiarities of knowledge management at SMEs (Awazu et al. 2004) as:

- Dominance of socialisation in the SECI Cycle:
- Common knowledge: In SMEs, there is a prominence of common knowledge in terms of both depth and breadth.
- Knowledge loss is not a problem: Some of the mature SMEs in our sample had deliberate mechanisms in place to prevent knowledge loss from becoming a problem.
- Exploitation of external sources of knowledge: SMEs have a knack for exploiting foreign sources of knowledge.
- People centred Knowledge Management: SMEs knowingly or unknowingly, manage knowledge the right way – the humanistic way. Technology is never made part of the knowledge management equation. Knowledge is created, shared, transferred through people based mechanisms and immediately put into practice.

One of most significant research is the one undertaken by the West Midlands Knowledge Management Centre in the UK. This centre is a regional partnership between a university, local city council, and business support agencies, which identifies and addresses the business support needs for SMEs in developing their knowledge management practices. Based on analysis of patterns in more than 100 small businesses that have used the centre's business education and support services, its research director John Sparrow describes four aspects of knowledge management that feature strongly in small firm knowledge projects (Sparrow 2001):

- Appreciation of personal and shared understanding: This is reflected in management based on 'management by perception'. There is an ongoing recognition of the meaning and interpretation of events by others. There is strong evidence that businesses/owners do not act until there is compelling reason or a fear of difficulties.
- Effective knowledge bases and knowledge systems: Typically small firms are more ready to embrace technology when they have a good grasp of the importance of information management.
- Integrated and contextualised action: The knowledge approach is grounded in the way the small firm operates and is more strategic in its view of knowledge. An important element here is capturing and utilising intellectual property rights, with intellectual capital valuation being a consideration at times of succession.
- Effective learning processes: Small firms are very social organisations, yet owner managers may deliberately restrict diffusion of their core knowledge to protect their firm's competitiveness.

SME case studies from Australia (Hall 2003) suggest a relatively strong level of interest and sophistication in KM strategies and in the practices pursued by some SMEs. In general, the issues reported were no different than those encountered by

**Table 6.1**  Specific knowledge in different types of firms

| Type of firm | Most valuable form of knowledge |
|---|---|
| Accounting firm | Expertise of senior staff and partners |
| | Specialised and technical knowledge in procedures and manuals |
| | Partnership style relationships with clients |
| | Analytical knowledge, gained through experience |
| Risk management service firm | Developmental and procedural |
| | Tacit knowledge of its employees |
| | Market intelligence |
| | Customer knowledge |
| Manufacturing firm | Product knowledge, since a lot of knowledge is already a part of the product |
| | Process innovation knowledge |
| | Technology upgrade has a dynamic rather than a static conception of knowledge |

larger organisations. It was found that different SMEs found different kinds and forms of knowledge valuable as compiled in Table 6.1:

SMEs need to use knowledge at two levels: (a) in day-to-day operations and (b) at strategic level to define organisational goals.

SMEs need to broaden their customer base, add new products/services, penetrate the domestic market, and strive for overseas expansion in order to grow to the next stage of the lifecycle.

As a vibrant and increasingly competitive part of any economy, SMEs are forced to innovate to remain competitive. This means constantly searching for ways to improve products and services, develop new products and introduce improved working methods.

## Need for Harnessing Organisational Learning in SMEs

Most knowledge in a company is forgotten in relatively short time after it is invented or discovered. In an SME the core knowledge is normally with only one person who is the owner who deliberately or unconsciously retains all the knowledge with him due to lack of time or fear of 'theft' of idea. Furthermore, SMEs cannot retain talent in a highly competitive market, as they cannot match the salary 'packages' of large corporate: "*An organization's knowledge walks out of the door every night – and it might never come back*".

Organisational learning and personnel training are important activities of a modern company. In larger companies these procedures are well defined and thoroughly designed. In small and medium-sized enterprises the learning is far less supported and explored. The experience people gain during their employment is stored in their minds rather than in published documents.

*Succession planning* and preserving organisational memory in the event of attrition/death are two critical requirements for SMEs to survive in a competitive and dynamic market. SMEs that don't plan knowledge management measures to preserve organisational memory are therefore taking the risk of decline/elimination.

All is fine when the enterprise is small and an informal network provides all the knowledge required to execute tasks and evolve a business strategy. But what happens when these enterprises see a dip in their sales and yet want to move into global markets? They need to know how their products/services evolved, what was the marketing strategy that succeeded or the strategy that failed, the reasons for its failure, what are the global challenges, what are the risks involved, and so on.

With a relatively low effort in KM these enterprises will be able to manage risk and to innovate and constantly search for ways by which they can improve products and services, develop new products and improve work processes. It will be interesting to study two distinct but interconnected knowledge cycles (Skyrme 2002).

**Knowledge sharing cycle** shows the processes associated with gathering and disseminating existing knowledge, having a knowledge repository as its focal point. This forms the basis of any knowledge management strategy.

**Innovation cycle** represents a progression from idea creation, i.e. progression of unstructured knowledge into more structured and reproducible knowledge, embedded within processes, products or services. If one views knowledge management in its broader context of exploiting knowledge for the development and growth of a business, then the innovation perspective is likely to be a more fruitful one in the small business context.

**KM in the SME lifecycle:** SMEs experience a rapid rate of change as they move through their organisational lifecycles. Each stage in the lifecycle requires a different approach and emphasis on managing knowledge. These unique characteristics determine how these enterprises strategically manage knowledge. Researchers have defined a lifecycle stage as a unique configuration of variables related to organisational context and structure. A lifecycle stage can be defined as a loose set of organisational activities and structures, (Dodge et al. 1994; Hanks et al. 1993; Quinn and Cameron 1983).

SMEs are normally started through entrepreneurship which is a process of creating value by bringing together a unique combination of resources to exploit an opportunity. These organisations have a typical lifecycle starting from a start-up phase to a maturity phase. Firms, however, do not go through their lifecycle in a vacuum. Environmental context plays a large part in determining the challenges faced by growing firms (Quinn and Cameron 1983). Enterprises in various stages of organisational lifecycle need different knowledge processes. We could broadly look at three main stages initially to evolve a feasible KM strategy.

The *birth stage* marks the beginning of organisational development. The focus is on viability. Decision-making and ownership are in the hands of one, or a few who share the same vision. The organisational structure is very simple with hardly any barriers for communication and knowledge sharing.

After the initial stage the organisation sees an *explosive growth* where each person is trying to bring in more business with no formal organisational structure. It now becomes difficult to get all the employees together and share knowledge. The focus is on growth and faster decision-making. More skilled jobs are required, roles become more specialised and decision-making needs to be delegated. This is where a change starts happening in SMEs. Here, the knowledge no longer flows easily as neither the owner nor the start-up group has time to discuss and create a knowledge repository that can be used by others.

As the enterprise moves further ahead, the focus is on *effective management* and efficient delivery of products and services. Job descriptions, policies and procedures, and hierarchical reporting relationships need to be much more formal. Formal organisational structures are defined to serve wider markets. At this stage it becomes imperative to create formalised structures and exploit its organisational knowledge by converting ideas into productive services. Lack of a formal structure at this stage can trigger the 'demise' of the SME.

Diagnosis of problems facing an enterprise can be effective when the analysis is based on the stage at which the enterprise is. This helps them plan what will be required as the firm progresses from one stage to the next in the lifecycle (Kazanjian and Drazin 1990). Each stage in the firm's lifecycle requires emphasis on different knowledge managing practices. The need for a formal knowledge management programme does not come until quite late in the overall evolution

## Knowledge Management Strategies of SMEs

The success of any KM initiative is determined by its impact on the organisation's performance (Handzic and Hasan 2003). It is often said that one should not take a 'one size fits all' approach to knowledge management. A critical starting point for a successful KM initiative is a clear KM vision, which is aligned with the overall business strategy of each organisation. KM tends to be driven by business strategy – innovation and succession planning. It is built on efficient business processes and supported by people, organisational structures and information technology. A KM strategy should seamlessly intertwine people, processes and technology. Though it is difficult to evaluate the return on investments in knowledge management most organisations, including SMEs feel that there are significant payoffs associated with KM initiatives (see Fig. 6.5).

The Asian Productivity Organisation (APO, see box below) defines and provides guidance for using simple and practical means of KM to support the SMEs
...To satisfy Existing Customers and Attract More Customers
....To Improve Productivity and Quality of Products, Services, Processes
....To Develop New Products and Services (Accelerate Innovation)
....To Develop Skills/Motivation/Teamwork among Employees

**Knowledge Management Framework**

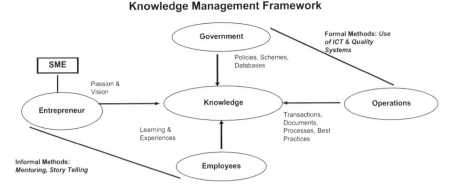

**Fig. 6.5** Knowledge management framework (Source: Kumta and Mukherjee 2010)

To support knowledge Management in SMEs the Asian Productivity Organisation (APO) has developed a series of three very useful publications:
- The Practical KM guide for SME owners and managers
- Knowledge Management Tools and Techniques Manual. This manual is also available on a website, as an example of a 'living knowledge base', in other words, as a wiki, for you to input and share your experiences, and to receive your feedback and comments at http://sites.google.com/site/apokmtools/home/.
- Knowledge Management Case studies for SMEs
    Download the manuals from: http://www.apo-tokyo.org/00e-books/IS-44_Practical-KM-Guide-for-SME-OwnerManager.htm

Regardless of sector, size, structure or maturity, organisations need to establish an appropriate management system to be successful. The Excellence Model is a practical tool to help organisations do this by measuring where they are on the path to Excellence; helping them understand the gaps and then stimulating solutions.

The Business Excellence Model originally developed by the European Foundation for Quality Management (EFQM) is a good model to map the KM initiatives. The Model is based on the premise that "Excellent results with respect to Performance, Customers, People and Society are achieved through Leadership driving Policy and Strategy, that is delivered through People, Partnerships, Resources and Processes".

The 'Knowledge Management process' therefore needs to assess three major components (Kumta 2008):
- *Business processes*– do these help or hinder knowledge management;
- *Infrastructure* – the support required putting in place the 'process' element to make knowledge management happen. This includes an organisational structure, an enabling technology and a content management strategy.

- *Environment* – A sharing culture and an environment that facilitates sharing.

In addition to the internal processes, knowledge in terms of environmental updates is required to support the development of SMEs. Being small in nature they need to know the environment in terms of government policies, standards, subsidies, development schemes, growing market space, avenues for financial help and procedures that would save time and eliminate reinventing the wheel.

KM supports and enhances the way the business operates. It does not replace one's strategy setting, but the strategy itself will be flavoured differently if one adopts a KM mindset. "KM will simply become M, a way of managing the business" (Bhatt 2000).

However, compared to large organisations, the successful SMEs were distinctive in the sense that they tended to be relatively agile, well integrated into international, national, professional and industrial associations and networks, and ready to learn from customers, clients, competitors, suppliers and providers (Handzic 2006). Knowledge was seen as information that could be used to act. It had to be in the form that is accessible, relevant and ready to use.

## Framework for Effective Implementation of KM in SMEs

Many SMEs have always regarded knowledge as the lifeblood of their organisation and have managed it effectively, often just through the usual sharing of knowledge that occurs naturally in small organisations where structures are flat and communication is part and parcel of daily operations. Empirical studies have shown that while the SMEs use a similar range of techniques and strategies for KM as those employed by larger firms (e.g. mentoring, maintaining databases for lessons learnt, standardising business processes), these are organised on a less formal basis.

Implementing a knowledge management strategy can initially appear to be a daunting and overwhelming task. The initiator often has some basic questions in his mind, more specifically in the SMEs.

- Where do I begin?
- How do I ensure the process is managed correctly?
- Should I use sophisticated technology?
- How do I measure the effectiveness of my knowledge management solution?

In recent times, there have been a number of efforts at developing KM frameworks to understand KM phenomena. In order to make sense of the variety of existing KM frameworks they have been categorised into descriptive and prescriptive frameworks. Descriptive frameworks attempt to characterise the nature of KM phenomena, while prescriptive frameworks attempt to direct methods to be followed in conducting KM (Standards Australia 2003).

David J Skyrme states, "In my own experience there are other determinants that guide when it makes sense to embark on a formal programme in an SME":

- The overall size of the business – If the personnel strength is less than 50, most staff will probably know each other fairly well; it probably therefore does not make sense to implement KM formally.
- Degree of dispersion – if the organisation is based at several locations, even when there are less than 50 employees, there are benefits achieved by putting key information into a shared repository.
- Number of distinct core documents – The repository may be able to handle only around 1,500 documents efficiently. Beyond that, the retrieval of documents becomes time-consuming and ineffective.
- Knowledge-intensity of business – In organisations like legal firms, consultancies, engineering, that blend high degree of internal expertise with outside knowledge, the benefits of knowledge management are more immediately obvious (Kogut and Zander 1992).

The following are three key phases in developing and implementing KM as suggested by Standards Australia (2003):

- Understanding the **context** (Vision, business strategy and the lifecycle stage) for knowledge management,
- Conducting a **knowledge gap** analysis with reference to the business strategy,
- Facilitating '**knowledge in action**' plan to explore and exploit knowledge to achieve the business strategy.

Most organisations develop their strategy around a well-recognised business model and it is therefore logical to map KM issues to a recognised business model. In order to be successful, organisations need to establish an appropriate management framework regardless of sector, size, structure or maturity.

The EFQM Excellence Model is a non-prescriptive framework based on nine criteria. Five of these are 'Enablers' and four are 'Results'. The 'Enabler' criteria cover what an organisation does. The 'Results' criteria cover what an organisation achieves. 'Enablers' cause 'Results' and 'Enablers' are improved using feedback from 'Results'.

Based on findings from SME case studies and related research one could conclude that knowledge management frameworks for SMEs should focus on key imperatives such as (Kumta 2008)

- Translation of individual knowledge held by key personnel into organisational knowledge through:
  - Embedding routine process and procedural knowledge into standard operating procedures,
  - Codifying implicit knowledge through "lessons-learnt" programmes,
  - Drawing on deep tacit knowledge through mentoring programmes, and
  - Using case studies as a means of knowledge transfer (Hall 2003).

- Generation of new knowledge and ideas leading to innovation which when exploited result in proposals for new products or services, new clients and improved business processes. This is a more free-flowing approach and is encouraged by the culture in the organisation.

- Creation of an eternal learning environment from concepts to practice to cope with new business processes, new products, the ever-changing business environment, and an increasingly dispersed workforce. E-learning will facilitate this process by drawing training content from frontline business applications in addition to providing modules on concepts.
- Providing access to external portals giving information about standards, regulations, statutory requirements, procedures and best practices. This will help build partnerships and networks that will support the business (Kumta 2008).

The relationships are summarized in Fig. 6.6.

A key point that results from research is that the more 'formal' knowledge management approaches of large firms should not be imposed on small businesses. Sparrow reports that in contrast to large firms, small firms benefit from the perspective of understanding their business in knowledge terms, i.e. the emphasis on the development of knowledge as a *lens* (as opposed to a knowledge management system) together with the emphasis on knowledge system *principles* (as opposed to ICT knowledge system elements). Many of the high value-added SMEs are likely to be knowledge intensive, either in the processes they deploy or the products and services they produce and sell.

Both internal and external sources of knowledge are important to entrepreneurs Internal knowledge comes from reorganising, accidents, experiments, and inventiveness. External knowledge comes from new people, acquisitions, joint ventures and social networks (Kogut and Zander 1992).

In developing the KM strategy, the focus should be on three key points to ensure its success:

- Map a knowledge management strategy to the business strategy based on a Business Excellence model.
- Similar to six-sigma concept, KM initiatives should be treated as projects and designed to help solve business issues, such as improving customer, employee, or partner relationship management, accelerating innovation, or improving a process to reduce cost and turn-around time.
- KM systems should start from people processes and use technology only to enable them.

Establishing a KM strategy can be much less daunting if one looks at KM as organising, locating and reusing actionable information. The KM initiative will depend on the lifecycle stage in which the organisation is and its future growth plans. The need for formal knowledge management comes in quite late in the overall evolution of the firm (Kumta and Mukherjee 2010).

Through the KM strategy of personalisation, SMEs will able to leverage upon its tangible and intangible assets, to learn from past experiences, whether successful or unsuccessful, and to create new knowledge (Hussain et al. 2010). The KM strategy needs to be implemented at three different levels in SMEs,

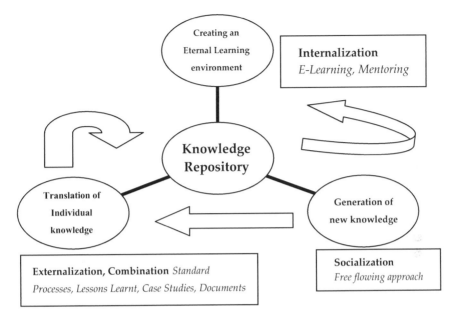

**Fig. 6.6** Knowledge repository (Source: *Knowledge Management Integrated: Concepts and Practice*, Heidelberg Press)

- People level: KM needs to emphasise on the competencies, education and learning abilities of organisational members to create KM awareness and make them more creative and innovative.
- Organisational level: KM is related to the development of a visionary leadership and a sound organisational culture to ensure maximum sharing of innovative and creative knowledge (Chan and Mauborgne 2003). Chan and Mauborgne also suggested constructive leadership behaviour and development of a healthy organisational culture as important enabler of KM.
- Technology level: Effective KM requires the efficient organisation of a suitable communication and information infrastructure based on suitable and relevant taxonomies and knowledge repositories.

Though commercialising knowledge is an important role of entrepreneurship, there are many challenges in doing it effectively (Bird et al. 1993).

## 6.3   Managing Knowledge at a Country or Regional Level

### Tangible Versus Intangible Assets

The quality of society is largely determined by its capacity to generate genuine learning and working together and to produce new visionary knowledge. This being the case, our society imposes entirely new requirements on work methods, work cultures, information validity, media literacy, etc. (Markkula 2010). Further, digitalisation and globalisation have changed business processes rapidly. Measuring this capacity is a prerequisite for having the intellectual capital high on the political agenda of the decision-making processes of nations.

The old paradigm of the Wealth of Nations which was focused on the tangible assets is now moving towards a new economic landscape based on intangibles, in terms of Knowledge. Today we see that the dimensions of what nations spend on welfare, health, education, R&D, or security at macroeconomic level are more and more intangible. Every innovation step starts with a small spending on intangibles. Sometimes this is referred to as "soft" dimension such us culture and values. In Japan they had coined this in Soft Economics way back in the 1980s. Today METI in Japan is calling this Intellectual Asset-based Management (Lin and Edvinsson 2011). But to a large extent the mapping is still done based on the tangibles. The knowledge gap or ignorance on the value of intangibles is still huge. So we need both a new perspective and new metrics for the mapping.

Today we have a lot of data as well as contextual reports for a deeper understanding of the role of Intellectual Capital of nations for future wealth creation. It is starting to reveal an ecosystem of both, drivers for the Social Capital as the larger holistic perspective, as well as new softer dimensions of Mind set, Culture and Values of Nations. The ability of a nation to use and create knowledge capital determines its capacity to empower and enable its citizens by increasing human capabilities.

Investments in information technologies may not necessarily correlate with increases in performance, (Strassmann 1997). Hence, in all such contexts, the emphasis should not only be on investments in relevant technologies, but effective utilisation of such technologies, keeping in perspective the outcomes driven focus of intellectual capital. This shift in perspective would certainly bring the focus closer to *performance*.

A study of the Skandia model for measuring Intellectual capital would help in evolving a strategic KM framework for a country. The model attempts to provide an integrated and comprehensive picture of both, financial capital and intellectual capital. Generally, national economic indicators supported by hard quantitative data are used for examining the internal and external processes occurring in a country. In this model, there are four components of intellectual capital: market capital (also denoted as customer capital), process capital, human capital, and renewal and development capital. In the context of the national intellectual capital assessment:

- Financial capital reflects the nation's history and achievements of the *past*,
- Process capital and market capital are components upon which the nation's *present* operations are based,
- Process renewal and development capital determines how the nation prepares for the *future*, and
- Human capital lies at the crux of intellectual capital. It is embedded in capabilities, expertise and wisdom of the people and represents the necessary lever that enables value creation from all other components.

# Skandia Framework for National Intellectual Capital

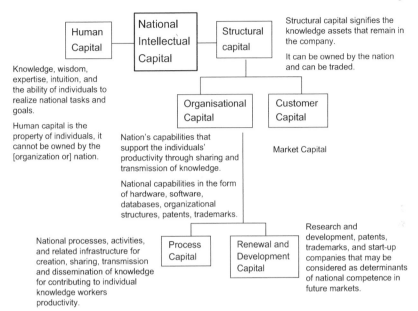

**Fig. 6.7** Skandia framework for National Intellectual Capital (*Adapted from the Skandia model for measuring intellectual capital* (Hess 2006))

The key determinants of hidden national value, or national intellectual capital, are human and structural capital. The framework is depicted in the following Fig. 6.7.

It is therefore necessary for a nation to build its human and structural capital to enhance its capacity and empower and enable its citizens. Governments should begin to undertake information and knowledge audits of the resources available and the ways in which they can be deployed to achieve competitive advantage (Durrant 2001).

**The manifesto of "The New Club of Paris" on the knowledge society and its economic foundations Extract**

Our society is undergoing a dramatic transition from the industrial & amp; information age towards a new era of brainpower industries, associated with upheavals in the global structure of the economy and accompanied by far-reaching demographic shifts and a transformation of social systems.

- A major challenge of such changes is that our economy is increasingly transforming into an "intangible" economy which is described as a "knowledge based economy".
- Indicators of this development at the time when this manifesto is issued initially are:
  1. The new relation between material (e.g. manufacturing) and nonmaterial (e.g. services) resources;

2. The sharing of commonly available knowledge such as open source information;

3. The insight that global competition can lead to rapid relocation of economic activities such as software, media creativity, healthcare and "mind-intensive" industries;

4. The radical change in work structure causing everyone to continuously change profession and type of employment throughout their working life, inducing lifelong learning and flexibility;

5. The increasing "knowledge divide", within societies, as well as among nations on a more global scale.

- Intellectual capital (comprising assets such as human abilities, structural, relational and innovation capital, as well as social capital) founded on clear, practiced values such as integrity, transparency, cooperation ability and social responsibility, constitute the basic substance from which our future society will nurture itself.

http://new-club-of-paris.org/mission/

## Attracting Talents to Regions

Regions with a high percentage of people employed in knowledge-intensive occupations have a higher per capita Gross National Product (GNP) than comparable regions (Lisbon Council policy brief: Ederer/Schuller/Wilms 2011). Knowledge work is becoming the growth engine of the region. The "Creative Class" (Florida 2002) has high purchasing power, is mobile and is well-informed. Regions worldwide have recognised this and are courting the best talents. The lack of qualified personnel, predicted with the demographic development, can be reduced in regions which manage to attract knowledge workers. The motto is "Brain gain" instead of "Brain drain". Figure 6.8 shows the factors which make a region attractive for knowledge workers. The availability of well-educated qualified personnel encourages the establishment of knowledge-based companies which in turn adds value to the region thus leading to a virtuous circle. In order to use this potential in a planned manner, metropolitan regions across the world have started adopting strategies for developing into a knowledge region by promoting research and development and training of skilled personnel, and linking companies, research and educational institutions. Florida's three T's: "Technology, Talent, Tolerance" form the characteristics of a creative region.

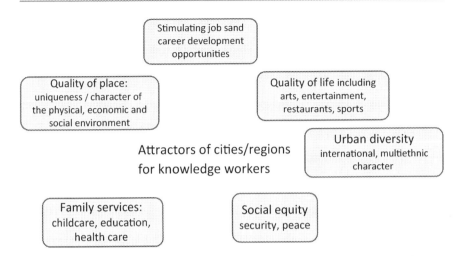

**Fig. 6.8** What makes a region attractive for knowledge workers (Source: Based on Florida (2002), Montreal Knowledge City Advisory Committee (2003), Yigitcanlar et al. (2007))

**Case: Indias National Knowledge Commission**

*For India to be globally competitive in the twenty-first century, a critical factor would be the ability to harness the knowledge potential. To make the best of the opportunities and respond to global challenges more strongly than ever before, the National Knowledge Commission (NKC) was constituted on 13th June 2005 as a high-level advisory body to the Prime Minister of India, with a mandate to guide policy and direct reforms.*

*NKC's overarching aim is to transform India into a vibrant knowledge-based society. This entails a radical improvement in existing systems of knowledge as well as the creation of avenues for generating new forms of knowledge In view of this, NKC developed appropriate institutional frameworks to strengthen the education system, promote domestic research and innovation and facilitate knowledge application in sectors like health, agriculture, and industry. It also highlighted the need to leverage information and communication technologies to enhance governance and connectivity. Its prime focus was on the on five key areas of the knowledge paradigm:*

- ***Access to knowledge**: Enhancing access to knowledge*
- ***Knowledge-concepts:** Reinvigorating institutions where knowledge concepts are imparted*
- ***Knowledge-creation**: Creating a world class environment for creation of knowledge*
- ***Knowledge application** :Promoting applications of knowledge for sustained and inclusive growth*
- ***Development of better knowledge services**: Using knowledge applications in efficient delivery of public services*
  *The methodology followed by the National Knowledge Commission involved*

- *Identification of focus areas through wide consultation, within and outside the government*
- *Identification of diverse stakeholders in these focus areas*
- *Constitution of Working Groups of specialists and practitioners to deliberate and prepare a report.*
- *Organising workshops and seminars periodically along with informal consultations with concerned entities and stakeholders to get as broad-based a point of view as possible.*
- *Communication of key recommendations to the Prime Minister*
- *Widespread dissemination of NKC recommendations to state governments, civil society and other stakeholders*
- *Implementation of the recommendations under the aegis of the Prime Minister's office along with coordination and follow up with various implementing agencies.*

## Knowledge Management for Rural Development

C. G. Hess in his paper *Knowledge Management and Knowledge systems for Rural Development* (2006) has brought out different perspectives for the rural segment. This segment requires knowledge networks, forums that facilitate exchange of learning, network of development agencies that can provide advisory services and technical co-operation which facilitates exchange of knowledge among various stakeholders in the value chain. Here Hess identifies that social, linguistic and cultural barriers impede effective communication between rural producers and outsiders which results in the clash of knowledge systems in many rural technology co-operation projects (Hess 2006). Agricultural experts acquire knowledge which is generated in formal educational settings (schools, universities, research institutes) and circulated through the global network of professionals, institutions and publications (Warren and McKiernan 1995) while farmers acquire knowledge by practice, trial-and-error and experience and usually receive little formal education.

An analysis of the maladies afflicting rural areas has brought out the need to develop an information and knowledge-led rural economy in order to promote rural prosperity. It has been found that knowledge transfers between and across rural communities, scientists, educators, administrators, health care providers and access to information on matters such as farming methods, health issues, rural credit and entrepreneurship opportunities could play a crucial role in such a process. The ancestral knowledge embedded in traditional crafts and agricultural methods needs to be captured and shared as some of these cannot be replaced by technology.

**KM Toolkit for local government organisations**

The Knowledge Management Toolkit has been developed to help local government organisations generate value from their intellectual and knowledge based assets. This value is unlocked when knowledge is shared across an organisation, among employees and departments and even with other organisations. In most organisations there are two types of knowledge assets:

- Information that the organisations hold and this can include business plans, client lists and databases. As a good rule of thumb this information can be stored either electronically or on paper.
- The more elusive asset is the knowledge, skills and experience that is in the heads of employees, which is often the most valuable asset that an organisation holds.

The major difficulty with unlocking this value is to work out an effective methodology to recognise, generate, share and manage that knowledge. This toolkit has been developed to assist organisations to identify their knowledge based assets and suggests strategies for sharing that knowledge across the organisation. This toolkit has been designed in two parts.

- Part One offers key definitions and knowledge statements that will help you to develop the skills necessary to undertake a knowledge management project and to determine how well your organisation manages its knowledge.
- Part Two contains six modules. By working through these you will help your organisation to move from being knowledge blocked to knowledge centred.

The how-to-guide comprises six modules and a number of checklists. Each of these modules will help local organisations to increase their capacity and success at harvesting the knowledge within, and potentially available to, their organisation.

Source: Australian Local Government Association  ALGA 2004. http://www.alga.asn.au/?ID=138

## 6.4    Key Insights of Chapter 6

- Knowledge-based management of a company in the international contexts poses two major challenges-integration of geographically scattered knowledge and complexity in acquiring, developing, transferring, using and safeguarding knowledge in the international context.
- Doz et al. described three approaches viz. projection, integration and orchestration. From the projection viewpoint, it is the function of management to find a balance between blind transfer of experience from the home country and over-conformity to the local conditions. This balance can rarely be determined beforehand. Integration not only involves learning from one's own company

worldwide but also from outside. Orchestration, in extreme case, means team-work of units of a company, alliance partners, customers and suppliers in a global network without a centre or headquarters.

- Opening new markets, developing global products, planning new factories or technical cooperation in development require knowledge-oriented project management the principles of which have been outlined. ADB's plan of action for knowledge management connotes a pragmatic, step-by-step approach. The Knowledge Management Results Framework is an important instrument at ADB to assess and improve performance and help identify problems and their solutions.

- In an SME the core knowledge is normally only with the owner, who deliberately or unconsciously has retained all the knowledge with him due to lack of time or fear of 'theft' of idea. When the enterprise is small an informal network provides all the knowledge required to execute tasks and evolve a business strategy. As the enterprise grows, it is imperative for these enterprises to plan the management of knowledge effectively to manage the risk and be able to innovate and constantly search for ways by which they can improve products and services.

- The quality of society is largely determined by its capacity to generate genuine learning and working together and to produce new visionary knowledge. The old paradigm of the Wealth of Nations which was focused on tangible assets is moving towards a new economic landscape based on intangibles in terms of knowledge.

## 6.5   Questions

1. What are the differences between the projection, integration and orchestration approaches to international management?
2. Managers, experts and organisations experience difficulties on learning and sharing knowledge across cultures. What are the reasons for misunderstanding and barriers to sharing/transferring knowledge?
3. What are strengths and weaknesses of small businesses in managing knowledge compared to big enterprises?
4. The knowledge and success of SMEs very often depends nearly exclusively on the owner. Which measures will allow this to change and create a team which is able to run the firm also in absence of the owner?
5. How can knowledge management contribute to regional development?

## 6.6   Assignments

1. **Exporting ornamental fish**

   Qian Hu Corporation Limited is a leading exporter of ornamental fish, exporting to more than 70 countries worldwide; Qian Hu's mission is to create a premium lifestyle experience in ornamental fish-keeping by providing a one-stop aquatic shop for both local and international wholesalers, retailers, and consumers. It engages in the full ornamental fish process: import and export; breeding and quarantine; conditioning and farming; and distribution activities. Qian Hu recognised the importance of knowledge in its early days, when the entire stock of guppies and loaches was lost. Knowledge is integral to improving the organisation's operational efficiency, enterprise planning, and decision-making, and to creating value for stakeholders.

*Sketch a knowledge management strategy and respective measures to be taken for this company.*

The full story you will find under: APO, knowledge management case studies for SMEs, p. 40 http://www.apo-tokyo.org/publications/files/ind-40-km_smes-2010.pdf

2. **Transferring manufacturing know-how**

A German company wants to open a new production line in India. Qualified people have been hired.

*In the project team you are responsible for training/know-how transfer. You are asked to give a presentation about the steps to take that the Indian associates will develop a deep understanding of the German production philosophy and the systems in order to adapt it to Indian circumstances.*

## 6.7   KM-Tool: Storytelling

**What is storytelling:**

The act of telling a story is a deceptively simple and familiar process, a way to evoke powerful emotions and insights. By contrast, working with stories in organisational settings – to aid reflection, build communities, transfer practical learning or capitalise on experiences – is more complicated. Storytelling has been used as a powerful way to share and transfer knowledge, especially experiential and tacit knowledge. For an example of a story see also case study "The inspiring pot" in Sect. 2.2.

**Why use storytelling?**

Storytelling **transfers the tacit part of knowledge:** Because it conveys much richer contexts through stories than other means of KM, storytelling by a vastly-experienced person in any field has the power to transfer his or her experiential knowledge.

Storytelling **nurtures good human relationships:** When someone tells his/her story, the action also conveys significant volume of the storyteller's personal information through the story itself, facial expressions, tone of voice, gesture, etc. This aspect nurtures trust between the storyteller and audiences that often becomes a seedbed for a community of the practice, which enables further sharing and creating of knowledge.

Storytelling **brings out the passion in audiences:** A great part of storytelling is that it is able to address the logical, as well as emotional, part of the brain. As a result, good storytelling can change people's mindset and behaviour to share and create more knowledge than before.

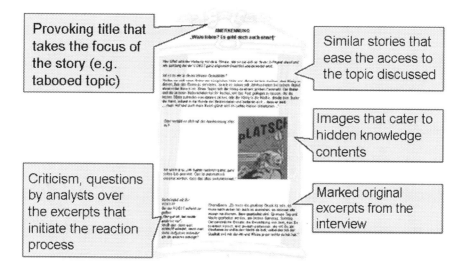

In the following we describe a storytelling process that results in a written story (or preparation as podcast) and therefore will be available organisation-wide. These are the steps:

*Planning phase:* Problem areas that always create difficulties in the company are identified (e.g. communication, team building or teamwork) and are fixed to typical results.

*Interview phase:* The experiences of all the participants are recorded, in order to get acquainted with different perspectives of one event by combining narrative and half-structured interviews.

*Extraction phase:* This phase involves evaluation of the interviews and extraction of important core statements. Statements that describe the problem areas appropriately are searched.

*Writing phase:* Now the story of the experience is written. The story begins with a provocative title that creates interest among the readers. The story is built in two columns so that it is possible to differentiate between the original excerpts in the right hand column from the comments of the author in the left hand column. Comments are meant to initiate the readers to think and reply.

*Validation phase:* The story is given to all the participants for reading with the option to make changes. This binds the interviewed employees in the process of creating the story.

*Circulation phase:* By circulating it one wants to achieve a company-wide discussion pertaining to the experience document; for instance in workshops (where the employees come together to develop methods of solution and also practice teamwork). The purpose of this phase is to trigger the learning and change processes in the entire company.

> **Case Study: Storytelling: The inspiring pot: The difference between a report and a story**
>
> **Version A:**
>
> In our evaluation of a project in Bangladesh we noted a wide variance in the competence of individual villages to develop sustainable and effective solutions to problems encountered, for example in replacing broken parts or developing low cost products such as new latrines. The lessons to be learned from this evaluation are that we should:
> - Work against over-dependence on donors;
> - Note and encourage entrepreneurial approaches to problems;
> - Identify existing and repeatable good practices;
> - Build and strengthen communication between villages to assist cross-fertilisation of ideas at the grassroots level.
>
> **Version B:**
>
> Bangladesh is a really impressive place… in a positive sense. I was in a village last year working in water and sanitation. We were trying to promote the use of improved latrines, but could not produce concrete slabs and rings locally for a low cost. Somebody told me to visit the latrines of a lady in the village, so I went along and said,
>
> "Can I see your latrines?" She had made a latrine out of a clay pot with the bottom cut off. Then with a potter from the area, she developed a small local production of bottomless pots and they became the latrines. Ingenious.
>
> A few weeks later I was in another village and saw a hand pump; it was broken, just a small piece missing. So I said to the villagers, "Why don't you repair your pump?" And they said, "Oh, we just wait for another donor to bring a new pump." So I said, "Why don't you visit the lady in the village over there? She finds ways of getting things done on her own."
>
> Source: Swiss Agency for Development and Cooperation 2006: Story Guide – Building bridges using narrative techniques.

Brown JS, Denning S, Groh K, Prusak L Storytelling in organisations. www.amazon.com/dp/0750678208

Stephen Denning's website at www.stevedenning.com/site/Default.aspx

Sources/links: Erlach, Thier, Neubauer 2005; Swiss Agency for Development and cooperation: Story Guide- Building bridges using narrative techniques www.youtube.com/watch?v=UFC-URW6wkU&feature=player_embedded.

Wikipedia. "Storytelling". Available at http://en.wikipedia.org/wiki/Storytelling

# How Can Information and Communication Technology Support Knowledge Work

**7**

*Enterprise 2.0 can't just be about a wiki here, a blog there forever. Taken together, the emergence and convergence of Web 2.0 and IP communications is what will determine whether there's truly an Enterprise 2.0. It's a new architecture defined by easier, faster, and contextual organisation of and access to information, expertise, and business contacts – whether co-workers, partners, or customers. And all with a degree of personalisation sprinkled in – Information Week* (edition 34, 26. 2. 2007)

**Learning Outcomes.** After completing this chapter

- You will know what the specific information and communication needs of knowledge workers are,
- You will be able to name the components and functionalities of a high performance workplace;
- You will know what needs to be considered to implement ICT successfully.
- You will be able to apply knowledge taxonomies and maps.

## 7.1 Needs of Knowledge Workers in Enterprise 2.0

To what extent does information and communication technology (ICT) support knowledge workers in accomplishing their work in a productive way?[1]

A 'creative' knowledge worker in an advertising agency needs very special creative phases in his work. For this, the systems too have to be supportive and enable a screened workplace environment (selectivity by controlling communication).

---

[1] Chapter 7 is based on a text prepared by Rupert Petschina.

K. North and G. Kumta, *Knowledge Management,*
Springer Texts in Business and Economics, DOI 10.1007/978-3-319-03698-4_7,
© Springer International Publishing Switzerland 2014

A knowledge worker who often works in the role of an 'external consultant' controls his work output mainly by using the interaction possibilities at the client's site combined with maximum possible availability. Special requirements of his workplace radius, controlled reachability, uncomplicated coordination of schedule and efficient bridging of spatial distance with colleagues all aid him optimally to be successful in his work.

System support for *'internal consultant'* should increasingly be aimed at making high-quality information available as the basis for decision-making (e.g. information systems, business intelligence). As regards information intensity, screening unnecessary information gains importance.

Employees whose work is highly characterised by *processing and forwarding of structured information* ('info-crunchers') require maximum possible process support on the one hand and on the other hand, high availability and accessibility of information in knowledge management systems.

What a knowledge worker requires for *analytical tasks* is optimal access to the knowledge and information basis of the company. In order to get efficient work results, one must not reinvent the wheel, and a good collaboration within the network of experts is one of the factors that ensures this. Here, systems must support the know-how pool and the network of experts.

The aforementioned cases are examples; in day-to-day work we often come across mixed forms of several task types. But what they have in common is that they jointly shape communication and teamwork in the company. Particularly challenging are meeting situations, shared data storage and data forwarding, project-oriented teamwork, mail and telephone communication across the boundaries of different business processes. Users, business processes and ICT equipment form a closed system: All three spheres of influence are necessary for working productively and efficiently. Massive shortcomings of the user, the processes or the system equipment can rarely be compensated by the other two respectively.

With McAfee's (2006) publication: Enterprise 2.0: The Dawn of Emergent Collaboration the enormous potentials of interaction of people by means of digital platforms became clear.

**Enterprise 2.0** is the use of emergent social software platforms within companies, or between companies and their partners or customers. **Social software** enables people to rendezvous, connect or collaborate and create communities through computer-mediated communication (http:// andrewmcafee.org/2006/05/enterprise_20_version_20/).

Enterprise social networking applications are becoming increasingly popular (Turban et al. 2011) and along with the private use of facebook, Twitter and others change communicative behaviours in firms as shown in Fig. 7.1.

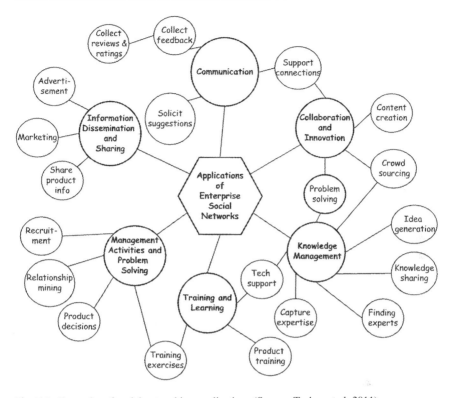

**Fig. 7.1** Examples of social networking applications (Source: Turban et al. 2011)

This puts high demands on those designing ICT systems: The art lies in balancing individual user requirements and requirements of a coherent and robust system landscape from the perspective of an organisation. Particular emphasis on systems enables knowledge sharing and use among the community that works together using collaborative technology at anytime, anyplace and anywhere, as shown below (Abdullah et al. 2005). The following criteria should be considered:

*Individualisation and demand-orientation: Does the system design suit the knowledge workers work/function requirements?*

In many companies, the information and communication processes of knowledge workers are geared towards technology (user requirements follow the system). However, a premise for successful productive knowledge work requires the ICT systems to be aimed completely at the requirements of knowledge workers (system follows user requirements).

However, pronounced orientation towards demand involves a risk of emergence of numerous individual software islands and approaches to finding solutions. The heterogeneity of system and application landscapes creates loss of productivity of interfaces. Users require a high degree of individualisation. However, a company is often reluctant to use necessary resources for individualisation. It wishes to retain its system landscape in a standardised and supposedly cost-effective and efficient form. One of the examples of individualisation is providing information to knowledge workers. Productivity is increased not only by the optimum availability of information in the systems, but also by filtering irrelevant information. However, systematic identification and evaluation of knowledge and its transformation in the systems is considered as increased resource expenditure for personalisation by the company.

### Integration: To what extent is the ICT system integrative in terms of practical use?

Does the ICT system itself cause waiting times and productivity loss in interfaces to other systems or activities?

Employees who have to operate a whole variety of systems have to struggle to a certain extent with multiple logins, heterogeneous structures and possibly even system crashes in interfaces. The systems that are not used very often are neglected. Experience shows that maximum two to three core systems are imposed on an employee.

When it comes to the level of integration of ICT's working environment, a user wishes to be at maximum ease with fewer interfaces. For the company, this means considerable expenditure on integrating and bridging interfaces. If the integrative character of systems is not considered sufficiently, the users' flexible productivity factors such as acceptance, user know-how or motivation – that are controlled by the user himself – are affected more intensely. The human factor influences the overall productivity decisively in a direct interplay with the usability of the entire system landscape.

### Acceptance and use: How easy is it to use the ICT system?

What are the barriers in application? What are the implementation barriers in changing processes during new installation of ICT systems?

Each of us has already heard of IT projects or has been closely associated with such projects wherein person years are spent in the development of individual software. In the end they were further developed for the user according to the requirements and important acceptance factors. Knowledge workers should be actively involved in all phases of development and implementation. An objectively measured performance of the system can be a clear performance indicator. This application efficiency can be evaluated only through a definite result. It helps to consider acceptance factors and implement incentive systems beforehand. Training and coaching is neglected by the companies and even the employees demand fewer skills. An 'error-culture' of identifying and admitting mistakes is not particularly popular.

### Performance: How well does the ICT-system perform?

Performance and productivity of ICT systems is not an issue as long as everything functions well. Things become critical only in the event of a breakdown. Many IT managers should take this challenge. Often, clear goals and measurable results also fail in achieving goals of the entire IT department. As a result, in a "normal" working situation, information and communication systems are rarely considered as productivity factors for a knowledge worker. In the end, what exists is a latent conflict of interest (to be optimised) between the requirements of knowledge workers and use of resources for ICT systems.

## 7.2    High Performance Workplace

How can an entire system be designed for supporting knowledge workers to optimise their performance and productivity? Austin et al. (2005), analysts at Gartner Inc., coined the term 'High Performance Workplace' (HPW) for this purpose. He described a productivity concept for knowledge workers. This concept sketched the integrative and knowledge-oriented character accurately in an optimised work environment:

High-performance workplaces augment the capabilities of their skilled staff for activities such as exploring data, developing innovative processes or products, and working with suppliers to respond to the requests for proposals. This support helps workers locate the right people, find the right content, support the right communication channels and focus on where to create maximum returns. In some cases, combining automation and augmentation may generate the highest returns – for example, adding expertise location to call centre applications.

Austin et al. (2008) supplemented this with an overview of components of a High Performance Workplace for supporting "non-routine work"; of work that cannot be standardised – the main criterion for knowledge work (See Table 7.1).

Such productive environments for knowledge workers are designed individually on demand in the company and on demand of the users. Therefore, they cannot be described in 100 % standardised form. For the benefit of knowledge workers, such environments supplement personal workplace with personalised information, knowledge components and communication tools. However, the system environment not only supports knowledge transfer and sharing of common documents and information but also supports flexible teamwork. The task is facilitated across distances using web conference solutions and integrating all available means of communication. This means knowledge transfer and mutual learning is supplemented by a common work platform for synchronous teamwork.

The structure and the functioning of virtual supra-regional project teams, competence teams and innovation teams or units in topic-based networks and virtual project rooms can be enabled by the operative work instrument of "High Performance Workplace".

**Table 7.1** Components of high performance workplace for supporting non-standardised work (Austin et al. 2008)

| Non-routine behaviour category | Example | Technology's role – augment, not automate |
|---|---|---|
| Discover | Threats and opportunities | Communications, search, predictive analytics, BI, business activity monitoring, modelling tools (Excel), 3-D visualisation tools, predictive markets |
| | Pattern recognition | |
| | Competitive intelligence | |
| Innovate | New processes, products, services, segments | Automatic contextual search, agents, professional communities, open innovation sites |
| Team | Find the right people, brainstorm, norm, bond, orchestrate | Expertise location, social network support, social network analysis, brainstorming, idea tracking, informal project management, communication and collaboration in general |
| Lead | Execute change plan, manage unstructured process, reward key behaviours | Web conferencing, group project management, soft corporate performance management |
| Learn | From experience | E-learning suites, communities of expertise (and related video, audio and other Web technologies) |
| Relate | Establish a working relationship with other people | Explore interests, background, common activities to speed bonding, consensus building and trust |

## Goals and results of introducing such work environment:

- Optimisation of productivity by improvement of information flow, communication and teamwork
- Increase in performance capacity of employees
- Increase in efficiency of communication
- Extending workplace radius by enhancing mobile working ability
- Reduction and substitution of travel activity with internal coordination
- Dynamic sampling of business processes (e.g. sales)
- Increase in productivity of employees
- Ideal effect and learning effect of best practices
- Efficient knowledge transfer and knowledge access through active participation of team members.

### Case: A normal research day at a global business software development company

Sven Kalberg is a project manager of a research project NextGenKM in a research department of the globally positioned business software developer, BusinessSoftware AG. BusinessSoftware AG is an international concern with a strong presence in Germany, USA and India. Its research department comprises of ten locations worldwide. Every location, also called as a lab, has a research centre which is assigned different relevant research projects.

For Sven, **teamwork goes beyond the boundaries and time zones**. Cooperation partners are located in other time zones and some even have different work culture. Sven's tasks as a project manager of NextGenKM comprise coordination and management of NextGenKM on behalf of BusinessSoftware AG.

The project wishes to build a new generation of knowledge-based systems that would be better at supporting knowledge workers in their work with daily flood of tasks. In this process, Sven coordinates four employees of BusinessSoftware AG in the NextGenKM project with regard to content and leads the team. A closing report is to be generated in the project. Below, we shall see how Sven managed to create the closing report of NextGenKM with his colleagues in Bangalore. Sven has some supporting tools to coordinate the teamwork effectively.

### Shared calendar

Sven uses the shared calendar to organise the first discussion on the closing report with his colleagues Brian and Ian. The shared calendar helps him overcome the limitations posed by location and time. He has shared his calendar with his colleagues for them to check his availability for any discussion. Likewise, if Sven wants to initiate the discussion, he can check his colleagues' availability. While sending a discussion request he can automatically attach a calendar entry for the selected appointment.

### Telephone conference and communication infrastructure

Sven has to communicate a lot to complete his regular project work. Regular phone calls are inevitable, especially to remain in sync with his colleagues in Bangalore. Sven has allotted fixed time slots for this purpose in the calendar of his colleagues. BusinessSoftware AG provides some technical facilities with its communication infrastructure. Thus, Sven has the option of either reserving a telephone conference service or making a phone call through Skype (Voice-over IP, calling *via* the internet).

### Application sharing

Yet another important aspect for Sven while preparing a closing report is that he not only hears the voice of his colleagues but also sees the presentation or the object being discussed. For instance, there are some screenshots of the transferred prototypes. Here, Sven has the option to select from number of Application Sharing Services. Using this option, he can share the application on his desktop with the participants of a conference.

### Collaboration rooms

Sven's team also has a collaboration room for exchanging documents, bookmarks and opinions on a particular topic. This enables the invited participants to exchange files and use the forum. Access to the collaboration room is integrated directly in the portal of every participant. Sven can comfortably share files using the collaboration room through his WebDAV browser, a tool that makes the file located in the collaboration room available in the file manager of his desktop. However, he generally finds it relatively cumbersome to upload the files in such closed system through a web interface.

### Simultaneous creation of documents

Sven wishes to work closely with his colleague Brian in Bangalore in order to create a closing report. He has already developed the outline from the information of an old report and made suggestions for some chapters to which even Brian can contribute. Sven and Brian have different options to create the report together. One method that has been practiced by them very often is the chapter-wise creation of the document in a document format such as Microsoft Word or LaTex and sharing of chapters through a file share or even a version control system. In the latter case, both can work simultaneously on the chapters and have open document format version at the same time. Sven has already tried creating collaborative documents with a Web 2.0 application such as Google Docs. This application helps several participants to work together on a document even in one section and the software synchronises the individual sections.

### Wikis

Sven can use wikis as yet another practised alternative. Wikis are available not only in BusinessSoftware AG but also in NextGenKM. Wikis have become particularly popular in the last 1.5 years. Therefore, there are multiple relevant Wikis in Sven's working environment. He visits at least one of these wikis daily to get an update on different aspects. The research project alone has two wikis. One of them contains information of the developed components of the project and makes it freely accessible. The other wiki is not for general public and serves in coordination and knowledge exchange of members of the research project. For instance, the weekly conference calls are documented or examinations of components are discussed. At present new wikis are surfacing almost every week. Some research locations have their own wiki and other development groups operate their own respective wikis.

Many efforts were made to curtail the uncontrolled growth at least within BusinessSoftware AG by specifying wiki technology. In order to create the closing report on NextGenKM, Sven, Brian and Ian are working with wiki sites and chapter-wise distributed documents. At first, Sven and Brian created and discussed an outline of the content. After a week, they had a stable structure of the contents and are now in a position to create the actual content of the report. They create the actual content chapter-wise in Microsoft Word documents and store it in a folder in the version control system project.

For the participating researchers, the successful teamwork in this exciting working environment essentially depends on the support provided. With the help of an example of BusinessSoftware AG, the case study shows different options for supporting knowledge work in the research project, NextGenKM. Different problems pertaining to support – motivated by technology or organisation – were explained in this case study.

Author:  Olaf Grebner (shortened version).

## 7.3    ICT Applications for Knowledge Workers: An Overview

The following is an overview of individual options for supporting a knowledge worker. A clear differentiation between operational systems and ICT for knowledge worker is not always possible or advisable because ICT manufacturers try consistently to enhance functionalities and position these in the overall company systems. Software vendors seized this opportunity to introduce new tools termed as "KM tools" which can be integrated with the existing systems to support the company's productivity.

The systems for knowledge workers are considered from the following perspectives of productive knowledge work: individual efficiency, teamwork, information supply, active information search, cooperative use of knowledge and planning and control (cf. Table 7.2).

### Individual Efficiency

Individual efficiency of an employee can be increased particularly by enhancing his workplace radius in the work situation, communication situation and teamwork situation. Blackberry or smart phones with Windows Mobile and push function for email and appointments enable independent asynchronous communication. Simultaneously, the marginal working time is extended and administrative activities such as setting up an appointment are made easy.

For knowledge workers, the work structures shift in such a manner that a full-fledged work environment that is independent of place always becomes critical for success (especially for sales, consultants, management or other specialised employees with high flexibility outside the company location). A decisive factor here is a possible complete access to company's core systems, possibly through a safe connection in the company network (virtual private network, VPN) and mobile internet access. A laptop comes first as an end device. However, mobile applications for PDA are a suitable productivity tool for selective groups in field work.

How do we support knowledge workers in conceptual activities? This purpose is served by some individual software solutions that help us get thoughts structured on paper or in a notebook (e.g. mind manager). Time management is always decisive for distinguishing "urgent" from "important" even for personal work organisation and personal working techniques. Systems based on personal working techniques support individual work by coordinating, handling and completing the tasks in a team.

Efficiency can also be increased by ensuring that knowledge workers do not have to act in accordance with their communication tools. Efforts must be taken to ensure that the communication environment is structured to be "adaptive" to individual changing work situations. Thus, in the age of IP telephony with complete integration option of mobile telephones, it has become easier to regulate appointment status in the calendar as basic information for changing the defined availability

**Table 7.2** Overview of system categories

| Category | Problem | Solution |
| --- | --- | --- |
| A. Individual efficiency | Poor accessibility, repetition of work, idle power and unused work time, loss by mobility | A1. Mobile devices for increasing communication ability |
| | | A2. Mobile solutions for extending the workplace radius |
| | | A3. PAT systems (personal working techniques) |
| | | A4. Adaptive communication solutions |
| | | A5. Unified Messaging Services |
| B. Teamwork | Inadequate teamwork, too long planning times, too long coordination periods, integration gaps, vulnerability to errors | B1. Shared workspaces |
| | | B2. Conference solutions |
| | | B3. Groupware functionalities |
| | | B4. Teleworker |
| | | B5. Presence information / instant messaging |
| | | B6. Workflow support (ECM, Ticketing, ...) |
| C. Information supply | No information about caller, lack of availability of information with competitive advantages, quality assurance | C1. Customer information system |
| | | C2. Enterprise resource planning |
| | | C3. Portals (Intranet, Extranet) |
| | | C4. Context information on communication partner (Xing) |
| D. Active info search | The wheel is reinvented. Knowledge from experience and expert know-how is not used efficiently | D1. Corporate directory |
| | | D2. List of experts |
| | | D3. Desktop and enterprise search |
| | | D4. Archiving |
| E. Use of cooperative knowledge | Knowledge of employees as the biggest capital of the company is not available explicitly and cannot be strengthened collectively | E1. E-learning |
| | | E2. Company's info channel (TV, MA magazine, Newsletter) |
| | | E3. Business community (WIKI, forum, ...) |
| | | E4. Company's blog |
| | | E5. Community knowledge games |
| F. Planning and control | Inadequate planning and control (incl. knowledge controlling) | F1. Management Information System (MIS) |
| | | F2. Business intelligence (Data-Warehouse) |
| | | F3. System knowledge controlling |

profiles (forwarding, representing, putting on silent mode or prioritising a call from a fixed group of persons). Many random statuses are predefined and the behaviour of the communication environment in situations such as meeting in house, appointment while travelling, travelling time, absence, vacation, illness, 'busy', 'do not disturb', and many more, is adjusted. There are many possibilities. Considering the individual requirement situation of the concerned work group, it is necessary to decide what can be used sensibly and usefully.

Another challenge is integrating different medium of receiving messages. Unified Messaging is a method of bringing incoming or outgoing messages of any form (e.g. voice-mail, email, fax, SMS, MMS, etc.) into a single form and allowing the user to access them through different access-clients (landline or mobile phone, email client, etc.).

## Teamwork

Supporting communication and teamwork is a topic that was developed by well-known software and system houses under the key term "collaboration". Burton (2005) defines Collaboration "as people working together on non-routine cognitive work". Effective collaboration requires the convergence of traditional communication tools like telephones, email, fax, etc.

Groupware solutions with common mail-management, schedule-management and task-management are constantly extended by platforms or portals for cooperation. For example, Share Point Portal Services of Microsoft, Quicktime of IBM or Oracle Collaboration Suite.

An important starting point is the type of filing structure. In reality, filing structure ranges from "controlled chaos" to a common structure (possibly with archiving) wherein knowledge is systematically evaluated in documents and emails at the same time.

If a team uses a common workspace in the intranet or internet, it can go a step further using common data filing and data organisation. This enables the knowledge worker to even process the documents together. The criteria for this are version control during asynchronous processing and synchronous access to one and the same application or document. In this process, a second processor – who might be sitting in some other location – is invited to share a monitor screen with the document owner and discuss simultaneously.

In most cases, the web conference solutions are compatible with shared workspace and groupware solution can be combined for the purpose of convergent and integrative development. There are many special providers of services ranging from web conference to virtual meeting rooms wherein camera, microphone and monitor are completely integrated. By now, development and supply of collaboration tools is affected significantly by Voice over IP internet services for private customers. These services are also growing continuously in the business market. That is how Skype offers a presence overview and simultaneous processing of documents for its users. Google developed itself from being a search engine to becoming a platform for communication and teamwork.

From many practical discussions, we notice that the subject of availability gains importance to the extent of change in the workplace radius of the knowledge worker. Maintaining 'presence information' in a company is a possible way of closing this information gap and giving information quickly about "when is my business partner available for me again?" Thus, one can avoid unnecessary and futile attempts to call or call-back. An important point to be considered while using presence information is to opt for a leading system in the entire company. Another success factor is at the behavioural level; semi-automatic adjustment for availability of suggested information should be possible. The knowledge worker can choose when he wants to work undisturbed even if the system suggests something else.

If one focuses on a process while considering communication and teamwork, one can define not only the information flow and use of diverse communication systems in every business process but also the document flow. Systems that enable systematic relaying and automation of business process reproduce workflows for processing and decisions in the company. We notice that the higher the knowledge intensity in a process, the more difficult the standardised implementation of a workflow. Yet structuring in the form of a workflow system is a good parameter for knowledge work processes and contributes significantly to safety and quality of process as well as reduction and measurability of processing time.

### Case Study: Teamworks – United Nations Development Program's (UNDP's) networking and knowledge platform

Teamworks is a secure, globally available Web 2.0 Extranet platform that will enable UNDP to leverage the collective knowledge of communities, individuals, programmes and projects and engage with partner UN agencies and selected non-UN partners in secure online exchange. Teamworks ensures global distribution of knowledge, while also giving users the capacity for identifying and connecting with peers and partners wherever they are located, as well as for contextualising, sharing and finding knowledge when it's needed.

Teamworks allows the creation of collaborative online spaces for communities of practice and working groups among UNDP staff, as well as with external partners. It facilitates One UN cooperation with other UN agencies to service clients with innovative, timely, results-oriented development solutions.

**What Teamworks users can do:**
- Feature professional knowledge, experience and skills of staff through user profiles;
- Connect to peers by professional networking with staff and external partners for knowledge exchange across HQ/regional/country office levels;
- Stay on top of the work of business teams using just-in-time and transparent communication via status updates, comments and instant messaging;
- Join and contribute to Communities of Practice;

- Create ad hoc online spaces to capture knowledge and foster innovation, communication and collaboration;
- Invite UN colleagues and external partners into a secure online environment for One UN collaboration;
- Obtain advisory services and find experts and consultants;
- Share insights and innovative solutions through files, bookmarks, pictures, videos, news articles and blogs;
- Collaborate and develop community content on wikis;
- Conduct effective searches to access knowledge assets;
- Obtain project information and share project achievements, evaluations and good practices.

Source: https://undp.unteamworks.org.

## Information Supply

What influences the success of a knowledge worker who renders his main service in direct cooperation with his customers or in partner networks?

He requires the minutest details about the activities of "his" customers. In most cases, they are not just "his" customers. Many employees and colleagues communicate with these customers or render services to them. The success of the work and the result depend directly on how well they are connected and co-ordinated.

Preventing customer information from flowing for a limited sales area and allowing it to flow along the customer contact points of the company's customers is a challenge and a key to significant increase in efficiency. The Customer Relationship Management systems are used for this purpose. Along a sales cycle, the sales approach in campaign management compiles plenty of customer information through lead management, supply management, contract management and service management. This information can flow back in the business process to have a decisive effect on its success.

Today, apart from the information in company's internal systems, even context information in Web 2.0 platforms, such as Xing etc., is being resorted to increasingly. The key question here is not "what is technically possible?" but "what can be implemented at a behavioural level and adopted by employees or users".

Based on the customer information system, we have already come quite close in a giant circle under the business relevant company systems, ERP – Enterprise Resource Planning. At this point many will wonder, "How is ERP associated to knowledge work? Isn't ERP primarily process and function oriented?"

Today, ERP enjoys such a crucial place in a company that the knowledge workers have to work with it. Supporting knowledge work should be incorporated in core business and core functions of an employee. Knowledge and relevant information should be systematically evaluated and identified wherever there is action and not in newly devised systems. In short, we incorporate requirements and specific work situations of a knowledge worker in integrated company systems such as ERP along the knowledge work process.

Last but not least, it is necessary to mention "portals" while talking about systems for supplying information to knowledge workers. The term 'portal' has gone through many ups and downs in the last 10 years. In different definitions, it was very difficult to distinguish whether a website could be called a portal for external or internal use. From the perspective of knowledge work, the following core capabilities are our concern:

1. The ability of processing content efficiently by decentralised use of content management system and passing the processed content further by categorising and evaluating it systematically.
2. A user administration with authorisation system for write and read access rights based on a central directory (Directory, e.g. LDAP)
3. The technological ability to establish interfaces through portal components (cf. portlet or webpart) for integrating external applications, services and databank contents.
4. The ability of supporting searching and finding information on internet/intranet through personalisation.

## Active Information Search

Knowledge workers like to control active information searches through experts or other knowledge bearers. Tacit knowledge and knowledge from experience is transferred in personal discussions. A business partner gets his information quickly and in a processed form. But how do I identify and reach a desired contact person and expert?

A common directory of employees not only enables display of contact data right in the telephone book but also shows its availability status. What counts against it is adding an overview of the contact information along with competencies, experiences, personal publication and capabilities of the mentioned person. Thus, networking of experts in a company not only takes place in an informal way but also in a structured and systematic way. If the already maintained employee information is available, it is easily possible to link it with employees' master data and authorisation data (LDAP directory). The effect gets bigger when the directory also turns into a contact network outside the company and employees share their personal networks with their colleagues. However, even in this case it is true that technical solution alone does not mean that half the battle is won. A lot depends on inducing the employees to start an in-house network and give away something to get something from others. This change in culture turns out to be more difficult than what it sounds because knowledge or even 'my own' contacts supposedly represent job guarantee or desired power for a lot of employees.

A common search: A search field wherein I enter the desired term and the search finds the desired document – be it on the same PC, fileserver, in the intranet or even in a document archive. In many companies, this vision makes a few employees sweat. The very presence of information on the availability of a document (e.g. with the name "staff reduction list") is cited as an argument against the introduction of an intelligent company search. Obviously, an authorisation system considers which results should be shown on demand in an archive.

### Case: Finding and binding experts at Sanofi-Aventis

In the pharmaceutical industry, the development of a drug – starting from the discovery of an acting agent up to its licensing – takes 10–15 years. Yet, saving even small amounts of time is important. The time saved shows up in the turnover and contributes in refinancing the innovative research. An agent with medium or good profitability (e.g. 365 million euros a year) generates *one million euros per day* on an average. Thus, reduction in the development time alone is beneficial for the turnover. On the one hand, the access to the right information at the right time can help in reducing the development time frame. On the other hand, there is also an option to improve the access to the researcher himself. This is applicable especially when different experts are working or have worked in different areas on similar problems. It is possible to avoid double work. This results in increase in productivity and the corresponding exchange of knowledge helps to reduce the investment in experts.

#### Analysing emails

Intranet-based software like "*KnowledgeMail*" create expert profiles by analysing emails. Furthermore, they can be supplemented by documents that are made available explicitly for the profiling system. The profiles can also be supplemented with a free description of the job profile in one's own words.

The emails are analysed in the background. The user, for whom the profile is created, need not be active. The profiles are based on keywords and phrases that are extracted automatically from the documents and linked to the names of the experts. The expert has complete control over the visibility of his profile to the others. However, the expert profile is searchable beyond the private profile without displaying the name by adhering to the data protection norms. The expert stays anonymous and can be contacted virtually using the software.

#### Innovative elements in the approach of knowledge management

The knowledge mail system has remarkable advantages over the manually maintained systems, like yellow pages and knowledge databases such as automatic profile creation and update, appraisal of the employee, network building and prevention of copyright problems as every employee decides what information he wishes to make accessible to the other employees. Such a system requires an extensive security model which protects privacy as well as ensures data security.

To a certain extent, the introduction of the knowledge management approach of "*find and bind experts*" means that the employees do not have to make an extra effort. The following is expected of the employees:

- Readiness to share available knowledge
- Readiness to accept the expert knowledge of the others ("*not invented here*" syndrome)

- Accepting storage of personal data
- Establishing contacts between persons beyond the boundaries of departments, countries and languages. This applies particularly when persons, who have neither seen nor known each other, come in contact with each other.

Source: (Oldigs-Kerber et al. 2002)

## Cooperative Knowledge Use

With its pioneering changes pertaining to who produces content for whom, Web 2.0 has initiated a radical upheaval of communication and teamwork for knowledge workers.

This development has taken root in the internet and multiplied to a large extent by now. However, the number of active users in a business community has to be much higher because the user group is innately much smaller. Presently, the demographic composition differs fundamentally thus posing further challenges in implementing business community projects.

The real challenge in establishing knowledge systems for cooperative use of knowledge does not lie in its technical implementation. It lies in editing of the content. Content editing is counted among the most resource-intensive activities and is generated optimally by number of individuals of a community, i.e. by the users. ICT systems that focus on procurement of learning content are increasingly moving together with the sections "collaboration" and "social networks in Internet and Intranet".

E-Learning comprises all forms of learning that involve use of digital media for presenting and distributing learning material and/or for supporting interpersonal communication. E-learning is also synonymous to online learning, tele-learning, computer-based training, multimedia-based learning, open and distance e-learning, computer-aided learning etc. The course and learning environment are organised using a separate LMS (Learning Management Systems) that has been developed as Content Management Systems for e-education.

Newspaper, TV and newsletter are used increasingly as convergent media for getting targeted employee information. These information and learning courses are tailored exactly for a target group. Furthermore, business TV presents a very effective method of motivating a group (employee, suppliers and customers) to learn.

Another form of knowledge-oriented Web 2.0 applications are weblogs (blogs) that have take root since the beginning of 2002 as an indispensable information and communication medium for knowledge workers.

Robes (2005) discussed different perspectives of weblogs:

- Weblogs as primarily private journals that give information about personal sensitivities and activities of its author
- Weblogs as a new journalistic form of expression that perform control function against established media
- Weblogs as marketing and communication instruments that enable the company to enter new dealings with their customers and employees
- Weblogs as a new learning medium using which people can deal with a certain topic systematically and thus make this process transparent to themselves and others

## Management Systems for Planning and Control

Management Information Systems (MIS) are IT information systems for managerial planning and control of a company. In most cases, the database for this model comes from a data warehouse.

BI systems use the same database with an additional focus on reporting. Thus, supporting tools that help the company to optimise the business results or ensure the quality of results are also the tools for knowledge workers. They make the following contributions to achievement of defined company goals:

- Establishing a contextual basis for making decisions
- Structuring the decision-making processes
- Contributing to quality assurance of work results
- Even knowledge management itself is a management discipline that has to be planned and controlled.

According to Deming's PDCA-cycle (PDCA: Plan, Do, Check, Act), it is possible to set knowledge controlling in a cycle oriented by key figures. For knowledge goals operationalised by key figures, it is recommended to incorporate quantifiable usage parameters of knowledge management systems and contents in addition to structural, human and relation key figures of an intellectual capital statement. How intensively is the ad hoc communication used in teamwork? What is the level of integrity of systematically classified storage of documents as knowledge sources? Which proportion of users work can be incorporated into a company's wiki? All these questions can be answered only by a continuous evaluation and accessing statistics in the ICT systems for knowledge workers.

## Success Factors for ICT Implementation

Optimum interplay of user, structure (operational and organisational structure) and ICT systems is a basic requirement for increasing the efficiency of the knowledge worker. In the following presentation of utilisation effects, quantitative usage dimensions are highlighted even if it is not always possible to quantify the usage dimension effectively.

The following principles should be considered for productive and user-friendly conception of ICT systems:

**Orientation to productivity**: In knowledge work, we have to deal with new, productivity-enhancing influential factors that should be organised. I particular this includes the daily work environment of knowledge workers with all the accompanying and supporting tools, knowing the right knowledge sources, facilities to access knowledge of colleagues and their readiness to share it, right equilibrium between concentrated individual work and common work and last but not least, productive use of knowledge (and knowledge-bearers in his working hours).

**Incorporation in business processes, working processes and operational procedures:** We have to deal with processes and systems that are to be implemented permanently. Accordingly, it is possible to create, store, distribute and use knowledge for the company. This is accompanied by balanced organisational structures and working environments. A one-time technology-oriented solution would go well in this structure. These processes and operations cannot be planned and simulated for individual persons as in case of productive work. Accordingly, it is necessary to design them in such a way that a knowledge worker follows them gladly because he knows the utility of his work. He can provide knowledge in a simplified form and become more capable of accessing experts and their knowledge based on optimised communication processes.

**Strengths of knowledge culture and readiness of an individual:** This determines the inner satisfaction of the participants, their interest and their motivation, and a company culture that stimulates and rewards the corresponding behaviour positively. Setting of incentives will become necessary here but not effective. However, knowledge management will become a part of life when the knowledge workers recognise the direct benefits of knowledge sharing and play a part in the system, for instance, by providing their own knowledge. An individual should be ready to share his knowledge and he should have the trust to rely on and use the already available information in a productive way. The company culture necessary for this has to be built for the long-term. This begins with developing the readiness of knowledge-bearers by implementing dedicated/ focused measures. This readiness has to be developed alongside the process of implementation.

**Establishing circular dependencies in implementation:** Knowledge management lives and get its benefits from knowledge that can be shared and used. On the other hand, creation and storage can begin only when it is present technically and organisationally. Thus, in knowledge management processes it is necessary to overcome a "dry spell". This raises technical, organisational and cultural challenges. But the dry spell can be overcome only with the help of spearheads. Again, spearheads are not just the management and seniors with specialisations. Even experts have a lot of decisive knowledge. For implementation, it is necessary to identify potential spearheads and plan measures beforehand.

**Management attention for knowledge objectives:** Knowledge objectives should be in tune with the overall strategy of the company or should be derived from it. They primarily present the stakeholders' perspective of the company. This process should not be performed once but should also be implemented permanently in order to build a learning organisation.

**Identification and creation of analogies**: A significant factor for success and acceptance of collaborative systems for knowledge workers is the ability of the employees to develop analogies between themselves and others. This step from anonymisation, a trustful behaviour of knowledge workers among themselves, should be supported clearly by ICT systems in units and cells of personal communication and teamwork. As the user of the system, a knowledge worker depends to a great extent on his motivation that is boosted by personal grading of his work.

For a successful ICT system usage, it is necessary to manage user expectations from IT projects. The belief that a problem is solved by installing a comprehensive and expensive ICT solution is detrimental to the success of the knowledge management initiative.

---

**Case: KM at eClerx – an example of knowledge Process Outsourcing**

*eClerx in India is a specialist Knowledge Process Outsourcing (KPO) company that provides data analytics and customised process solutions to global enterprise clients across a wide range of industry sectors from its offshore delivery centres in India. Incorporated in 2000, the company has four delivery centres across Mumbai and Pune and onshore support and client engagement operations in Austin (Texas), New York, Dublin and London.*

*With each passing year since its inception, eClerx has entered into more short-term and higher-complexity engagements; concurrently, the collective knowledge base and organisational capabilities of the company have continued to grow. By late 2003, it was clear that one-on-one apprenticeship and nurturing of the transfer of tacit knowledge needed to be supplemented with a broader framework of KM.*

*In the absence of such a framework, new staff were tossed into a whirlpool of process execution and expected to perform without any substantial introduction to the firm's history, culture, processes and lessons learned. Senior management thus proposed KM as a solution for moving ahead, acknowledging constraints and remodelling to a world where cutting-edge technology and intelligent processes must partially displace approaches used in the start-up years at eClerx.*

*It was also felt that KM would address concerns about the company's ability to retain knowledge when staff moved on. In line with others companies in the knowledge-intensive professional services space, the firm's annual employee attrition averages about 30 %. Without KM, an employee's departure could mean that strategic advantage might be depleted, not only through loss of human capital, but also accumulated experiential knowledge.*

*Today, the KM team at eClerx has a decentralised and "cellular" structure. Each operations unit has dedicated knowledge anchors (KAs) to provide localised support. The premise is that learning is more than "vanilla" classroom training. It's not always possible or optimal for staff to abandon core work duties every time they require support. Also, the dynamic nature of eClerx's business means that waiting for explicit knowledge (to be documented) before acting is inadequate. Instead, spontaneous learning opportunities are created by leveraging Web 2.0 technologies to connect consumers with creators of knowledge.*

*All offline and online learning programs are consolidated under a single umbrella – a "virtual university" that offers over 3,000 courses. This in-house university supports:*

- *Domain-specific knowledge on areas such as derivatives, risk management, trade processing, key regulations and so on for financial services clients, and online retail and analytics.*
- *Functional knowledge that is core to the eClerx business, programs on data mining and warehousing, advanced business statistics, Business Objects, SQL Server 2008.*
- *Business process training that delivers process execution know-how. The emphasis here is on application rather than mere acquisition of knowledge of processes.*
- *Training on supporting competencies, including analytical thinking and problem solving, six sigma, team management, interpersonal communication, strategic orientation, leadership, time management, quality management, and project management.*

*Since documented knowledge must typically be reviewed and quality assured, the cycle of publishing documented knowledge may not be quick enough to take action for gaining competitive advantage. Instead, taxonomies, shared platforms, an ask-an-expert system, blogs and wikis, discussion forums and simple contact lists act as smart "push" options that code knowledge and learning into the work of each knowledge worker at eClerx.*

*eClerx has deployed Microsoft Office SharePoint Server 2007 (MOSS 2007). The MOSS 2007 implementation enables:*

- *Content Management: Document management, version control, check-in/check-out document locking, auditing, and role-based-access controls at the document library, folder, and individual document levels.*
- *Enterprise Search: Efficient search and retrieval of relevant content saves time.*
- *Team Portals: Multiple portals that mirror the organisational structure and facilitate collaboration at team level.*
- *Collaboration: With offices in the US, UK and India, the Web 2.0 capabilities of MOSS 2007 enable eClerx employees to leverage workspaces, tasks, surveys, forums, blogs, wikis and RSS.*
- *Wikis and blogs: Wikis provide eClerx employees with a forum where they can contribute and build on the existing knowledge base of the firm. Blogs, on the other hand, catalyze the socialisation process by trapping experiences and lessons learned as they happen.*

*Source:* Makhija (2009).

## 7.4    Key Insights of Chapter 7

- In order to carry out analytical activities, a knowledge worker has a distinct need for an optimum access to company's "knowledge and information bases". There is no need to reinvent the wheel for efficient results. Good teamwork in expert network is one of the success factors. In such cases, the systems should encourage know-how pool and networking of experts.
- The systems for knowledge workers are considered from the following perspectives of productive knowledge work: individual efficiency, teamwork, information supply, and active information search, cooperative use of knowledge and planning and control.
- Users, business processes and ICT settings build a close system. All three influential factors are necessary for productivity and efficient working. Massive weaknesses in users, organisations of business processes or system settings can rarely be compensated by the remaining two factors.
- High-performance workplaces augment the capabilities of their skilled staff for activities such as exploring data, developing innovative processes or products, and working with suppliers to respond to the requests for proposals. This support helps workers locate the right people, find the right content, support the right communication channels and focus on where to create maximum return.
- A knowledge-oriented company is unimaginable without efficient information management. Providing, storing and distributing information is a basic requirement for creation and transfer of knowledge in phase 1 where explicit knowledge has to be made sharable.
- The art of designing ICT systems lies in balancing individual user requirements and requirements of a coherent and robust system landscape from the perspective of an organisation. The human factor influences the overall productivity decisively in direct interplay with usability of the entire system landscape.
- A knowledge-oriented company should protect its knowledge from outside but allow employees a free access to most of the information. Distrust towards one's own employees and the restricted information access thereof, hinder the process of knowledge transfer.

## 7.5    Questions

1. Discuss why Knowledge Management initiatives inspired by Information Technology alone do not result in successful Knowledge Management.
2. What are the characteristics of an "enterprise 2.0"? What does this mean for the ICT system and what are the implication for users/contributors?
3. "Information empowerment is a full equation for information sharing. One half of the equation is getting the right information to the right people at the right time. The other half of the equation is making sure that people can do something with the information when they get it". Discuss.

4. Which ICT tools can enhance teamwork?
5. As a student you are a knowledge worker: Draw a mindmap of your information and communication systems.

## 7.6    Assignments

1. **An information junkyard**

    A large consumer products company decided to restructure the organisation so as to be able to improve professional work. The professional staff was instructed to document their key work processes in an electronic database. It was a despised task. Most staff felt their work was too varied to capture in a set of procedures. After much debate and motivation the task was completed. Within a year the database was populated but it resulted in creating an expensive and useless information junkyard.

    *Discuss the lacunae in designing the knowledge management system and suggest a framework that would help the organisation in improving professional work.*

2. **The challenge to find high quality information**

    'People in large corporations face the same challenges finding information on their organisations' intranets as they do finding it on the Internet: there is too much to search from and searches can yield as much nonsense as helpful material'.

    Discuss this in the framework of Knowledge Management processes highlighting the imperatives and the challenges.

## 7.7    KM-Tool: Knowledge Taxonomy and Knowledge Map

**What is a taxonomy and knowledge map?**

    A taxonomy is a technique that provides the structure to organise information, and documents in a consistent way. Information and knowledge is put in hierarchical or contextual order (like a folder structure in your windows explorer or a mind map).

**Why use taxonomies and knowledge maps?**

    This structure assists people to efficiently navigate, store, and retrieve needed data and information across the organisation. It builds a natural workflow and knowledge needs in an intuitive structure.

**How to develop a taxonomy or knowledge map?**

    Developing a taxonomy involves finding an appropriate breakdown for the diverse forms of information contained and used by different actors within an organisation.

1. Start with a general category for the area of work being addressed, e.g. "processes" or competences

2. Establish the subcategories for this category. These can be developed by answering the question 'what types of, for example, processes or competences are there?' Repeat the process of division, based on the planned application of the taxonomy, and the users concerned. The division used should be consistent with the expectations of the users, otherwise it becomes hard for them to navigate the system intuitively. Decide on standard terms and naming of documents. These should follow the same logic and consistency across different types of item, following the same pattern for similar situations so that, once learned, the user can reasonably predict how it will apply in a new situation.
3. Decide on the kind of visualisation of the taxonomy. (e.g. folder hierarchy, Mind map, knowledge tree, etc)
4. Optional: Assess the maturity and depth of information/knowledge in each "branch" of the structure.

| Type of knowledge | Reference "Lighthouse" | Maturity 1–5 (low to high) | Where is the knowledge documented, who is responsible for the topic? |
|---|---|---|---|
| | | | |

Sources and links:

A useful video on Taxonomy is available on YouTube at www.youtube.com/watch?v=qGymV0ZCme4&feature=player_embedded

**Useful Links**

http://drupal.org/project/modules

www.apqc.org

# Measuring and Safeguarding Intellectual Capital

8

> *Despite important contribution of knowledge and services to value creation and growth of modern companies and nations, our management control systems, our economic models and our social measuring instruments concentrate – baring a few exceptions – on physical and financial assets and physically and financially measurable outputs* – J.B. Quinn (Adapted from Quinn 1992, p. 243)

**Learning Outcomes.** After completing this chapter
- You will know what the challenges to evaluating intangible assets are,
- You will be able to differentiate between deductive summarising and inductive analytical approaches to evaluate intellectual assets;
- You will know how to use a Balanced Scorecard as a multidimensional measuring instrument;
- You will be able to assess risks of loss and know how to protect intellectual assets;
- You will be able to establish a knowledge inventory.

## 8.1 Finding Measures for Intangible Assets[1]

"What is not measured is not managed" is an often made statement in business practice. The measurement and evaluation system is thus the core system for the perceptions of any company. This system, directly influences the performance measurement and evaluation of the top management and of all employees, and

---

[1] This chapter is based North and Gueldenberg (2011) and on North (1999, pp. 184).

K. North and G. Kumta, *Knowledge Management*,
Springer Texts in Business and Economics, DOI 10.1007/978-3-319-03698-4_8,
© Springer International Publishing Switzerland 2014

indirectly influences the strategic decisions. Each organisation thinks and functions through its measurement system even if many decision-makers may be unaware of it. The measurement system can be considered as a strategic map which reflects the organisational reality in a certain manner. We all know that the basic difference between various kinds of maps is the purpose they serve; thus we have road maps, hiking maps, flight maps, and climate maps. But all good maps have the following things in common:

- They give an orientation: In a complex environment, maps help us to focus on the important things and to find our path which lies in the future.
- They are rational and goal-oriented models of reality: Maps never depict the reality one to one. For one, it is impossible to do so, and secondly it would not serve the underlying goal to provide orientation, because the complexity of the maps would overburden the cognitive capacity of human beings and the organisation.

So what do the orientation maps in today's organisations look like? On which significant parameters do they help us focus? Do these parameters help us find a suitable strategy? And how is the strategic performance of an organisation defined?

Classic approaches answer these questions with the help of various financial indicators. Starting with turnover, net income or EBIT, these indicators include traditional returns figures such as ROI or ROS up to the new estimates of shareholder value (ROCE, EVA, DCF, CFROI, etc.). The disadvantage of all these financial indicators is that they are not enough to adequately consider the resource "knowledge" and its significance in the framework of the knowledge economy. These figures thus lead to mismanagement, which in turn negatively affects the success of the organisation in the long run.

According to the disadvantages of the existing performance measurement systems can be summarised in several key statements:

**We too often measure the wrong things:**

- To start with, we measure what is easy to measure, without questioning the strategic purpose the results of such a measurement are supposed to provide us. This way, we become prisoners of our indolence and our bounded rationality.
- Financial indicators are the parameters which, in today's organisations, are the easiest to collect. In doing so, we invest all our energy in aggregating these financial parameters to meaningful indicators. Here, usually the mathematical computability dominates the cause-effect chain and the chronological order of the strategic development is overlooked. During all this we also forget the non-financial, intangible aspects.
- Very often we are inclined to measure only the inputs. Input factors usually have very little significance in predicting to the output achieved with them. This is generally decided in the organisation (through its structure and processes).
- We concentrate too much on stock figures and too little on flow figures. In this way, we strengthen our static view about things and loose the perception for the processes in the course of time.

- We try too hard to divide the organisation into individual units, and forget about its synergies and correlations which characterise every organisation and are in fact its raison d'être.

**Too often we measure using the wrong scale:**

- Often we measure for the short-term: Our time scale is too short. This way, we end up getting static measurements and not dynamic. We get to look at a series of snapshots instead of the complete film. Thus, for strategic decisions and business understanding, we miss out on noticing important dynamic processes such as delay effects or feedback loops.
- Our measurements are solely quantitative and not interlinked and qualitative. This unnecessarily reduces the quality of the information available to us. We fail to see cause-and-effect relationships and trust the supposedly objective numbers more than our own experience.
- We measure with an absolute standard and not with relative. By their definition, however, absolute parameters are always control-oriented and not learning-oriented, because findings can be drawn only from the relative interplay with other parameters.
- We measure only internally and relate very little between the organisation and its environment. This leads to a distorted perception and blinkered attitude to one's work. Concentration on internal mediocrity distorts the view of the possible potentials.

**We do not measure what is important:**

- Intangible assets are generally hardly measured or not measured at all. As a result, we rely mainly on tangible assets while making strategic decisions.
- We hardly know the knowledge base of our organisation and its strategic value. We are unaware of the areas in which we have a knowledge-edge over our competitors. We do not know how widespread knowledge is in the market. It is therefore difficult for us to form sustainable knowledge strategies.
- We do not know how effective our knowledge management system is and what its strategic contribution is. This makes it difficult for us to define a knowledge management strategy.
- We know nothing about the quality and nature of the learning potential of our organisation. Are we in a position to learn faster than our competition?
- We know nothing about the extent and strategic edge of our organisation-specific intelligence. In which areas do we have structural advantages? Which areas are our strongholds? What constitutes our competitive advantage?

**We measure without realising why:**

- Though a number of indicators are available to us, we find it difficult to link these to our strategy. We therefore use indicators to exercise operational control instead of using them for strategic learning.
- We find it difficult to interpret deviations. We therefore concentrate on correcting these deviations. But in doing so we overlook strategic opportunities and risks.

**Case: Intellectual capital statement of Austrian Research Centre, Seibersdorf (ARCS)**

The Austrian Research Centre of Seibersdorf (ARCS) is the biggest extramural research company of Austria. Being found as a nuclear research institute, its field of activity was developed into a broad spectrum of different natural sciences, technology and social sciences with about 700 employees at numerous locations.

Intellectual Capital reporting is supposed to document the future value creating potential and present its progress along the strategic re-orientation of the company. Being a largely publicly financed organisation management wanted to increase transparency of resource use and results achieved for the community and A Balanced Scorecard was developed before the project of intellectual capital statement. This Balanced Score card was supposed to deliver specific information for the internal research and knowledge management.

With the implementation of intellectual capital statement, a three-member team was created apart from the control team which comprised members from different parts of the company and external specialists. This three-member team was made up of two employees of ARCS and an advisor. The ARCS intellectual capital statement is based on a process model that illustrates a knowledge cycle within the company over a certain period of time. The broad threefold classification of intellectual capital in human, structural and relational capital was selected for this purpose. Using this model, it is possible to trace the three capital forms that represent the input for the actual value-creation process (see Fig. 8.1).

The most important core processes of this research organisation are the order and programme research. Three knowledge-based resources are transformed into knowledge within the framework of these processes that are organised in form of projects in the organisation. This model can be illustrated with the following example: A talented researcher (human capital) works in one of the laboratories in Seibersdorf (structural capital) within the research network of ARCS (relational capital). He works not only on problems pertaining to fundamental research (programme research) but also on industrial projects for application development (order research).

Thus, on the one hand, new findings arise in form of publication and methods and on the other hand new products or solutions come into being. The employee learns by himself and enhances his experience. Apart from these findings, there are also financial refluxes that are parallel to the business area of ARCS. For this purpose, detailed indicators are developed that can be retrieved just like the complete intellectual capital statement from www.arcs.at.

Source: Bornemann and Leitner (2002) and www.arcs.ac.at.

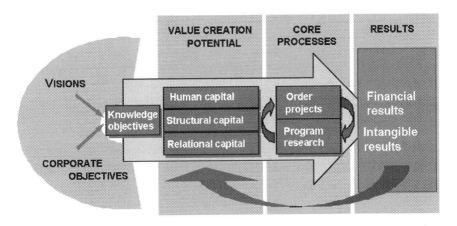

**Fig. 8.1** Process model of ARCS

## 8.2    Intellectual Capital Reporting

Making the effectiveness of knowledge work measurable means to analyse the end result of knowledge work, i.e. the intellectual assets or the knowledge capital generated. Since the beginning of the 1990s there have been efforts to extend the existing, mainly financially oriented, measurement system to non-financial or intangible assets. Knowledge reporting in companies always has an internal and an external dimension. The internal dimension has mainly to do with strategic control and internal accounting.

The external dimension deals with external accounting and reporting, and thus stresses the significance of communication with external stakeholders of the company, especially with its shareholders.

In the following we will not enter into a discussion of International Accounting Standard (IAS 38), where some intellectual assets and their valuation are regulated but refer instead to the relevant accounting literature.[2] A key argument against the recognition of intangible assets in balance sheets still is the uncertainty of future economic flows from such assets.

We distinguish two categories of approaches to evaluating intellectual capital:

*Deductive summarising approaches* rate the difference between a company's market value and book value. Some examples are indicators such as market-to-book value ratios, Tobin's q and Calculated Intangible Value (CIV). Such derived indicators evaluate the intangible assets in monetary form but either fail to explain or explain only partially the difference between the market and the book value. Therefore, from a knowledge viewpoint, they are not suitable as sole variables for operative and strategic control of a company.

---

[2] See for example Lev et al. (2005).

**Table 8.1** Methods for analysing the intellectual capital

| Approach | Description |
|---|---|
| Direct intellectual capital methods (DIC) | Estimate the $-value of intangible assets by identifying its various components. Once these components are identified, they can be directly evaluated, either individually or as an aggregated coefficient |
| Market capitalisation methods (MCM) | Calculate the difference between a company's market capitalisation and its stockholders' equity as the value of its intellectual capital or intangible assets |
| Return on assets methods (ROA) | Average pre-tax earnings of a company for a period of time are divided by the average tangible assets of the company. The result is a company ROA that is then compared with its industry average. The difference is multiplied by the company's average tangible assets to calculate an average annual earning from the Intangibles. Dividing the above-average earnings by the company's average cost of capital or an interest rate, one can derive an estimate of the value of its intangible assets or intellectual capital |
| Scorecard methods (SC) | The various components of intangible assets or intellectual capital are identified and indicators and indices are generated and reported in scorecards or as graphs. SC methods are similar to DIS methods, expect that no estimate is made of the $-value of the Intangible assets. A composite index may or may not be produced |

Table based on: http://www.sveiby.com/articles/IntangibleMethods.htm

In contrast to deductive approaches, *inductive analytical approaches* describe and evaluate and aggregate components of intellectual assets with the purpose to arrive at an overall value. One such approach is an intellectual capital statement as an instrument for targeted presentation and development of intellectual capital of an organisation. It shows the correlation between the organisational objectives, the business processes, the intellectual capital and the success of the organisation and describes these elements by means of indicators.[3]

Sveiby (2010) has developed a somewhat wider systematisation summarised in Table 8.1.

In the following we will explain some of the approaches relevant for practice.

## Deductive Summarising Approaches

### "Market-to-Book Value" Relation

The simplest indicator of the value of an intangible asset is the difference between the market value and the book value. For companies listed on stock exchange, the market value can be calculated easily as share price multiplied by number of shares. The book value can be taken from the annual balance sheet. This happens under the assumption that everything that is not attributed to the book value is based on the

---

[3] www.akwissensbilanz.org

components of intangible assets. Thus, if a company such as Microsoft is worth approximately 86 billion US dollars and the book value is approximately 7 billion US dollars, the value of its organisational knowledge base is 79 billion US dollars.

Though this calculation is easy, it is not very helpful because of the following three reasons (Stewart 1997):

- The stock exchange value changes rapidly and is not characterised by rational and suggestible factors. A 5 % drop in the stock exchange price without any change in the book value of an asset does not mean that the value of knowledge base has reduced by 5 % .
- A company's book value and even market value to a certain extent are set too low. Through extensive use of depreciation, the book value appears to be lower than its real value (keyword: hidden reserve).
- The informative value of the sentence "the intangible assets of Microsoft are worth 79 billion US dollars" is restricted. What can a manager or an investor deduce from this sentence?

Instead of considering the difference between market value and book value, it makes more sense to analyse the quotient that is obtained when market value is divided by book value. With this quotient, a company can compare itself better with similar competitors. If they operate in the same economic zone and are exposed to similar exogenous factors, a benchmark between different companies appears to be meaningful and informative. A diminishing market-to-book value quotient can be an indicator of a warning that enough investment has not been made in organisational knowledge base, maintenance of brand or development of an image and its transparent presentation.

## Tobin's q

James Tobin, winner of the Nobel Prize for Economics, developed a quotient that relates market value of an asset to its replacement value. If $q < 1$, the market value of an asset, a building for instance, is lower than the replacement cost. As a result, the company will ensure that such assets are purchased or held as funds in as less numbers as possible. If $q > 1$, it means that the market value of the asset is higher than the replacement cost. This is particularly applies to knowledge or experts. A high value of q reflects the value of investment in technology and employees. If q is very high, e.g. $q = 2$, the use of this asset is considered to be very profitable. In this respect, q can be seen as a measurement for "monopoly return". The company gains high profits with such resources because it is the only one that uses them. Hence, q is also a measurement of inimitableness and sustainable competitive advantages. Thus, for example, a company can buy young researchers "*at a good price from the market*". The company's ability to integrate and motivate these employees in a functional development team gives rise to technological solutions that are far too valuable than the sum of market value of individual researchers. Imagine the calculation of Tobin's q to get the value of a football team. Tobin's q can be calculated for the entire company as market value divided by the replacement value of fixed assets. The advantage of Tobin's q is that unlike the market-to-book value ratios, it neutralises the effects of different depreciation practices. The informative value of this indicator is highest if similar companies are compared over a longer period of time.

## Calculated Intangible Value (CIV)

This evaluation method was developed by NCI Research (Kellogs School of Business, Stewart 1997) to encourage knowledge-intensive companies. Even here, the basic consideration is that a transparent presentation and financial evaluation of intangible assets should encourage the readiness to invest in knowledge-intensive companies. The approach is built analogous to rating of market value. While evaluating brands, if one assumes that instead of similar products, higher price can be achieved through the brands alone, then in case of calculated intangible value one assumes that companies that develop and use their organisational knowledge base in a better way, gain higher owned-capital returns than similar companies with a less developed organisational knowledge base.

While the deductive summarising evaluation manages to assign a value to the organisational knowledge base, they are – as aggregate values – not in the position to shape the cause-effect relation between interventions and changes in the knowledge base. Thus, this class of indicators is suitable only for strategic and operative control of a company from knowledge viewpoint. The inductive analytical method explained below is more suitable for this purpose.

## Inductive Analytical Approaches

The analytical description and evaluation of different components of organisational knowledge base as well as other components of intangible assets as described by Sveiby (1997) under the term "*intangible assets monitor*", by Stewart (1997) as "*intellectual capital navigator*" and by Roos et al. (1998) as IC index. The concept of the Austrian Research Centre Seibersdorf (Leitner et al. 2000) has also found its way in creation of intellectual capital statement in Austrian universities. The Seiberdorf model inspired a "*Intellectual capital statement – Made in Germany*" and the European Intellectual Capital Statement (INCAS). In Denmark, approximately 20 companies created intellectual capital statements for a pilot project by following Sveiby's approach (Mouritson et al. 2001). Based on this, the Danish Ministry of Economics published "*The Danish Guideline for Intellectual Capital Statements*" (Danish Agency for Trade and Industry 2000).

> **Downloads of guidelines for intellectual capital statements:**
> - "*Intellectual capital statement – Made in Germany*": http://www. akwissensbilanz.org/Infoservice/Infomaterial/Leitfaden_english.pdf
> - The Danish Guideline for Intellectual Capital Statements: http://en.fivu. dk/publications/2001/a-guideline-for-intellectual-capital-statements
> - European Intellectual Capital Statement (INCAS): www.incas-europe.eu/

There are some approaches that integrate financial as well as non-financial indicators into a complete system for operative and strategic control of the company. The most prominent representative is the "*balanced scorecard*" developed by Kaplan and Norton (1996). The *multi-stage indicator model* according to North et al. (1999) in particular tries to make the cause-effect chain visible and present the correlation between the financial and intangible resources.

The financial valuation of individual elements of intellectual capital statement is still in its early stages but is already practiced in a due diligence in Mergers and Acquisitions.

The following are some of these approaches that have gained importance in theory and practice.

## Intangible Assets Monitor

Sveiby assumes that the market value of a company is made up of visible equity and intangible assets. Intangible assets are composed of components of "external structure", "internal structure" and "competence of the employees". The external structure contains relationships with customer and suppliers. The internal structure covers processes and technologies, in short, everything that remains when an employee leaves the company (Sveiby 1997).

The intangible assets monitor evaluates these elements of organisational knowledge base from the perspective of growth/renewal, efficiency and stability related to employees, internal structure, external structure. Sveiby set his approach to practice in a Swedish company Celemi, which develops and sells learning tools (cf. Fig. 8.2). From the aspect of their contribution to the knowledge base, the customers are divided in to three categories:

*Image-enhancing customers* who ease Celemi's task of acquiring new customers and reducing marketing costs come under the "external structure" category in the intangible assets monitor. *Organisation-enhancing* customers who demand "state of the art" solutions, who are relatively new for Celemi and promote development of new products, are posted under growth/renewal section of the internal structure. *Competence-enhancing* customers challenge the knowledge of Celemi's employee and stimulate a common learning process. These customers are posted under the growth/renewal section of the employees.

However, this classification simultaneously brings forth the problem of limitations of indicators. One could argue that organisation-supporting customers should also be considered from the perspective of efficiency wherein, for example, they support just-in-time deliveries or zero-error quality and a 24-h service. In turn, the competence-supporting customer could also be classified under the growth/renewal section in the internal structure.

**Fig. 8.2** Indicators of
"intangible assets monitor"
(Source: Sveiby 1997, p. 165)

|                   | External structures | Internal structures | Employee competence |
|-------------------|---------------------|---------------------|---------------------|
| Growth/ renewal   |                     |                     |                     |
| Efficiency        |                     |                     |                     |
| Stability         |                     |                     |                     |

**Case: Intangible Assets Monitor applied to a cricket team**

Let us consider the intangible assets of a first division cricket team. Firstly, the players of the team are the employees that gain a market value by their transfer fee and success in the game in the ongoing season. The players not only have an individual value as "*experts*" but also as a team. Furthermore, a value can also be assigned to the trainer as an employee as well as to the assistants etc. who could also be described in the internal structure and processes (guiding processes, team development processes) and can be quantified admittedly with some difficulties. Externally, the customer and relations with (loyalty of the fans) have a high value.

## Intellectual Capital Navigator

Stewart (1997, p. 243ff.) suggested that companies should be evaluated under the same perspectives as mentioned by Sveiby and the result should be presented as shown in Fig. 8.3 – in a target-performance comparison. The indicators for human capital, structural capital (according to Sveiby's internal structure) and customer capital (the supplier relations are not considered) are shown in addition to the market-to-book value relationships. Three key figures are suggested for each of the latter three categories. However, Stewart does not differentiate between growth/ renewal, efficiency and stability. Yet, he implicitly focuses mainly on the indicators of growth and renewal. Motivational measures are taken to create scales for every indicator in such a way that the target value in the graphical presentation rests on the arc. This diagram provides a simple target-performance comparison as a starting point for targeted intervention in organisational knowledge base.

## The Intellectual Capital (IC) Index

The IC index of Roos et al. (1998, p. 89) is based on classification of intellectual capital into relational, innovation, human and infrastructural capital. Indicators are built for each of these capitals. Analogous to the cost-utility analysis, they are

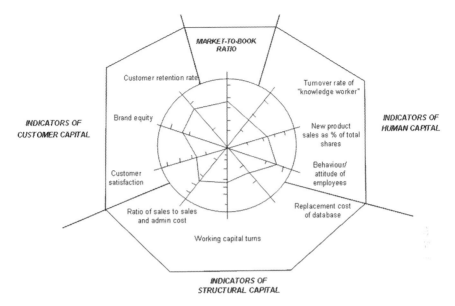

**Fig. 8.3**  The "intellectual capital navigator" (Source: Stewart 1997, p. 245)

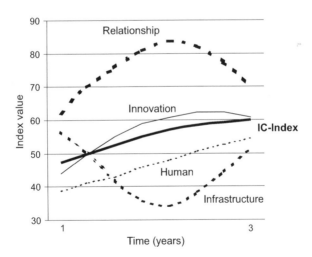

**Fig. 8.4**  The "intellectual capital index" (Source: Roos et al. 1998, p. 89)

weighed and aggregated – into an index and an IC index, and presented over a course of time. On the one hand, this presentation of intellectual capital takes into account the need for simplified key figures but on the other hand its significance is restricted only to new trends. Furthermore, the relative weightage of individual key figures is not based on concrete examples (see Fig. 8.4).

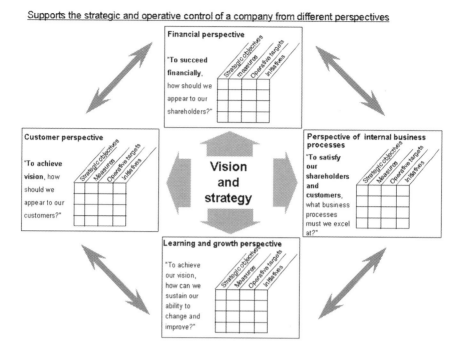

**Fig. 8.5**  Structure of Balanced Scorecard (Source: Kaplan and Norton 1996, p. 76)

## The Balanced Scorecard

The Balanced Scorecard developed by Kaplan und Norton (1996) is a result of one of the surveys in the USA supported by the KPMG auditing and consulting firm in order to increase the informative value of traditional financially-oriented key figures. The model (see Fig. 8.5) views a company from four perspectives – customer perspective, financial perspective, perspective of internal business processes, and perspective of learning and growth.

The Balanced Scorecard is a strategic management system that can be used to support the operative implementation of a long-term strategy. Different perspectives of the company are not only juxtaposed but also shown in their cause-effect correlation. Strategic objectives, measurement categories, operative targets and initiatives are specified for each of the perspectives. Kaplan and Norton compare the balanced scorecard in their application with a flight simulator wherein a complex number of cause-effect relations of critical variables are considered that describe the flight-route as well as a strategy to reach a destination.

However, there is the awareness that every organisation should compile its own, custom-made and context-specific set of indicators in order to capture and control the dimensions that are relevant for them. Simultaneously, the Balanced Scorecard supports the dense connection of knowledge objectives and knowledge measurement which will ideally lead to fast feedback processes.

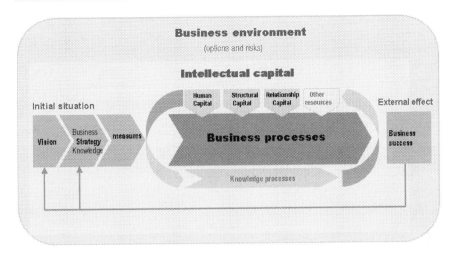

**Fig. 8.6** The intellectual capital statement model developed by the Intellectual Capital Statement Project Group (AK-WB)

## InCaS Intellectual Capital Statement: Made in Europe

Based on the Austrian methodology (see case on p. 256) the German Federal Ministry of Economics and Labour supported the trial of a methodology called *"Intellectual capital statement – Made in Germany"* which was then tested and adapted in the European context by pilot companies. The *"Intellectual capital statement-"*[4] developed is considered as an instrument for medium-sized enterprises to present their intangible assets in a structured form and evaluate these assets. As an instrument for strategy development and organisational development, the intellectual capital statement allows systematic deduction of measures for optimised internal controlling of business processes. As an instrument for external communication, the intellectual balance sheet facilitates the decisions pertaining to banks and investors for instance, because future potentials of the company are made transparent.

The intellectual capital statement comprises intangible assets in form of human capital (employee competence, employee behaviour), structural capital (IT, intellectual property, organisational culture, process organisation etc.) and relational capital (relationships with customers, suppliers, others partners and public).

Figure 8.6 shows the intellectual capital statement model. The statement starts with the initial situation of vision and strategy of the organisation and gives an overview of options and risks in the business environment. From this, the organisation derives a range of measures on how it wishes to position itself according to the different dimensions of intellectual capital, namely human, structural and relational capital.

The interaction of business and knowledge-based processes, together with the other tangible and financial resources which are not observed in the intellectual

---

[4] Further information under www.akwissensbilanz.org.

capital statements, leads to business success. From this result, the organisation draws conclusions for the future which can lead to changes in visions and strategies. The knowledge gained from the intellectual capital statement on the knowledge processes and the relevant resources make it easier to derive measures in a new cycle and to facilitate the sustained orientation of the organisation.

The complete intellectual capital statement is created using five steps with four milestones:

- *Milestone I* presents the intellectual capital statement in its simplest form. Three steps are needed to achieve this milestone: assessing the initial situation relating to business environment and strategy, recording intellectual capital, and self-evaluation of intellectual capital. The target group of Milestone I is the management of the organisation which can define measures for improvement on the basis of the results.
- *Milestone II* targets the same group but goes one step further in supporting self-evaluation with indicators. Thus, self-evaluation is given further concrete form and supported using facts. The collection and assessment of indicators is, at the same time, preparation for internal or external communication.
- *Milestone III* provides a processed document or a presentation of the organisation's intellectual capital. It is tailored for a specific (external and/or internal) target group and describes the most important information attractively and in a structured form.
- *Milestone IV* works out a full intellectual capital statement which is also suited to monitor the organisation. It integrates amongst other things correlation analyses and assessments which provide information on where the measures should be initiated in order to optimise business success.

The first draft of the intellectual capital statement is best implemented in a cohesive step-by-step project over a period of between 4 and 12 weeks. Different time allocations can be calculated for the effort, depending on the initial situation and number of individuals involved. As a minimum, Milestone I demands an effort of half a work-month. Up to three work-months can be required for full implementation up to Milestone IV. The goals pursued with the intellectual capital statements should always be synchronised with the milestones. This makes it possible to implement the intellectual capital statement in a cost-effective, result oriented and step-by-step manner.

### Danish Guideline for Intellectual Capital Statements

Following a 2-year research project, Danish Agency for Trade and Industry published the first *"Guideline for Intellectual Capital Statements"* in November 2000.[5]

---

[5] Danish Ministry of Science, Technology and Innovation (Hrsg.) (2002), "Intellectual Capital Statements in Practice – Inspiration and Good Advice", p. 3. http://www.videnskabsministeriet.dk/fsk/publ/2002/intellectualcapstatements/intcapst.pdf [15-08-2002].

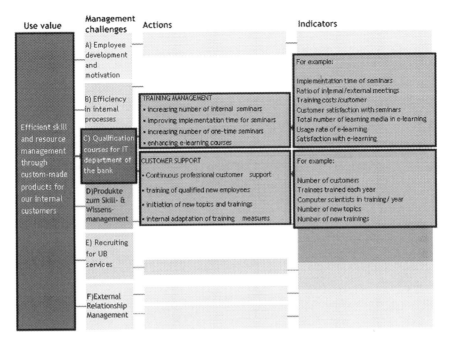

**Fig. 8.7** Implementation of Danish guideline for IT skill resources department of a bank (an extract)

The intellectual capital statement begins with a *knowledge narrative*. Based on the customer requirements, the *use value* of a company's product is presented to the customer. This gives an idea of the extent to which the features of the product, that create value for the customer, depend on the company's intellectual capital.

This future knowledge-oriented strategy is subsequently broken down in a set of different objectives – *the management challenges*.

In the third step, *actions* are derived from such challenges. Actions are operative measures necessary for achieving knowledge objectives. In order to make their effect measurable with reference to the set objectives, actions are supported with *indicators*. The development of the intellectual capital in the previous period can be read and new goals can be set for the following period from the realisation level of the ascertained goals.

The findings of these processes are interpreted in the intellectual capital report and presented to the internal and external target groups in different details.

The implementation of these process components within IT skill resources is shown with examples in Fig. 8.7. Based on the guidelines, certain goals, measures and indicators were defined with the respective team leaders. Finally, 84 different key figures were measured considering two deadlines. An intellectual capital statement is divided into human capital (objective A), structural capital (objective B) and relational capital (objective C with F) along the formulated objectives. In order to achieve the objective of "qualification courses for the IT area of the bank", it is necessary to take different measures in the field of training management and customer service (cf. Fig. 8.7). They are measured by means of the described indicators and evaluated within the intellectual capital statement. By means of this intellectual capital statement, it is possible to read the development of intellectual capital of a unit over the course of time as well as with reference to the goals set for oneself.

## 8.3    The Multi-stage Indicator Model

The model developed by North, Probst and Romhardt (1998) is composed of a multi-stage indicator system that separates the indicators of knowledge base, interventions, transfer effects and results of business activity. This model (Fig. 8.8) shows how company objectives can be achieved through targeted interventions in the organisational knowledge base and whether the results can be measured/can be made measurable.

Considering our processes of measuring knowledge, there are four classes of indicators.

*Indicator class 1* describes the organisational knowledge base.

*Indicator class 2* describes inputs and processes as measurable factors of interventions for changing the organisational knowledge base.

*Indicator class 3* measures intermediate results and transfer effects.

*Indicator class 4* measures financial as well as non-financial results.

Using this model, it is possible to create a cause-effect correlation and measure changes in the organisational knowledge base with reference to business results.

We will use the aforementioned indicator system to explain the following example of a case study of a home and savings association.

### Case: Intellectual capital statement of a home loan bank
#### Initial situation

A home and savings association with 800 part-time external staff wishes to improve customer service and contract contingent for two of its most popular construction-financing products by introducing an expert system built on modern information and communication technology. For this purpose, the following company objectives should be operationalised:

• Improved quality of advice,
• Lower cancellation rate,
• Higher premium volumes
• Reduced consulting expenses

The intellectual capital statement at the beginning of the business year, (time $T_0$, indicator class 1), shows for the employees a training level between secondary school (two third of employees) and school leaving examination, with subsequent administrative training (one third of employees), conservative attitudes that confront the use of experts system sceptically in absence of customer, a high variance of product competence measured through self-evaluation and a competence for using information and communication technology that is marked by the dominance of the popular windows applications.

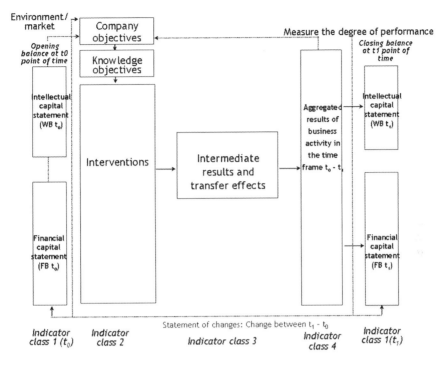

**Fig. 8.8**  Process of measuring and transforming knowledge

In the internal structure, the process of advising and closing deals are less structured and supported rudimentarily by information and communication technology. The ICT structure is characterised by individual laptops of external advisors who have not yet been linked and do not have access to a central server. In the external structure, the customer relationships are affected not only by ample loyalty but also by a certain amount of dissatisfaction over the lack of ability of the external staff to provide information.

**Actions**

The following interventions (indicator class 2) were made in the organisational knowledge base for achieving the knowledge objectives:

- An expert system was developed.
- 800 PCs of the field staff were made capable of multimedia.
- In 3 days, all the 800 external staffs were trained to use the new software and the changed method of desired customer dialogue.
- Over a year, the competence of the field staff in dealing with the new software and the desired behaviour towards the customer was improved in a coaching process wherein the regional groups shared their experiences.

At this level of intervention, the indicators measure the input that can also be expressed in monetary form. In our example, the input indicators appear as follows:

- Development of software: 16 employee months, information and communication inputs, and creation of a CD-ROM.
- Upgrading the PCs: 800 multimedia upgrade sets for laptops.
- Training: Cost of trainer, cost of rent of premises/logistics, unpaid investment of external staff, 3 days of training × 800 – 2,400 employee days and coaching user groups: X days experienced coach.
- Travelling cost, logistics and 800 external staff.
- Unpaid expenses of external staff: 4 × 0.5 days × 800 = 1,600 days.

**Intermediate result**

The intervention in the knowledge base of a company creates measurable intermediate results (indicator class 3) of quantitative and qualitative form. We can describe them as follows: Availability of expert system across the group, 760 external personnel passed the counselling interview with test-customers successfully, 20 employees were retrained and 20 others were rejected because they were not willing to work or were incapable of working with the expert system. The third quarter of the year witnessed an increase in business volumes and reduction in contract cancellations. In their own log sheet, the external staff recorded reduction in time taken by them to close a deal.

The following business results (indicator class 4) were seen at the end of the business year $(T_1)$:

- Business volume increased by 15 % but volume per employee increased only by 17.5 % because the rejected external employees were not replaced.
- External product testing of home and savings association and insurance companies reveals an improved image and a higher customer satisfaction with the quality of advice.

Thus, the set company objectives are achieved. The change in organisational knowledge base is reflected in the year-end intellectual capital statement (final balance sheet). The external staff confronts the multimedia-supported deals and customer dialogue positively. They have improved their product competence for selling products A and B. Simultaneously, they have also improved their competence pertaining to information and communication technology. The value of the internal structure has increased by PC upgrades, information and communication structure and improvement in processes of customer counselling and closing deals. But none of these processes can be evaluated detached from the employees. However, employee experience is documented and codified in an expert system so that it is possible to train new employees quickly. This "shortened learning curve" accelerates the growth process of the company. The changes to the external structure refer to an improvement in the customer relations by increasing customer satisfaction and gaining new customers (15 % increase in volume refers to new customers). The value of the brand increases due to the image of the company as a modern service provider. These new customer relationships can also have financial implications, e.g. increase of value of a customer of a home and savings association.

## Evaluation of IC Reporting Approaches

Which conclusions can be drawn from the explanation of the IC reporting models above?

There is no *one* particular model yet for accounting the intellectual capital because each approach has strengths and weaknesses. The weaknesses particularly refer to standardisation and objectified methods as well as informative value for internal and external target groups.

All the models evaluate intellectual capital with the help of a set of indicators as opposed to aggregated key figures and present cause-and-effect relation to a certain extent. Thus, the models prove to be advantageous for evaluating internal processes are of limited value to an outsider.

The present communication of results is a central aspect of IC reporting because companies publish Intellectual Capital Reports willingly without any statutory provisions. Thus, today many companies balance their intellectual capital to position themselves externally as an innovative company rather than for internal purposes. Accordingly, there is a lot of interest in presenting positive results. Intellectual capital statements may be a marketing instrument in danger of "window dressing".

The size of the company is a restrictive factor. Today, primarily smaller companies or units are balancing their intellectual capital. The desire for objectivity incorporates a number of objectives, success factors, data clusters and correlation between these elements in the analysis. Therefore, the models should be oriented at smaller units within this company.

Publishing sensitive, internal data has a negative effect on competitive advantages of a company. Often, the extent of this effect goes unnoticed. The field of innovations itself comprises this aspect that clearly pleads for a differentiation between creation of internal and external reports. Even if the necessity for such differentiation is mentioned in the model, it does not provide any approaches for a concrete course of action. Hence, there is a risk that the published balance sheets would include only those values that have little informative significance or would have been derivable anyway from other sources. This would contradict the original approach of uncovering hidden assets which use knowledge accounting and are largely responsible for creating explanatory gaps between market value and book value of a company.

Even the investors should make themselves familiar with this new type of capital and its accounting. This is because the intellectual capital statement is actually generated only if it is read and interpreted by management and investors correctly. The present debate on the implementation of new rules for lending by banks offers a big chance of bringing the topic of intellectual capital statement out in public. The Brazilian Development Bank BNDES, for example, evaluates Intellectual Capital and intangible assets to determine prospects of competitiveness as a basis of giving major loans. The extent of success in developing transparent, comparable and significant levels will decide whether the intellectual capital report will find its place or will remain purely a marketing instrument.

## 8.4    Protecting Knowledge

As a result of the measurement of Intellectual Capital, companies are often more aware of what significance is being assigned to their intangible assets. Companies often wonder about ways to protect themselves against complete loss or loss in value of knowledge as well as prevent or reduce knowledge-related risks. As we have seen in the previous chapters, knowledge lives in the brains of employees, is stored as information in the respective systems, takes a concrete form in processes as well as technologies and is legally safeguarded by patents, licences and corresponding contracts.

The dilemma of knowledge protection and knowledge sharing is of particular interest in a increasingly networked economy (Hurmelinna-Laukkanen and Tarkiainenen (2011). The conflicts between the two are easy to pinpoint: if certain intangibles are protected against copying and imitation, the firm is typically not willing to let others use those assets freely, and certainly not without compensation. Moreover, many protection mechanisms inherently make knowledge exchange impossible or highly difficult, and firms relying on those mechanisms are often bound to keep the knowledge within the firm – whether they want it or not. On the other hand, the firm can choose to provide other firms with an access to its knowledge assets, in which case it typically needs to put keeping secrets aside. Networking and collaboration for innovation presents one area, where knowledge exchange is imperative for reaching the wanted outcomes.

Considering the chances of an enterprise to reap profits from its know-how, the first thought is that it should reach the position of the sole beneficiary of the knowledge assets – or at least being the one to control the use of these assets. In other words, appropriability mechanisms should enable keeping certain technological or operational advances secured from the use of anyone else. Intellectual property rights (IPRs) are by definition designed to protect intellectual creations and aim at granting the creator the rights that provide certain ownership over the intangibles and at fostering diffusion of ideas and further innovative creations IPRs create barriers against harmful imitation. However, intellectual property protection is only one among many barriers to imitation.

## Loss of Knowledge: The Organisation Forgets

The knowledge asset can suffer damage either because it is lost due to changes of employees and employee teams or because it loses its value due to innovations. The effect of loss of knowledge and unavailability of knowledge are similar. Figure 8.9 describes the forms of knowledge loss based on individual and collective loss of employees as well as loss and unavailability of electronically stored information.

| Mode \ Type | | Individual | Collective | Electronic |
|---|---|---|---|---|
| Memory has been deleted | | ❏ Termination ❏ retirement ❏ death ❏ ... | ❏ dissolving adjusted teams ❏ reengineering ❏ outsourcing functional areas | ❏ Irreversible data loss through: ❏   virus ❏   hardware errors ❏   system crash ❏     insufficient back up |
| Access not possible | Limited | ❏ overload ❏ transfers ❏ illness/vacation ❏ inadequate training ❏ service according to regulations | ❏ making taboo of routines ❏ collective sabotage | ❏ reversible data loss ❏ overload/limited ❏ interface problems |
| | Permanent | ❏ overload ❏ no awareness of importance of own knowledge ❏ inner termination | ❏ sales of company divisions ❏ migration of teams ❏ ... | ❏ permanent incompatibility of systems ❏ overload/permanent ❏ wrong codification |

**Fig. 8.9**  How do organisations forget? (Source: According to Probst et al. 1997, p. 311)

## Ways of Safeguarding Knowledge

A company can protect itself from loss or devaluation of knowledge by taking three types of measures – employee-related, technical and legal.

*Employee-related measures* establish conditions to ensure that qualified employees are retained in the company, knowledge is constantly passed on to colleagues and as far as it is relevant, continues to be available even after an employee leaves the company. The value of employees' knowledge can be safeguarded by continuous training and development combined with practical application of knowledge. Furthermore, knowledge can be safeguarded by identifying key employees and evaluating the value of their knowledge for the company. Employees should have a feeling that their knowledge is at least as valuable in the company as outside. This not only involves matters of compensation but also handling competent employees in the company and their job and labour facilities. Allocating positions at the right time, familiarising new employees with the work and using valuable knowledge of employees after they leave the company are some other ways of preventing loss of knowledge.

Systematic transfer of knowledge to the next generation of employees has gained a lot of importance, especially against the backdrop of demographic development.

The following are some principles that should be considered during knowledge transfer:

- *Motivation*: Senior management should highlight the need and trigger and control the process of sharing knowledge across generations of employees.
- *Recognition*: Reward successful knowledge transfer by way of monetary incentive if need be or in target-setting for present and newly recruited employees if necessary.
- *Involving in work groups*: Organise the tasks in such a way that an experienced employee is included in a work group, mentoring or shadowing concepts are helpful.
- *From push to pull*: Do not ask the leaving employee to "*just write everything down*" and push-out his knowledge. Instead, ensure that successors may pull relevant experience.
- *From managing to advising*: Use the experience gained by working on projects to provide advice to new project teams. For example the construction manager will step aside sometime before retirement and become a consultant of the construction team.
  - *Future-orientation*: In a fast changing business environment many past experiences are not longer relevant in the future. Rather address questions like: What would you have willingly implemented if you had time? What potential business strategies do you perceive?
- *Integration in business processes*: Make knowledge transfer an integral part of daily business by defining clear organisational measures.

### Case: Volkswagen's knowledge relay

With the knowledge relay, the experts of the Volkswagen's knowledge management team have developed an instrument that ensures optimum transfer of specialist, expert and project knowledge to the successors and assures valuable learning to the company. Custom-made expert interviews are the main highlight of this process. They are organised, moderated and documented by a team of specialists so that the participants can concentrate completely on communicating and receiving knowledge. Three different methods were developed under knowledge courier. The first method for change in discipline focuses on transfer of specialist knowledge, the second method for change in leadership emphasises transfer of "relational knowledge" and experience, and the third method for project closure is based on identifying the lessons learnt.

The course of such methods is explained below with help of an example of change in leadership:

The quality assurance manager at VW plant in China was just about to retire. His successor, who came from a managerial position of another company, should give his best in this new position – but how? A new company, a new plant, new colleagues and a predecessor who was about to retire were all waiting for him. VW plant wanted to retain the knowledge of their long-tenured quality assurance manager within the company. His experience primarily comprised important contacts, experiences, processes and organisational procedures.

A handover session was organised between the predecessor and the successor as well as between the successor and his seniors. The session helped the participants to get to know each other, exchange experience, build trust and establish a positive relation. This dialogue was designed and prepared very well by the specialists beforehand. By means of a subject catalogue and support of advisors, the predecessor and successor decided independently over topics that were important from their perspective and about which they wanted to talk to each other. The successor invested five evenings with advisors of Volkswagen management to filter out questions that were important for him and to identify the persons to whom these questions were to be asked. They worked with mind maps. A tree was generated from each topic and every branch corresponded to a sub-topic, a question. The questions were checked for redundancy and it was ensured that the questions were not repeated. The actual handover discussion not only included numbers, organigram, quality and budget but also involved important key persons or dealing with a secretary. A one-day seminar – a Transition Workshop – was held with the new manage, the outgoing manager and all employees. This created a foundation for interaction between the new management and the employees. The employees bombarded the new comer with questions like 'How do you encourage your employees?' or 'What is unacceptable to you?' In doing so, the new comer could learn something about his team. Supported by a competent moderator and coupled with knowledge of the predecessor, the successor managed to make an optimum start in the new role. In case of a change in discipline, the knowledge management team calls for IT-supported documentation in addition to personal interviews and expert interviews.

Source: www.volkswagen-coaching.de.

The second form of safeguarding knowledge is using **technical systems.** Elements of explicit knowledge can be stored as information in the databases such as project profile, customer contacts, presentations, etc. Furthermore, knowledge of employees becomes an integral component of processes or technologies. Knowledge becomes explicit and is given a concrete form as employees contribute in increasing productivity and quality in continuous improvement processes. Technical systems are capable of storing explicit knowledge. Implicit knowledge takes a concrete form in the behaviour of employees. Technical systems are also suitable for controlling selective access to information, laboratories, buildings, etc. thus allowing only specific employees to access information and knowledge. Thus, information and knowledge are protected from unauthorised use.

Knowledge is **legally protected** by patents, license contracts, franchising contracts or know-how contracts of external knowledge bearers with alliance partners, suppliers and customers. However, contracts alone cannot provide complete protection against loss of knowledge as knowledge is held by employees who perceive it as power. The loss of implicit knowledge caused by leaving employees is generally more significant than the loss caused by the illegal transfer of documented explicit knowledge. Generally, legal safeguarding protects companies against imitation only for a certain period of time and ensures exclusive use of innovation for this period. Patents have less importance in industry sectors having a very high rate of innovation such as electronic industry, as against pharmaceutical or chemical industries which have long development time frames and product lifecycles.

Harvey and Lusch (1997) suggest a security plan for intangible assets similar to the one for tangible assets. Such a plan should analyse and find out which knowledge losses are most consequential for a company. Based on this, it is necessary to determine preventive options of knowledge protection and execute them systematically. Among other things, Harvey and Lusch suggest that the company should think about how much they spend on protecting their tangible assets considering the value of these assets and they transfer this percentage even on the intangible assets. This approach can contribute to the awareness that the intangible assets of a company should be protected as much as tangible assets. It is also advocated to create the role of an "intangible assets risk manager".

### Case Study: Better use of patents at Dow Chemical (Petrash 1996)

Dow manufactures approximately 2,000 chemical products in 15 business units over 40 joint ventures worldwide. With a turnover of approximately 20 billion US dollars (of which approximately 1 billion goes in R&D) and about 4,000 employees, Dow owns approximately 25,000 patents and spends about 30 million US dollars every year for patent management. Because of inadequate overview of the patents, Dow set a goal of using its patent know-how in a better way and developing it systematically. Dow chose the following procedure for this purpose:

1. *Creating patent portfolio for every business unit*: Identify all the patents. Find out whether they are still active. Find the business unit that gains benefit from the patent or sponsors it (i.e. bears the costs related to the maintenance of the patent).
2. *Rating the use of patents*: Rate the patents as per the criteria such as "is used", "will be used", "will not be used" etc. Take decisions pertaining to the patents belonging to the categories "will not be used", "abandon patents", "search possible licence numbers", etc.
3. *Integrating the patent portfolios in the company strategy*: Check how the existing patents can be integrated in the business strategy in order to use the knowledge optimally. Identify 'know-how gaps' that arise while implementing the business strategy. Think how the missing know-how can be obtained externally or developed and stored internally.
4. *Supporting the strategy by reviewing technology and conducting technological analysis of competition*: Estimate the value of the existing patents and the possible cost of purchasing external know-how or developing the know-how. Systematise the patents as per technological criteria and conduct a technological analysis of the competition (Dow uses a "patent tree" for systemisation).

5. *Investments in the patent portfolio*: Decide about acquiring and developing additional know-how according to the points 3 and 4. Use the 'not required' patents existing externally (waiver, licensing). Since many of the 'not required' patents have a little value, Dow took the path to abandon these patents by bestowing them on universities and similar institutions so that they can perhaps be used in such institutions.

6. *Managing the patent process*: Install decentralised responsibility for the patent management. Dow has launched over 75 "*Intellectual Asset Management Teams*". These teams are responsible for managing patents at the business unit level. The management of different functional areas of a business unit meets 2–3 times every year to discuss about improving the patent process and using patents. This team of managers is lead by an Intellectual Asset Manager.

7. *Supporting the decentralised patent management by a central technology management*: Through a tech-centre, Dow supports the decentralised activities of the developing technology by systematising knowledge as per the themes, building networks of experts, updating information systems, conducting training and advance training and supporting the decentralised patent management process. Furthermore, the tech-centre should plan and systematise the business strategy keeping the development of "intellectual assets" in mind.

As per the information provided by the company, the improved patent management has yielded over 40 million US dollar to the additional capital and reserve for the business areas until now.

Source: Petrash (1996), S. 365–373.

## 8.5 Key Insights of Chapter 8

- With the increasing sensitisation for the importance of knowledge as a resource, the companies are looking for options for describing and evaluating knowledge and measuring the excellence of a knowledge-oriented management process.
- There are a number of approaches to structuring and evaluating intellectual capital. The "one best method", however does not exist. The implementation of these new approaches in practice is impeded not only by concrete description of organisational knowledge base of a company but also by lack of available of data.
- It is not possible to create a universally valid set of "ten most important knowledge indicators". Each organisation has to define organisation-specific and context-specific indicator systems.
- A company can secure itself from loss or devaluation of knowledge by means of employee related measures, technical systems and legal measures.

## 8.6     Questions

1. 'What can be measured is not always important and what is important cannot always be measured'. Discuss this in the context of intellectual capital reporting.
2. Traditional lending models look for a history of profitability, tangible assets and a reasonably predictable business environment. Knowledge-based businesses do not fit this paradigm'. Discuss.
3. Which components of intellectual capital are usually considered in intellectual capital reporting?
4. Identify the major knowledge assets/components of intellectual capital in an educational institution/university/business school and indicate why you consider them to be assets
5. What can an organisation do in order not to lose important knowledge?

## 8.7     Assignments

1. **Intellectual capital reporting**
   Establish an outline of an intellectual capital report for a business school based on the INCAs- methodology.

2. **Intellectual capital risk management**
   You have been assigned the new position of "Intellectual capital risk officer". Your mission is to identify risks to loss and devaluation of intellectual assets and propose preventive measures.
   **You are asked to develop an action plan**

## 8.8     KM-Tool: Knowledge Inventory

**What is a knowledge inventory?**
   A knowledge inventory is a form of stock taking used to identify and locate knowledge assets around the organisation. This includes the explicit and the very difficult to locate tacit knowledge sources. We suggest that the inventory be focused on specific topic and knowledge areas; for example "What do we know about customers, where is this knowledge located? How and where is it available?"

**Why use a knowledge inventory?**
- Provides a mapping or quick overview over your existing knowledge assets
- Identifies gaps ("What we should know and do not know")
- Gives us hints hoe to improve availability and accessibility of knowledge
- Can be a preparation for a more elaborated intellectual capital reporting

**How to develop a knowledge inventory?**

1. Demarcate a clear topic area (e.g. products, technologies, processes, customers, etc.)
2. The best way to make a comprehensive list of knowledge sources is to segregate it by explicit and tacit knowledge.
3. Some of the questions you might want to ask when **identifying explicit knowledge sources** are:
   - What explicit knowledge already exists? – Categories of documents, databases, intranet libraries, links etc.
   - Where this knowledge is located? – Locations in the organisations and the various systems that house the information.
   - Access and Organisation – How is the knowledge structured and how easy of difficult is it for people to locate this information, and do they have access to it as well.
   - Purpose and relevance – why does the information exist? How relevant is it to the users?
   - Usage – who uses them? How often?
        **Identifying tacit knowledge sources** is an entirely different proposition. Unlike explicit knowledge, tacit knowledge is much more difficult to quantify. Though there are a few questions you could ask to create a rough map of where it exists.
   - Who we have – The numbers and categories of people working in the organisation.
   - Where they are – Identifying where people are located is extremely important when building a tacit knowledge map
   - What they do and what they know – job profiles, expertise areas and so on.
        The above questions should give you an excellent place to start collating the list of knowledge sources you have in your organisation. Once this is done you can move on to the next step of identifying the gaps after comparing this information to the information you've garnered from the knowledge audit.

Source/link:        http://itsallkm.wordpress.com/2007/03/12/what-is-a-knowledge-inventory/

   http://www.kmtalk.net/article.php?story=20060905001530455

# How to Put Knowledge Management into Practice

9

*The greatest danger in times of change is not the turbulence –*
*it is to act with yesterday's logic* – Peter Drucker

**Learning Outcomes.** After completing this chapter
- You will know what the challenges and governance options of KM are in organisations;
- You will be able to select a KM implementation framework that suits the need of your organisation;
- You will know which eight steps should be considered in leading change;
- You will be able to name the key competences of knowledge workers;
- You will be able to carry-out a work-out session.

## 9.1 Shaping the knowledge organisation of the future

In a constantly turbulent and complex environment, knowledge management should be able to support organisations in developing their "dynamic capabilities" for reconfiguring, redirecting and integrating core competencies with external resources. (*"Dynamic capabilities are the ability to reconfigure, redirect, transform, and appropriately shape and integrate existing core competences with external resources and strategic and complementary assets to meet the challenges of a time-pressured, rapidly changing Schumpeterian world of competition and imitation."*) (Teece et al. 2000, p. 339)

At the same time, this "dynamization" is the core process of future KM. In an environment that is characterised by unpredictable, varying and "unexpected" crisis situations, knowledge management encourages swift problem solving, permanent experimenting, and quick collective learning as well as living with mistakes. This also implies a series of changes to how organisational knowledge management should be designed in the future.

K. North and G. Kumta, *Knowledge Management,*
Springer Texts in Business and Economics, DOI 10.1007/978-3-319-03698-4_9,
© Springer International Publishing Switzerland 2014

**Table 9.1** Differences between KM in stable and turbulent contexts

| Knowledge management in stable context | Knowledge management in turbulent context |
|---|---|
| Codify knowledge and document process | Share tacit knowledge |
| Build on experiences | Develop ability to learn fast and "turbo problem-solving" |
| Disseminate 'Best Practices' | Develop "Next Practices" |
| Ensure knowledge transfer across employee generations | Facilitate ad-hoc availability of knowledge |

Organisations will need to give up attempts to force knowledge into an orderly manageable and achievable form. In the future, organisations would need to carefully consider when it is worth the effort to make knowledge explicit and document it or whether it is more effective to switch over to creating collective implicit knowledge (process of socialisation) in rapidly changing situations.

*The knowledge organisation of the future* will need to further increase its learning ability and develop methods for finding quick solutions across organisational boundaries. How much energy should be spent in identifying and transferring "Best Practices", if rapid changes instead demand the development of "Next Practices"? Table 9.1 displays some of the challenges of practising KM in turbulent environments.

Knowledge management of the future is hence closely coupled with strategy, innovation management and personnel development which encourage the dynamisation of organisations. It

1. Focuses on competition-relevant knowledge and supports competency ("Selective Knowledge Management" Howald et al. 2004);
2. Defines and complies with normative standards and routines of documentation, of knowledge exchange, of learning and of knowledge protection (e.g. when should After Action Reviews be carried out and how should their results be integrated in future value creating process?);
3. Offers professional services for "dynamization of knowledge" (turbo problem solving, innovation workshops, knowledge carriers, organising exchange forums such as knowledge markets, support of CoP, etc.)

These tasks can be accomplished by different *governance options of KM functions* in an organisation.

The task of *focusing on competition-relevant knowledge and supporting relevant competency development* can be accomplished by setting-up an "expert organization" which includes *competence centers* for priority areas relevant for supporting present business and relevant for future business development, naming *subject matter experts* charged with systematisation and dissemination of relevant know-how as well as *communities of practice* linking expertise across the organisation and to the outside. As those professionals having technical expertise usually do not have experience about ways to document, share and learn they need either to be trained on these issues or be supported by professional KM services (see below).

The task of *setting and monitoring compliance* with normative standards and routines can be best accomplished if KM is attached to functions already in charge of standards and procedures such as quality management, process & information management or organisational development. In these functions usually a central unit and decentralised roles are combined to ensure implementation in all units of the organisation. This means for example having a central knowledge manager attached to quality or information management and a network of quality or information managers in the business units who depending on the size of the unit might be a full-time job or a role occupying 10 % of a professional's time.

The task of providing *professional KM services* can be accomplished by different options. An effective one is to attach KM services to in-house consulting services. Another is to place KM services within the context of corporate universities and training/coaching functions, thus strengthening the link between organisational learning and KM. A third option is to link KM to business development and innovation management.

Independent from the organisational anchoring the end point should be integration of KM in the daily practices of each employee, in each unit and the management structures of the organisation, just like other management disciplines such as financial, people, project or quality management. And just like these other disciplines, KM needs a management framework within which it can be embedded. Furthermore, knowledge workers need to develop the relevant skills to manage their information and knowledge.

## 9.2  KM Implementation Frameworks

A framework is a defined set of technologies and processes, embedded into business activity, and a defined set of roles embedded into the organisational structure, all under an umbrella of governance. Like other management systems, effective KM is a framework of roles, processes, technologies and governance which has been embedded into the business.[1] It is a change process which is not gradual but a step-change. It is a remodelling of the organisation; a make-over, a new way of thinking that needs to be treated and measured as a change process. Don't go into KM thinking that it is about a new IT tool, or just "trying out communities" – you won't get far if you don't start to address the hearts and minds. This also means that KM implementation must be structured like a change program (including a piloting component), and must have a strong team of change agents to implement the change.[2]

Introducing KM into an organisation will not happen by accident. It will only happen if someone makes a deliberate decision. Very few CEOs wake up one morning and 'decide' to implement KM. Instead, like any other practice,

---

[1] For an overview of KM frameworks see Wong and Aspinwall (2004); Liebowitz and Megbolugbe (2003).

[2] Knoco stories: Top 7 tips for knowledge management success http://www.nickmilton.com/2011/09/top-7-tips-for-knowledge-management.html.

implementation of KM results from a series of decisions, and each decision rests on evidence (Milton and Young 2007).

Implementing a KM system can be complex and dynamic, no matter how well planned and developed it might be. Inevitably a degree of organisational inertia is focused on the *current* rather than the *new*. Within an enterprise, personal and group interests can adversely affect the commitment needed to successfully implement such a system. The best way to ensure KM system value and overall proper implementation is to focus on enterprise performance as it relates to customer benefit (Bixler 2002).

In the following we will present some frameworks for KM implementation.

## Business Excellence Models as an Overarching Framework

One option is to integrate KM initiatives in a Business Excellence framework. Business Excellence (BE) aims at developing and strengthening the management systems and processes of an organisation to improve performance and create value for stakeholders. BE is about achieving excellence in everything that an organisation does (including leadership, strategy, customer focus, information management, people and processes) and most importantly achieving superior business results.

Business Excellence Models – first called Total Quality Management Models – are now used in around 90 countries as a key mechanism to help businesses to improve.[3]

There are several quite similar models in use around the world: The Baldrige Criteria for Performance Excellence (CPE) which is used in the United States but has been adopted in many countries in Asia. The leading model in Europe is the EFQM Model (European Foundation of Quality Management, www.efqm.org). For the public sector a "Common assessment Framework" (CAF, www.eipa.eu) based on the EFQM Model is in use in many European countries. These excellence models usually start with a self-analysis followed by the determination of priority actions and a change and implementation process along the PDCA-cycle (Plan, Do, Check, Act). In order to integrate KM initiatives in a Business Excellence framework in Table 9.2 we summarise KM objectives in relation to the Baldrige Criteria for Performance Excellence which are also closely related to the criteria used by the EFQM Model.

---

[3] Adapted from http://www.apo-tokyo.org/coe/files/Understanding-Business-Excellence.pdf

**Table 9.2**  Knowledge management objectives linked to the Baldrige criteria for performance excellence

| Baldrige criteria for performance excellence | Link to knowledge management |
| --- | --- |
| 1. *Leadership*: examines how your organisation's senior leaders' personal actions guide and sustain your organisation. Also examined are your organisation's governance system and how your organisation fulfills its legal, ethical, and societal responsibilities and supports its key communities | Leaders recognise the link between KM and performance, the right attitudes exist to share and use others' know-how, leaders reinforce the right behaviour and act as role models |
| 2. *Strategic Planning*: examines how your organisation develops strategic objectives and action plans, how your chosen strategic objectives and action plans are implemented and changed | Clearly identified Intellectual assets KM strategy is embedded in the business strategy. Framework and tools enable learning before, during and after |
| 3. *Customer Focus*: examines how your organisation engages its customers for long-term marketplace success. This includes how your organisation listens to the voice of its customers, builds customer relationships, and uses customer information to improve and identify opportunities for innovation | Networks and CoPs and open innovation with customers, effective learning routines with and from (potential) customers |
| 4. *Measurement, Analysis, and Knowledge Management*: examines how your organisation selects, gathers, analyses, manages, and improves its data, information, and knowledge assets and how it manages its information technology | A KM action plan and resources for KM exist, Knowledge is easy to get to, easy to retrieve. It is constantly refreshed and distilled |
| 5. *Workforce Focus*: examines your ability to assess workforce capability and capacity needs and build a work force environment conducive to high performance | Skill/competence management is linked to business objectives and personal development goals. A wide variety of learning formats are in use Incentive systems contribute to align behaviour |
| 6. *Operations Focus*: examines how your organisation designs, manages, and improves its work systems and work processes to deliver customer value and achieve organisational success and sustainability. Also examined is your readiness for emergencies | Processes are documented, "Best Practices" are systematically identified and disseminated; quick problem solving routines tapping all required knowledge (e.g. work out approach) are applied |
| 7. Results: examines your organisation's performance and improvement in all key areas – product and process outcomes, customer-focused outcomes, workforce-focused outcomes, leadership and governance outcomes, and financial and market outcomes | Indicators measuring the quality of knowledge management are in use; intellectual assets are evaluated regularly. Competitive Benchmarking allows to learn from best performers |

## Step Approach Frameworks to KM

KM initiatives require a change process in the organisation. Therefore several frameworks define a sequence of steps inspired by change management approaches to guide the implementation of KM practices within an organisation. Wiig's "Building Blocks", North's "knowledge ladder" and Nihilent's $MC^3$ are such frameworks

### Building blocks according to Wiig

Wiig (1999) introduced a set of 16 common building blocks in a step-wise manner to guide the introduction of KM practices in an organisation. They were presented in the following order of implementation:

1. Obtain management buy-in.
2. Survey and map the knowledge landscape.
3. Plan the knowledge strategy.
4. Create and define knowledge-related alternatives and potential initiatives.
5. Portray benefit expectations for knowledge management initiatives.
6. Set knowledge management priorities.
7. Determine key knowledge requirements.
8. Acquire key knowledge.
9. Create integrated knowledge transfer programmes.
10. Transform, distribute and apply knowledge assets.
11. Establish and update a KM infrastructure.
12. Manage knowledge assets.
13. Construct incentive programmes.
14. Coordinate KM activities and functions enterprise-wide.
15. Facilitate knowledge-focused management.
16. Monitor knowledge management.

Accompanying these building blocks, Wiig discusses the purpose and characteristics of each building block and provided examples of KM activities to introduce them.

## A KM Implementation Framework Based on the "Knowledge Ladder"

In Chap. 2 we have explained the "knowledge ladder" visualising the steps of knowledge based value creation. The knowledge ladder has also proved a practical framework to implement knowledge management in a modular way. The challenge of implementing KM is on the one hand to provide "quick wins" addressing priority problems and on the other hand to integrate these actions into a longer and more comprehensive perspective towards a learning organisation.

Therefore we have defined five modules or components which can be used as work packages for a KM project. As a result of a KM self-analysis (see Chap. 1) objectives for each work package as well as measures can be defined. Below you will find a suggestion for formulation of objectives as well as typical measures related to achieving the objective. You can start at any step of the knowledge ladder provided you do not lose a long-term perspective of completing all five components (see Fig. 9.1).

### *1st Component: knowledge strategy*

*Objective:* Knowledge and learning are integral components of corporate strategy. Core competencies and knowledge goals are derived from the strategy and turned into measures for developing competencies and safeguarding knowledge.

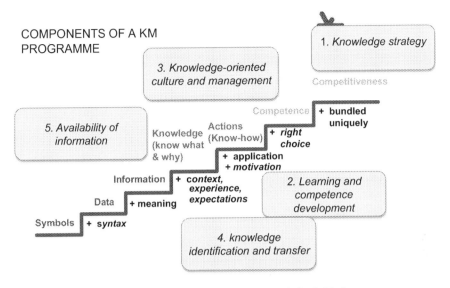

COMPONENTS OF A KM PROGRAMME

*1. Knowledge strategy*

*3. Knowledge-oriented culture and management*

Competitiveness

*5. Availability of information*

Knowledge (know what & why)

Actions (Know-how)

Competence

**+ bundled uniquely**

**+ right choice**

**+ application**
**+ motivation**

Information

**+ context, experience, expectations**

Data **+ meaning**

*2. Learning and competence development*

Symbols **+ syntax**

*4. knowledge identification and transfer*

**Fig. 9.1**  KM implementation framework based on the "knowledge ladder"

*Measures for example:*

1. Identification, examination and communication of core competencies, periodical execution of a "strategic knowledge analysis" or development of an intellectual capital statement.
2. Competence centres or communities ensure development of core competencies and their incorporation in the performance process ("key topics").
3. Personal development is oriented towards core competencies and knowledge goals derived from them.

### 2nd Component: Learning and competence development

*Objective:* Competences of employee are evaluated systematically and their development is encouraged. Collective learning is integrated in business routine.

*Measures for example:*

1. Identifying competences and developing them by a systematic skill management and different forms of learning
2. Identifying key experts and integrating them into a team
3. Establishing competence centres for key themes and comprehensive performance processes.
4. Encouraging informal learning through CoP (communities of practice) and initiatives such as "colleagues learn from and with colleagues."
5. Learning in and from projects (project briefing/lessons learned) and integrating in quality management
6. Living in an "error culture" ("The error of the month")

### 3rd Component: Knowledge-oriented culture and management

*Objective:* A culture of sharing knowledge and cooperation is encouraged and followed systematically ("Sharing knowledge is power"). Management takes up the task of setting an example. Teamwork is the lived value of an open organisation.

*Measures for example:*

1. Creating reasons for exchange of knowledge (e.g. common breakfast, brown bag lunch, lunch bingo, etc.)
2. Encouraging exchange over levels of hierarchy (e.g. skip level meeting)
3. Incorporating competence development and knowledge transfer in employee appraisal
4. Encouraging knowledge transfer by rotating jobs, organising teams and planning substitutions
5. Providing time for exchange of knowledge
6. Playful motivation: "sharing knowledge earns you miles" and establishing awareness
7. Office architecture and communication zones encourage exchange of knowledge

### 4th Component: Knowledge identification and transfer

*Objective:* "Knowbodies" are identified and approachable ("Knowing who knows what"). Handover situations (orientation, preparation) are attended to systematically.

*Measures for example:*

1. Yellow pages, expert finder, company Facebook, or knowledge mail for identifying expertise
2. Orientation concept and orientation package for new employees
3. Accompanying handover situations

### 5th Component: Information availability

*Objective:* Information strategy is demand-oriented (role concept), easily accessible and retrievable (pull system), selected information is forwarded in structured and coherent form to potentially interested persons (push system) High-priority information is supervised by moderators who are responsible for regular updating and consolidating of information.

*Measures for example:*

1. User-based structuring of information and overall concept for decentralised databases as well as re-launching intranet
2. Implementing cross-departmental wikis and blogs
3. Cleanup day of databases: clearing, discarding, giving away, etc.

These components can be adapted according to necessity and can be implemented in a phased mid-term strategy.

**Case: Suggestions for knowledge management in a small to medium law firm**

1. Discuss KM challenge with partners. Choose one partner as KM officer, manager or coordinator (not to act in directive manner, but as driving force, coordinator and adviser behind the KM effort). KM needs to be recognised and started as a meaningful activity, important to the future of the firm. Inform all colleagues.

2. Defining key (major) areas of KM interest should be key practice and competency areas that the firm wants to develop may be 4–7 major areas of legal business, meaningful and prospective from client's and firm's point of view. KM will focus on these areas. All firm activities need not be covered.

3. Appoint 1–2 partners responsible for KM in each area in addition to doing client work and promotion.

4. Define objective(s) of KM for each area (becoming market leaders, offering new services, catching up with competition, improving quality, etc.) related to real business and firm strategy objectives, and client needs and requirements

5. Define key terms (taxonomy, thesaurus) for KM effort in each area – a limited number of key issues

6. Define database (traditional + computerised), including: project (case) profiles, presentations, literature, web links, directories, internal expertise, external experts and other sources, etc.)

7. Choose software solution adequate to coverage, objectives, volume and resources

8. Develop competency profile for each partner and lawyer in chosen key areas, e.g., rating knowledge of each in each area as basic-good-expert level (e.g. competence matrix)

9. Define individual development targets by areas (becoming a top expert, just keeping up-to-date, acquiring basic knowledge, ignoring the area, etc.). Link KM with individual development efforts.

10. Define with partners and all lawyers their individual roles and responsibilities for making inputs in the database and contributing to KM more generally

11. Focus the whole effort on future, from existing (past) documents and sources include selectively only essential know-how and sources that will remain important in the future

12. Among completed projects (client contracts) focus on those that were really important, that offer a lot of learning, that were in prospective markets, that could be easily replicated to save time, where the firm could develop its own internal standard, etc.

13. Do not produce any documents and files just for the sake of it; be very selective and rational

14. Organise (regular) knowledge-sharing events offering significant learning – on important current or completed projects, outcome of conferences, new legislation, new business trends and demands with new implications to legal work – always sticking to the key areas of business

15. Circulate only a minimum of information to all or most lawyers, but make sure that they get all the information that is imperative for them to know
16. Circulate and exchange some well-selected information and tips of wider professional and intellectual interest beyond the defined areas of business (ethics, conflict of interest, new trends in business and law, etc.).
17. Periodically, discuss the functioning and effectiveness of your system at partner meetings and with other lawyers and take corrective measures. Flexibility and adaptability are essential. Make sure that the system is alive!

## Nihilent's MC$^3$ Framework[4]

Organisations are like living organisms. In rapidly changing scenarios, they need to be constantly aware of their environment, sense opportunities and adapt quickly in order to win in the marketplace. This is the fundamental belief that gave birth to MC$^3$ – the world's first patented holistic learning and innovation framework that brings about knowledge-enabled transformation in organisations. MC$^3$ is the first patented framework of its kind focusing on Learning and Innovation (South Africa Patents Act 1978, No. 2002/1681) introduced by Nihilent, a global Consulting and Solutions Integration company headquartered in Pune, India.

The framework adopts a cybernetic (cause and effect) approach, since similar to the laws that govern nature everything a company does is governed by what it is. It is a framework that integrates people, process and technology, has a direct impact on business results and brings about not just an incremental change but a transformation in an enterprise.

The MC$^3$ framework truly transcends conventional change management boundaries. It emphasises the need to create a context for learning, problem solving and innovation through curiosity, thus increasing its capability to create new knowledge in terms of innovations, process improvements and better services.

When rephrased, the four constituents that symbolise MC$^3$ are (see also Fig. 9.2):

- **Motivation** to seek and collaborate
- **Capability** to create, capture and disseminate knowledge and information
- **Capacity** to leverage and institutionalise best practices
- **Calibrate** performance against predefined goals

The MC$^3$ framework aligns and percolates strategy to all levels in the organisation. It enables organisations to leverage their intellectual capital and, supported by appropriate technology, achieve business results. While application of the MC$^3$ framework is tailored to suit each organisation's requirements, it addresses the following constituents:

---

[4] Our Model http://www.mc3consulting.com/html/ourmodel/Framework.

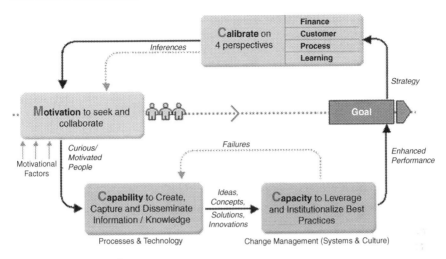

**Fig. 9.2** Nihilent's MC³ framework (Copyright © 2007 Nihilent Technologies Pvt. Ltd)

**Intent Management:** Create a mindset for learning and define a learning agenda tied to the business goal and encourage individuals to learn better and perform better.

**Content Management:** Facilitate capture of tacit knowledge from suppliers, customers and internal experts and acquire competitive and business intelligence.

**Action Management:** Apply the learning and thus change the way in which the organisation performs and,

**Performance Management:** Re-aligning individual goals with organisational goals and assessing and analysing performance based on these metrics.

**Calibration** is the first stage in the implementation of the framework.

It does the following:

- Calibrates the organisation across four crucial perspectives, namely: finance, customer, process and learning
- Generates learning agendas within the business context and
- Acts as an overall Performance Management System for the organisation.

The Calibration stage consists of three distinct processes:

- Balanced Scorecard Implementation
- Competency Assessment
- Knowledge Mapping

The Balanced Scorecard implementation provides clear and measurable targets to the organisation as a whole, the various departments within it, and to the roles within these departments. This provides the business context to everyone within the organisation. Competency assessment and knowledge mapping help in defining the learning agendas for individuals in this business context.

At the end of the **Calibration** exercise, individuals know what they are supposed to do and also become aware of the gaps in their capabilities and knowledge levels that could possibly hinder their progress in achieving their goals.

The **Motivation** exercise follows the calibration and motivates individuals to perform through group workshops and individual counselling.

It takes inputs from:

- The Competency Assessment exercise, which identifies gaps in the "soft" skills of the individual (like attitude, team building, etc.)
- The $MC^3$ Assessment exercise which identifies motivational gaps in the organisation as a whole.

Based on these inputs, people are categorised with respect to motivational levels (High, Medium and Low) and interventional workshops or individual counselling sessions are introduced depending on these categories. This exercise generates a highly focused and motivated work force that knows exactly what it has to do and how it is going to be measured in the business context.

The **Capability** exercise equips the organisation with the ability to aid this motivated, focused work force to learn, share, innovate and therefore bridge their knowledge gaps and the knowledge gaps of the organisation as a whole. Inputs are taken from the knowledge mapping exercise in the Calibration phase. This is typically a knowledge management exercise and breeds the essential learning habit within the organisation.

This phase requires two interventions:

**Non-technological interventions include**:

- Tacit knowledge to explicit knowledge externalisation
- Creating repositories of knowledge
- Inculcating Communities of Practice
- Gathering Competitive Intelligence
- Ideation and brainstorming techniques, etc.

**Enabling technology** also plays a large role in the knowledge management initiative. Examples of technology interventions are Collaborative tools, Employee portals, Business intelligence tools, Data marts, Document management systems and E-learning systems.

**Capacity** is the final stage of the $MC^3$ implementation process, where the organisation develops the capacity to institutionalise the successes from the previous exercise (Capacity) and scale it across the organisation. Processes which build sustained successes and augment the transformation of the enterprise are created.

This stage is also called Change Management because it equips the organisation with processes that manage the change that takes place in the organisation. $MC^3$ involves Change Management diagnostics which are immensely useful in this process.

"Change champions" are identified within the organisation and are instrumental in continuing the cycle and developing the sustained transformation that is so essential to excellence.

Even though this is the final stage of the $MC^3$ framework, it doesn't end here. Change management leads to Recalibration of performance. Newer and higher levels are targeted and the cycle repeats itself. The cycle has to repeat itself for the organisation to survive.

### Case: Share TRAnsactions Totally Electronic (STRATE)

Monica Singer, CEO of STRATE, the organisation that performed the electronic settlement of all equity trades in South Africa, was planning the way forward for the balanced scorecard driven knowledge management intervention that STRATE had implemented over the past 8 months. At the beginning, most of the knowledge about STRATE's business had resided with the consultants that had helped establish STRATE and the IT systems that were so critical to its functioning. What she initially thought to be a simple knowledge transfer exercise had actually resulted in a comprehensive organisational transformation and she was delighted with the outcome.

STRATE is the authorised Central Securities Depository (CSD) for the electronic settlement of financial instruments in South Africa. It is a regulated body formed by JSE Securities Exchange and five major banks of South Africa. Its core competencies include an IT infrastructure and application to serve the needs of the security trading market. Initially, STRATE handled only equity market operations. It then acquired Universal Exchange Corporation Ltd. (UNEXcor), which handles bond market depository, clearing and settlement operations. UNEXcor was entrusted with the responsibility of developing Money Market Clearing, settlement and depository operations. With this acquisition STRATE would be a major player in the electronic settlement of financial instruments in South Africa.

STRATE experienced amorphous growth in its short span of time. It outsourced most of its projects to external service providers and consultants especially in the Information Technology area including a world-class settlement system namely SAFIRES (South African Financial Instruments Real Time Electronic Settlement System). Most of the knowledge and expertise was with third party providers/consultants and STRATE paid high outsourcing costs.

Another challenge that STRATE faced was that business and technology experts were wrapped in silos affecting productivity and hence "time-to-market". There were low levels of communication between staff and management leading to divided focus on long term and short-term goals across various divisions.

The $MC^3$ framework for learning and innovation was used at STRATE to transform STRATE into a learning organisation. To ensure client comfort, reduced risk and to capitalize on experience, the following were built:

- A clear and flexible performance model aimed at accomplishing business goals in line with the vision.

- A process for creating and utilising intellectual capital towards driving its sustainability as a viable service provider.
- A process for transfer of required knowledge to role holders within the organisation.
- A dynamic organisation in order to respond to the changes in the market

"The process opened my eyes to where we are and where we want to go. This process has standardised the applicability of HR processes across the organisation and clearly brings out the issues that contribute to the company's progress. We are very pleased. Now we know that KM is not a theory." says Brutus Molefe, Head-HR, STRATE.

Source: http://www.nihilent.com/casestudies/STRATE.pdf.

## 9.3  Implementing KM: A Change Project

As discussed earlier the implementation phase
- Needs to be someone's responsibility,
- Needs a change strategy and a plan,
- Needs a special team and budget,
- Has a start and an end, and
- Has objectives and deliverables.

So it needs to be managed as a project. Whatever process you use internally for managing projects, apply it to your KM implementation.

Based on KM models, control projects model and a continuous improvement cycle, Erfani et al. have defined a KM implementation Model considering the five phases of Project Management. The model is shown below in Fig. 9.3:

It has been shown that while implementing the managerial models many interested organisations don't pay attention to the initiating phase and go directly into the execution phase. These organisations face problems because of neglecting preliminary requirements such as budgeting. Moreover they do repetitive work since they don't consider closing the phase in their models and don't have a method to document the results and procedures of their projects (Erfani et al. 2010). Organisations wishing to implement KM initiatives should be aware that this requires in most of the cases a change of behaviour. This is why **_KM projects are fundamentally change projects_**. To increase the probability of successful change those leading KM initiatives should be aware of the principles of change management.

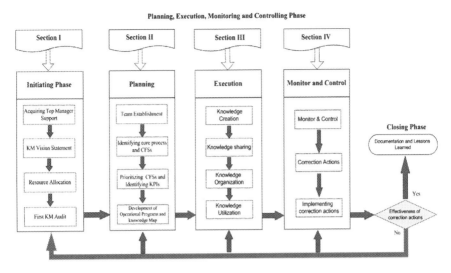

**Fig. 9.3** Five phase implementation model of project management (Source: http://idosi.org/wasj/wasj11(1)10/6.pdf)

## Kotter's Eight Steps of Change

There are many theories about how to "do" change. A widely accepted model was introduced by Harvard professor Kotter with his eight-step change process in his 1996 book, *"Leading Change."* We look at his eight steps for leading change below.[5]

1. **Establish a Sense of Urgency**

   Talk of change typically begins with some people noticing a vulnerability in the organisation. The threat of losing ground in some way sparks these people into action, and they in turn try to communicate that sense of urgency to others. Kotter notes that over half the companies he has observed have never been able to create enough urgency to prompt action. "Without motivation, people won't help and the effort goes nowhere [. . .]. Executives underestimate how hard it can be to drive people out of their comfort zones". In the more successful cases the leadership group facilitates a frank discussion of potentially unpleasant facts: about the new competition, flat earnings, decreasing market share, a lack of communication and knowledge sharing other relevant indicators. It is helpful to use outsiders (consultants) who can share the "big picture" from a different perspective and help broaden the awareness of people. When is the urgency level high enough? Kotter suggests it is when 75 % of your leadership is honestly convinced that business as usual is no longer an acceptable plan.

---

[5] Adapted from http://siriusmeetings.com/files/8steps1.pdf

2. **Form a Powerful Guiding Coalition**

Change efforts often start with just one or two people, and should grow continually to include more and more who believe the changes are necessary. The need in this phase is to gather a large enough initial core of believers. Regardless of size of your organisation, the "guiding coalition" for change needs to have 3–5 people leading the effort. This group, in turn, helps bring others on board with the new ideas. The building of this coalition – their sense of urgency, their sense of what's happening and what's needed – is crucial. Involving respected leaders from key areas of your church in this coalition will pay great dividends later.

3. **Create a Vision**

Successful transformation rests on "a picture of the future that is relatively easy to communicate and appeals to stakeholders. A vision helps clarify the direction in which an organisation needs to move". The vision functions in many different ways: it helps spark motivation, it helps keep all the projects and changes aligned, it provides a filter to evaluate how the organisation is doing, and it provides a rationale for the changes the organisation will have to weather. "A useful rule of thumb: if you can't communicate the vision to someone in five minutes or less and get a reaction that signifies both understanding and interest, you are not yet done with this phase of the transformation process".

4. **Communicate that Vision**

Kotter suggests the leadership should estimate how much communication of the vision is needed, and then multiply that effort by a factor of 10. Leaders must be seen "walking the talk" – another form of communication – if people are going to perceive the effort as important. "Deeds" along with "words" are powerful communicators of the new ways. The bottom line is that a transformation effort will fail unless most of the people understand, appreciate, commit and try to make the effort happen. The guiding principle is simple: use every existing communication channel and opportunity.

5. **Empower Others to Act on the Vision**

This entails several different actions. Allow people to start behave and act in the new ways and to make changes in their areas of involvement. Allocate budget money to the new initiative. Carve out time on the agenda to talk about it. Change the way your organisation is organised to put people where the effort needs to be. Free up key people from existing responsibilities so they can concentrate on the new effort. In short, remove any obstacles there may be to getting on with the change. Nothing is more frustrating than believing in the change but then not having the time, money, or support needed to effect it. You can't get rid of all the obstacles, but the biggest ones need to be dealt with.

6. **Plan for and Create Short-Term Wins**

Since real transformation takes time, the loss of momentum and the onset of disappointment are real factors. Most people won't go on a long march for change unless they begin to see compelling evidence that their efforts are bearing fruit. In successful transformation, leaders actively plan and achieve some short-term gains which people will be able to see and celebrate. This provides prove that their efforts are working, and adds to the motivation to keep the effort going. "When it becomes clear to people that major change will take a long time, urgency levels can drop. Commitments to produce short-term wins help keep the urgency level up and force detailed analytical thinking that can clarify or revise visions".

7. **Consolidate Improvements and Keep the Momentum for Change Going**

   As Kotter warns, "Do not declare victory too soon". Until changes sink deeply into an organisation's culture – a process that can take time – new approaches are fragile and subject to regression. Again, a premature declaration of victory kills momentum, allowing the powerful forces of tradition to regain ground. Leaders of successful efforts use the feeling of victory as the motivation to delve more deeply into their organisation: to explore changes in the basic culture, to expose the systems relationships of the organisation which need tuning, to move people committed to the new ways into key roles. Leaders of change must go into the process knowing that their efforts will take a while to produce results.

8. **Institutionalise the New Approaches**

   In the final analysis, change sticks when it becomes "the way we do things around here", when it seeps into the bloodstream of the corporate body. "Until new behaviors are rooted in social norms and shared values, they are subject to degradations as soon as the pressure for change is removed". Two factors are particularly important for doing this. First, a conscious attempt to show people how the new approaches, behaviors, and attitudes have helped improve the life of the organisation. People have to be helped to make the connections between the effort and the outcome. The second is to ensure that the upcoming leaders believe in and embody the new ways. Kotter writes, "There are still more mistakes that people make, but these eight are the big ones. In reality, even successful change efforts are messy and full of surprises".

## Implementation Paths of Knowledge Management

KM implementation is long-term issue as in most cases it requires a change towards an open, self-organised enterprise model. Such a change process can have different starting points. In a survey of German companies four main implementation paths of KM were identified (North and Papp 2001). Most of the knowledge management initiatives of the companies surveyed resulted from pressure to change or need to improve (path 3).

Ask yourself a question: How and where should we begin? Below we will explain the four implementation paths. We found several companies that switch from one path to another or combined paths over time (Ref. Fig. 9.4).

### Implementation Path 1: ICT Orientation

The first path implements new information and communication systems in order to improve access, documentation and interaction. Best-practice databases, discussion forums or yellow pages are established as a starting point. In the second phase, a central coordinator or a coach motivates the interested individuals to cooperate.

| | **Phase I** | **Phase II** | **Phase III** |
|---|---|---|---|
| **1st path** | • New ICT systems are implemented<br>• Databases, discussion forums or yellow pages are introduced | • Interested individuals are motivated by knowledge-authorities to contribute to the process<br>• Informal and formal networks are developed | • Creation and transfer of knowledge is further encouraged by incentive systems and active support of management |
| **2nd path** | • A coordinator is appointed to transfer knowledge; he motivates exchange of information sets a positive example | • Topic-related networks are formed. They are then supported by IT infrastructure | • Informal teamwork is formalised, rewarded by incentive systems and supported by company's management |
| **3rd path** | • Internal or company-wide benchmarking survey → pressure to change<br>• Best practices are shared | • Network of interested individuals is formed. They store the information in databases and maintain discussion forums | • Company culture undergoes a change<br>• Incentive systems changed from knowledge perspectives |
| **4th path** | • Business management takes up the goals of knowledge management →research groups are called up<br>• Pilot project are motivated | • Informal networks are formed<br>• IT infrastructure is built as per goals<br>• Knowledge-authorities motivate employees for usage | • Creation and transfer of knowledge is supported by incentive systems and continuous internal marketing |

Knowledge-oriented company

**Fig. 9.4**  Implementation paths of knowledge management (Source: North and Papp 2001)

This builds informal and formal networks. In the following phase, creation and transfer of knowledge is further encouraged by suitable incentive systems and active management support. Sceptics are convinced that teamwork is worthwhile, organisation culture changes gradually and existing organisation structures are adapted to new working methods.

### Implementation Path 2: Knowledge Manager as an Evangelist

The second implementation path begins with appointment of a coordinator for knowledge transfer. This coordinator motivates exchange of experiences, is supposed to keep a record of "*who knows what in the company*", exemplifies knowledge exchange and demonstrates that teamwork is worthwhile by means of small concrete examples. Inspired exchange of experience gives rise to relevant networks that are then supported by IT infrastructure. Following the snowball system, more and more employees are included. Informal cooperation is formalised, rewarded by incentive systems, and supported by the company management. For instance, a knowledge manager of a pharmaceutical company is responsible for "*the business development of the company. Projects are established in this context and persons who are suitable worldwide are recruited. In the future, efforts will be taken to enhance the networks internally as well as externally*".

### Implementation Path 3: Pressure to Change

The third implementation path is linked directly to internal and external pressure of competition, e.g. through benchmarking surveys. A pressure to improve is developed. Business units find out that they are facing similar problems. Best practices are exchanged. Units start working together in comprehensive projects, improvement goals are set and networks with similar interests are generated. These networks store their information systematically in databases and maintain discussion forums. The company culture changes. Organisational structure and incentive systems are changed from knowledge perspectives.

### Case: Competence networks in an electronics company

A pilot project was started in the computer-chip developing division of an electronics company in cooperation with the central process consultation. The project primarily aimed at linking experts who worked on the same subject. A meeting was organised every 6 months in which the interest groups (20–30 people, international) discussed common problems under the guidance of a moderator.

While organising the activities, it was always ensured that needs of network members were met and functioning as an "instructor" was strictly avoided. This gave rise to the requirement for an efficient form of communication (primarily in international context). Communication technology was adapted by installing a suitable video conference system. Since the initiatives offered relatively fast results for quite a huge number of participants, there was an increased interest in teamwork at the employee level and the project also enjoyed desired and necessary support of the top management.

Today, efforts are being made to link interest groups formed earlier. Communities of Practice are implemented which consists individuals with similar experience and interest. Presently, efforts are being made to connect 1,500 employees. A major task in the process of connection is removing barriers and reconstructing information and communication systems accordingly. Roles should be defined (community manager, administration, etc.) and the entire system should be integrated in day-to-day business.

## Implementation Path 4: Top-Down Initiative

The fourth implementation path is a top-down initiation and begins with ambitious goals of the company or comprehensive strategic programmes that require cooperation or motivate cooperation. A company's internal "*knowledge alliances*" and cooperative projects are established and they become components of daily work. Information and communication infrastructure is built and rebuilt and networks are formed. Success in the achievement of ambitious goals further encourages teamwork, particularly when greater attention is paid to rewarding the overall success of a company than satisfying particular interests of individual business units.

## Which Is the Most Effective Path?

Depending on the implementation path and phase, the implementation of knowledge management is subject to different levels of difficulties. Companies following the first path complete a long stretch quickly but do not reach very high. One can also call this way as "*quick win*" way. Quick results like increasing interest and increasing number of users obscure the view of much difficult part of the path, i.e. the necessary adaptation of incentive systems and a corresponding change in the corporate culture. Many companies rest on this intermediate goal for a long time, thus risking their authenticity and creating useless IT graveyards.

In many surveyed companies, internal marketing was and continues to be at the top in the plan of activities. Internal marketing aims at sensitising people for knowledge management and motivating them to use knowledge management tools. However, these important measures for stimulating the exchange of knowledge should not serve as an end in itself. Words should be followed by actions. The management and/or the spokesperson of knowledge management should consistently exemplify the communicated and encouraged image of an "*ideal employee*".

Findings from the second round of interview made it clear that knowledge management initiatives often depend on individual employees connected to the subject. These initiatives are doomed to fail if these promoters leave the company or devote their time to other activities. In 5 of the 30 surveyed companies, the position of such promoters or contact persons remained vacant after the existing contact persons quit the company.

Knowledge management requires a professional organisation that ensures sustainable and systematic use of knowledge. There are different ways of integrating knowledge management organisation in formal structures in a given case. In the early times of KM implementation it was often advocated that creation and transfer of knowledge does not require active control. This perception is no longer true. A vast majority of those who were interviewed admitted that a formally established knowledge manager should promote, coordinate and monitor knowledge management activities. Experiencing knowledge-oriented management of a company is like entering into a new territory and experimenting.

## 9.4    Implementing KM at Individual Level: Key Competencies for Knowledge Workers[6]

Independent from the organisational anchoring and implementation path the ultimate objective is the integration of KM in the daily practices of each employee, in each unit and the management structures of the organisation.

This requires the development of skills and competences to at individual level. The following five key competencies are essential for knowledge workers:

1. **Structuring and evaluating knowledge domains**
   "*Finally I understand what you do!*", exclaimed the CEO of an international organisation after the employees had structured important topics and fields of

---

[6] This subchapter has been adapted from North and Gueldenberg (2011).

**Table 9.3**  Structuring and evaluating knowledge domains

| Field of intervention, service module, method | Specific knowledge | Reference "lighthouse" | Maturity level (1 crude – 5 developed) | Documentation and availability |
|---|---|---|---|---|
| . . .. | | | | |
| . . .. | | | | |

knowledge for each service module and had systematised reference projects, documents, publications and methods according to a standard pattern.

The challenge lies in presenting one's own knowledge domain in such a way that others understand what their colleagues do. An even greater challenge lies in working together in one department:

- What is the core knowledge of our group or department?
- How do we distinguish ourselves from the others?
- What are the methods specific to our work?

While structuring knowledge domains and while visualising, e.g. with a mind map or in the form of a process presentation, it does not make much sense to start with the question, "What do we know?" Instead, a more useful question would be, "Which services do we provide to our customers and what is the knowledge required for providing these services?" (See also tools knowledge taxonomy and knowledge inventory).

It is also practical to evaluate knowledge domains on the basis of their maturity; for instance from "crude" (knowledge under development) through "mature" (tried and tested) up to "excessively mature" or "obsolete" (i.e. this knowledge is not required anymore and thus can be discarded). Structuring knowledge domains and evaluating them is also important in order to realise which knowledge we, as a group for instance, lack and how we can acquire it. Table 9.3 shows a practically tested structure of knowledge domains with reference to specific services, fields of intervention or methods.

2. **Learning teamwork: find a common language**

   *"It took me much time to find a common language and a common method of working in the team, but it was worth it"*, said a young engineer who worked in a development project along with social scientists, doctors and business economists. Several disciplines further train lone fighters and when work groups are formed during training they are mostly comprised of people from the same discipline: Engineers work with engineers, doctors with doctors and so on.

   Thus, it is important to have interdisciplinary work groups already at the stage of training. With the interdisciplinary aspect also comes the intercultural aspect. For instance, if a German engineer has to work with a French engineer both have to understand the way of thinking of the counterpart, which has been developed by different cultural traditions. Thus, the ability to work together has to be learnt. There should be room for reflecting on methods, implicit assumptions and role allocation. We talk a lot about what we do, but very little about how we work together.

3. **Using information and communication media intelligently**

A lawyer once said, *"When I am not reachable, I somehow feel excluded. But when I take time-off it's business as usual even without me"*.

During a routine working day, we rarely think about how we communicate.

Handling communication tools consciously and developing one's own communication strategy is a skill of knowledge workers and this skill has to be learnt.

4. **Self-management**

*"I had no idea what to do with the newly found freedom"*, said a project engineer who had moved from a tightly controlled conglomerate to a small engineering firm.

Utilising available freedom is difficult for many; even for students it is more difficult than executing more or less predefined tasks. Using freedom effectively requires the ability to manage oneself. This means structuring tasks, setting goals for oneself, finding a certain work rhythm, making decisions, and coping with uncertainty. All this was taught and learnt insufficiently until now in the dominant education system.

Self-management also means taking responsibility for developing one's own competencies. Knowledge workers should be able to upgrade their competency profile and proactively develop further.

Marketing one's own competencies also falls under the domain of self-management. Thus, young consultants need to learn quickly that they have to market their abilities in order to get interesting projects, while perhaps their education trained them to wait until they are approached.

Self-management also includes the ability of self-reflection, i.e. to think, 'How do I deal with myself and with others?'

5. **Mindfulness**

*"While working, I always think about the next step and the step after that. What I do now seems like a hindrance only to get to the next step"*, said a manager in a seminar. Being mindful means to observe internal and external processes calmly and with undivided attention. Being mindful means to fully concentrate and appreciate the things one is doing, or to pay undivided attention to a partner in a discussion. Judging people and things in peace and without being prejudiced is not always easy, especially when a quick decision is required. Being mindful can be practiced, e.g. as shown through a number of techniques of Zen Buddhism. What do you do to develop these key competencies for yourself and for your organisation, and probably also for students and managers in further training?

## 9.5 The 12-Point Programme for Knowledge-Oriented Management of a Company

At the end of the book we would like to summarise our implementation suggestions by the following *12-point programme which* was developed in a project with small and medium enterprises. You can start at any random point. Under a mid-term perspective you should complete all 12 points one by one. You can also use the

*12-point programme* as a checklist to examine the latest status of knowledge-oriented management of your company.

1. Sensitise your employees for knowledge management and carry out a problem analysis: Where are we falling short of knowledge? Where could we avoid errors through a better flow of knowledge? How could we improve our innovation performance?

2. Derive knowledge strategies from the organisational strategy. Which competences do you want to develop in the coming years?

3. Create enabling conditions that encourage creation and exchange of knowledge, e.g. through incentive systems, knowledge criteria in employee appraisals or employee agreements on teamwork

4. Make arrangements for knowledge flows and learning from external sources, i.e. from customers, suppliers, competitors, universities, research centres or other external experts. This can also be done by creating technology teams and customer forums. Cooperate with other companies.

5. Pay attention to targeted competence development of your employees. For instance, create a competence profile and control the results of development measures.

6. Enable knowledge transfer across employee generations so that the company does not lose any valuable know-how. This is possible through godparent model following the motto *"employees train employees"* or checklist for orientation of the successors.

7. Encourage creativity and innovation of your employees by introducing non-bureaucratic employee suggestions, making small improvements immediately beforehand or initiating competitions of ideas for new products.

8. Support the learning process within and across projects by after action reviews, debriefing (neutral persons document the project experiences of employees) and through project discussions and lessons-learnt databases.

9. Integrate knowledge management in your business processes. The key question here is: How can we make process knowledge transparent and accessible?

10. Create opportunities for facilitating personal exchange of knowledge. This can be done by regular meetings, departmental breakfast, info zones of knowledge markets.

11. Bring structure to your documents, databases and intranet. Create guidelines on documentation and define precisely which employee is responsible for which content. Give incentives to your employees for actually using the systems.

12. Provide for an open and trustworthy atmosphere of teamwork so that the employees are ready to share their knowledge with others.

   ***Cogitate Incognita Think the unthinkable, think something new and put it into practice***

## 9.6    Key Insights of Chapter 9

- KM needs to be introduced as a management framework consisting of technologies and processes, embedded into business activity along with a set of roles embedded into the organisational structure – all under an umbrella of governance. Once embedded, the management framework will deliver sustained organisational KM, but needs to be accompanied by a change in behaviour and culture too. Different frameworks have been introduced.
- The best way to ensure KM system value and overall proper implementation is to focus on enterprise performance as it relates to customer benefit.
- Knowledge management of the future is hence closely coupled with strategy, innovation management and personnel development which encourage dynamisation of organisations
- KM needs to be managed as a change project. Whatever process you use internally for managing projects apply it to your KM implementation and be aware of Kotter's eight principles leading to change.
- The following five key competencies are essential for knowledge workers: Structuring and evaluating knowledge domains, learning teamwork: find a common language, using information and communication media intelligently, self-management and mindfulness.

## 9.7    Questions

1. What are the elements of a KM framework?
2. Discuss the pros and cons of the four KM implementation paths.
3. How can you measure the effectiveness of the KM initiative in an organisation?
4. What are the tasks of a knowledge manger (refer also to Chap. 5)?
5. Where do you see differences in implementing KM in a firm, public administration and a non-profit organisation?

## 9.8    Assignments

1. **Implementing KM in a hospital**

   The medical field in recent years has been facing increasing pressures for lower cost and increased quality of healthcare. An organisation can lower its cost through elimination of non value-added activities and enhance quality of service through process control. It is perceived that knowledge management can significantly increase the efficiency of operations.

   *As a consultant, you have been assigned the task of implementing knowledge management at a large hospital to improve the quality of service. Identify the knowledge assets of the hospital and formulate a KM strategy that would help them improve their efficiency and brand name.*

## 2. KM vision

*Formulate a vision, what you want to achieve with implementing a KM project in a company? Conduct an internet search for published KM visions and compare them.*

## 9.9 KM-Tool: Work-Out (General Electric)

### What is a Work-out?

This problem solving methodology was developed by General Electric:

*"Work-Out was based on the simple belief that people closest to the work know more than anyone; how it could be done better. It was this enormous reservoir of untapped knowledge, and insight, that we wanted to draw upon. Across GE today, holding a Work-Out session is as natural an act as coming to work. People of disparate ranks and functions search for a better way, every day, gathering in a room for an hour, or eight, or three days, grappling with a problem or an opportunity, and dealing with it, usually on the spot - producing real change instead of memos and promises of further study. Everyone today has an opportunity to have a voice at GE, and everyone who uses that voice to help improve things is rewarded"* (General Electric, Annual report 1995, p. 5)

### Why do a Work-out?

Work-Out is not just a cost-cutting process. It rather helps companies grow along five key dimensions:

First, it *provides a focus on stretch.* By forcing people to rethink what they are doing, it also encourages them to stretch to a goal or challenge that is significantly beyond their current performance level.

For example, the stretch goal might be to cut the time to develop a new product in half, or to reduce the number of customer complaints by 30 % in the next year.

Second, Work-Out helps to *develop systems thinking.* Work-Out encourages people to take a systems perspective. In the initial design phase of Work-Out, the design team creates a comprehensive map that describes the steps, processes, and subprocesses involved in producing current results.

Third, Work-Out *encourages lateral thinking.* With the process map as a starting point, participants brainstorm ways to achieve the goal and sort through ideas, select the best ones, and develop them into recommendations. Work-Out begins by focusing on the *"low-hanging fruit,"* the easy fixes that can be made to virtually any process. Every organisation develops clutter or inefficiency over time.

### How to do a work-out?

No matter what the challenge, the process remains the same, with four basic steps:
1. Bring together the people who know the issues best.
2. Challenge them to develop creative solutions.
3. Make yes or no decisions on the solutions immediately in a public forum.
4. Empower people to carry out the solutions.

Work-Out particularly addresses "RAMMPP" inefficiencies, short for reports, approvals, meetings, measures, policies, and practices. These are relatively easy to find and remove.

The simple RAMMPP Matrix illustrated below lists each type of clutter and the places where it might exist.

**CONTROL**

| | Self | Department | Group | Company | External |
|---|---|---|---|---|---|
| Reports | | | | | |
| Approvals | | | | | |
| Meetings | | | | | |
| Measures | | | | | |
| Policies | | | | | |
| Practices | | | | | |

Could it be:

1. Eliminated?

2. Partially eliminated?

3. Delegated downward?

4. Done less often?

5. Done in a less complicated/time-consuming manner?

6. Done with fewer people involved?

7. Done using a more productive technology?

8. Other?

Sources/Links: Ulrich et al. (2002), a free @*GE WORK-OUT* KIT can downloaded from www.scribd.com/.../3240020-GE-WORKOUT

# Multilingual Glossary

In the following core terms related to managing knowledge are explained. Translation into German (DE), French (F), Spanish (E) and Portuguese (P) languages are provided.

An **After Action Review** (AAR) is a process used by a team to capture the lessons learned from past successes and failures, with the goal of improving future performance. It is an opportunity for a team to reflect on a project, activity, event or task so that they can do better the next time. It can also be employed in the course of a project to learn while doing.

DE: After Action Review, Lessons Learned; F: revue après action; E: Lecciones aprendidas; P: revisão depois de ação, lições aprendidas

**Benchmarking** is the structured comparison of processes and activities. Camp (1994) defines it as "the continuous process of measuring products, services, and practices against the company's toughest competitors or those companies renowned as industry leaders."

DE/F/E/P: Benchmarking

**Best practices** are those practices that have been shown to produce superior results; selected by a systematic process; and judged as exemplary, good, or successfully demonstrated. "Best Practices" are a moving target as they change with experience and innovation.

DE: Best Practices; F: meilleures pratiques; E: mejores practicas; P: melhores práticas

The term **competence (or competency)** of a person or a group basically describes the relationship between the tasks assigned to or assumed by the person or the group and their capability and potential to do meet these requirements. People mobilise knowledge, skills and behaviours to "do the right thing" at the right moment.

DE: Kompetenz; F: competence; E: competencia, P: competência, habilidade

**Core competencies** are a combination of skills and technologies that deliver value to the customer. This combination is based on explicit and hidden knowledge and is characterised by temporal stability and influence on the products. Core competencies

1. Are not easy for competitors to imitate.
2. Can be re-used widely for many products and markets.
3. Must contribute to the end consumer's experienced benefits.

K. North and G. Kumta, *Knowledge Management*,
Springer Texts in Business and Economics, DOI 10.1007/978-3-319-03698-4,
© Springer International Publishing Switzerland 2014

DE: Kernkompetenzen; F:compétences clés; E: competencias esenciales; P: competências essenciais

**A Community of practice** is a group of people who share a concern, a set of problems, or a passion about a topic, and who deepen their knowledge and expertise in this area by interacting on an ongoing basis (Wenger/McDermott/ Snyder 2002).

DE: Wissensgemeinschaft; F: communauté de pratiques; E: comunidad de practica; P: comunidade de prática

**Dynamic capabilities** are the ability to reconfigure, redirect, transform, and appropriately shape and integrate existing core competences with external resources and strategic and complementary assets to meet the challenges of a time-pressured, rapidly changing Schumpeterian world of competition and imitation (Teece et al. 2000).

DE: Dynamische Fähigkeiten, F:capacités dynamiques,E: capacidades dinámicas, P: capacidades dinâmicas

**Epistemology** is a branch of philosophy that investigates the origin, nature, methods, and limits of human knowledge. It raises questions such as: (1) how reality can be known, (2) the relationship between the knower and what is known, (3) the characteristics, the principles, the assumptions that guide the process of knowing and the achievement of findings, and (4) the possibility of that process being shared and repeated by others in order to assess the quality of the research and the reliability of those findings. Epistemological reflection is what enables us to elucidate the different paradigms which give different answers to the questions raised by epistemology (see Vasilachis 2011).

DE: Erkenntnistheorie; F: épistémologie ; E: epistemología; P: epistemologia

**Information** is organised data adding a meaning to a message.

DE: Information; F: informations; E: información; P: informação

**Innovation** is the successful exploitation of new ideas. In other words: creating value from a new combination of knowledge.

DE: Innovation; F: innovation; E: innovación; P: inovação

**Intangible Assets**: According to International Accounting Standard (IAS 38) "an identifiable non-monetary asset without physical substance". Comprises assets such as reputation, brand value, monopoly rights and other non-balance sheet items such as "potential" – i.e. the capacity to generate competitive advantage in the future.

DE: Immaterielle Vermögenswerte; F: immobilisations incorporelles; E: activos intangibles; P: ativos intangíveis

**Intellectual Capital:** Intellectual Capital (IC), a subset of the intangible assets including three sub-categories: Human Capital, Structural Capital, Customer Capital. IC can include the knowledge of employees, data and information about processes, experts, products, customers and competitors; and intellectual property such as patents or regulatory licenses. (CEN)

DE: Intellektuelles Capital; F: capital intellectual; E: capital intelectual; P: capital intelectual

**Knowledge** refers to the tacit or explicit understanding of people about relationships among phenomena. It is embodied in routines for the performance of activities, in organisational structures and processes and in embedded beliefs and behaviour. Knowledge implies an ability to relate inputs to outputs, to observe regularities in information, to codify, explain and ultimately to predict (Carnegie Bosch Institute 1995).

De: Wissen; F: connaissances, savoir; E: conocimiento; P: conhecimento

**Tacit knowledge** represents the personal knowledge of an individual. It is based on education, ideals, values and feelings of the individual person. Subjective insights and intuition embody tacit knowledge that is deeply rooted in the actions and experiences of the particular person.

DE: implizites Wissen; F: connaissances implicites; E: conocimiento tácito; P: conhecimento tácito

**Explicit knowledge** is methodological and systematic and is present in an articulated form. It is stored in the media outside the brain of an individual (disembodied knowledge).

DE: Explizites Wissen; F: connaissances explicites; E: conocimiento explícito; P: conhecimento explícito

**Knowledge management** enables individuals, teams and entire organisations as well as networks, regions and nations to collectively and systematically create, share and apply knowledge to achieve their strategic and operational objectives. Knowledge management contributes to increase the efficiency and effectiveness of operations on the one hand and to change the quality of competition (innovation) on the other by developing a learning organisation.

DE: Wissensmanagement; F: gestion des connaissances; E: Gestión del conocimiento ; P: gestão do conhecimento

**Knowledge work** is an activity based on cognitive skills that has an intangible result and whose value added relies on information processing and creativity, and consequently on the creation and communication of knowledge.

DE: Wissensarbeit; F: travail du savoir; E: trabajo de conocimiento; P: trabalho de conhecimento

**Knowledge workers** are people who primarily engage in knowledge work. Also called "Creative Class" (Florida) or "white collar", "gold collar" workers.

DE: Wissensarbeiter, F: Les travailleurs du savoir; E: trabajadores del conocimiento; P: trabalhadores do conhecimento

**Leadership** is the process by which a person influences others to accomplish an objective (Akhil Shahani).

DE: Führung; F: leadership, direction; E:liderazgo; P:chefia

**Learning organisations** are organisations where people continually expand their capacity to create the they truly desire, where new and expansive patterns of thinking are nurtured, where collective aspiration is set free, and where people are continually learning to see the whole together (Senge).

DE: Lernende Organisation, F: organisations apprenantes; E: organizaciones que aprenden; P: organizações de aprendizagem

**Management** according to Drucker means: (1) Making people's strengths effective and their weaknesses irrelevant. (2) Enhancing the ability of people to contribute. (3) Integrating people in a common venture by thinking through, setting and exemplifying the organisational objectives, values and goals. (4) Enabling the enterprise and its members to grow and develop through training, developing and teaching. (5) Ensuring everyone knows what needs to be accomplished, what they can expect of you, and what is expected of them Management allows us to coordinate hundreds or thousands of people with different skills and knowledge to achieve common goals.

An **Ontology** is the study of entities and their relations used p.e. in the semantic web as a basis for search.

DE: Ontologie, F: ontologie; E: ontología; P: ontologia

**A Taxonomy** is the classification of objects (information) in an ordered system A taxonomy provides the structure to organise information, and documents in a consistent way. Information and knowledge is put in hierarchical or contextual order.

DE: Taxonimie, F: taxonomie; E: taxonomía, P: taxonomia

## Knowledge Management Resources

## KM Related Journals

Journal of Knowledge Management,
Journal of Knowledge Management Practice,
Electronic Journal of Knowledge Management,
Knowledge Management Research and Practice,
International Journal of Knowledge Management,
Knowledge Management,
Knowledge Management Review,
Knowledge and Process Management,
Interdisciplinary Journal of Information, Knowledge, and Management
International journal of knowledge culture and change management
Knowledge management for development journal,
Journal of Intellectual Capital,
International Journal of Learning and Intellectual Capital,
Learning Organization
E-Journal of Organizational Learning and Leadership
International Journal of Intelligent Enterprise
International Journal of Innovation and Learning
International Journal of Innovation and Knowledge Management in Middle East & North Africa

## Knowledge Management Toolkits[1]

### Toolkits in English

| Toolkits | Target group | Number of tools | Web links |
|---|---|---|---|
| APO toolkit | SMEs | 26 | www.apo-tokyo.org/00e-books/IS-44_Practical-KM-Guide-for-SME-OwnerManager.htm |
| Knowledge sharing toolkit | All organisations | Over 30 | http://www.kstoolkit.org |
| DBA toolkit | Companies in design practices | 7 | http://www.usablebuildings.co.uk/Pages/Unprotected/SpreadingTheWord/SharingKnowledge.pdf |
| IDEA tools and techniques | Local governments | 8 | http://www.idea.gov.uk/idk/aio/8595069 |
| ODI toolkit | International agencies | 30 | http://www.odi.org.uk/sites/odi.org.uk/files/odi-assets/publications-opinion-files/188.pdf |
| SDC toolkit | SDC partner countries | 23 | http://www.sdc-learningandnetworking.ch/en/Home/SDC_KM_Tools |
| UN CPR | UNDP offices | 15 | http://www.undp.org.ye/reports/Knowledge%20Management%20Toolkit%20for%20the%20Crisis%20Prevention%20and%20Recovery%20Practice%20Area.pdf |

### Toolkits in Spanish and Portuguese

| Toolkits | Target group | Number of tools | Web links |
|---|---|---|---|
| Bain & Company – Ferramentas de Gestão | Enterprises | 25 | http://www.bain.com/offices/saopaulo/pt/Images/Management_tools_2009_POR.pdf |
| EoiAmérica Toolkit (America Grau) | Multinational enterprises | 82 | http://docencia.udea.edu.co/ingenieria/semgestionconocimiento/documentos/Mod7_HerrTec.pdf |

### Toolkits in German

| Toolkits | Target group | Number of toolsik | Web links |
|---|---|---|---|
| SIHK | SMEs | 15 | http://www.sihk-wissensbilanz.de/wissensaktivitaeten.htm |
| 12 Punkte programm | SMEs | 20 | http://www.ihk-lahndill.de/share/wissen/12punkte.html |

---

[1] Prepared by Renia Babakhanlou

## Toolkits in French

| Toolkits | Target group | Number of tools | Web links |
|---|---|---|---|
| Service public fédéral de Belgique, | Public administration | 15 | http://www.fedweb.belgium.be/fr/a_ propos_de_l_organisation/gestion_des_ connaissances/ |
| FAO (IDEA) | Local governments | 8 | http://www.fao.org/knowledge/ networksandcommunities/knrepositories/ fr/?tx_mblnewsevent_organizer=29320 |

# Bibliography

Abdullah R, Selamat MH, Sahibuddin S, Alias RA (2005) A framework for knowledge management system implementation in Collaborative Environment for Higher Learning Institution. J Knowl Manag Pract 6. March 2005. http://www.tlainc.com/articl83.htm

Adler PS, Cole RE (1993) Designed for learning: a tale of two auto plants. Sloan Manag Rev 35 (1):85–94

Agarwal R, Nisa S (2009) Knowledge process outsourcing, India's emergence as a global leader. Asian Soc Sci 5(1):82–92, http://ccsenet.org/journal/index.php/ass/article/view/539/0

ALGA (2004) KM Toolkit for local government organizations. http://www.alga.asn.au/?ID=138

Alter A (2005) Knowledge workers need better management. http://www.cioinsight.com/c/a/Expert-Voices/Knowledge-Workers-Need-Better-Management/

Alwert K, Bornemann M, Will M (2009) Does intellectual capital reporting matter to financial analysts? J Intellect Capital 3:354–368

Anand A, Singh MD (2011) Understanding knowledge management – a literature review. Int J Eng Sci Technol 3(2):926–939, http://www.ijest.info/docs/IJEST11-03-02-090.pdf

Andriessen D (2004) Making sense of intellectual capital. Butterworth Heinemann, Amsterdam

APO (2010) The practical KM guide for SME owners and managers. Asian Productivity Organisation, Tokyo

APQC (American Productivity and Quality Centre) (1996) Knowledge management – consortium benchmarking study. Final report. APQC, Houston

APQC (2013) Gamification in knowledge management – an APQC overview. http://www.apqc.org/knowledge-base/documents/gamification-knowledge-management-apqc-overview

Argyris C, Schön D (1978) Organizational learning: a theory of action perspective. Addison-Wesley, Reading

Argyris C (1999) On organizational learning, 2nd edn. Blackwell Business, Malden

Arthur DL (ed) (1998) Knowledge managment: reaping the benefits. Prism (ADC), Second Quarter 98

Austin T et al (2005) Introducing the high performance workplace: Improving competitive advantage and employee impact. Gartner, Stamford. ID Number G00127289

Austin T et al (2008) Key issues for the high performance workplace 2008–2009. Gartner, Stamford. ID Number: G00156556

Awazu Y, Desouza KC (2004) Knowledge management at SMEs: five unique peculiarities. Submitted to Organizations and Society in Information Systems (OASIS) workshop

Baddracco JL (1991) The knowledge link: how firms compete through strategic alliances. Harvard Business School Press, Boston

Barney J (1992) Integrating organizational behaviour and strategy formulation research. Adv Strateg Manage 8:39–61

Barringer BR, Bluedorn AC (1999) The relationship between corporate entrepreneurship and strategic management. Strateg Manage J 20:421–444

Bartlett CA, Ghoshal S (1989) Managing across borders: the transnational solution. Harvard Business School Press, Boston

K. North and G. Kumta, *Knowledge Management*,
Springer Texts in Business and Economics, DOI 10.1007/978-3-319-03698-4,
© Springer International Publishing Switzerland 2014

Bartlett CA, Ghoshal S (1993) Beyond the M-form: toward a managerial theory of the firm. Strateg Manage J 14:23–46

Bateson MC (1994) Peripheral visions – learning along the way. Harper Collins, New York

Berryman SE (o.J.) Designing effective learning environments: cognitive apprenticeship models. http://frc.fvtc.edu/wids/teaching%20strategies/in-class%20delivery%20strategies/designing%20effective%20learning%20environments.pdf

Bhatnagar J, Budwar P, Srivastava P, Saini DS (2010) Organizational change and development in India: a case of strategic organizational change and transformation. J Organ Change Manage 23(5):485–499

Bhatt D (2000) EFQM excellence model and knowledge management implications, Jan 2000. http://www.comp.dit.ie/dgordon/courses/researchmethods/Countdown/3Elements.pdf

Bianchi P, Labory S (2004) The economic importance of intangible assets. Ashgate, Aldershot

Bird BJ, Hayward DJ, Allen DN (1993) Conflicts in the commercialization of knowledge: perspectives from science and entrepreneurship. Entrep Theory Pract 17(4):57–78

Bixler CH (2002) Knowledge management: practical aspects of implementation. KMWorld 11(7)

Blair J (1997) Knowledge management leverages engineering at Chrysler: Gardner Group. Research note case studies CS-CS-219

Bleicher K (1992) Das Konzept integriertes management. Campus (2. Aufl.), Frankfurt am Main

Bontis N (1996) There's a price on your head: managing intellectual capital strategically. Bus Q 60 (4):40–47

Bornemann M, Leitner K-H (2002) Entwicklung und Realisierung einer Wissensbilanz für eine Forschungsorganisation. Eine Fallstudie zum Forschungszentrum Austrian Research Centers Seibersdorf. In: Pawlowsky P, Reinhardt R (eds) Wissensmanagement für die Praxis: Methoden und Instrumente zur erfolgreichen Umsetzung. Luchterhand, Neuwied, pp 335–367

Bowersox D (1990) The strategic benefits of logistics alliances. Harv Bus Rev, July–August: 36–45

Bridges W (2003) Managing transitions: making the most of change. Da Capo Press, Cambridge, MA

Brinkley I et al (2009) Knowledge workers and knowledge work. The Work Foundation, London, http://www.theworkfoundation.com/Assets/Docs/Knowledge%20Workers-March%202009.pdf

Brooking A (1999) Corporate memory. International Thomson Business Press, London

Brown JS (Dec 1996–Jan 1997) "The Human Factor", Information strategy

Brown JS, Duguid P (2000) The social life of information. Harvard Business school Press, Boston

Brown JS, Gray ES (1999) The people are the company. http://www.fastcompany.com/26238/people-are-company

Brown JS, Collins A, Duguid P (1989) Situated cognition and the culture of learning. Educ Res 18(1):32–42

Burton B (2005) How to define a collaboration strategy that drives business value. https://www.gartner.com/doc/483308

Buckingham M, Coffman C (1999) First, break all the rules: what the world's greatest managers do differently. Simon & Schuster, New York

Buckley PJ, Carter MJ (1997) Managing cross border complimentary knowledge: the business process approach to knowledge management in multinational firms. Carnegie Bosch Institute, Pittsburgh

Bukowitz W, Williams RL (1999) The knowledge management framework. Financial Times/ Prentice Hall, London

Burgelmann RA (1994) Fading memories: a process theory of strategic business exit in dynamic environments. Adm Sci Q 39:24–56

Camp RC (1989) Benchmarking – the search for industry best practices that lead to superior performance. APQC Quality Press, Milwaukee

Carleton K (2011) How to motivate and retain knowledge workers in organizations: A review of the literature. Int J Manage 28(2):459–469

Castells M (1996) The rise of the network society. Blackwell, Oxford

CBI (Carnegie Bosch Institute) (1995) Knowledge in international corporations – outline of research area. CBI, Pittsburg

Chan Kim W, Mauborgne R (1997) Fair process: managing in the knowledge economy. Harv Bus Rev, July–Aug:65–75

Chan KW, Mauborgne R (2003) Fair process: managing in the knowledge economy. Harv Bus Rev 81(1):127–136

Chawla D, Joshi H (2011) Impact of knowledge management on learning organization practices in India: an exploratory analysis. Learn Organ 18(6):501–516

Chesbrough H, Vanhaverbeke W, Wet J (eds) (2006) Open innovation: researching a new paradigm. Oxford University Press, Oxford

Ciborra CU (1996) The platform organization: recombining strategies, structures and surprises. Organ Sci 7(2):103–118

Coase R (1937) The nature of the firm. Economica 4(16):387–405

Collison C, Parcell G (2004) Learning to fly: practical knowledge management from leading and learning organizations. Capstone, Chichester

Contractor FJ, Kumar V, Kundu SK (2010) Global outsourcing and offshoring: an integrated approach to theory and corporate strategy. Cambridge University Press, Cambridge, UK

Crestanello P, Tattara G (2009) A global network and its local ties: restructuring of the Benetton Group. University Ca' Foscari of Venice, Dept. of Economics Research Paper Series No. 11/WP/2009. http://ssrn.com/abstract=1397103 or http://dx.doi.org/10.2139/ssrn.1397103

Daft RL, Weick KE (1984) Toward a model of organizations as interpretation systems. Acad Manage Rev 9(2):284–295

Danish Agency for Trade and Industry (ed) (2000) A guideline for intellectual capital statements. Danish Ministry for Trade and Industry, Copenhagen, p 1

Das G (2010) Indian Express Finance, Monday 22 Nov 2010

Davenport TH (1997) The principles of knowledge management and four case studies. Knowl Process Manage 4(3):187–208

Davenport TH (2005) Thinking for a living: how to get better performance and results from knowledge worker. Harvard Business School Press, Boston

Davenport TH, Probst G (2000) Knowledge management case book (Siemens). Wiley, München

Davenport TH, Prusak L (1998) Working knowledge – how organizations manage what they know. Harvard Business School Press, Boston

Davenport TH et al (1996) Improving knowledge work processes. Sloan Manage Rev 37:53–64

Deepak C, Himanshu J (2011) Impact of knowledge management on learning organization practices in India: an exploratory analysis. Learn Organ 18(6):501–516

Deiser R (1996) Vom Wissen zum Tun und zurück. In: Schneider, U. (Hrsg), Wissensmanagement. FAZ, Frankfurt, pp 49–76.

Denning S (2001) The springboard – how storytelling ignites action in knowledge-era organizations. Butterworth-Heinemann, Boston

Dertouzos M (1997) What will be. Harper Edge, San Francisco

Despres CJ-N (1996) Work, management and the dynamic of knowledge. Sabin J Manage 2:1–13

Dierkes M et al (1999) Handbook of organizational learning. Oxford University Press (in Vorbereitung), Oxford

Dodge H, Fullerton S, Robbins J (1994) Stage of the organizational life cycle and competition as mediators of problem perception for small businesses. Strateg Manage J 15:121–134

Donoghue LP, Harris JG, Weitzman BA (1999) KM strategies that create value. http://www.accenture.com/SiteCollectionDocuments/PDF/knowledge2.pdf

Dopson S, Stewart R (1990) What is happening to middle management? Br J Manage 1:3–16

Dostal W, Parmentier K, Plicht H, Rauch A, Schreyer F (2001) Wandel der Erwerbsarbeit. Qualifikationsverwertung in sich verändernden Arbeitsstrukturen, vol 246, Beiträge zur Arbeitsmarkt- und Berufsforschung. Bundesanstalt für Arbeit, Nürnberg

Doz YL et al (1997) The metanational corporation, vol 97/60, INSEAD (working paper). INSEAD, Fontainebleau

Draganidis F, Mentzas G (2006) Competency based management: a review of systems and approaches. Info Manag Comput Secur 14(1):51–64

Drucker P (1993) Post-capitalist society. Econ, New York

Drucker P (1997) The future that has already happened. Harv Bus Rev, Sept–Oct:20–24

Drucker PF (1999) Management challenges for the 21st century. Harper Business, New York

Durrant F (2001) Knowledge management in the context of government, Caribbean regional ministerial consultation & high level workshop: e-government, information and communication Technologies in Public Sector Management, Montego Bay, 10–14 Dec 2001

Earl M (1997) Knowledge as a strategy. In: Prusak L (ed) Knowledge in organisations. Butterworth-Heinemann, London, pp 1–15

Earl MJ, Scott IA (1999) The role of the Chief Knowledge Officer; Financial Times Supplement "Mastering Information Management", 8 Mar 1999, pp 7–8

Ederer/Schuller/Wilms (2011) How Europe's regions and cities can drive growth and foster social inclusion. Lisbon Council Policy Brief V(1)

Edvinsson L, Malone MS (1997) Intellectual capital. Harper Business/Harper Collins, New York

Edvinsson L, Sullivan P (1996) Developing a model for managing intellectual capital. Eur Manag J 14(4):356–364

Erfani SZ, Akhgar B, Ramin F (2010) A novel knowledge management implementation model for mobile telecommunication industry. World Appl Sci J 11(1):29–37, ISSN 1818–4952 © IDOSI Publications, 2010

Erlach C, Thier K, Neubauer A (2005) Story telling. Durch Geschichten zur Seele des Unternehmens. http://www.community-of-knowledge.de/fileadmin/user_upload/attachments/Story_Telling_NARRATA.pdf

Escher FU, Bajenaru C (1997) Increasing Organisational Capacity through Knowledge-Based Work Design. http://www.ikmagazine.com/xq/asp/sid.0/articleid.35A3005B-D167-4FF0-A201-28E897A26679/eTitle.Increasing_Organisational_Capacity_through_Knowledge_Based_Work_Design/qx/display.htm

Falk A (2008) Empirische Haltlosigkeit. Wirtschaftswoche 11(10.03.2008):54

Fariselli P (2001) Policies for SMEs in the digital economy: from policy assessment to policy innovation. Inputs to 2nd policy group meeting, pp 21–24. http://citeseerx.ist.psu.edu/viewdoc/download?doi=10.1.1.136.8588&rep=rep1&type=pdf

Flood RL (2009) Rethinking the fifth discipline: learning within the unknowable. Routledge, London

Florida R (2002) The rise of the creative class. Basic Books, Cambridge, MA

Fornengo Pent G (1992) Product differentiation and process innovation in the Italian clothing industry. In: van Liemt G (ed) Industry on the move. ILO, Geneva, pp 223–233

Galbraith JR (1995) Designing organizations. Jossey-Bass, San Francisco

Galvin R (1996) Managing knowledge towards wisdom. Eur Manag J 14(4):374–378

Gardner H (1995) Leading minds: An anatomy of leadership. Basic Books (Harper Collins), New York

General Electric (1995) Annual report, p. 5

Ghosh L (2010) How Eureka Forbes uses Indian Parliamentary model to connect with its staff 12 Nov 2010, ET Bureau

Gettier E (1963) Is justified true belief knowledge? Analysis 23(6):121–123

Ghoshal S, Barlett CA (1997) The individual corporation. Harper Collins, New York

Ghoshal S, Bartlett CA (1995) Building the entrepreneurial corporation: new organisational processes, new managerial tasks. Eur Manag J 13:139–155

Giarini O, Liedtke PM (1998) Wie wir arbeiten werden. Hoffmann u Campe, Hamburg

Goffee R, Jones G (1996) What holds the modern company together? Harv Bus Rev, Nov–Dec:133–148

Goleman D (1997) Emotional intelligence. Bantam Books, New York

Goold M, Campbell A (1998) Desperately seeking synergy. Harv Bus Rev, Sept–Oct:131–142

Graham AB, Pizzo VG (1996) A question of balance: case studies in strategic knowledge management. Eur Manag J 14(4):338–346

Grant RM (1996) Toward a knowledge-based theory of the firm. Strateg Manage J 17(1996, Winter Special Issue):109–122

Grassmann O (1997) Organisationsformen der internationalen F&E in technologieintensiven Großunternehmen. Zeitschrift für Führung und Organisation 66:332–339

Grübel D, North K, Szogs G (2004) Intellectual capital reporting – ein Vergleich von vier Ansätzen. Zeitschrift Führung und Organisation (ZfO) 1:19–27

Halal WE (1994) From hierarchy to enterprise: internal markets are the new foundation of management. Acad Manag Exec 8(4):69–82

Hall R (2003) Knowledge management in the new business environment, Acirrt. University of Sydney, Sydney

Hamel G (1991) Competition for competence and inter-partner learning within international strategic alliances. Strateg Manag J 12:83–103

Hamel G, Heene A (eds) (1994) Competence based competition. Wiley, Chichester

Hamel G, Prahalad CK (1994) Competing for the future. Harvard Business School Press, Boston

Hammer M, Champy J (1993) Reengineering the corporation. Nicholas Brealey, London

Hampden-Turner C, Trompenaars F (2000) Building cross-cultural competence – how to create wealth from conflicting values. Wiley, London

Handzic M (2006) Knowledge management in SMEs: practical guidelines. Knowledge Management Research Group (KMRG) – CACCI Journal, Vol. 1 (reprinted from Asia-Pacific Tech Monitor, Jan–Feb 2004, pp. 21–34). Available online at: http://www.cacci.org.tw/Journal/ 2006%20Vol%201/Handzic-mar2004.pdf

Handzic M, Hasan H (2003) Continuing the knowledge management journey, chapter 16. In: Hasan H, Handzic M (eds) Australian studies in knowledge management. UOW Press, Wollongong, pp 520–554

Hanks S, Watson C, Jansen E, Chandler G (1993) Tightening the life cycle construct: a taxonomic study of growth stage configurations in high technology organizations. Entrep Theory Pract 18:5–29

Hansen MT (2009) Collaboration.; Boston (Mass.): Harvard Business School Press. Harvard Business Review (ed) (1998) Harvard Business Review on Knowledge Management. Harvard Business School Press, Boston

Hansen MT, Nohria N, Tierney T (1999) What's your strategy for managing knowledge? Harv Bus Rev, March–April:106–116. http://www.itu.dk/~kristianskriver/b9/Whats%20your%20strat egy%20for%20managing%20knowledge.pdf

Harvey M, Lusch R (1997) Protecting the core competencies of a company: intangible asset security. Eur Manag J 15(4):370–380

Hedlund G (1994) A model of knowledge management and the N-form corporation. Strateg Manag J 15:73–90

Hedlund G, Nonaka I (1993) Models of knowledge management in the West and Japan. In: Lorange P et al (eds) Implementing strategic processes, change, learning and cooperation. Basil Blackwell, London, pp 117–144

Henn G (1995) Management-Kommunikation formt Raumstruktur. Leonardo 4/95:68–71

Henn G (1996) Das Büro als Wissensbörse. Henn Architekten, München

Herzberg F (1966) Work and the nature of man. World Publishing Company, New York

Hess CG (2006) READER: GTZ knowledge management. GTZ Sector Project Knowledge Systems in Rural Development. http://www.gtz.de/agriservice

Hope J, Hope T (1997) Competing in the third wave. Harvard Business School Press, Boston

Howald J, Klatt R, Kopp R (Hrsg.) (2004) Neuorientierung des Wissensmanagements – Paradoxien und Dysfunktionalitäten im Umgang mit der Ressource Wissen. Deutscher Universitäts-Verlag, Wiesbaden

Howe J (2006) The rise of crowdsourcing. Wired, 14 June. Available at http://www.wired.com/ wired/archive/14.06/crowds.html

Hube G (2005) Beitrag zur Beschreibung und Analyse von Wissensarbeit. Dissertation am Institut für Arbeitswissenschaft und Technologiemanagement (IAT), Universität Stuttgart. Jost-Jetter Verlag, Heimsheim

Huws U (2005) The transformation of work in a global knowledge economy: towards a conceptual framework. Report of Works Project. http://worksproject.be/documents/WP3synthesisreport-voorpublicatie.pdf

Hurmelinna-Laukkanen P, Tarkiainen A (2011) Knowledge protection and knowledge sharing – benefits and problems in networked innovation. http://www.imp2011.org/add_articles/Knowl edge%20protection%20and%20knowledge%20sharing%20-%20benefits%20and%20problems% 20in%20networked%20innovation.pdf

Hussain I, Si S, Ahmed A (2010) Knowledge management for SMEs in developing countries. J Knowl Manag Pract 11(2)

INCaS (no year) Intellectual capital statement –Made in Europe. http://www.incas-europe.org

Itami H, Roehl T (1987) Mobilizing invisible assets. Harvard University Press, Cambridge, MA

Janjua FJ, Naeem MA, Kayani FN (2012) The competence classification framework – a classification model for employee development. Interdiscip J Contemp Res Bus 4(1):396–404

Johnson LW, Frohmann AL (1989) Identifying and closing the gap in the middle of organizations. Acad Manag Exec 3:104–114

Kanter RM (1989) The new managerial work. Harv Bus Rev 67:85–92

Kanter RM (1994) Collaborative advantages: the art of alliances. Harv Bus Rev 72(4):96–108

Kaplan RS, Norton DP (1996) The balanced scorecard. Harvard Business School Press, Boston

Karlenzig W (1999) Chrysler's new know mobiles. http://kmmag.com/kmmagn2/km199905/fea ture1.htm

Kazanjian RK, Drazin R (1990) A stage-contingent model of design and growth for technology based new ventures. J Bus Venturing 5:137–150

Kieser A, Kubicek H (1992) Organisation. De Gruyter (3. Auflage), Berlin

Kim WC, Mauborgne R (2003) Fair process: managing in the knowledge economy. Harv Bus Rev, Jan 2003, pp 3–11

Klein DA (ed) (1998) The strategic management of intellectual capital. Butterworth-Heinemann, Boston

Klodt H et al (1997) Tertiarisierung in der deutschen Wirtschaft. Institut für Weltwirtschaft an der Universität Kiel, Kiel

Kogut B, Zander U (1992) Knowledge of the firm, combinative capabilities and the replication of technology. Organ Sci 3(3):383–397

Kotter JP (1996) Leading change. Harvard Business Review Press, Cambridge, MA

Kruthiventi D, Gajjar M, Awasthi B (2009) Using listeners to capture tacit knowledge at Tata Chemicals. Knowledge Management Review, June Edition, 2009. http://www.videndanmark. dk/fileadmin/Diverse_dokumenter/http___www.melcrum.com_kmreview_kmreview_0609.pdf

Kulkki S (1997) Knowledge creation of multinational corporations. Helsinki School of Economics and Business Administration, Helsinki

Kumta G (2008) Knowledge management in small & medium enterprises. In: Cader Y (ed) Knowledge management integrated: concepts and practice. Heidelberg Press, United Arab Emirates, pp 117–130

Kumta GA, Mukherjee S (2010) Managing organizational learning in small & medium enterprises in India. In: Legardeur J, North K (eds) Towards new challenges for innovative management practices, vol 3, no. 1. Available at http://www.erima.estia.fr/2010/proceedings/proceedings_ 2010.pdf

Kuriakose KK, Raj B, SatyaMurty SAV, Swaminathan P (2010) Knowledge management maturity models – a morphological analysis. J Knowl Manag Pract 11(3), Sept 2010

La Barre P (1996) Knowledge brokers. Industry Week, 1 April 1996, p 50

Latham GP, Pinder CC (2005) Work motivation theory and research at the dawn of the twenty-first century. Annu Rev Psychol 56:485–516

Lave J (1991) Situating learning in communities of practice. In: Resnick LB, Levine JM, Teasdale SD (eds) Perspectives on socially shared cognition. American Psychological Association, Washington, DC, pp 63–82

Lave J, Wenger E (1991) Situated learning: legitimate peripheral participation. Cambridge University Press, Cambridge, UK

Leitner K-H et al (2000) Entwicklung eines Bilanzierungssystems. Forschung Austria Report_A.03_08/00, Forschung Austria, Wien

Leonard D, Straus S (1997) Putting your company's whole brain to work. Harv Bus Rev 75 (4):111–121

Leonard D, Swap W (2005) Deep smarts – how to cultivate and transfer enduring business wisdom. Harvard Business School Press, Boston

Leonard-Barton D (1992a) Core capabilities and core rigidities: a paradox in managing new product development. Strateg Manage J 13:111–125

Leonard-Barton D (1992b) The factory as a learning laboratory. Sloan Manag Rev 34(1):23–38

Leonard-Barton D (1995) Wellsprings of knowledge. Harvard Business School Press, Boston

Lev B, Cañibano L, Marr B (2005) An accounting perspective on intellectual capital. http://www.uam.es/personal_pdi/economicas/lcanibano/2007/Tema%207%20Contabilidad%20Intangibles/Accounting%20Perspective%20on%20IC%20_Lev%20Canibano%20Marr_.pdf

Liebowitz J, Megbolugbe I (2003) A set of frameworks to aid the project manager in conceptualizing and implementing knowledge management initiatives. Int J Proj Manag 21(3):189–198

Lin CY-Y, Edvinsson L (2011) National intellectual capital – a comparison of 40 countries. Springer, New York. doi:10.1007/978-1-4419-7377-1

Luhmann N (1995) Social systems. Stanford University Press, Stanford

Lutz CH (1997) Der Arbeitnehmer ist tot es lebe die Lebensunternehmerin. In: Hensch CH, Wismer U (Hrsg.), Zukunft der Arbeit. Schäffer-Poeschel., Stuttgart, pp 129–135

Machlup F (1962) The production and distribution of knowledge in the United States. Yale University Press, Princeton

Maier R (2007) Knowledge management systems: information and communication technologies for knowledge management, 3rd edn. Springer, Berlin

Maier R, Hädrich T, Peinl R (2009) Enterprise knowledge infrastructures, 2nd edn. Springer, Berlin/Heidelberg/New York

Maister DH (1993) Managing the professional service firm. The Free Press, New York

Makhija A (2009) Building a KM function from the ground up at eClerx. KM Review, Sept 2009. http://www.videndanmark.dk/index.php?id=62&tx_mininews_pi1%5BshowUid%5D=3208&cHash=79b3797f96

March JG (1991) Exploration and exploitation in organizational learning. Organ Sci 2:71–87

Markkula M (2010) Policy recommendations – Committee of the Regions (CoR), Plenary Digital Agenda Opinion 6 Oct 2010, EU 2020 Strategy

Marshall C, Prusak L, Shpilberg D (1996) Financial risk and the need for superior knowledge management. Calif Manag Rev 38(3):77–101

Martins E (2010) Psychological ownership in Organisationen. R.-Hampp, Mering

McAfee A (2006) Enterprise 2.0: the dawn of emergent collaboration. MIT Sloan Manag Rev 47(3):20–28

McDermott R (1999) Nurturing three-dimensional communities of practice – how to get the most out of human networks. Knowl Manag Rev 2(5):26–29

McMaster M. Communities of practice – an introduction. http://www.co-i-l.com/coil/knowledge-garden/cop/mmintro.shtml

Mehrotra N (2005) Business process outsourcing – the Indian experience. ICFAI, Hyderabad

Meister JC (1997) Corporate universities: an opportunity or threat to higher education. In: Proceedings, seminar on knowledge management and the European Union, Utrecht, May 1997

Meyer C (1997) Relentless growth. The Free Press, New York

Milton N, Young T (2007) Masterclass KM implementation. Inside Knowledge. Feature 10(5). Posted 31 Jan 2007

Montreal Knowledge City Advisory Committee (2003) Montreal: Knowledge City. Report of the Montreal Knowledge City Advisory Committee

Moore K, Birkinshaw J (1998) Managing knowledge in global service firms: centres of excellence. Acad Manag Exec 12(4):81–92

Morin J (1985) L'Excellence Technologique. Picollec, Paris

Morin J, Seurat R (1989) Le management des ressources technologiques. Les éditions d'organisation, Paris

Mouritsen J, Bukh PN et al (2003) Intellectual capital statements – the new guideline. Danish Ministry of Science, Technology and Innovation, Copenhagen

Mouritson J, Larsen HT, Bukh PND (2001) Intellectual capital and the capable firm: narration, visualization and numbering for numbering knowledge. Report Copenhagen Business School and Aarhus School of Business

Nalebuff BJ, Brandenburger AM (1996) Co-opetition. Harper Collins Business, London

Nefiodow LA (1990) Der fünfte Kondratieff – Strategien zum Strukturwandel in Wirtschaft und Gesellschaft. Gabler, Wiesbaden

Nelson RR, Winter SG (1982) An evolutionary theory of economic change. Harvard University Press, Cambridge, MA

Nicolini D, Powell J, Conville P, Solano LM (2008) Managing knowledge in the healthcare sector. A review. Int J Manag Rev 10(3):245–263

Nonaka I (1991) The knowledge-creating company. Harv Bus Rev 69:96–104

Nonaka I, Konno N (1998) The concept of "Ba" – building a foundation for knowledge creation. Calif Manag Rev 40(3):40–53

Nonaka I, Takeuchi H (1995) The knowledge creating company. Oxford University Press, Oxford

North K (1997) Localizing global production. International Labour Office, Geneva

North K (1998) Wissensorientierte Unternehmensführung:Wertschöpfung durchWissen, vol 147. Gabler Verlag, Wiesbaden (5th edition 2010)

North K, Probst G, Romhardt K (1998) Wissen messen. Ansätze, Erfahrungen und kritische Fragen. Zeitschrift für Führung und Organisation 67(3):158–166

North K, Papp A (2001) Wie deutsche Unternehmen Wissensmanagement einführen – Vergleichsstudie 1998 bis 2000. REFA-Nachr 54(1):4–12

North K (2003) Das Kompetenzrad. In: Erpenbeck J, von Rosenstiel L (eds) Handbuch Kompetenzmessung. Erkennen, verstehen und bewerten von Kompetenzen in der betrieblichen, pädagogischen und psychologischen Praxis. Schäffer-Poeschel, Stuttgart, pp 200–212

North K (2005) Wo geht's lang zur wissensorientierten Unternehmensführung – Praxiserprobte Rezepte für kleine und mittlere Unternehmen. Wissensmanagement 1/2005:16–19

North K, Aukamm T (1996) "Think global - Actlocal" – Neuansätze zur Planung von Auslandsproduktionsstätten der Automobilindustrie. REFA-Nachr 49(2):15–21

North K, Grübel D (2005) Von der Intervention zur Wirkung: Das mehrstufige Indikatorenmodell. In: Mertins K, Alwert K, Heisig P (eds) Wissensbilanzen. Springer, Berlin, pp 109–119

North K, Gueldenberg S (2011) Effective knowledge work. Emerald, London

North K, Hornung T (2003) The benefits of knowledge management – results of the German Award "Knowledge Manager 2002". J Univ Comput Sci 9(6):463–471

North K, Kares S (2005) Ragusa or how to measure ignorance: the ignorance meter. In: Bounfour A, Edvinsson L (eds) Intellectual capital for communities. Elsevier, Amsterdam, pp 253–264

North K, Papp A (2000) Wie deutsche Unternehmen Wissensmanagement einführen – Vergleichsstudie 1998 bis 2000. REFA-Nachr 54(1):4–12

North K, Schmidt A (2004) Nutzenbeurteilung von Wissensmanagement. REFA-Nachr 5/2004:23–30

North K, Romhardt K, Probst G (2000) Wissensgemeinschaften – Keimzellen lebendigen Wissensmanagements. IO Manag 69(7/8):52

North K, Franz M, Lembke G (2004) Wissenserzeugung und –austausch in Wissensgemeinschaften, vol 85, QUEM-Report Heft. Arbeitsgemeinschaft Betriebliche Weiterbildungsforschung, Projekt Qualifizierungs-Entwicklungs-Management, Berlin

O'Dell C, Grayson CJ (1998) If only we knew what we know. The Free Press, New York

O'Reilly CA III, Tushman ML (2004) The ambidextrous organization. Harv Bus Rev 82(4):74–81

O'Reilly CA, Tushman ML (2008a) Ambidexterity as a dynamic capability: resolving the innovator's dilemma. Res Organ Behav 28:185–206

O'Reilly CA III, Tushman ML (2008b) Ambidexterity as a dynamic capability: resolving the innovator's dilemma. Sci Dir 30(28):185–206

OECD (1996a) Measuring what people know. OECD, Paris

OECD (1996b) National Accounts, Volume II: detailed tables 1982–1994. OECD, Paris

OECD (2008) Intellectual assets and value creation. Synthesis report. OECD, Paris, http://www.oecd.org/sti/inno/40637101.pdf

Oldigs-Kerber J et al (2002) Experten finden und verbinden – ein Knowledge Management Ansatz bei Aventis Pharma. In: Wissensmanagement – Das Magazin für Führungskräfte, Artikel 04/2002:14–19

Palmer D, LuncefordS, Patton AJ (2012) The engagement economy: how gamification is reshaping businesses. Deloitte University Press, July 1, http://www.dupress.com/articles/the-engagement-economy-how-gamification-is-reshaping-

Penrose ET (1959) The theory of the growth of the firm. Wiley, New York

Perlow LA, Porter JL (2009) Making time-off predictable & required. Harv Bus Rev 87(10):102–109

Peters TJ (1987) Thriving on chaos. Alfred A. Knopt, New York

Peters TJ (1992) Liberation management. Macmillan, London

Peters TJ (1994) The Tom Peters seminar. Vintage Books, New York

Petrash G (1996) Dow's Journey to a knowledge value management culture. Eur Manag J 14(4):365–373

Pine JB II (1993) Mass customization: the new frontier in business competition. Harvard Business School Press, Boston

Pink D (2009) Drive: the surprising truth about what motivates. Riverhead, New York

Polanyi M (1966) The tacit dimension. University of Chicago Press, Chicago

Porter ME (1990) The competitive advantage of nations. The Free Press, New York

Porter Liebeskind J (1996) Knowledge, strategy and the theory of the firm. Strateg Manag J 17(1996, Winter Special Issue):93–107

Porter ME, Millar VE (1985) How information gives you competitive advantage. Harv Bus Rev 63(4):149–160

Porter M (1985) Competitive advantage. The Free Press, New York

Probst G, Raub S, Romhardt K (1997) Wissen managen. Gabler, Wiesbaden

Probst G, Borzillo S (2008) Why communities of practice succeed and why they fail. Eur Manag J 26:335–347

Quinn JB (1992) Intelligent enterprise. The Free Press, New York

Quinn R, Cameron K (1983) Organizational life cycles and shifting criteria of effectiveness: some preliminary evidence. Manag Sci 29:33–41

Quinn JB et al (1996) Leveraging intellect. Acad Manag Exec 10(3):7–27

Raisch S, Birkinshaw J (2008) Organizational ambidexterity: antecedents, outcomes, and moderators. J Manag 34(3):375–409

Raisch S, Birkinshaw J, Probst G, Tushman ML (2009) Organizational ambidexterity: balancing exploitation and exploration for sustained performance. Organ Sci 20(4):685–695

Reinmann-Rothmeier G, Mandl H (2000) Individuelles Wissensmanagement. Huber, Bern

Reinmann G, Eppler M (2008) Wissenswege – Methoden für das persönliche wissensmanagement. Huber, Bern

Rayport JF, Sviokla JJ (1995) Exploiting the virtual value chain. Harv Bus Rev 73(6):75–85

Richter F-J, Wakuta Y (1993) Permeable networks: a future option for the European and Japanese car industries. Eur Manag J 11(2):262–267

Robes J (2005) What's in it for me? Über den Nutzen von Weblogs für Wissensarbeiter. IM - Inf Manage Consult 3:2005

Roehl H (2002) Organisationen des Wissens – Anleitung zur Gestaltung. Klett-Cotta, Stuttgart

Romer P (1986) Increasing returns and long-run growth. J Polit Econ 94:1002–1037

Roos J, von Krogh G (1996) The epistemological challenge: managing knowledge and intellectual capital. Eur Manag J 14(4):333–337

Roos J et al (1998) Intellectual capital. New York University Press, New York

Rosenbaum D (2012) The games businesses play. CFO.com 14 Feb. http://www3.cfo.com/article/2012/2/it-value_gamification-marketing-knowledge-management-?currpage=1

Rubenstein-Montano B, Liebowitz J, Buchwalter J, McCaw D, Newman B, Rebeck K (2001a) The knowledge management methodology team. A systems thinking framework for knowledge management. Decis Support Syst 31(1):5–16

Rubenstein-Montano B, Liebowitz J, Buchwalter J, McCaw D, Newman B, Rebeck K (2001b) SMARTVision: a knowledge-management methodology. J Knowl Manag 5(4):300–310

Rumelt R (1994) Foreword. In: Hamel G., Heene A (eds) Competence based competition. Wiley, Chichester, pp XV–XIX

Saxenian A (1996) Regional advantage: culture and competition in Silicon Valley and route 128. Harvard University Press, Boston

SCANDIA (1998) Human capital in transformation (Intellectual capital prototype report). Skandia, Stockholm

Scharmer CO (2007) Theoryy U: Leading from the future as it emerges. Meine, Cambridge

Schindler M (2000) Wissensmanagement in der Projektabwicklung, Dissertation, Rosch-Buch Verlag, Schesslitz

Senge PM (1990) The fifth discipline. Doubleday Currency, New York

Seifert H (1996) Gewußt wie. Manager Magazin 132–134

Seufert A, van Krogh G, Bach A (1999) Towards knowledge networking. J Knowl Manag 3 (3):180–190

Simon H (2009) Hidden champions of the 21st century. Springer, New York

Singleton T (ed) (1978) The analysis of practical skills. MTP Press, Lancaster

Skyrme DJ (2002) Knowledge management: approaches and policies. This article was first published in The Business Times, Singapore, 23 Nov 2000

Sparrow J (2001) Knowledge management in small firms. Knowl Process Manag 8(1):3–16

Spender J-C (1996) Making knowledge the basis of a dynamic theory of the firm. Strateg Manag J 17(Winter Special Issue):45–62

Sreenivas T (2006) Globalisation and emerging India. Discovery Publishing, New Delhi

Stadler S (1995) Gaining advantage by "leaking" information. Eur Manag J 13(2):156–163

Standards Australia (2003) HB275-2000 – knowledge management: a framework for succeeding in the knowledge era. Standards Australia, Sydney

Starbuck WH (1992) Learning by knowledge-intensive firms. J Manag Stud 29(6):713–740

Stewart TA (1997) Intellectual capital. Nicholas Brealey, London

Strassmann PA (1997) The squandered computer: evaluating the business alignment of information technologies. Information Economics Press, New Canaan

Sveiby KE (1997) The new organizational wealth. Berret-Koehler, San Francisco, http://www.sveiby.com.au

Sveiby K-E (2001) A knowledge based theory of the firm to guide strategy formulating. J Intellect Capital 2(4):344–358

Sveiby K E (2010) Methods for measuring intangible assets. http://www.sveiby.com/articles/IntangibleMethods.htm

Swiss Development Agency (2006) Story guide. http://www.deza.admin.ch/.../resource_en_155620.pdf

Sydow J, van Well B (1996) Wissensintensiv durch Netzwerkorganisation – Strukturationstheoretische Analyse eines wissensintensiven Netzwerks. In: Schreyögg und Conrad 1996 a.a.O. pp 191–234

Szulanski G (1996) Exploring internal stickiness: impediments to the transfer of best practice within the firm. Strateg Manag J 17(Winter Special Issue):27–43

Teece DJ (1998) Capturing value from knowledge assets: the new economy, markets for know-how, and intangible assets. Calif Manage Rev 40:55–79

Teece DJ (2007) Explicating dynamic capabilities: the nature and microfoundations of (sustainable) enterprise performance. Strateg Manag J 4:1319–1350

Teece D (2009) Dynamic capabilities & strategic management. Oxford University Press, Oxford

Teece DJ, Pisano G, Shuen A (1997) Dynamic capabilities and strategic management. Strateg Manag J 18:509–533

Teece DJ, Pisano G, Shuen A (2000) Dynamic capabilities and strategic management. In: Dosi G, Nelson RR, Winter SG (eds) The nature and dynamics of organizational capabilities. Oxford University Press, Oxford, pp 334–362

The Conference Board (1995) New corporate performance measures. The Conference Board, New York

Thompson KR et al (1997) Stretch targets: what makes them effective? Acad Manag Exec 11(3):48–60

Thurow LC (1997) Needed: a new system of intellectual property rights. Harv Bus Rev, Sept–Oct;95–103

Tidd J et al (1997) Integrating technological, market and organizational change. Wiley, Chichester

Tissen R et al (1998) Value-based knowledge management. Longman, Amsterdam

Traecy M, Wiersema F (1993) Customer intimacy and other value disciplines. Harv Bus Rev 71(1):84–93

Tsai W, Ghoshal S (1998) Social capital and value creation: the role of intrafirm networks. Acad Manag J 41(4):464–476

Tsoukas H (1996) The firm as a distributed knowledge system: a constructionist approach. Strateg Manag J 17(Winter Special Issue):11–25

Turban E, Bolloju N, Liang T-P (2011) Enterprise social networking: opportunities, adoption, and risk mitigation. J Organ Comput Electron Commer 21(3):202–220, http://dx.doi.org/10.1080/10919392.2011.590109

Tushman ML, O'Reilly CA (1996) Ambidextreous organizations: managing evolutionary and revolutionary change. Calif Manag Rev 38(4):8–30

Ulrich D et al (2002) The GE work-out: how to implement GE's revolutionary method for busting bureaucracy and attacking organizational problems – fast! McGraw-Hill, New York

van Doren C (1991) A history of knowledge. Ballantine Books, New York

Vasilachis de Gialdino Irene (2011) Ontological and epistemological foundations of qualitative research [85 paragraphs]. Forum Qualitative Sozialforschung/Forum Qual Soc Res 10(2) Art. 30, http://nbn-resolving.de/urn:nbn:de:0114-fqs0902307

Volderba HW (1997) Strategic renewal in large multiunit firms: four dynamic mechanisms. OECD (Workshop on the development of practice tools for improving the innovation performance of firms), Paris

von Hipple E (1987) Cooperation between rivals: informal know-how trading. Res Policy (Amsterdam) 16:291–302

von Hipple E (1994) "Sticky information" and the focus of problem solving: implications for innovation. Manag Sci 40:429–439

von Krogh G, Roos J (1995) Organizational epistemology. MacMillan, London

von Krogh G, Roos J (1996) Five claims on knowing. Eur Manag J 14(4):423–426

von Krogh G, Nonaka I, Ichijo K (1997) Develop knowledge activists. Eur Manag J 15(5):475–483

von Krogh G, Ichijo K, Nonaka I (2000) Enabling knowledge creation. Oxford University Press, Oxford

Warren DM, McKiernan G (1995) CIKARD: a global approach to documenting indigenous knowledge for development. In: Warren DM, Slikkerveer LJ, Brokensha D (eds) The cultural dimension of development: indigenous knowledge systems. Intermediate Technology Publications, London, pp 426–34

Weick KE (1993) Organization re-design as improvisation. In: Huber G, Glick W (eds) Organizational change and redesign. Oxford University Press, New York

Wenger E (1998a) Communities of practice – learning as a social system. Published by System Thinker, 6/98

Wenger E (1998b) Communities of practice: learning, meaning, and identity. Cambridge University Press, Cambridge, UK

Wenger E, Snyder W (2000) Communities of practice: the organizational frontier. Harv Bus Rev, Jan–Feb, :139–145

Wenger E, McDermott R, Snyder W (2002) Cultivating communities of practice. Harvard Business Press, Boston

Wiersema F (1996) Customer intimacy. Knowledge Exchange, Santa Monica

Wiig KM (1999) Introducing knowledge management into the enterprise. In: Liebowitz J (ed) Knowledge management handbook. CRC Press, Boca Raton, pp 3.1–3.41

Willke H (1998) Systemisches Wissensmanagement. Lucius & Lucius (UTB), Stuttgart

Wunderer R (1996) Besonderheiten des "Human-Kapitals". Folgerungen für die Unternehmensführung und die Steuerung des Personalmanagements. In: SGO-Jahresbericht, pp 4–9

Womack JP et al (1990) The machine that changed the world. Rawson, New York

Wong KY, Aspinwall E (2004) Knowledge management implementation frameworks: a review. Knowl Process Manag 11(2):93–104

Yeong A, Lim TT (2010) Integrating knowledge management with project management for project success. J Proj Program Portfolio Manage 1(2):8–19

Yigitcanlar T, Baum S, Horton S (2007) Attracting and retaining knowledge workers in knowledge cities. J Knowl Manag 11(5):6–17

Zack M, McKeen J, Singh S (2009) Knowledge management and organizational performance. J Knowl Manag 13:392–409

# Index

K. North and G. Kumta, *Knowledge Management*,
Springer Texts in Business and Economics, DOI 10.1007/978-3-319-03698-4,
© Springer International Publishing Switzerland 2014